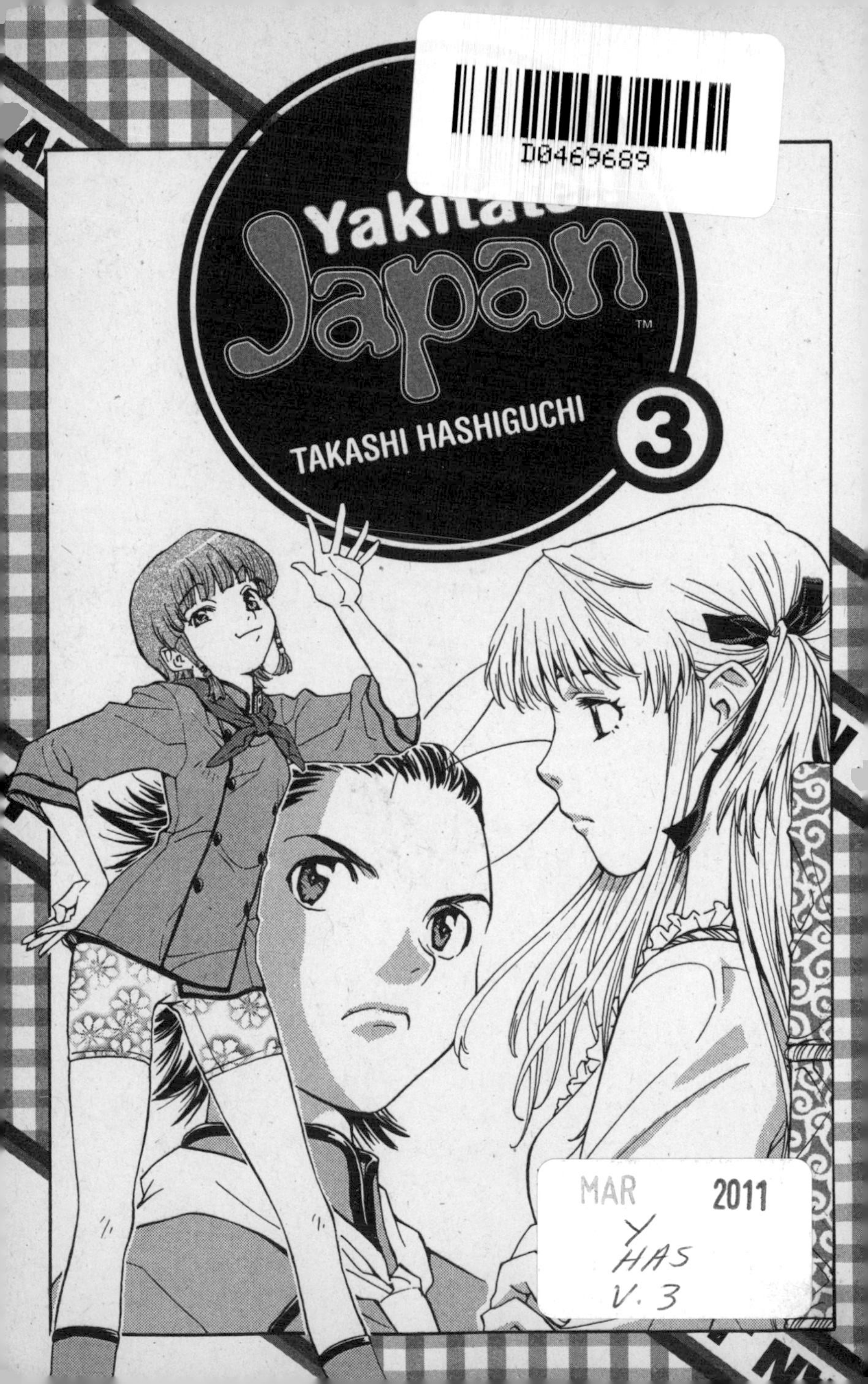
Japan
TAKASHI HASHIGUCHI
3

YAKITATE!! JAPAN
3
VIZ Media Edition

★The Story Thus Far★

Kazuma Azuma is obsessed with creating an iconic bread, or "Ja-pan," for his rice-obsessed homeland.

In pursuit of this dream, he marched into the Main Store of the Pantasia bakery with 55 experimental bread recipes fermenting in his head.

After a disastrous employment examination, he failed to win a spot at the Main Store. However, the owner's granddaughter, Tsukino Azusagawa, recruited him to work at Pantasia's South Tokyo Branch...

Every day at the store, Kazuma works hard alongside his colleague and rival Kyosuke Kawachi, and under the strict direction of the talented branch manager, Ken Matsushiro.

Now, the time has come for Kazuma and Kawachi to participate in Pantasia Group's annual Rookie Tournament. Kawachi comes to the sad realization that he is less talented than Kazuma, who possesses the fabled "Hands of the Sun." In desperation, he accepts Tsukino's offer to help him to develop his own "Gauntlets of the Sun"...

CONTENTS

Research Assistance: Aruru Sugamo, Andersen Aoyama, Shikishima-sei Pan (Pasco).

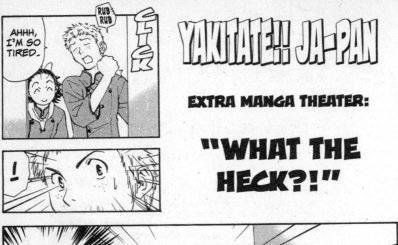

YAKITATE!! JA-PAN

EXTRA MANGA THEATER:

"WHAT THE HECK?!"

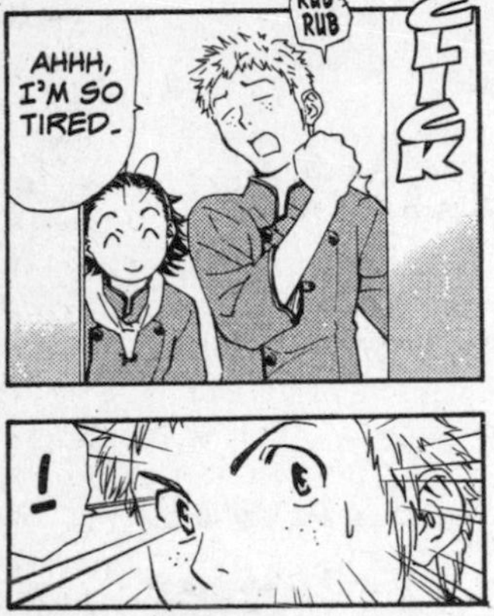
CLICK
RUB RUB
AHHH, I'M SO TIRED.
!

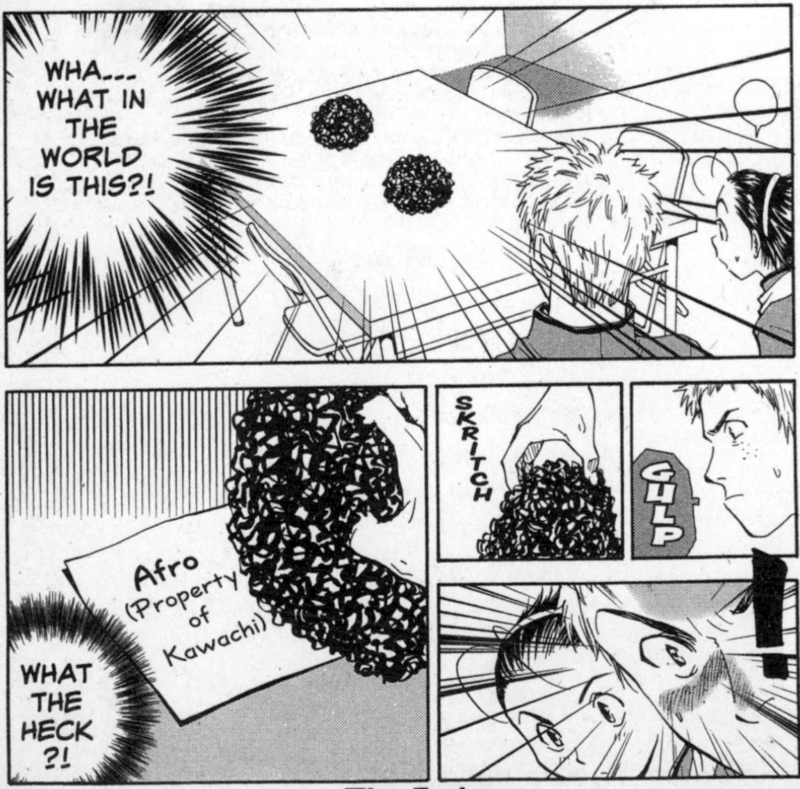
WHA... WHAT IN THE WORLD IS THIS?!
GULP
SKRITCH
!
Afro (Property of Kawachi)
WHAT THE HECK ?!

The End

Story 16: Loser

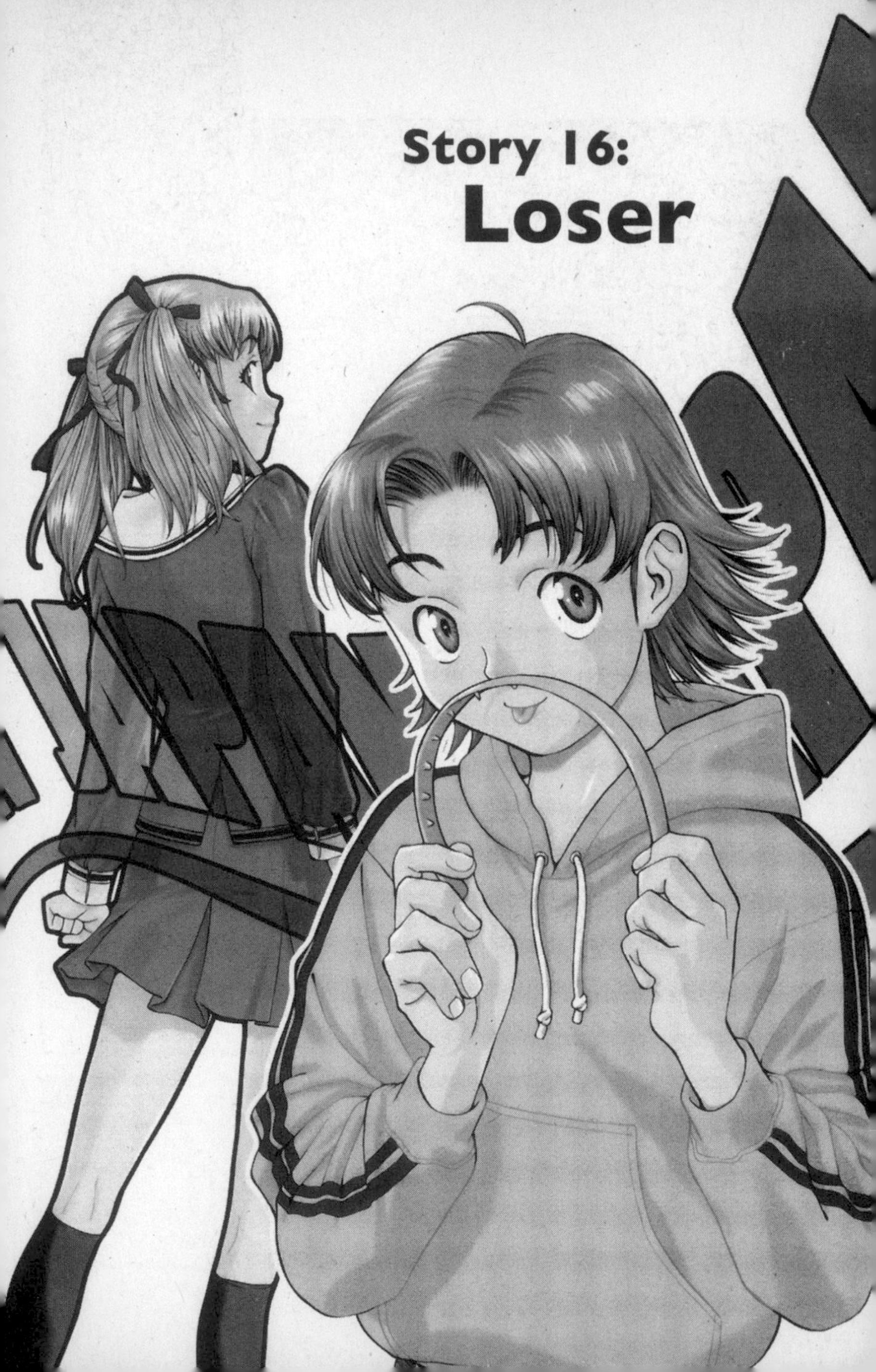

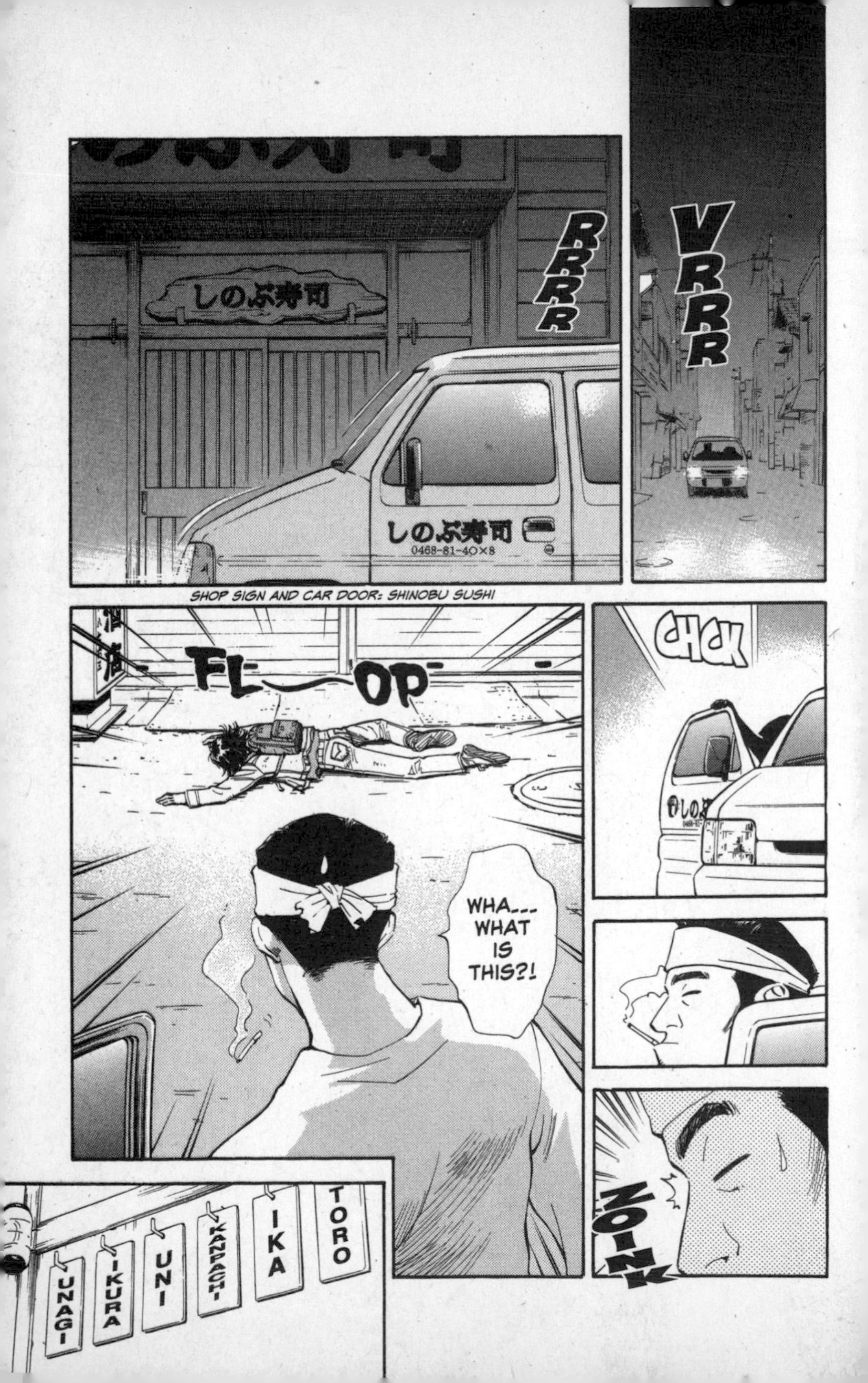
VRRR
RRRR
しのぶ寿司
しのぶ寿司
0468-81-40×8
SHOP SIGN AND CAR DOOR: SHINOBU SUSHI
CHCK
ZOINK
FL—OP
WHA... WHAT IS THIS?!
TORO
IKA
KANPACHI
UNI
IKURA
UNAGI

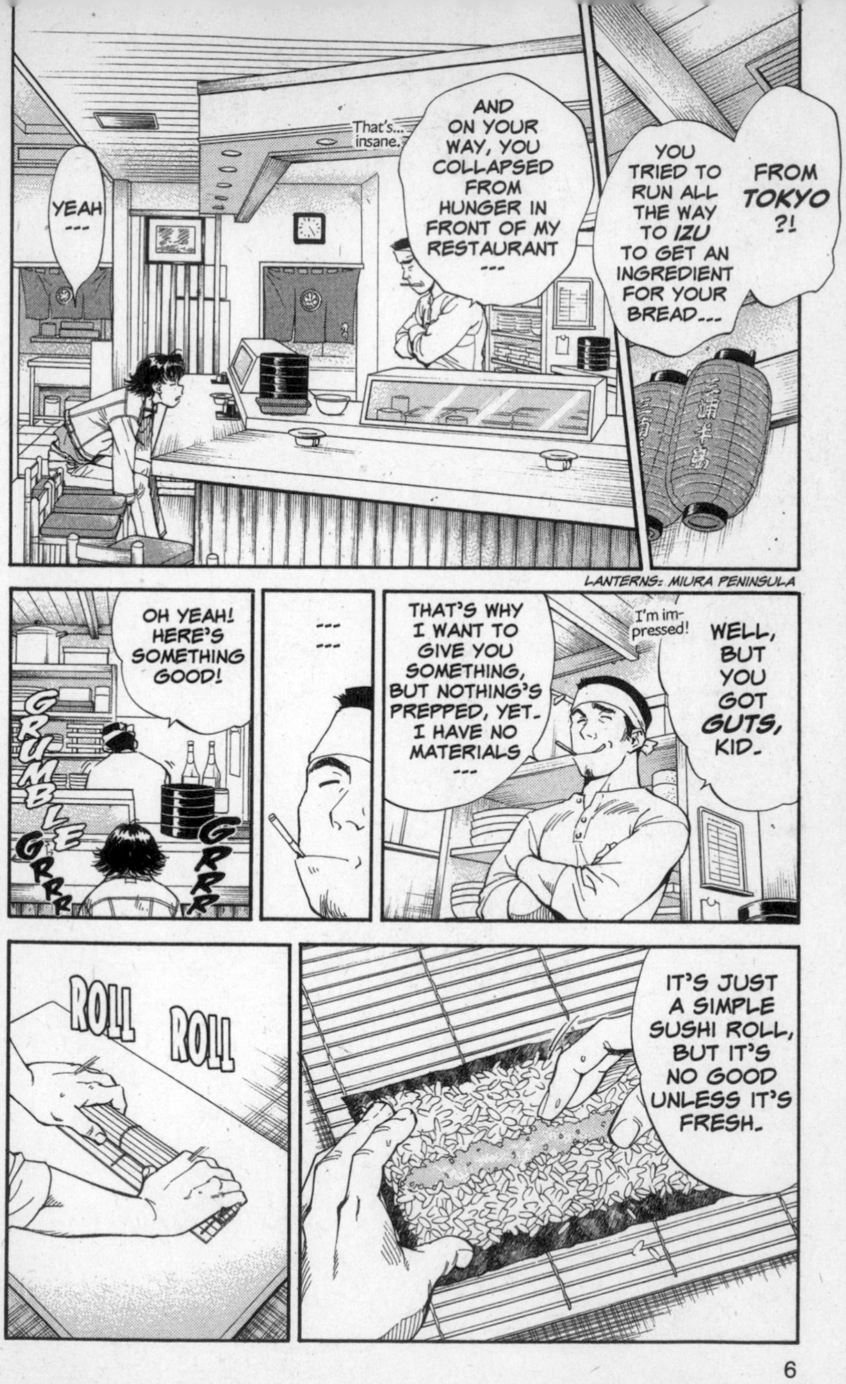
FROM TOKYO?!
YOU TRIED TO RUN ALL THE WAY TO IZU TO GET AN INGREDIENT FOR YOUR BREAD...
AND ON YOUR WAY, YOU COLLAPSED FROM HUNGER IN FRONT OF MY RESTAURANT...
That's... insane.
YEAH...
LANTERNS: MIURA PENINSULA
WELL, BUT YOU GOT GUTS, KID.
I'm impressed!
THAT'S WHY I WANT TO GIVE YOU SOMETHING, BUT NOTHING'S PREPPED, YET. I HAVE NO MATERIALS...
...
...
OH YEAH! HERE'S SOMETHING GOOD!
GRRR
GRUMBLE GRRR
IT'S JUST A SIMPLE SUSHI ROLL, BUT IT'S NO GOOD UNLESS IT'S FRESH.
ROLL
ROLL

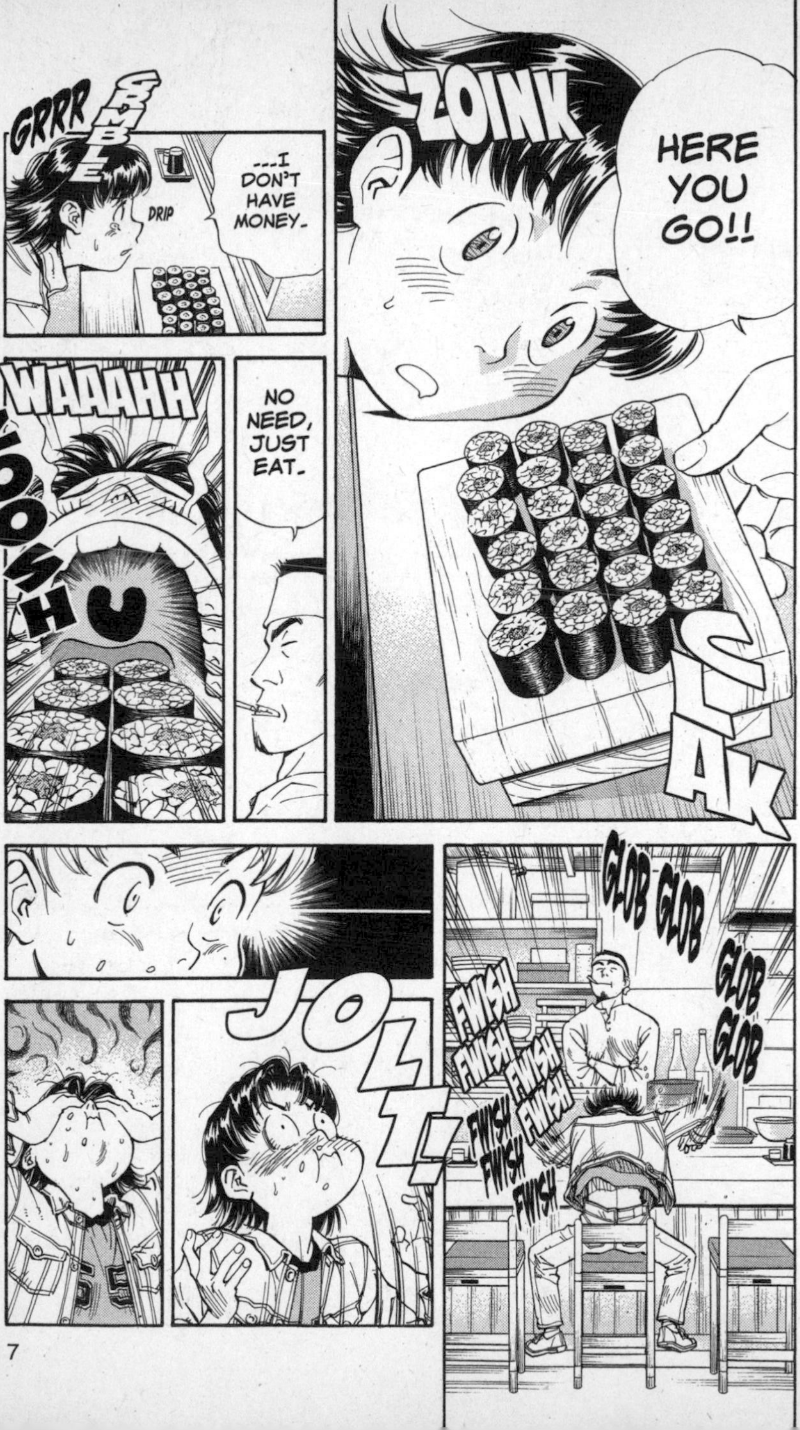
ZOINK
HERE YOU GO!!
CLAK
GRRR GRMBLE
...I DON'T HAVE MONEY...
DRIP
NO NEED, JUST EAT...
WAAAHH
NOOSH
GLOB GLOB GLOB GLOB
FWISH FWISH FWISH FWISH FWISH FWISH FWISH
JOLT!!

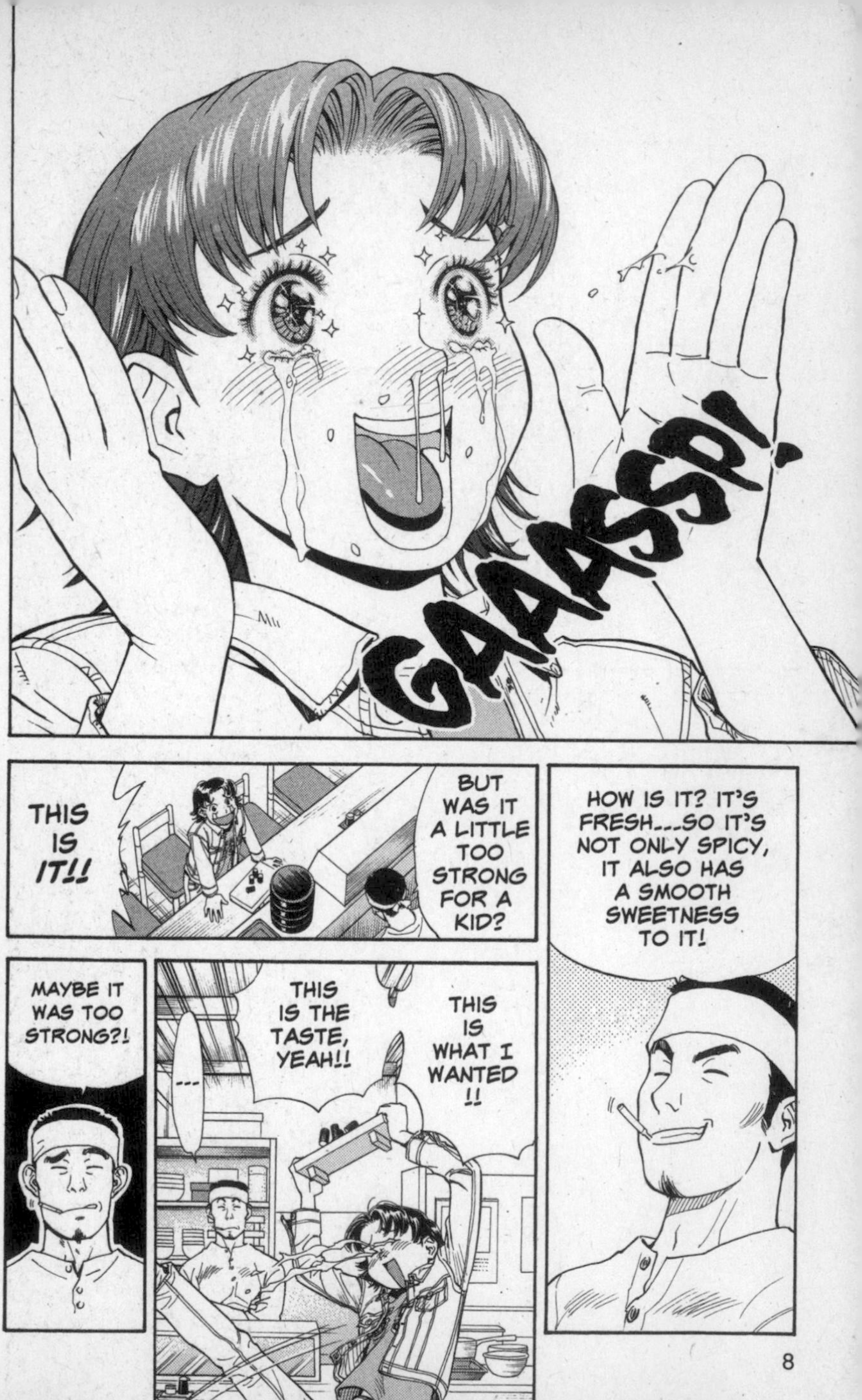
GAASP!
HOW IS IT? IT'S FRESH...SO IT'S NOT ONLY SPICY, IT ALSO HAS A SMOOTH SWEETNESS TO IT!
BUT WAS IT A LITTLE TOO STRONG FOR A KID?
THIS IS *IT!!*
THIS IS WHAT I WANTED !!
THIS IS THE TASTE, YEAH!!
...
MAYBE IT WAS TOO STRONG?!

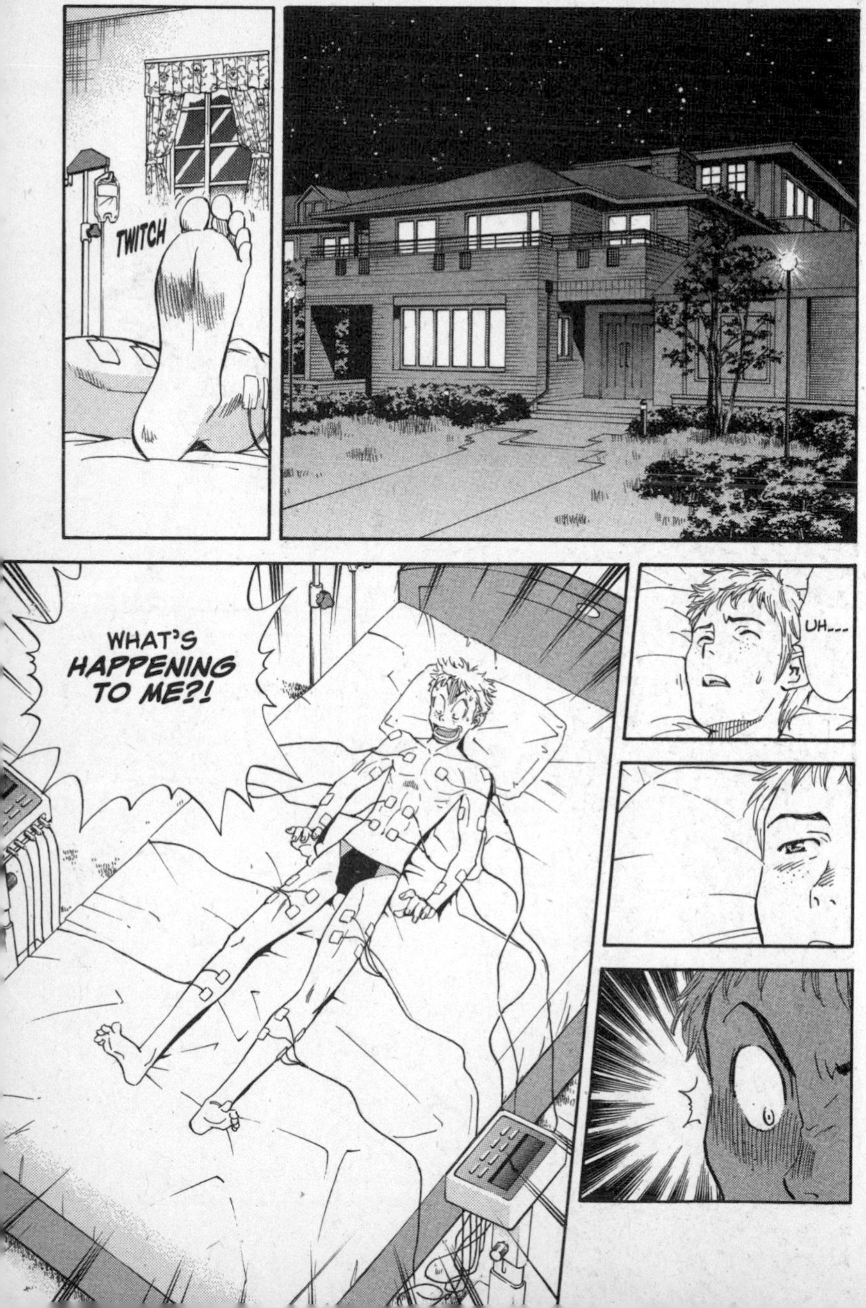
TWITCH
UH---
WHAT'S HAPPENING TO ME?!

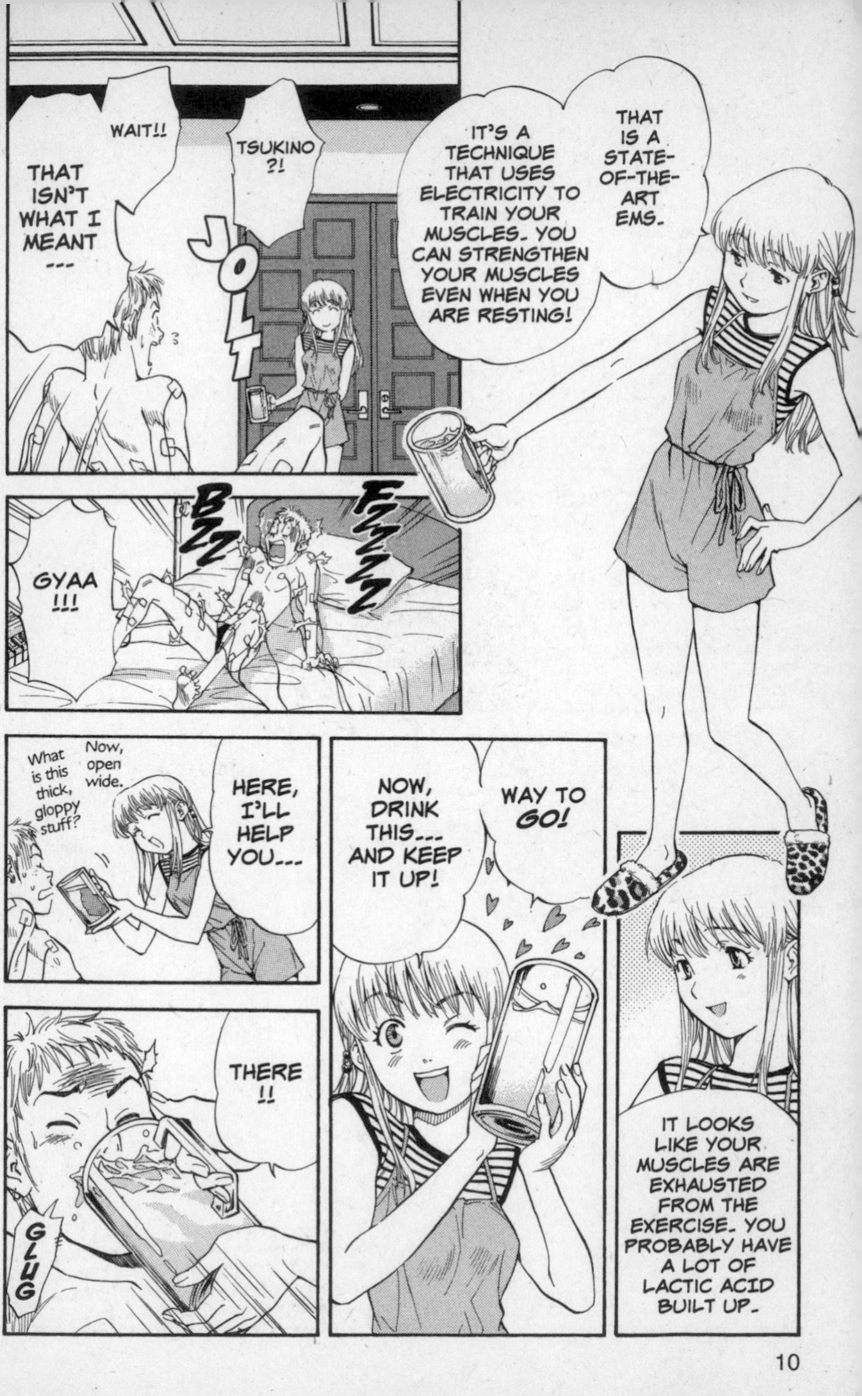
THAT IS A STATE-OF-THE-ART EMS.
IT'S A TECHNIQUE THAT USES ELECTRICITY TO TRAIN YOUR MUSCLES. YOU CAN STRENGTHEN YOUR MUSCLES EVEN WHEN YOU ARE RESTING!
TSUKINO ?!
WAIT!!
THAT ISN'T WHAT I MEANT ---
JOLT
FZZZZ
BZZ
GYAA !!!
IT LOOKS LIKE YOUR MUSCLES ARE EXHAUSTED FROM THE EXERCISE. YOU PROBABLY HAVE A LOT OF LACTIC ACID BUILT UP.
WAY TO GO!
NOW, DRINK THIS... AND KEEP IT UP!
HERE, I'LL HELP YOU...
Now, open wide.
What is this thick, gloppy stuff?
THERE !!
GLUG

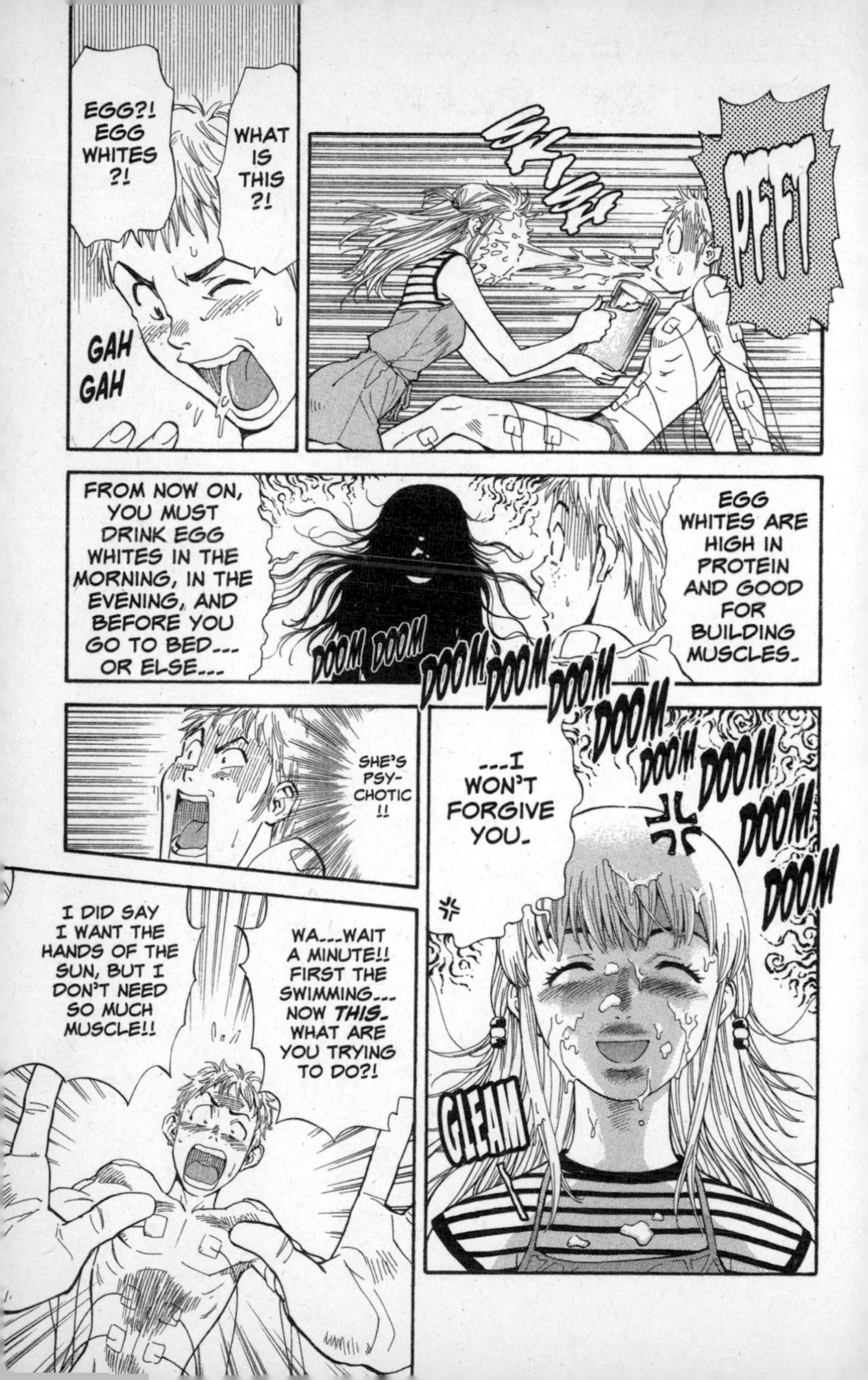
PFFT
WHAT IS THIS ?!
EGG?! EGG WHITES ?!
GAH GAH
EGG WHITES ARE HIGH IN PROTEIN AND GOOD FOR BUILDING MUSCLES.
FROM NOW ON, YOU MUST DRINK EGG WHITES IN THE MORNING, IN THE EVENING, AND BEFORE YOU GO TO BED... OR ELSE...
DOOM DOOM DOOM DOOM DOOM DOOM DOOM DOOM DOOM DOOM
...I WON'T FORGIVE YOU.
GLEAM
SHE'S PSY-CHOTIC !!
WA...WAIT A MINUTE!! FIRST THE SWIMMING... NOW *THIS*. WHAT ARE YOU TRYING TO DO?!
I DID SAY I WANT THE HANDS OF THE SUN, BUT I DON'T NEED SO MUCH MUSCLE!!

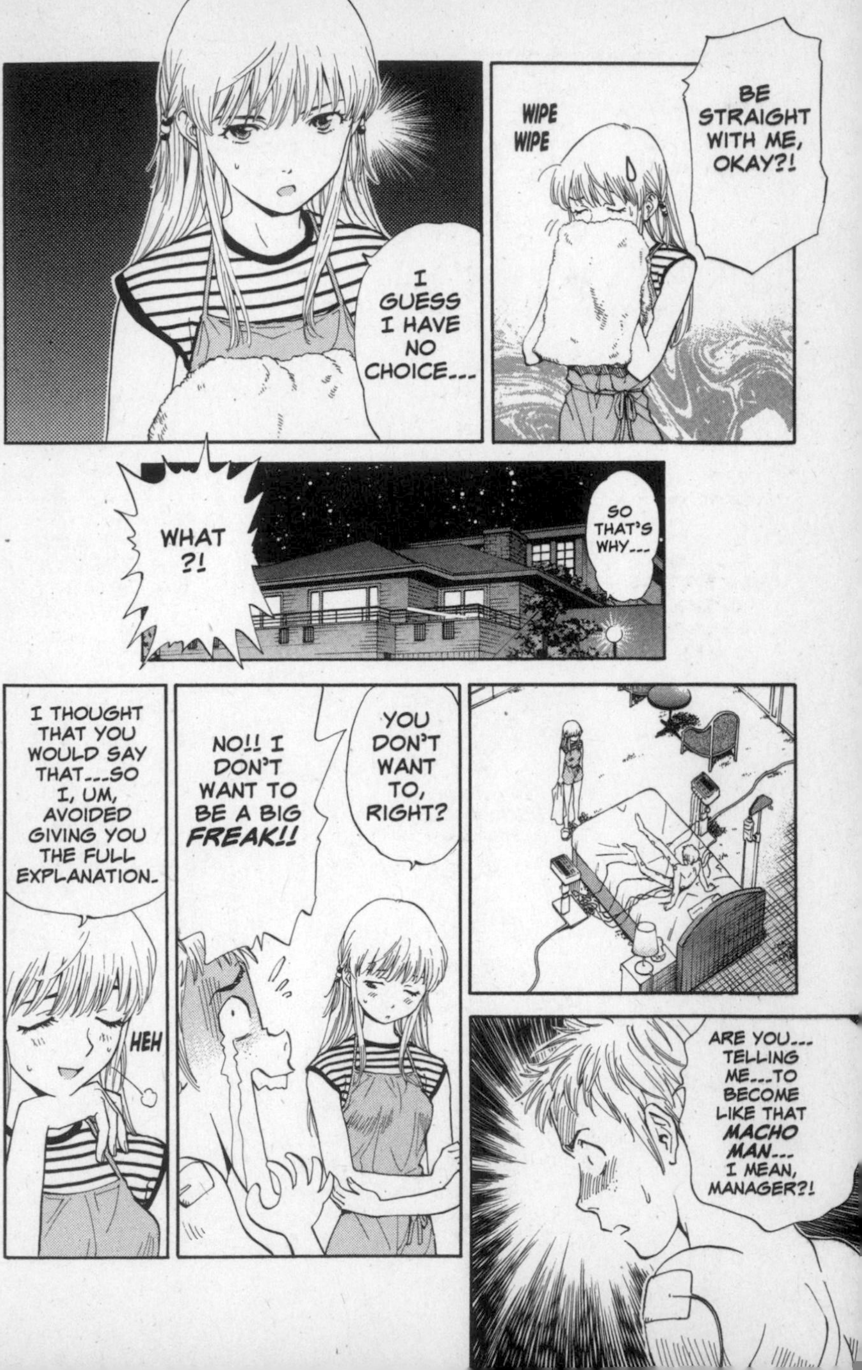
BE STRAIGHT WITH ME, OKAY?!
WIPE WIPE
I GUESS I HAVE NO CHOICE...
SO THAT'S WHY...
WHAT?!
ARE YOU... TELLING ME... TO BECOME LIKE THAT MACHO MAN... I MEAN, MANAGER?!
YOU DON'T WANT TO, RIGHT?
NO!! I DON'T WANT TO BE A BIG FREAK!!
I THOUGHT THAT YOU WOULD SAY THAT...SO I, UM, AVOIDED GIVING YOU THE FULL EXPLANATION.
HEH

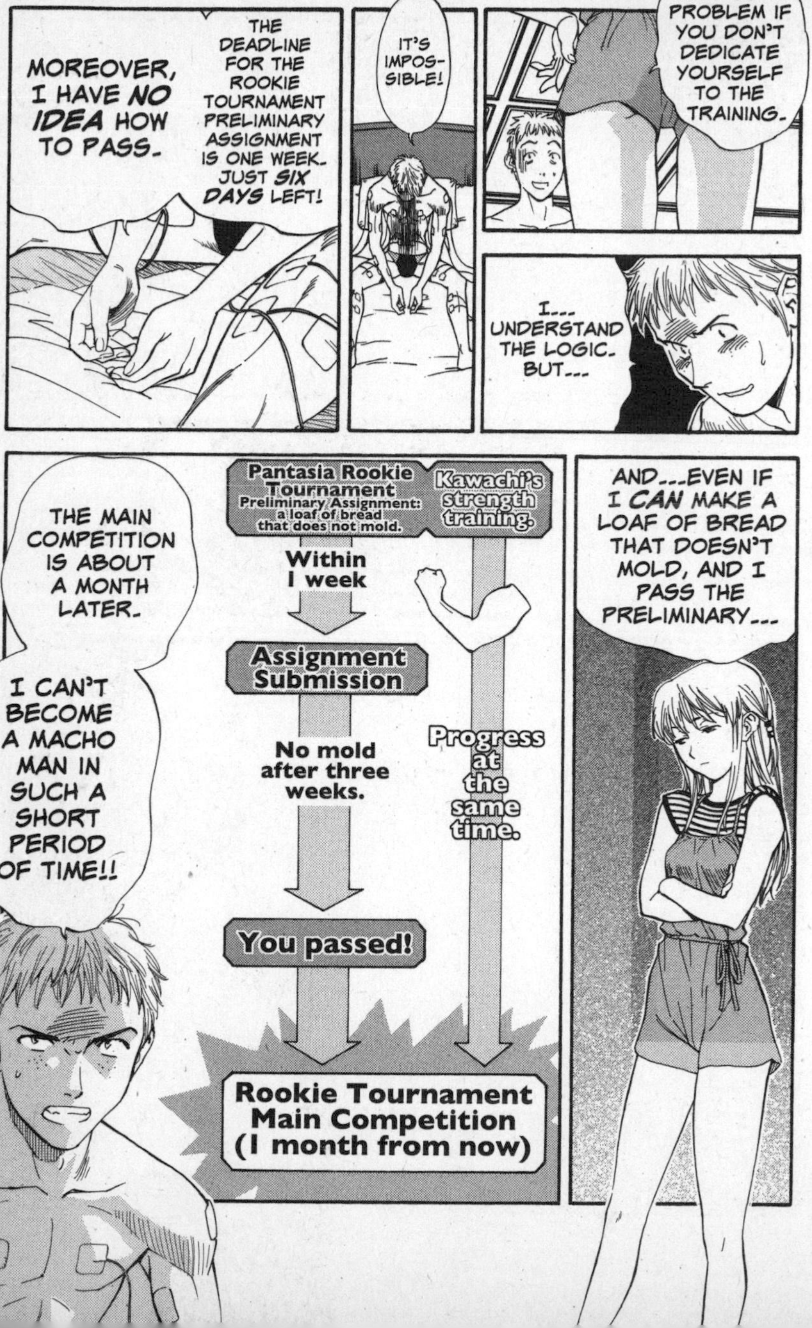

IT'LL BE A PROBLEM IF YOU DON'T DEDICATE YOURSELF TO THE TRAINING.
I... UNDERSTAND THE LOGIC. BUT...
IT'S IMPOS-SIBLE!
THE DEADLINE FOR THE ROOKIE TOURNAMENT PRELIMINARY ASSIGNMENT IS ONE WEEK. JUST SIX DAYS LEFT!
MOREOVER, I HAVE NO IDEA HOW TO PASS.
AND...EVEN IF I CAN MAKE A LOAF OF BREAD THAT DOESN'T MOLD, AND I PASS THE PRELIMINARY...
Kawachi's strength training.
Progress at the same time.
Pantasia Rookie Tournament Preliminary Assignment: a loaf of bread that does not mold.
Within 1 week
Assignment Submission
No mold after three weeks.
You passed!
Rookie Tournament Main Competition (1 month from now)
THE MAIN COMPETITION IS ABOUT A MONTH LATER.
I CAN'T BECOME A MACHO MAN IN SUCH A SHORT PERIOD OF TIME!!

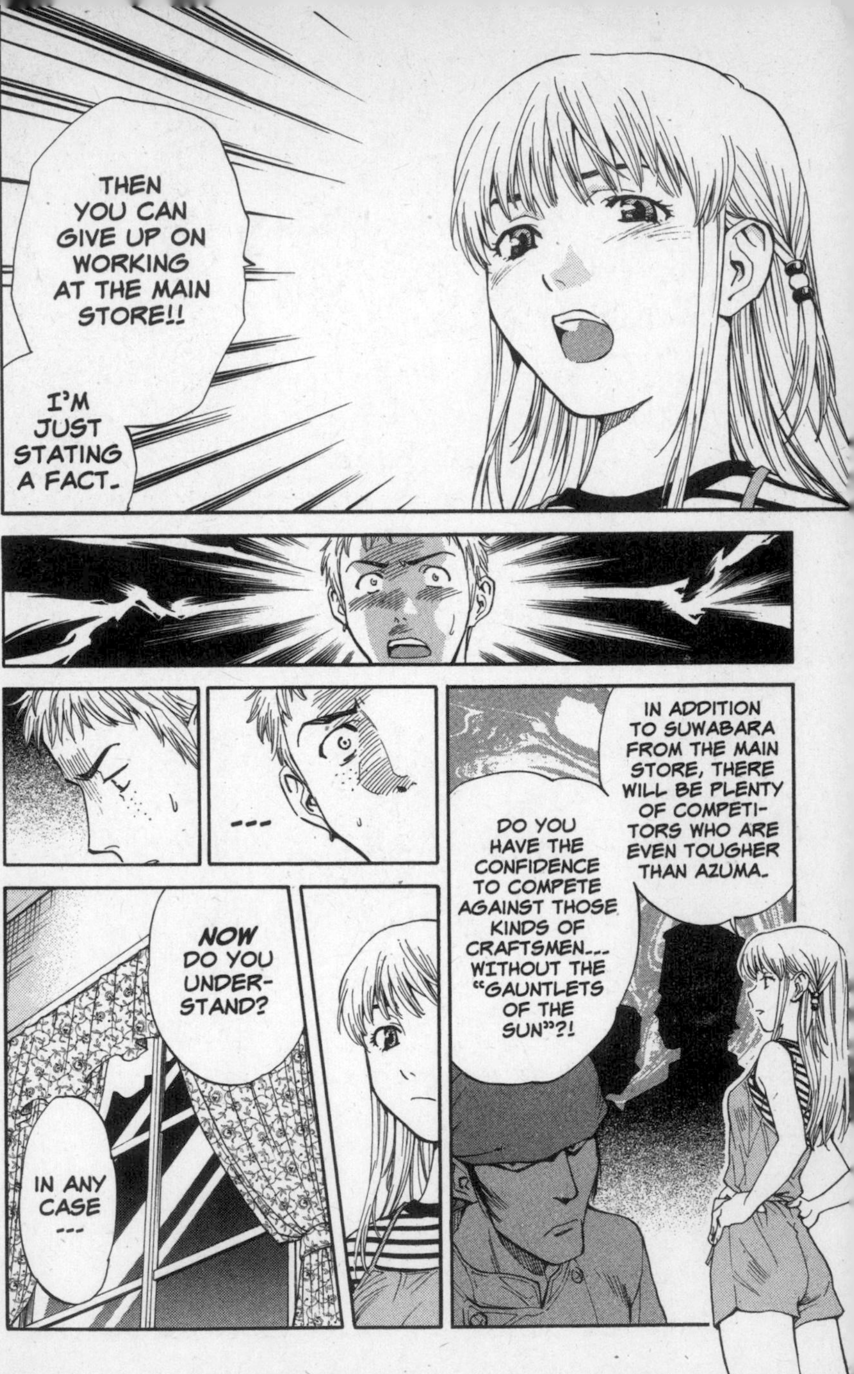

THEN YOU CAN GIVE UP ON WORKING AT THE MAIN STORE!!
I'M JUST STATING A FACT.
IN ADDITION TO SUWABARA FROM THE MAIN STORE, THERE WILL BE PLENTY OF COMPETITORS WHO ARE EVEN TOUGHER THAN AZUMA.
DO YOU HAVE THE CONFIDENCE TO COMPETE AGAINST THOSE KINDS OF CRAFTSMEN... WITHOUT THE "GAUNTLETS OF THE SUN"?!

NOW DO YOU UNDERSTAND?
IN ANY CASE ---

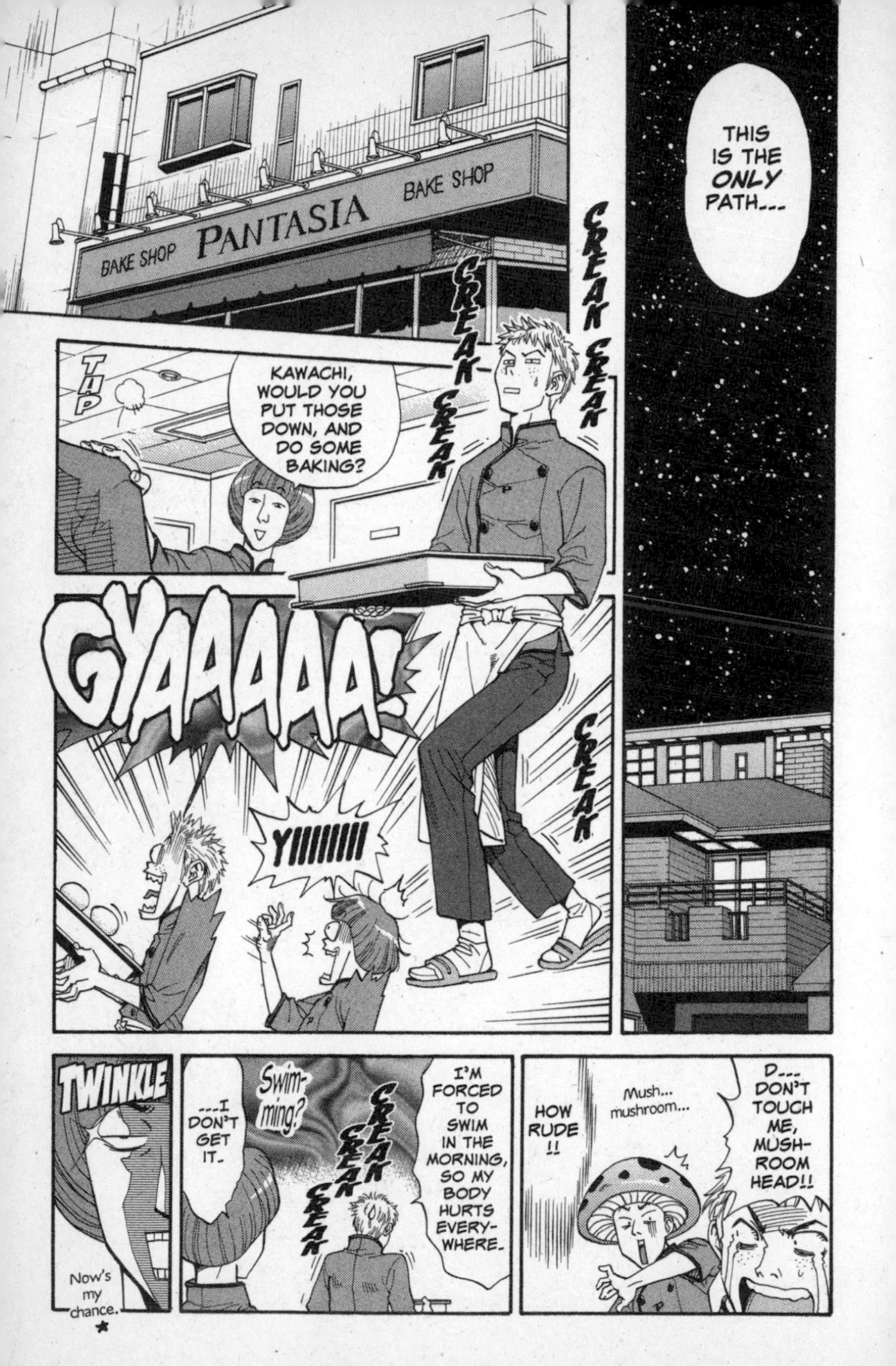
THIS IS THE ONLY PATH...
CREAK CREAK
BAKE SHOP
PANTASIA
BAKE SHOP
CREAK CREAK
TAP
KAWACHI, WOULD YOU PUT THOSE DOWN, AND DO SOME BAKING?
CREAK
GYAAAA!
YIIIIIIII
D... DON'T TOUCH ME, MUSH-ROOM HEAD!!
Mush... mushroom...
HOW RUDE!!
I'M FORCED TO SWIM IN THE MORNING, SO MY BODY HURTS EVERYWHERE.
Swim-ming?
CREAK CREAK CREAK
...I DON'T GET IT.
TWINKLE
Now's my chance.

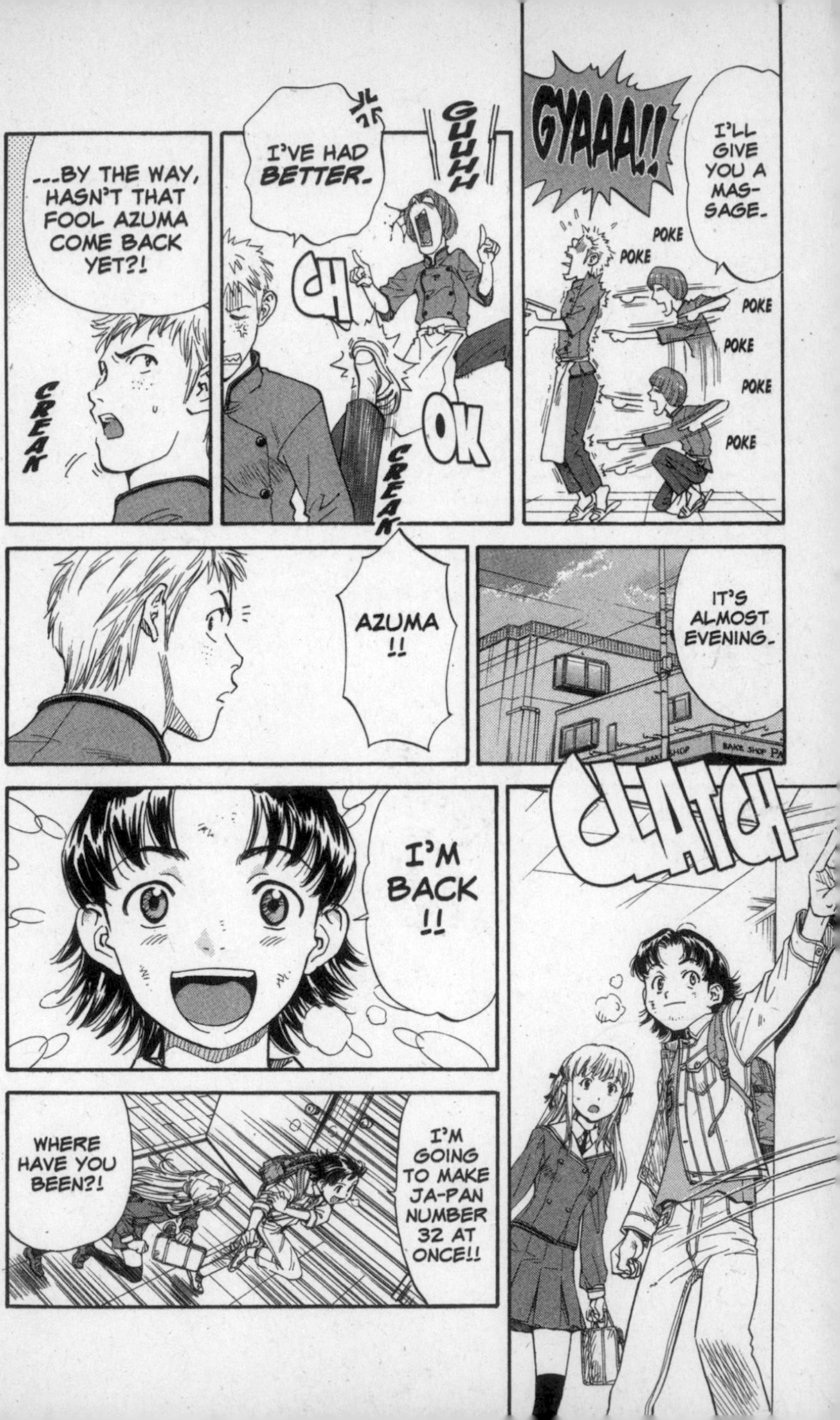
GYAAA!!
I'LL GIVE YOU A MAS-SAGE.
POKE
POKE
POKE
POKE
POKE
POKE
GUUHH
I'VE HAD BETTER.
CH
OK
CREAK
...BY THE WAY, HASN'T THAT FOOL AZUMA COME BACK YET?!
CREAK
IT'S ALMOST EVENING.
BAKE SHOP
BAKE SHOP PA
AZUMA!!
CLATCH
I'M BACK!!
I'M GOING TO MAKE JA-PAN NUMBER 32 AT ONCE!!
WHERE HAVE YOU BEEN?!

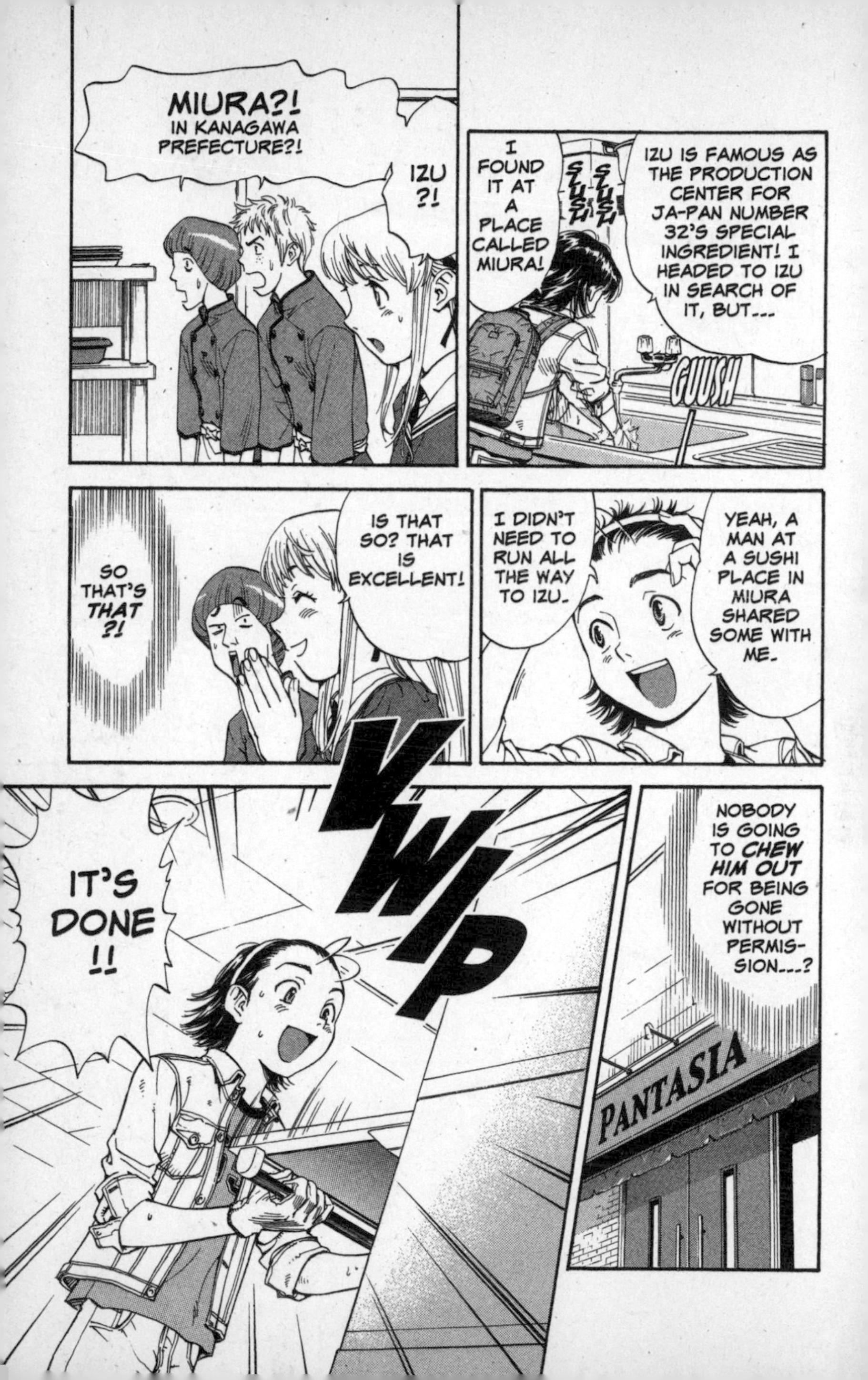
IZU IS FAMOUS AS THE PRODUCTION CENTER FOR JA-PAN NUMBER 32'S SPECIAL INGREDIENT! I HEADED TO IZU IN SEARCH OF IT, BUT...
I FOUND IT AT A PLACE CALLED MIURA!
SLUSH SLUSH
GUUSH
IZU?!
MIURA?! IN KANAGAWA PREFECTURE?!
YEAH, A MAN AT A SUSHI PLACE IN MIURA SHARED SOME WITH ME.
I DIDN'T NEED TO RUN ALL THE WAY TO IZU.
IS THAT SO? THAT IS EXCELLENT!
SO THAT'S THAT?!
NOBODY IS GOING TO CHEW HIM OUT FOR BEING GONE WITHOUT PERMIS-SION...?
PANTASIA
VWIP
IT'S DONE!!

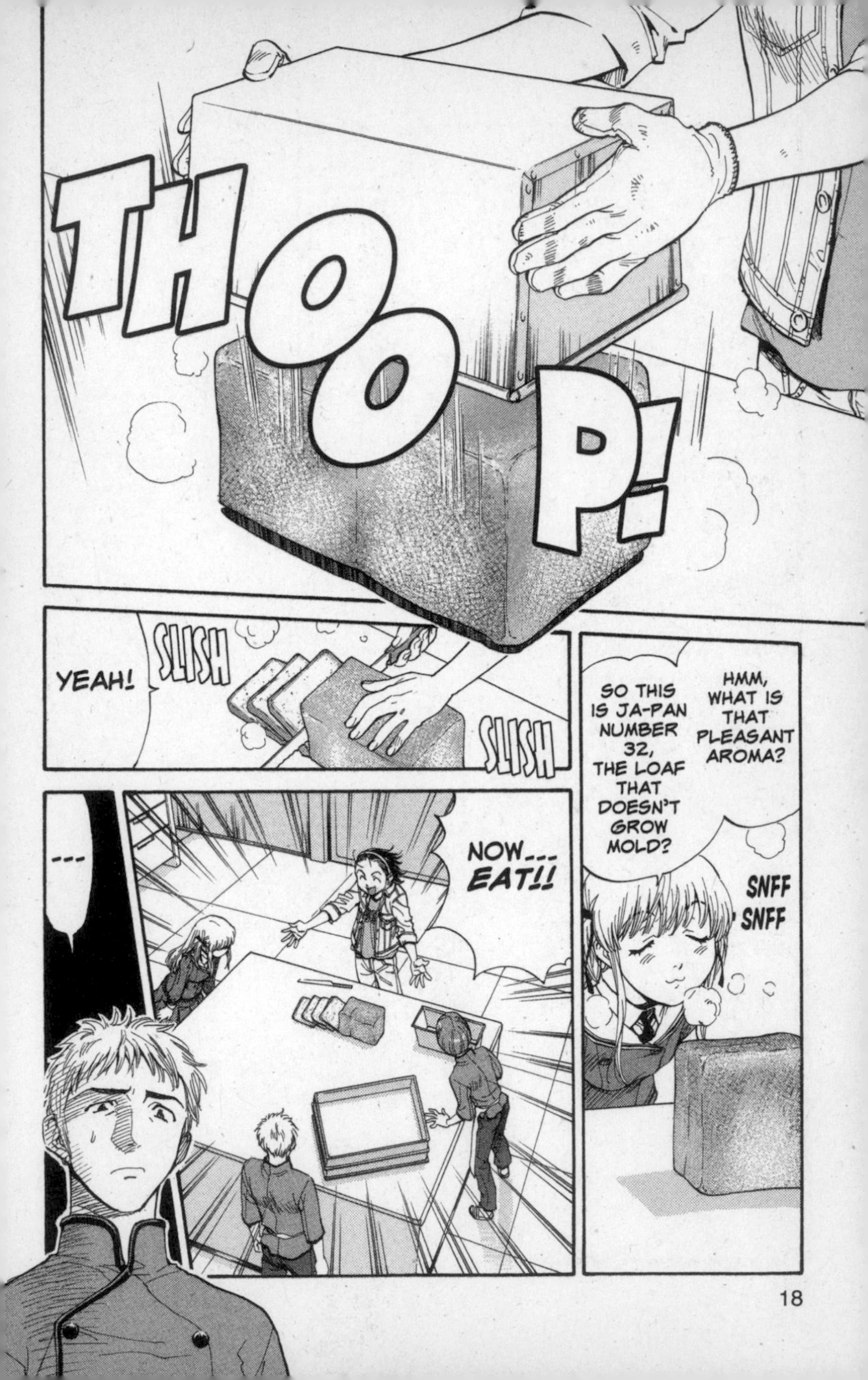

THOOP!
HMM, WHAT IS THAT PLEASANT AROMA?
SO THIS IS JA-PAN NUMBER 32, THE LOAF THAT DOESN'T GROW MOLD?
SNFF SNFF
SLISH
YEAH!
SLISH
NOW... EAT!!
...

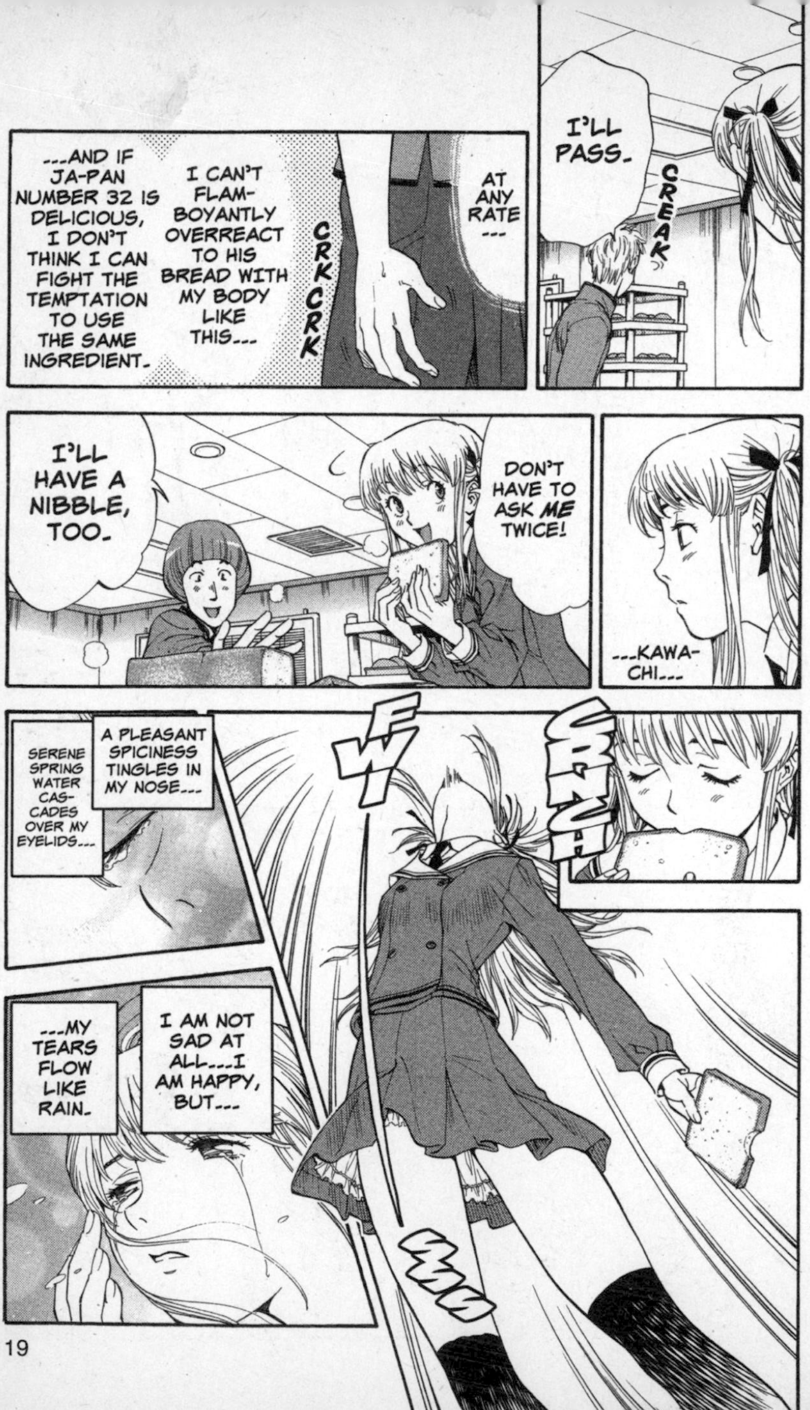
I'LL PASS.
CREAK
AT ANY RATE---
CRK CRK
I CAN'T FLAMBOYANTLY OVERREACT TO HIS BREAD WITH MY BODY LIKE THIS---
---AND IF JA-PAN NUMBER 32 IS DELICIOUS, I DON'T THINK I CAN FIGHT THE TEMPTATION TO USE THE SAME INGREDIENT.
---KAWACHI---
DON'T HAVE TO ASK *ME* TWICE!
I'LL HAVE A NIBBLE, TOO.
A PLEASANT SPICINESS TINGLES IN MY NOSE---
SERENE SPRING WATER CASCADES OVER MY EYELIDS---
I AM NOT SAD AT ALL---I AM HAPPY, BUT---
---MY TEARS FLOW LIKE RAIN.

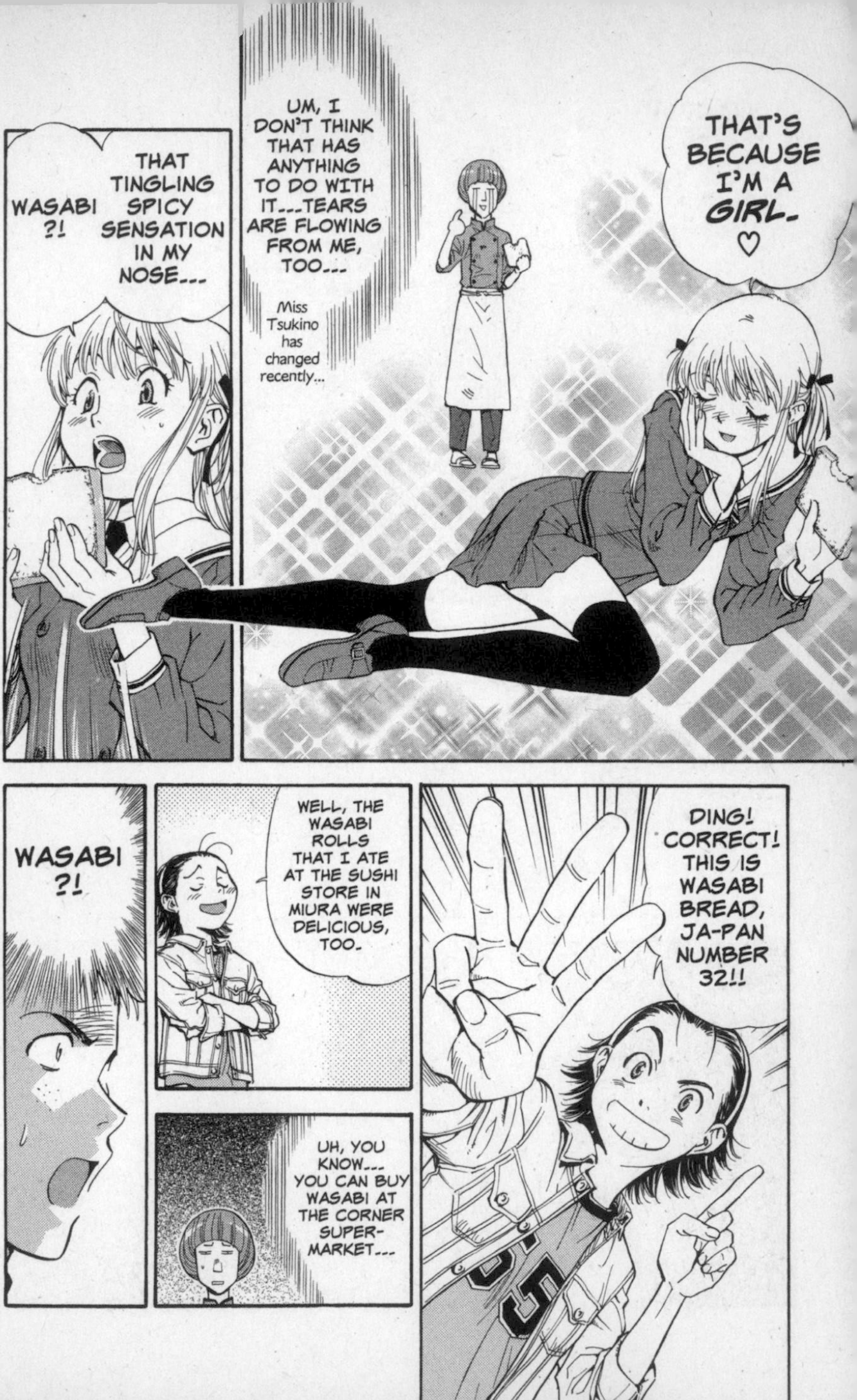
THAT'S BECAUSE I'M A GIRL. ♡
UM, I DON'T THINK THAT HAS ANYTHING TO DO WITH IT... TEARS ARE FLOWING FROM ME, TOO...
Miss Tsukino has changed recently...
THAT TINGLING SPICY SENSATION IN MY NOSE...
WASABI ?!
DING! CORRECT! THIS IS WASABI BREAD, JA-PAN NUMBER 32!!
WELL, THE WASABI ROLLS THAT I ATE AT THE SUSHI STORE IN MIURA WERE DELICIOUS, TOO.
UH, YOU KNOW... YOU CAN BUY WASABI AT THE CORNER SUPER-MARKET...
WASABI ?!

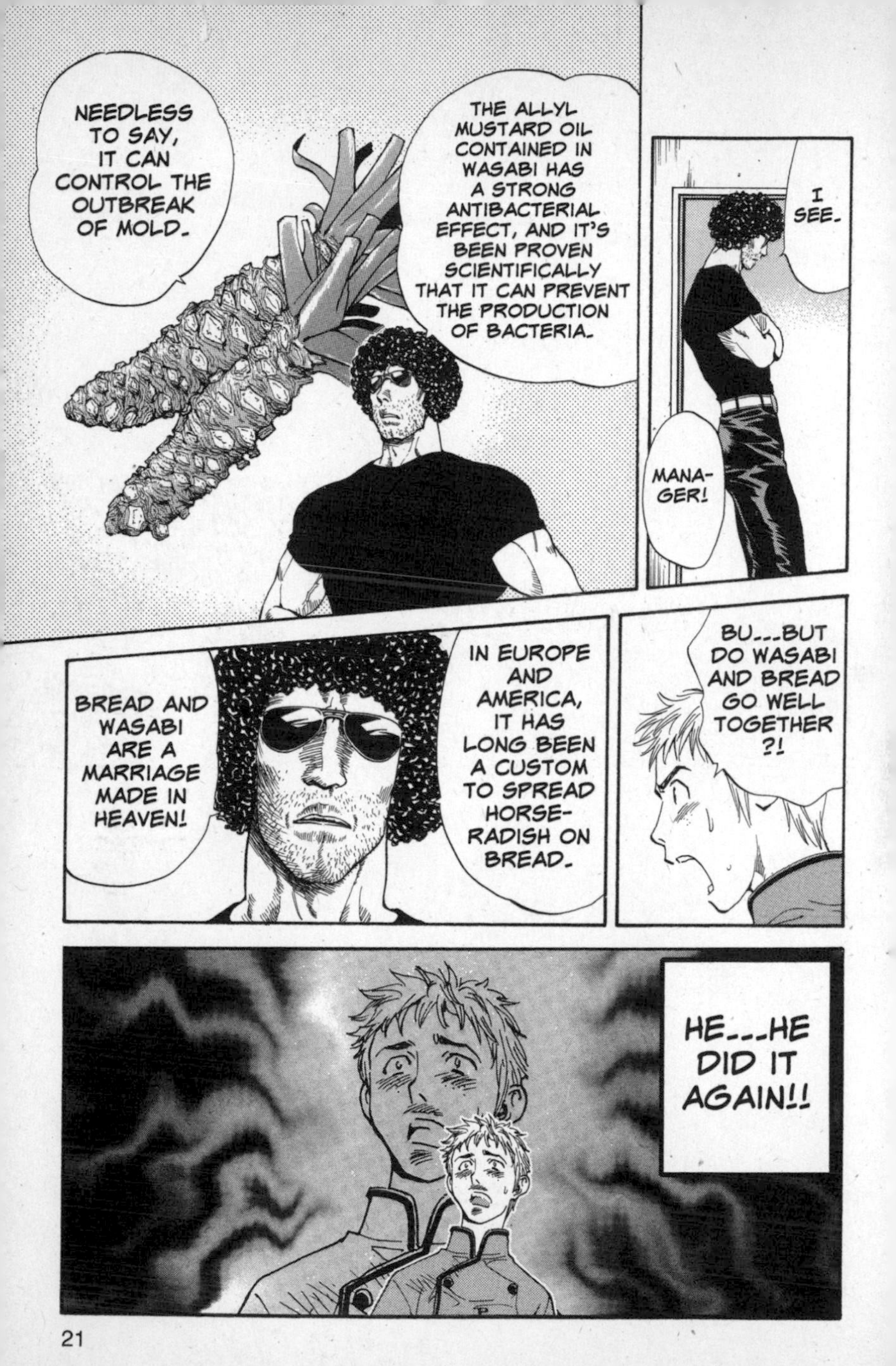

I SEE.
MANAGER!
THE ALLYL MUSTARD OIL CONTAINED IN WASABI HAS A STRONG ANTIBACTERIAL EFFECT, AND IT'S BEEN PROVEN SCIENTIFICALLY THAT IT CAN PREVENT THE PRODUCTION OF BACTERIA.
NEEDLESS TO SAY, IT CAN CONTROL THE OUTBREAK OF MOLD.
BU...BUT DO WASABI AND BREAD GO WELL TOGETHER?!
IN EUROPE AND AMERICA, IT HAS LONG BEEN A CUSTOM TO SPREAD HORSE-RADISH ON BREAD.
BREAD AND WASABI ARE A MARRIAGE MADE IN HEAVEN!
HE...HE DID IT AGAIN!!

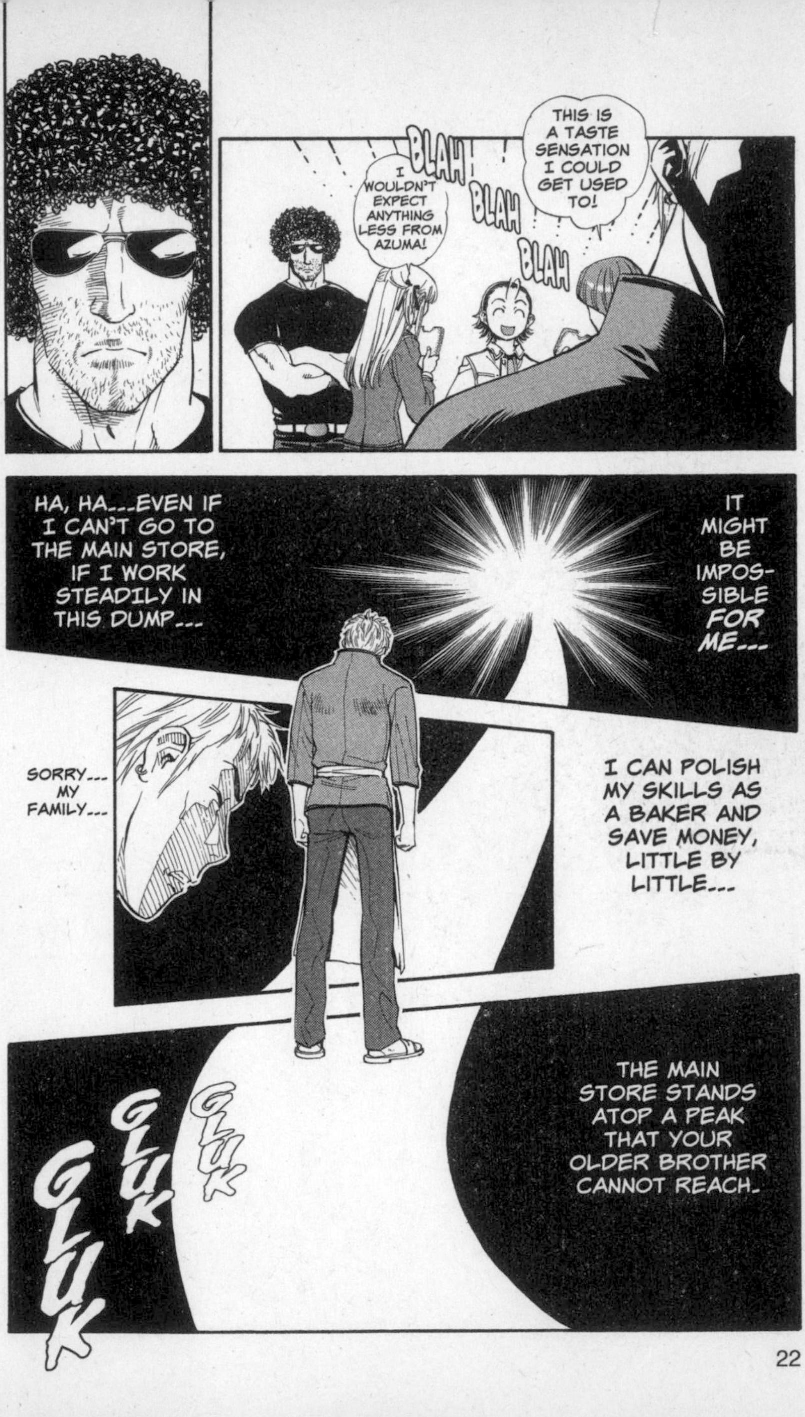
THIS IS A TASTE SENSATION I COULD GET USED TO!
BLAH
BLAH
BLAH
I WOULDN'T EXPECT ANYTHING LESS FROM AZUMA!
IT MIGHT BE IMPOS-SIBLE FOR ME...
HA, HA...EVEN IF I CAN'T GO TO THE MAIN STORE, IF I WORK STEADILY IN THIS DUMP...
I CAN POLISH MY SKILLS AS A BAKER AND SAVE MONEY, LITTLE BY LITTLE...
SORRY... MY FAMILY...
THE MAIN STORE STANDS ATOP A PEAK THAT YOUR OLDER BROTHER CANNOT REACH.
GLUK
GLUK
GLUK

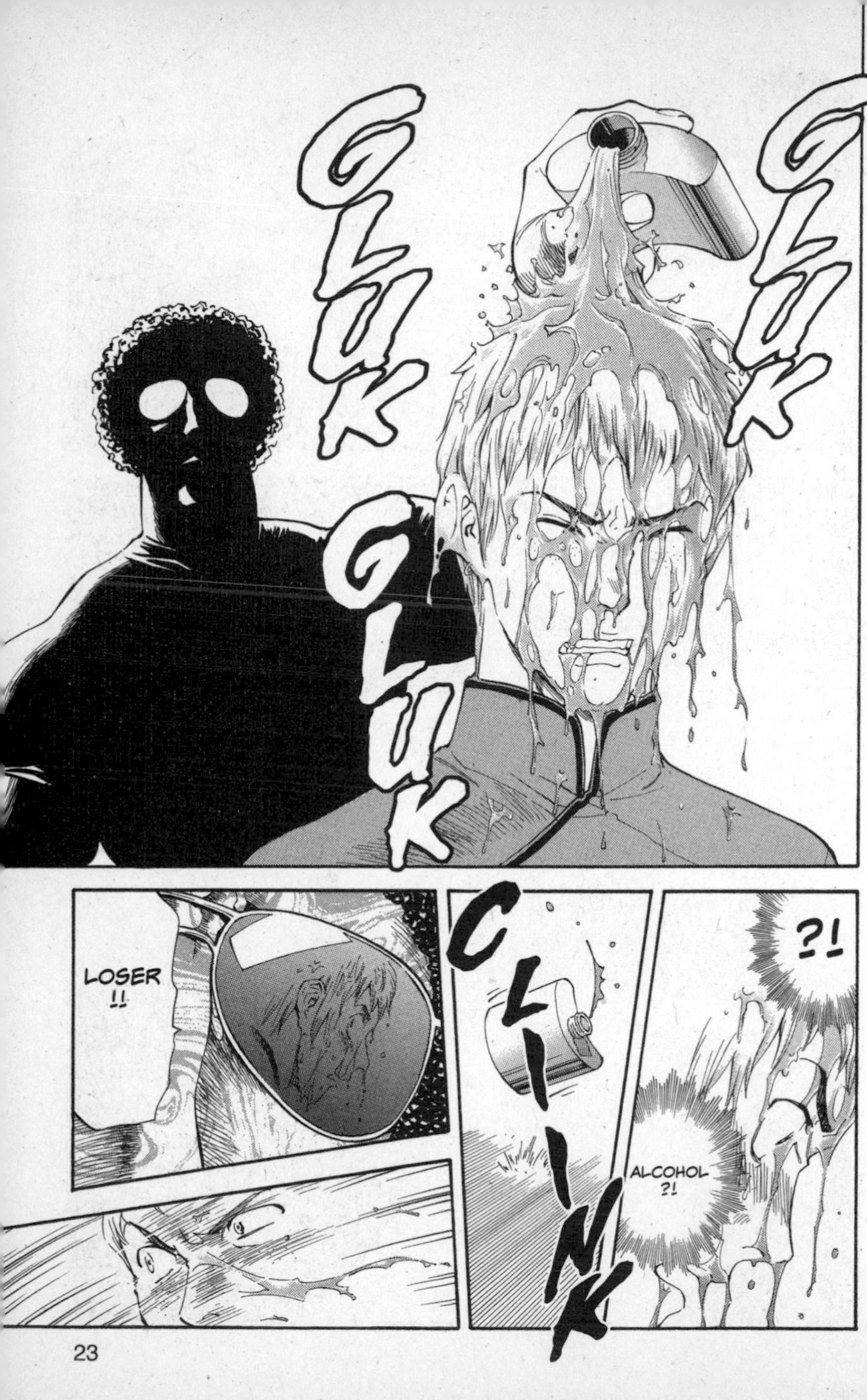
GLUK
GLUK
GLUK
?!
ALCOHOL ?!
CLINK
LOSER !!

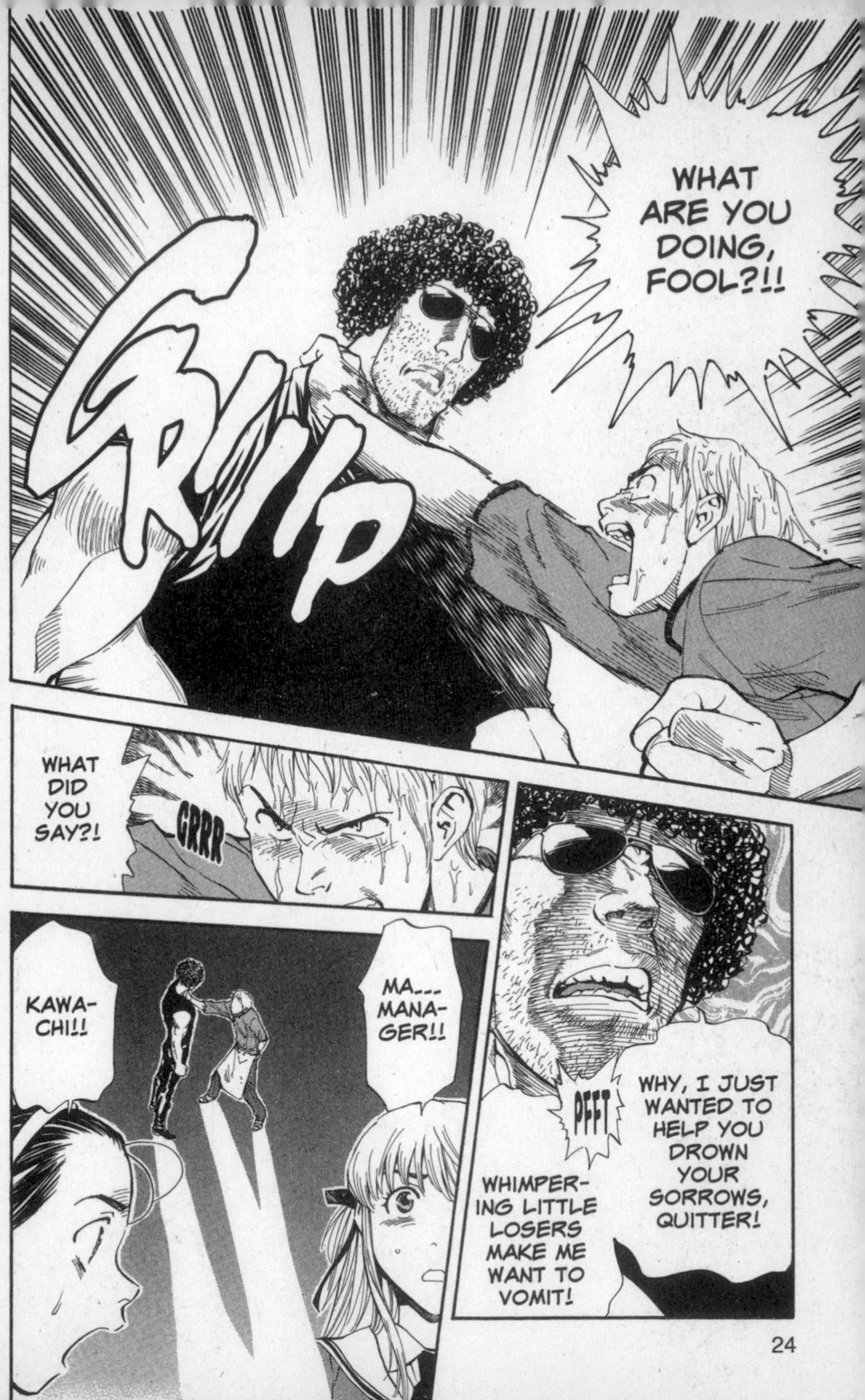
WHAT ARE YOU DOING, FOOL?!!
PFFT
WHY, I JUST WANTED TO HELP YOU DROWN YOUR SORROWS, QUITTER!
WHIMPER-ING LITTLE LOSERS MAKE ME WANT TO VOMIT!
WHAT DID YOU SAY?!
GRRR
MA... MANA-GER!!
KAWA-CHI!!

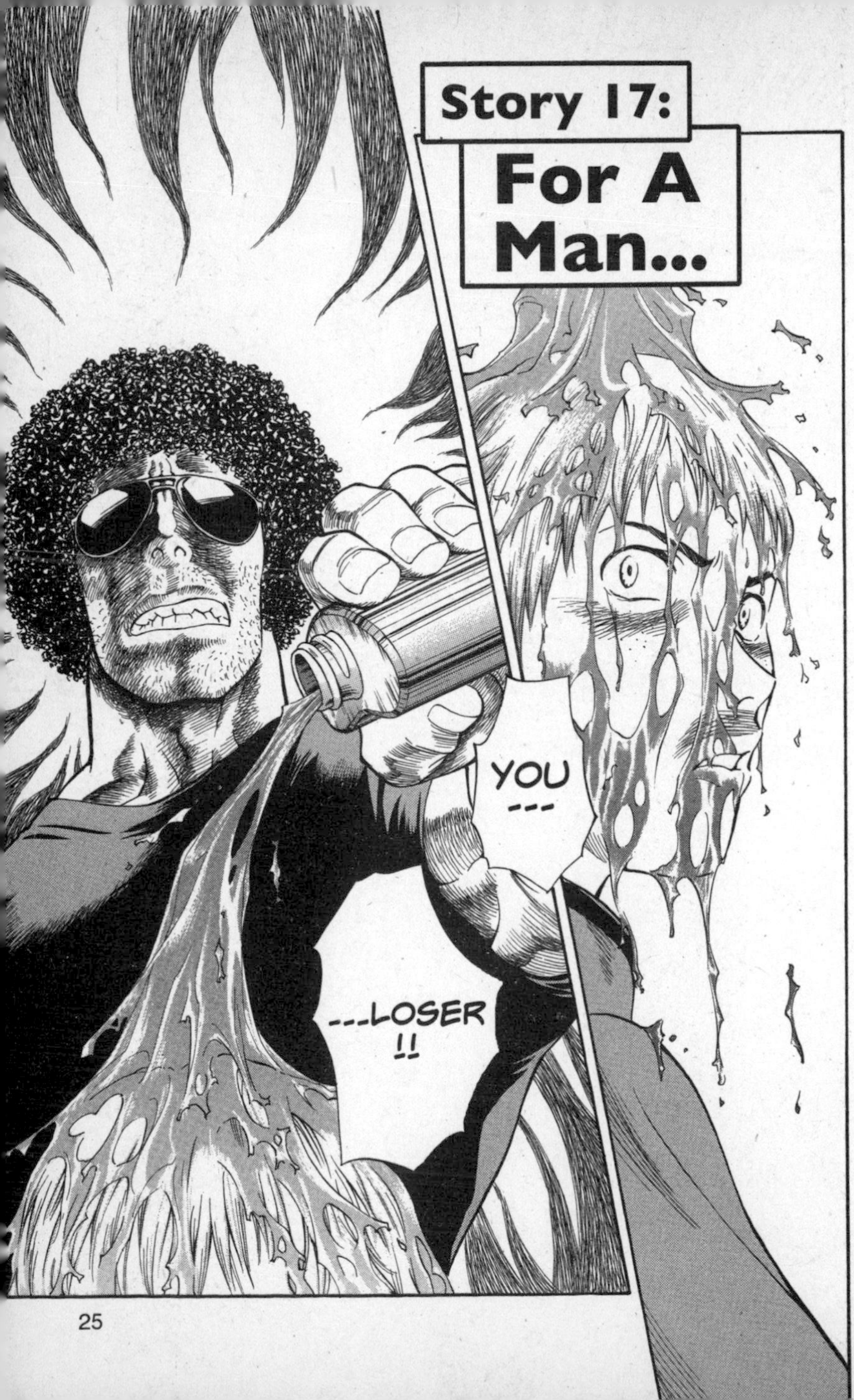
Story 17:
For A Man...
YOU ---
---LOSER !!

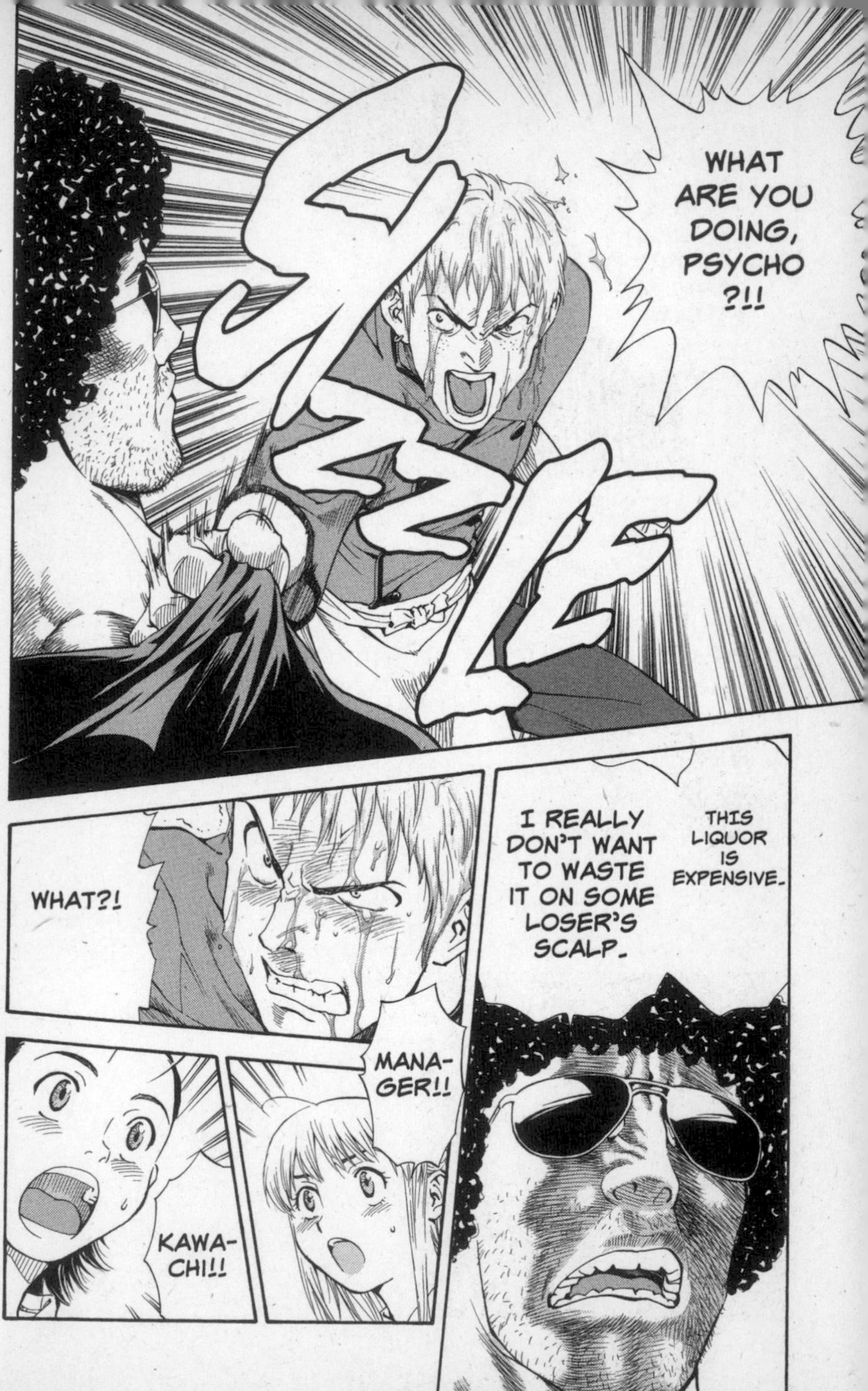
WHAT ARE YOU DOING, PSYCHO ?!!
THIS LIQUOR IS EXPENSIVE.
I REALLY DON'T WANT TO WASTE IT ON SOME LOSER'S SCALP.
WHAT?!
MANAGER!!
KAWACHI!!

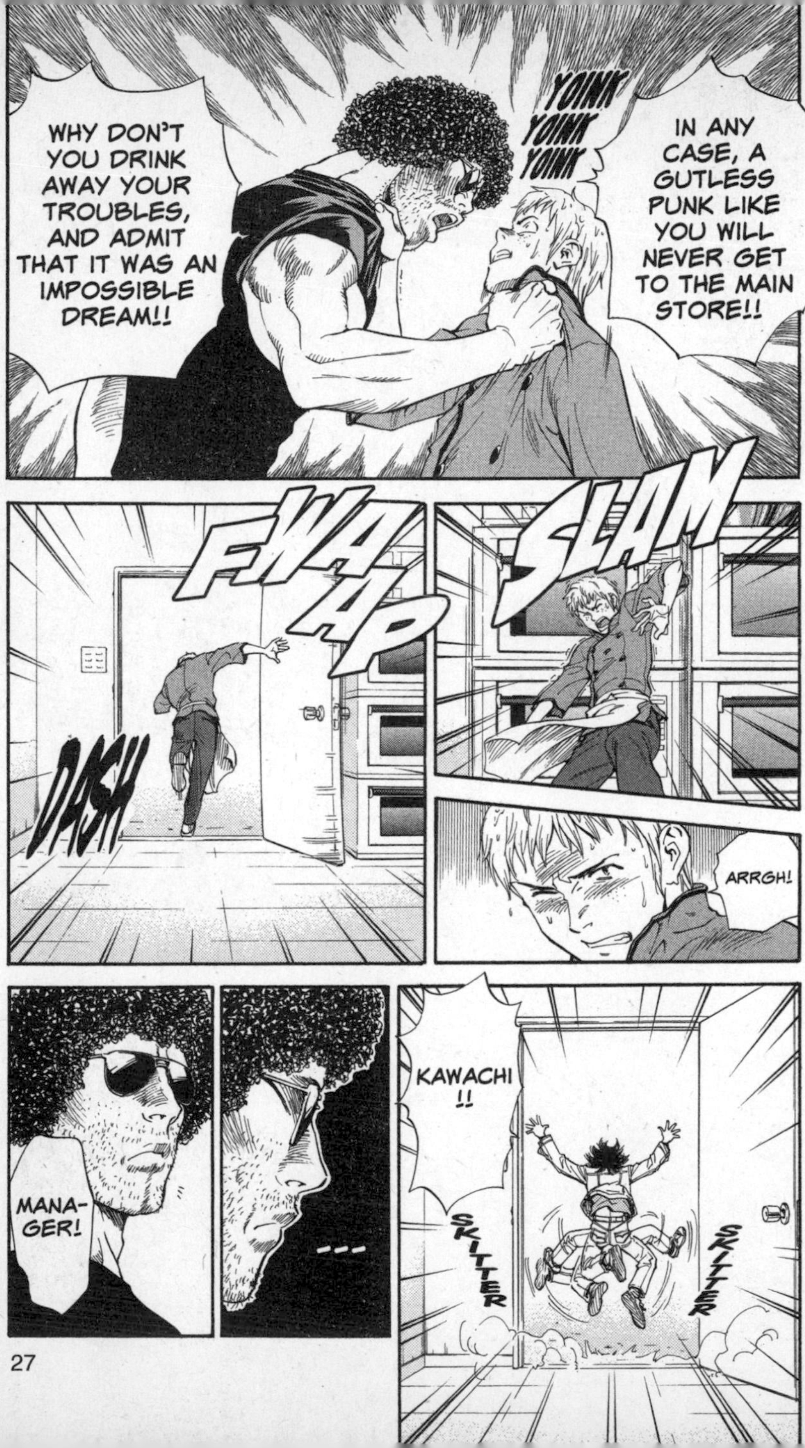
YOINK YOINK YOINK
IN ANY CASE, A GUTLESS PUNK LIKE YOU WILL NEVER GET TO THE MAIN STORE!!
WHY DON'T YOU DRINK AWAY YOUR TROUBLES, AND ADMIT THAT IT WAS AN IMPOSSIBLE DREAM!!
SLAM
ARRGH!
F-WAP
DASH
KAWACHI !!
SKITTER
SKITTER
...
MANA-GER!

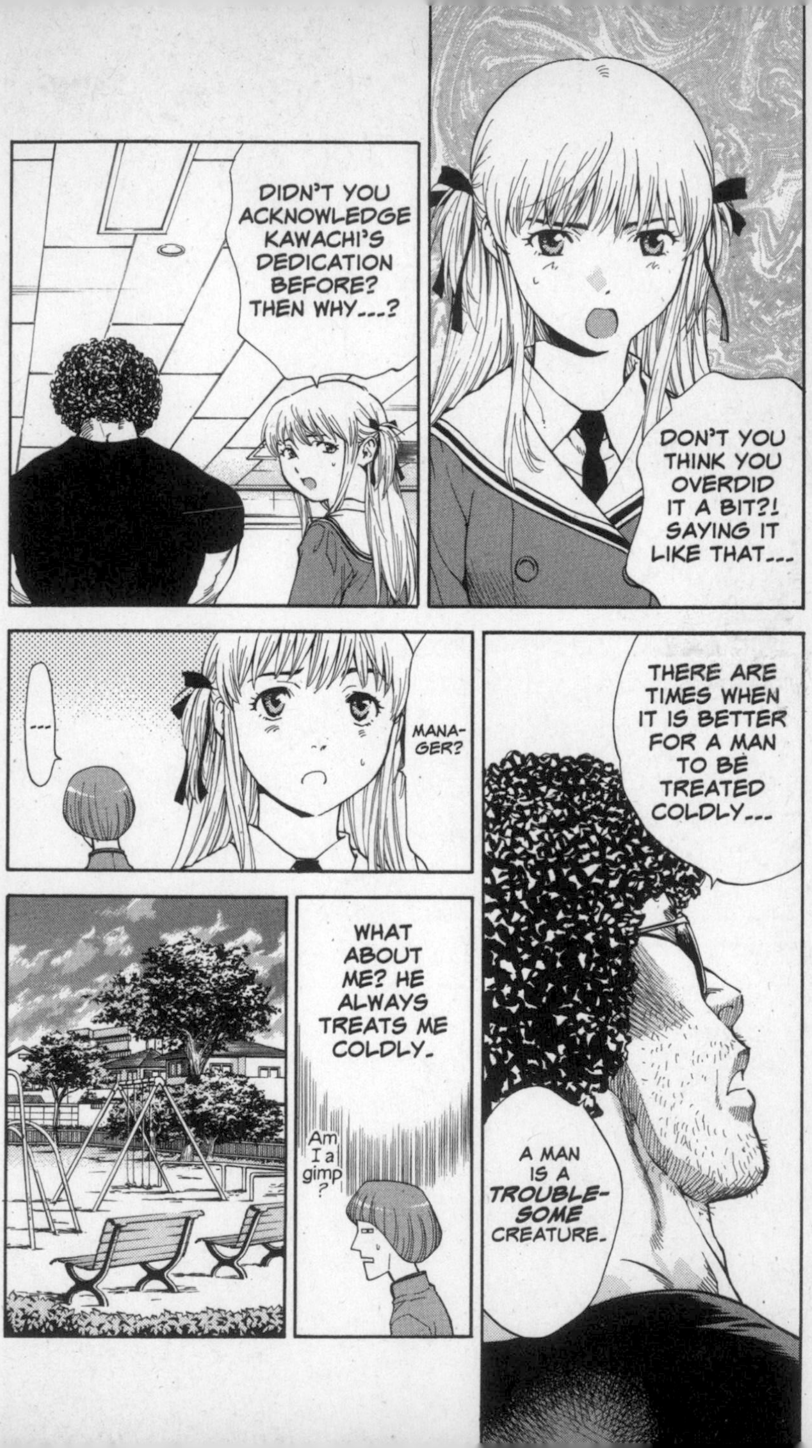

DON'T YOU THINK YOU OVERDID IT A BIT?! SAYING IT LIKE THAT...
DIDN'T YOU ACKNOWLEDGE KAWACHI'S DEDICATION BEFORE? THEN WHY...?
THERE ARE TIMES WHEN IT IS BETTER FOR A MAN TO BE TREATED COLDLY...
A MAN IS A *TROUBLESOME* CREATURE.
MANAGER?
...
WHAT ABOUT ME? HE ALWAYS TREATS ME COLDLY.
Am I a gimp?

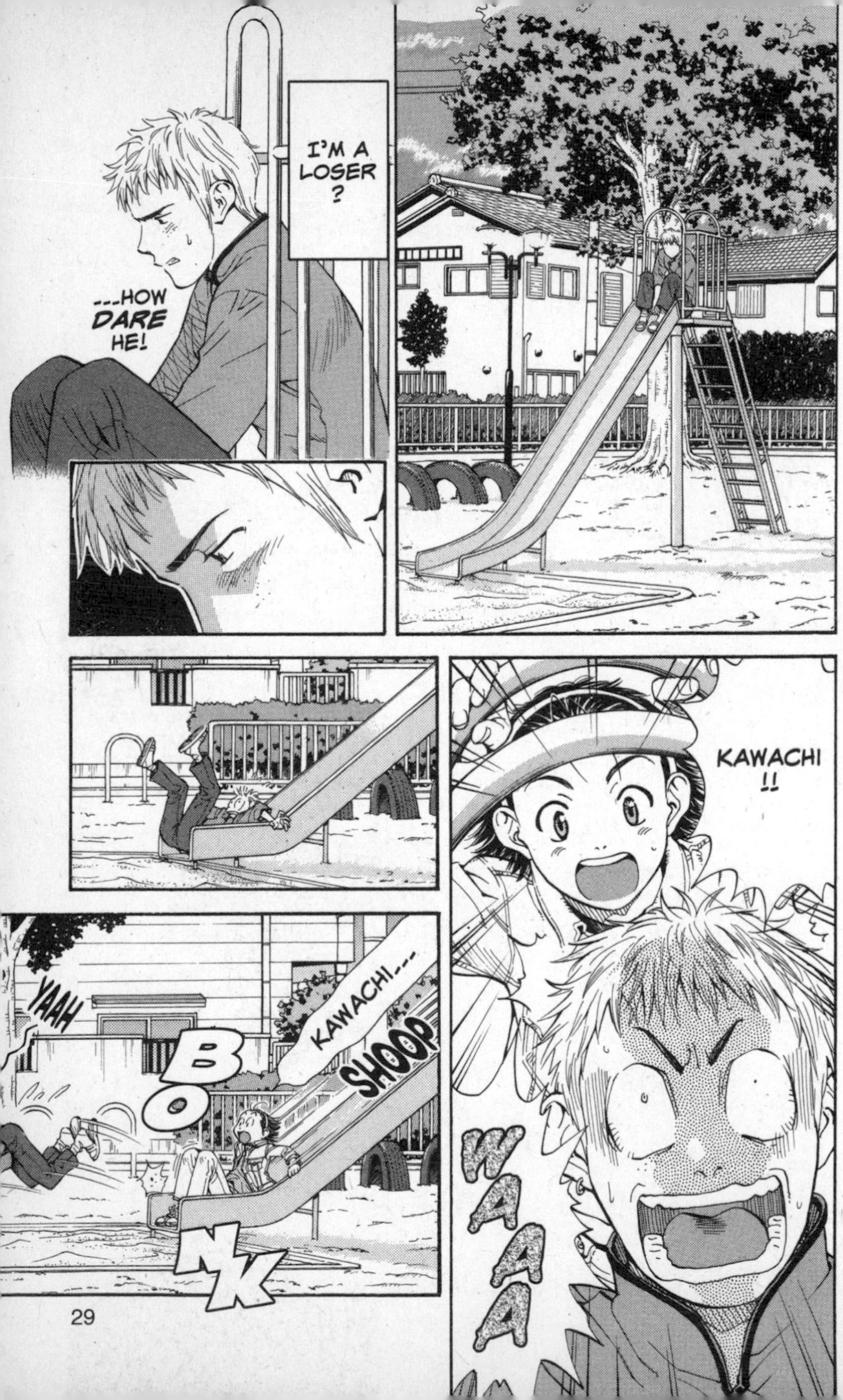
I'M A LOSER ?
...HOW DARE HE!
KAWACHI !!
WAAAA
KAWACHI...
SHOOP
YAAH
BONK

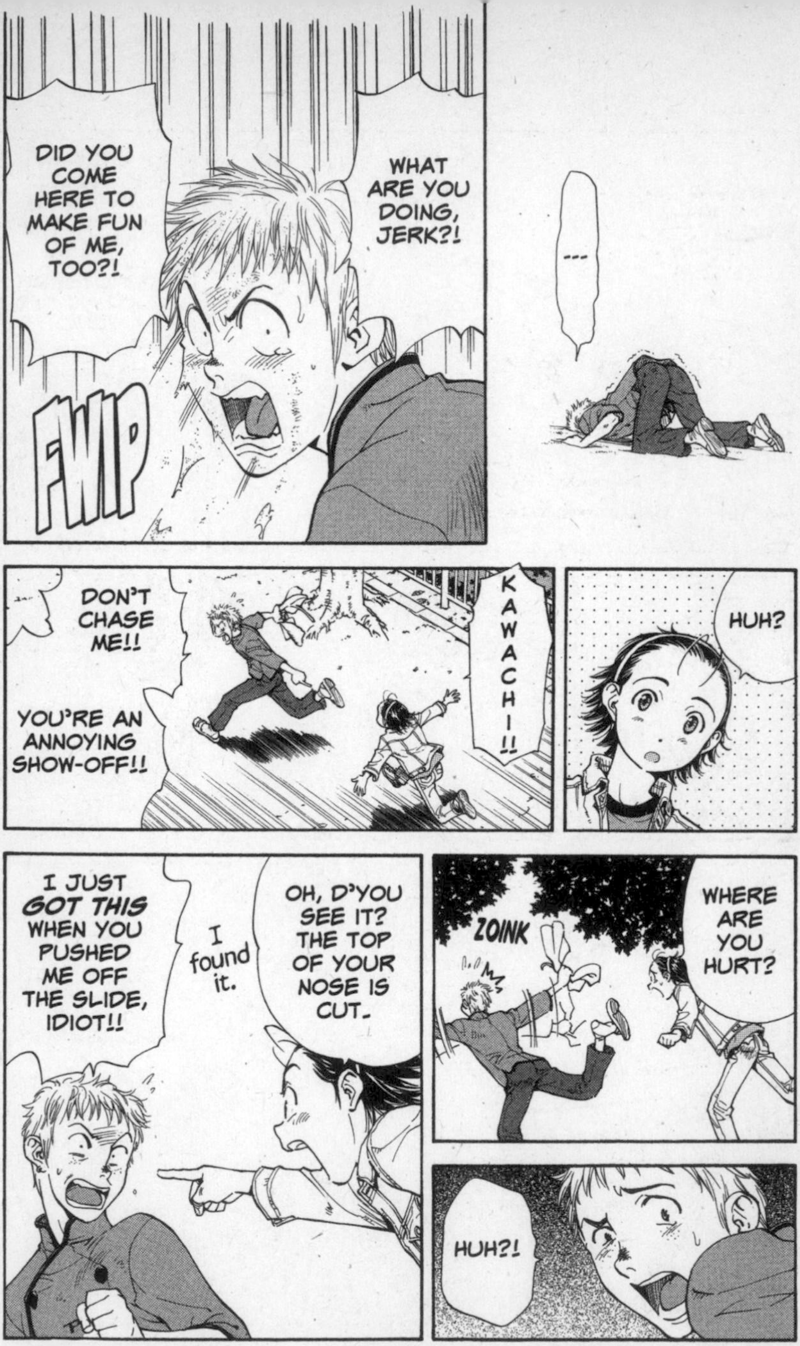
...
WHAT ARE YOU DOING, JERK?!
DID YOU COME HERE TO MAKE FUN OF ME, TOO?!
FWIP
HUH?
KAWACHI!!
DON'T CHASE ME!!
YOU'RE AN ANNOYING SHOW-OFF!!
WHERE ARE YOU HURT?
ZOINK
HUH?!
OH, D'YOU SEE IT? THE TOP OF YOUR NOSE IS CUT.
I found it.
I JUST ***GOT THIS*** WHEN YOU PUSHED ME OFF THE SLIDE, IDIOT!!

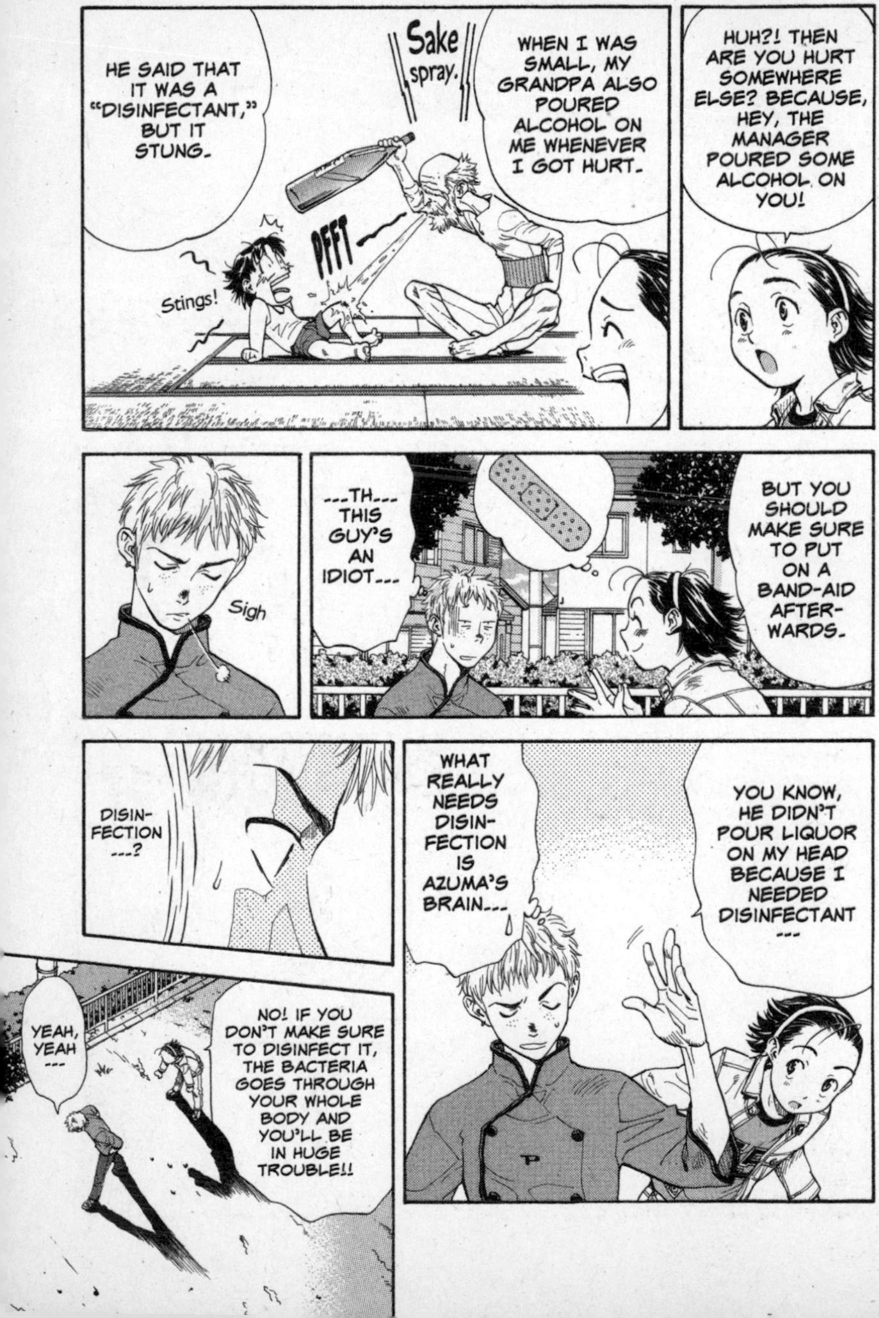
HUH?! THEN ARE YOU HURT SOMEWHERE ELSE? BECAUSE, HEY, THE MANAGER POURED SOME ALCOHOL ON YOU!
WHEN I WAS SMALL, MY GRANDPA ALSO POURED ALCOHOL ON ME WHENEVER I GOT HURT.
Sake spray.
PFFT
HE SAID THAT IT WAS A "DISINFECTANT," BUT IT STUNG.
Stings!
BUT YOU SHOULD MAKE SURE TO PUT ON A BAND-AID AFTER-WARDS.
...TH... THIS GUY'S AN IDIOT...
Sigh
YOU KNOW, HE DIDN'T POUR LIQUOR ON MY HEAD BECAUSE I NEEDED DISINFECTANT...
WHAT REALLY NEEDS DISIN-FECTION IS AZUMA'S BRAIN...
DISIN-FECTION...?
NO! IF YOU DON'T MAKE SURE TO DISINFECT IT, THE BACTERIA GOES THROUGH YOUR WHOLE BODY AND YOU'LL BE IN HUGE TROUBLE!!
YEAH, YEAH...

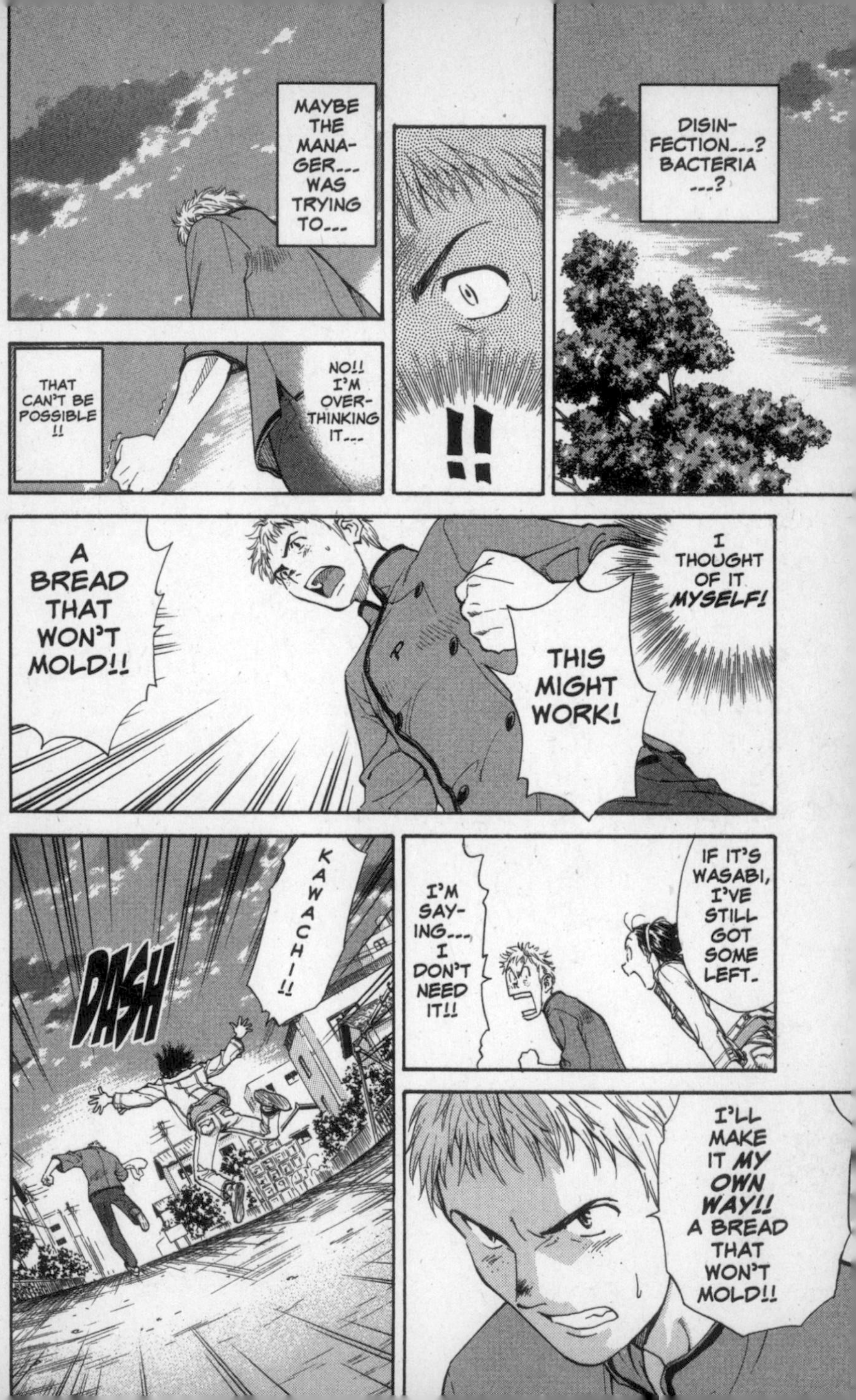
DISIN-FECTION...? BACTERIA...?
!!
MAYBE THE MANA-GER... WAS TRYING TO...
NO!! I'M OVER-THINKING IT...
THAT CAN'T BE POSSIBLE!!
I THOUGHT OF IT *MYSELF!*
THIS MIGHT WORK!
A BREAD THAT WON'T MOLD!!
IF IT'S WASABI, I'VE STILL GOT SOME LEFT.
I'M SAY-ING... I DON'T NEED IT!!
I'LL MAKE IT *MY OWN WAY!!* A BREAD THAT WON'T MOLD!!
KAWACHI!!
DASH

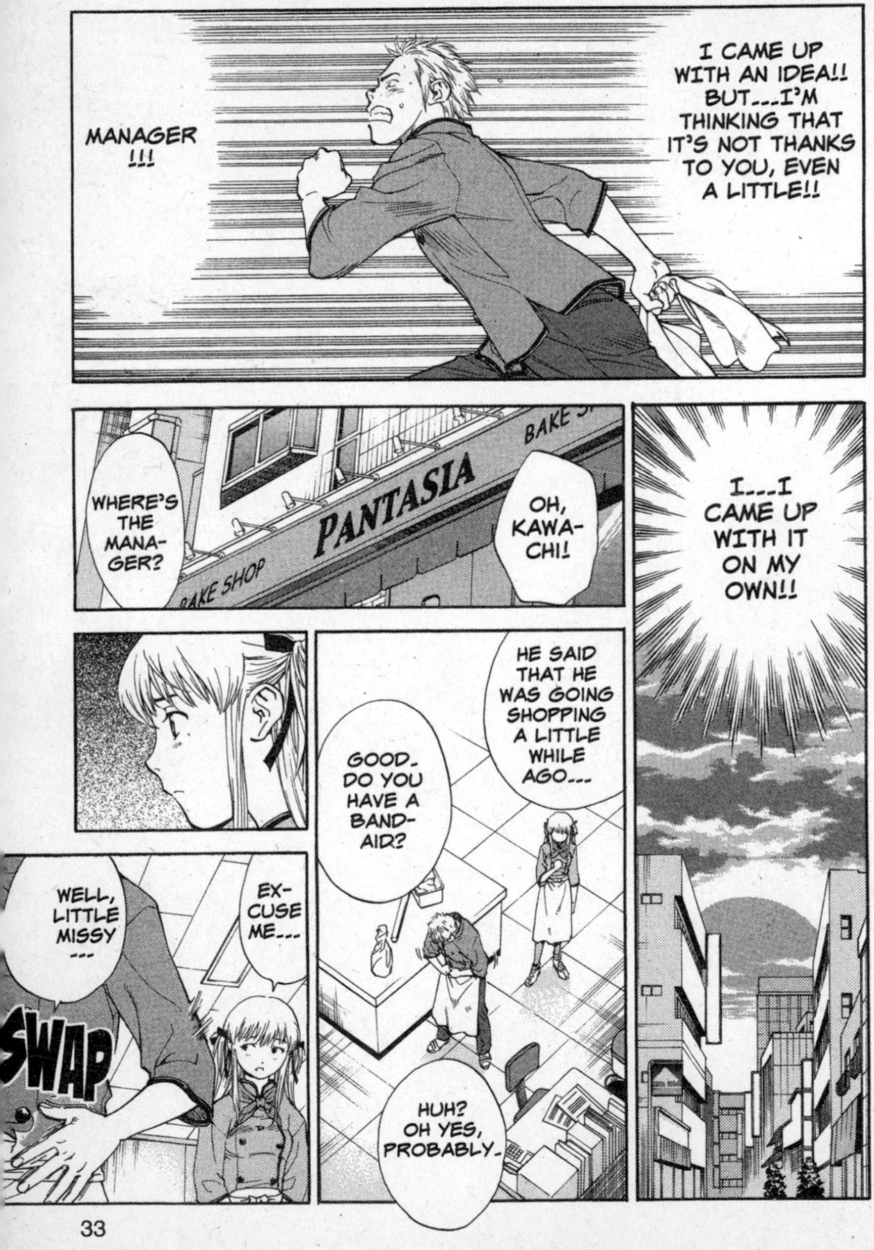
I CAME UP WITH AN IDEA!! BUT...I'M THINKING THAT IT'S NOT THANKS TO YOU, EVEN A LITTLE!!
MANAGER !!!
I...I CAME UP WITH IT ON MY OWN!!
BAKE SHOP
PANTASIA
BAKE SHOP
OH, KAWA-CHI!
WHERE'S THE MANA-GER?
HE SAID THAT HE WAS GOING SHOPPING A LITTLE WHILE AGO...
GOOD. DO YOU HAVE A BAND-AID?
HUH? OH YES, PROBABLY.
EX-CUSE ME...
WELL, LITTLE MISSY...
SWAP

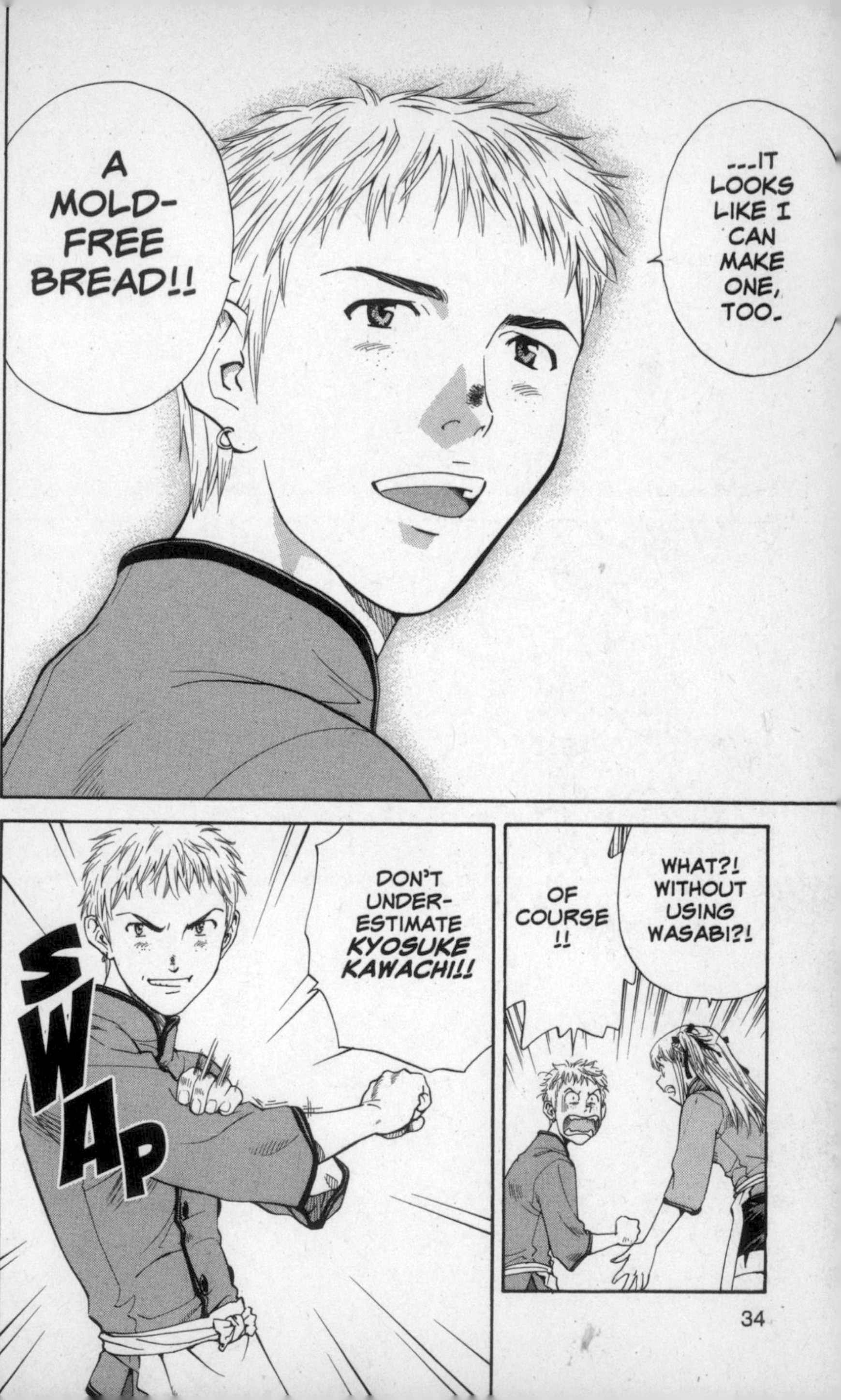
...IT LOOKS LIKE I CAN MAKE ONE, TOO.
A MOLD-FREE BREAD!!
WHAT?! WITHOUT USING WASABI?!
OF COURSE!!
DON'T UNDER-ESTIMATE KYOSUKE KAWACHI!!
SWAP

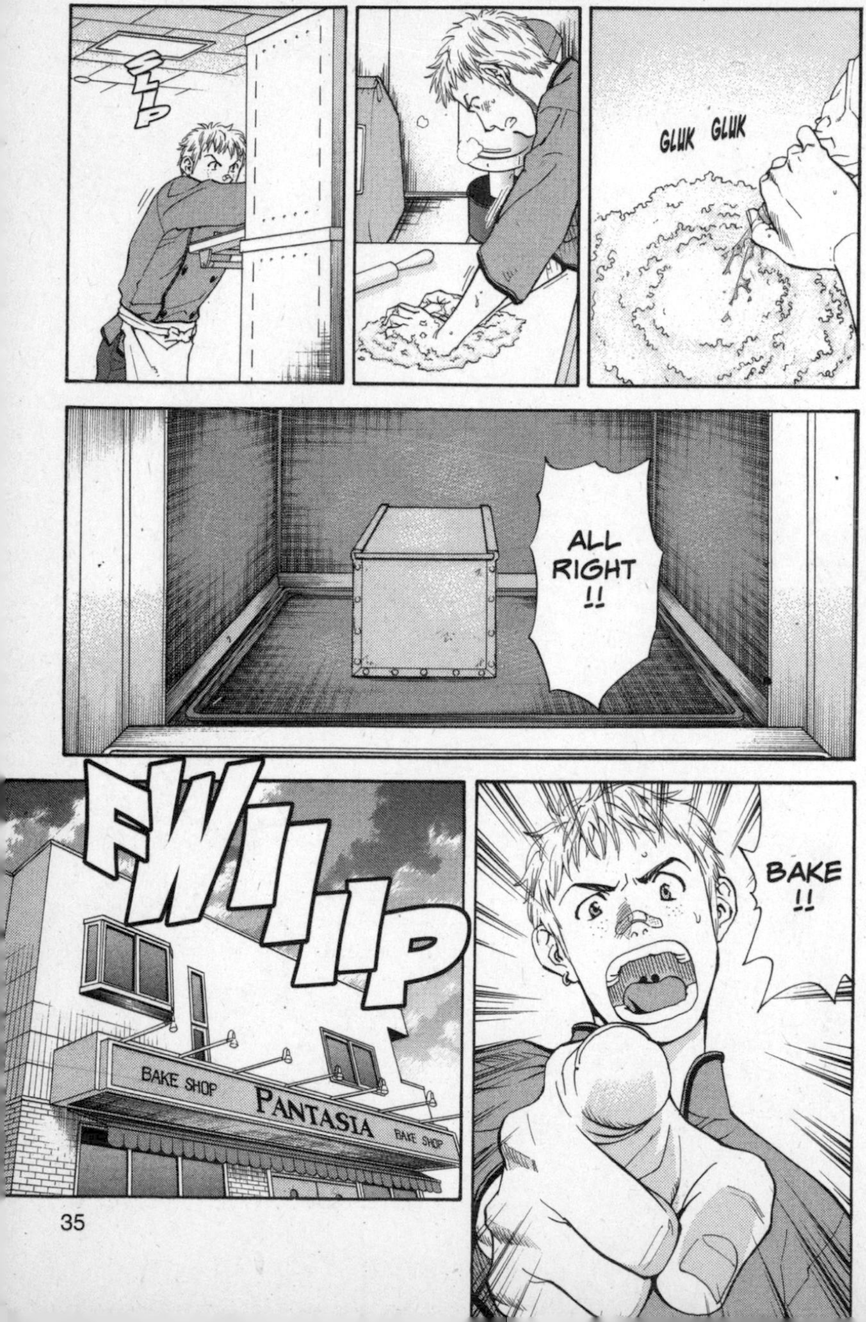
GLUK GLUK
SLIP
ALL RIGHT !!
BAKE !!
FWIIIIP
BAKE SHOP
PANTASIA
BAKE SHOP

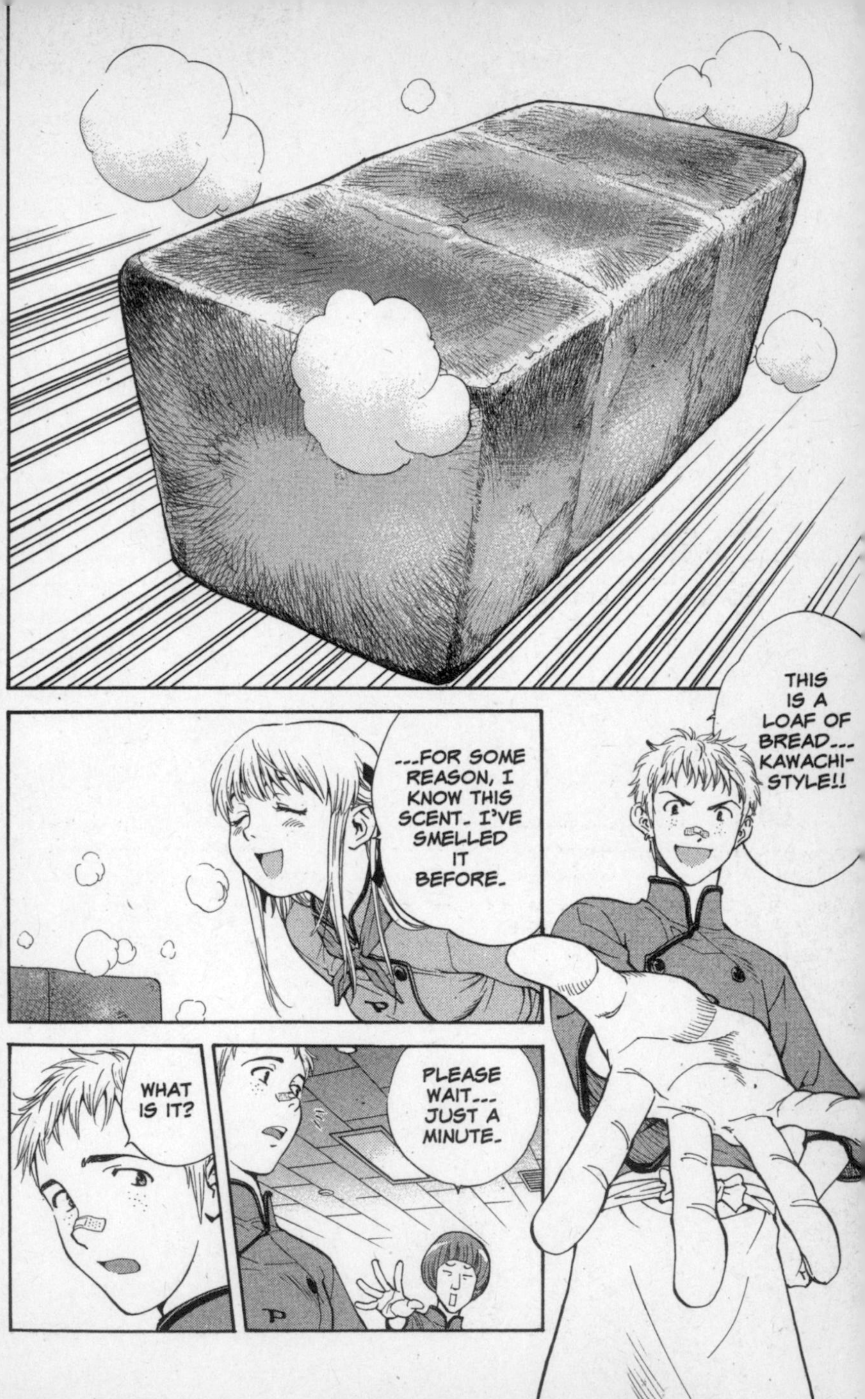
THIS IS A LOAF OF BREAD... KAWACHI-STYLE!!
...FOR SOME REASON, I KNOW THIS SCENT. I'VE SMELLED IT BEFORE.
PLEASE WAIT... JUST A MINUTE.
WHAT IS IT?

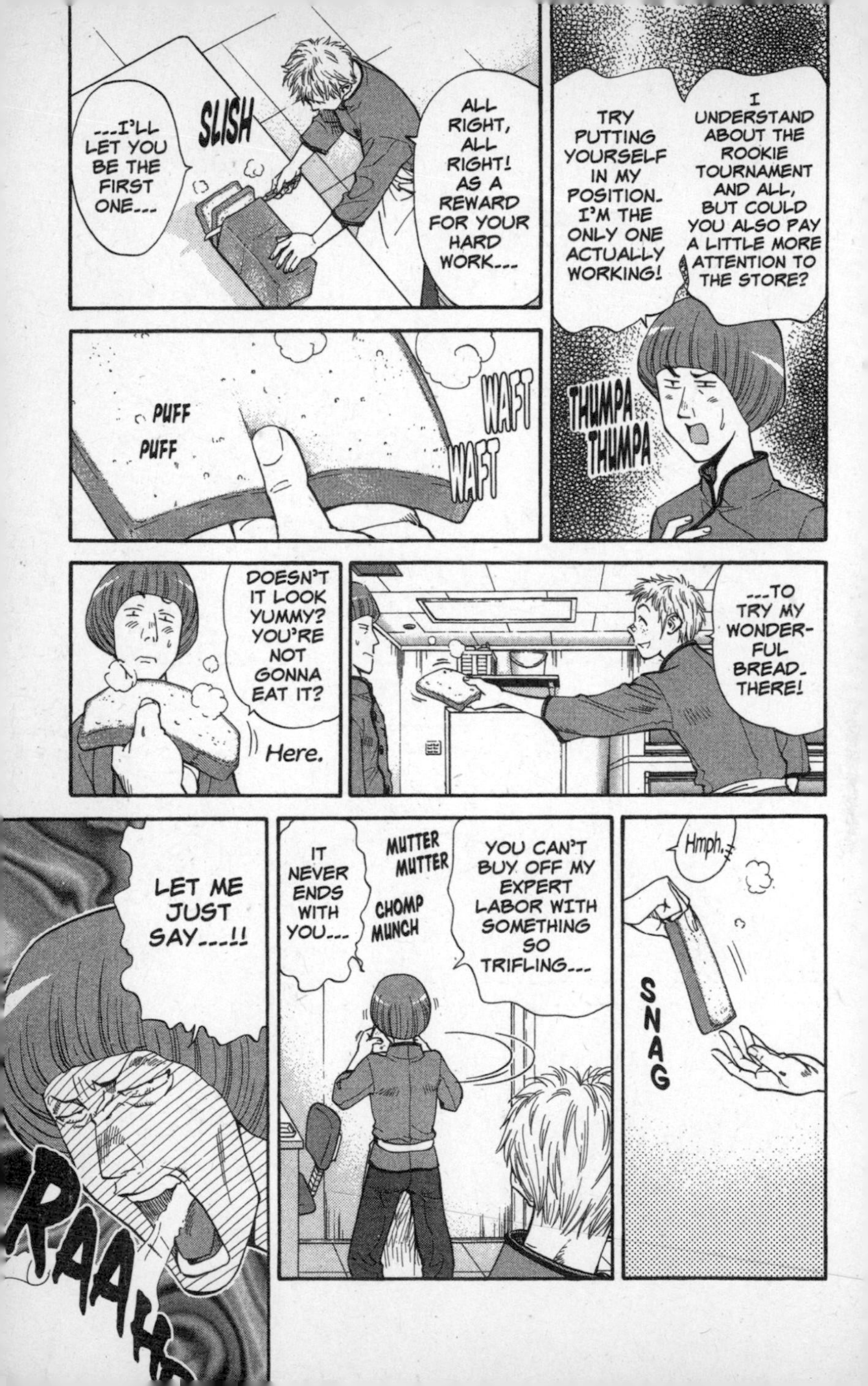
I UNDERSTAND ABOUT THE ROOKIE TOURNAMENT AND ALL, BUT COULD YOU ALSO PAY A LITTLE MORE ATTENTION TO THE STORE?
TRY PUTTING YOURSELF IN MY POSITION. I'M THE ONLY ONE ACTUALLY WORKING!
THUMPA THUMPA
ALL RIGHT, ALL RIGHT! AS A REWARD FOR YOUR HARD WORK...
SLISH
...I'LL LET YOU BE THE FIRST ONE...
WAFT
WAFT
PUFF
PUFF
...TO TRY MY WONDERFUL BREAD. THERE!
DOESN'T IT LOOK YUMMY? YOU'RE NOT GONNA EAT IT?
Here.
Hmph.
SNAG
YOU CAN'T BUY OFF MY EXPERT LABOR WITH SOMETHING SO TRIFLING...
MUTTER MUTTER
CHOMP MUNCH
IT NEVER ENDS WITH YOU...
LET ME JUST SAY...!!
RAAH

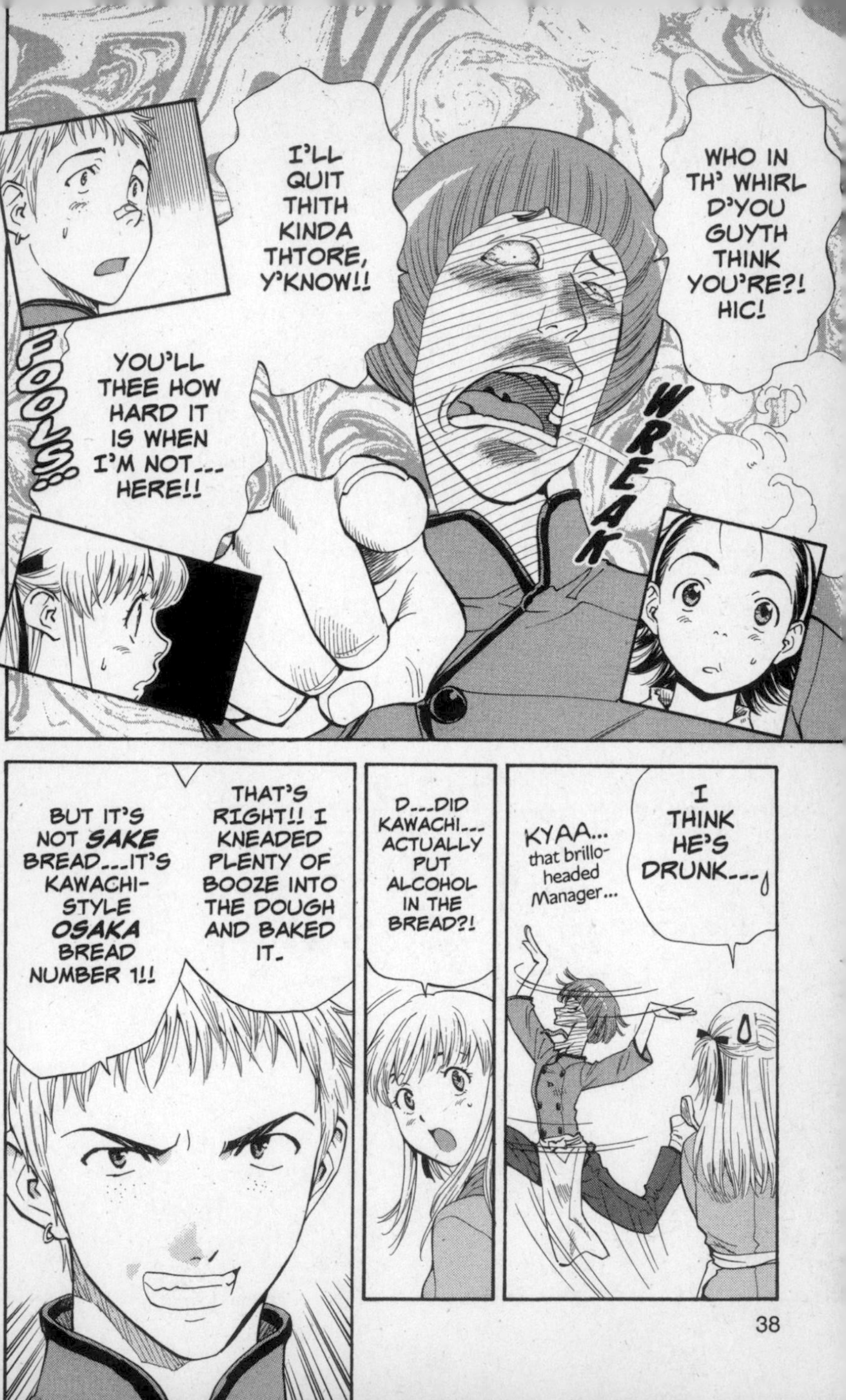
WHO IN TH' WHIRL D'YOU GUYTH THINK YOU'RE?! HIC!
I'LL QUIT THITH KINDA THTORE, Y'KNOW!!
WREAK
YOU'LL THEE HOW HARD IT IS WHEN I'M NOT... HERE!!
FOOLS!!
I THINK HE'S DRUNK...
KYAA... that brillo-headed Manager...
D...DID KAWACHI... ACTUALLY PUT ALCOHOL IN THE BREAD?!
THAT'S RIGHT!! I KNEADED PLENTY OF BOOZE INTO THE DOUGH AND BAKED IT.
BUT IT'S NOT SAKE BREAD...IT'S KAWACHI-STYLE OSAKA BREAD NUMBER 1!!

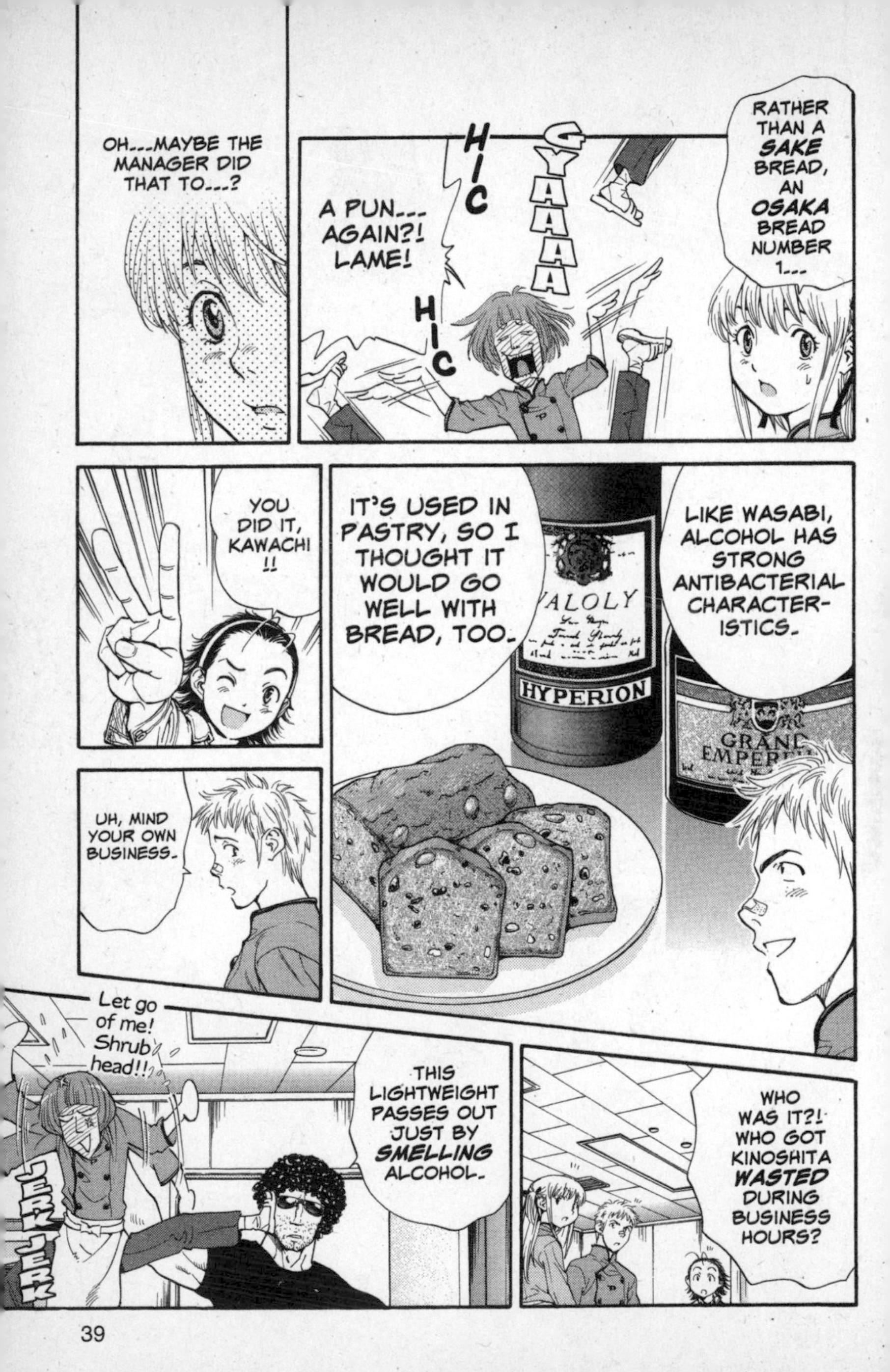
RATHER THAN A SAKE BREAD, AN OSAKA BREAD NUMBER 1...
GYAAAAA
HIC
HIC
A PUN... AGAIN?! LAME!
OH...MAYBE THE MANAGER DID THAT TO...?
LIKE WASABI, ALCOHOL HAS STRONG ANTIBACTERIAL CHARACTER-ISTICS.
IT'S USED IN PASTRY, SO I THOUGHT IT WOULD GO WELL WITH BREAD, TOO.
HYPERION
YOU DID IT, KAWACHI!!
UH, MIND YOUR OWN BUSINESS.
WHO WAS IT?! WHO GOT KINOSHITA WASTED DURING BUSINESS HOURS?
THIS LIGHTWEIGHT PASSES OUT JUST BY SMELLING ALCOHOL.
Let go of me! Shrub head!!
JERK JERK

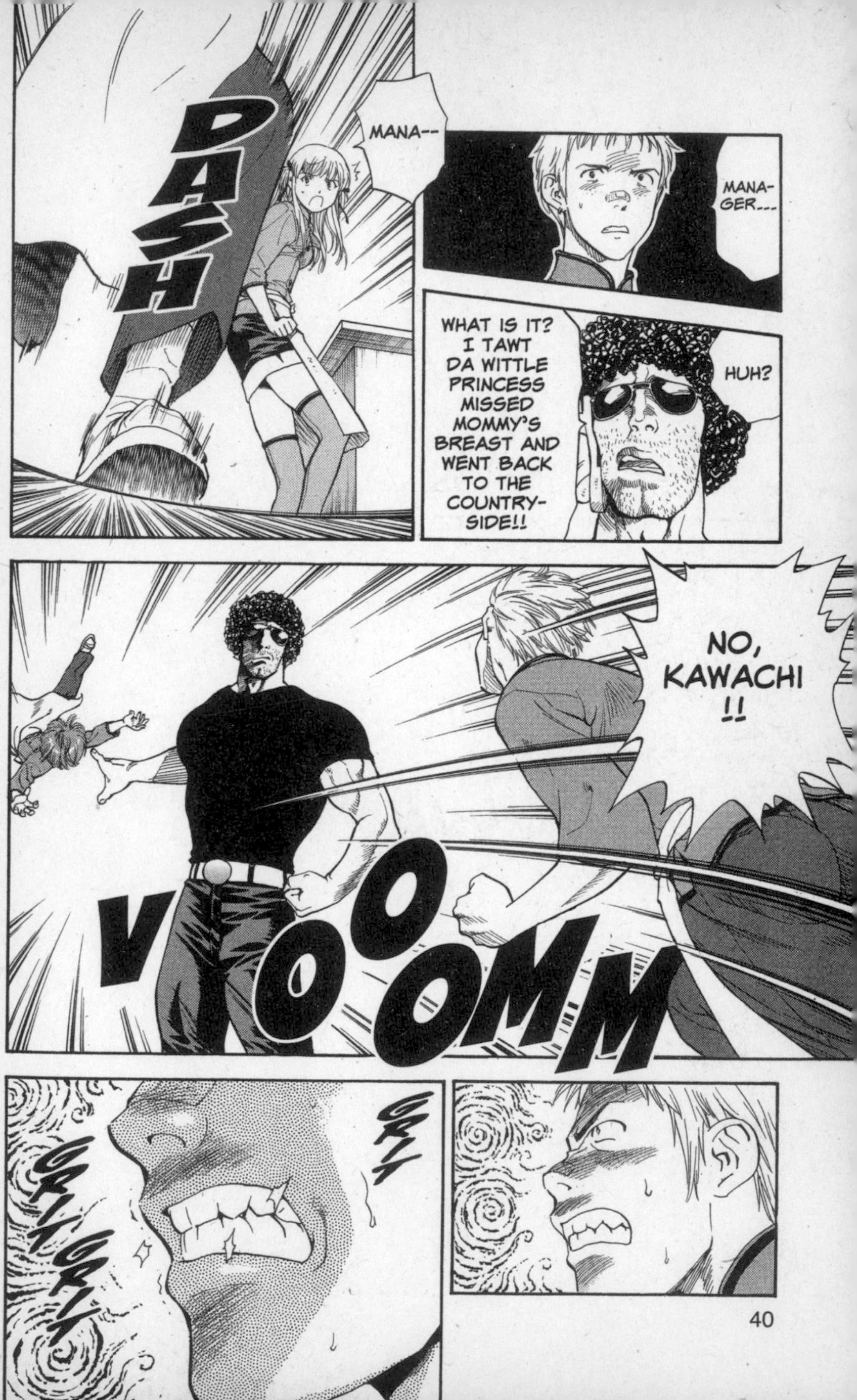

MANA--
MANA-GER...
HUH?
WHAT IS IT? I TAWT DA WITTLE PRINCESS MISSED MOMMY'S BREAST AND WENT BACK TO THE COUNTRY-SIDE!!
DASH
NO, KAWACHI !!
VOOOOMM

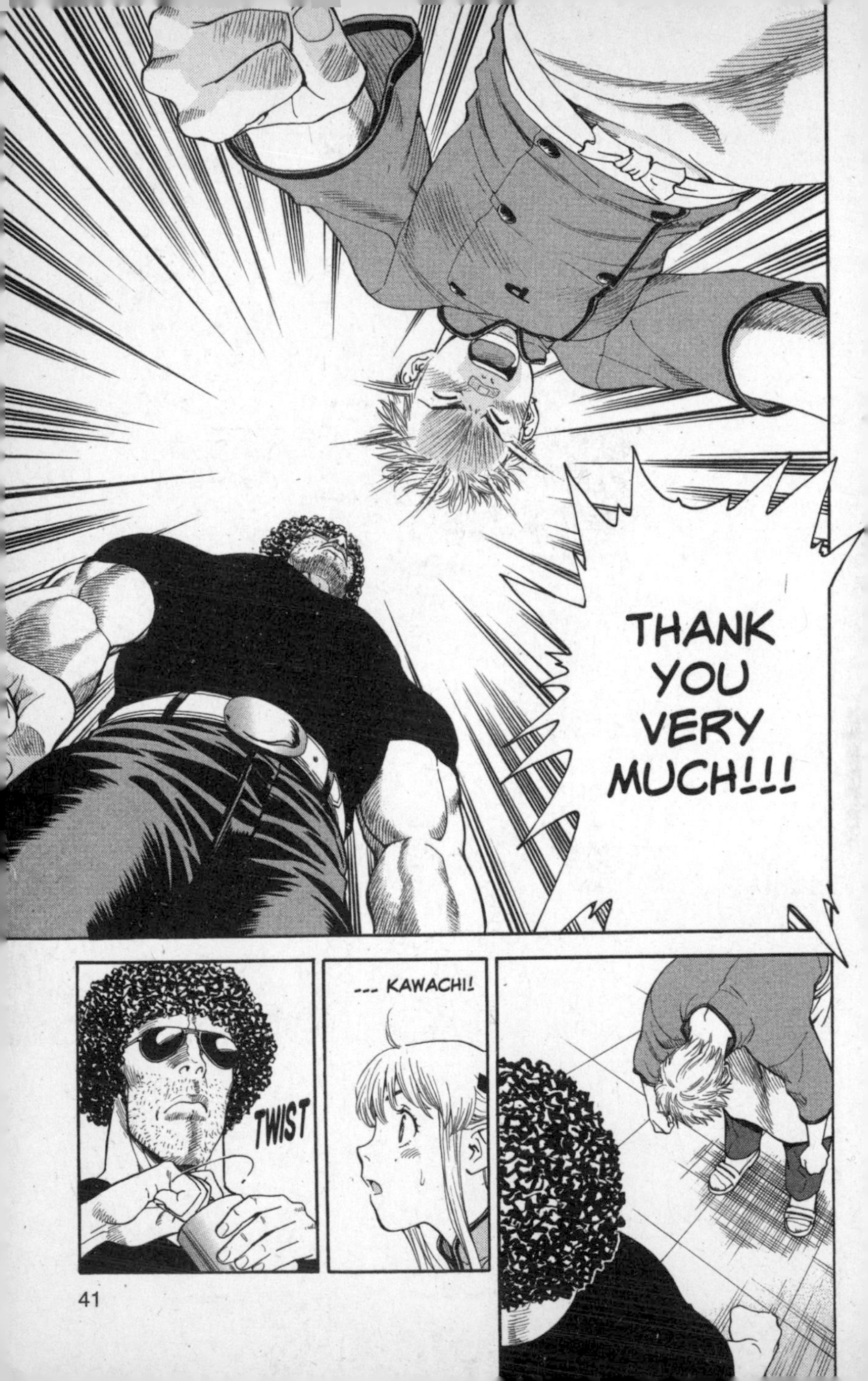
THANK YOU VERY MUCH!!!
--- KAWACHI!
TWIST

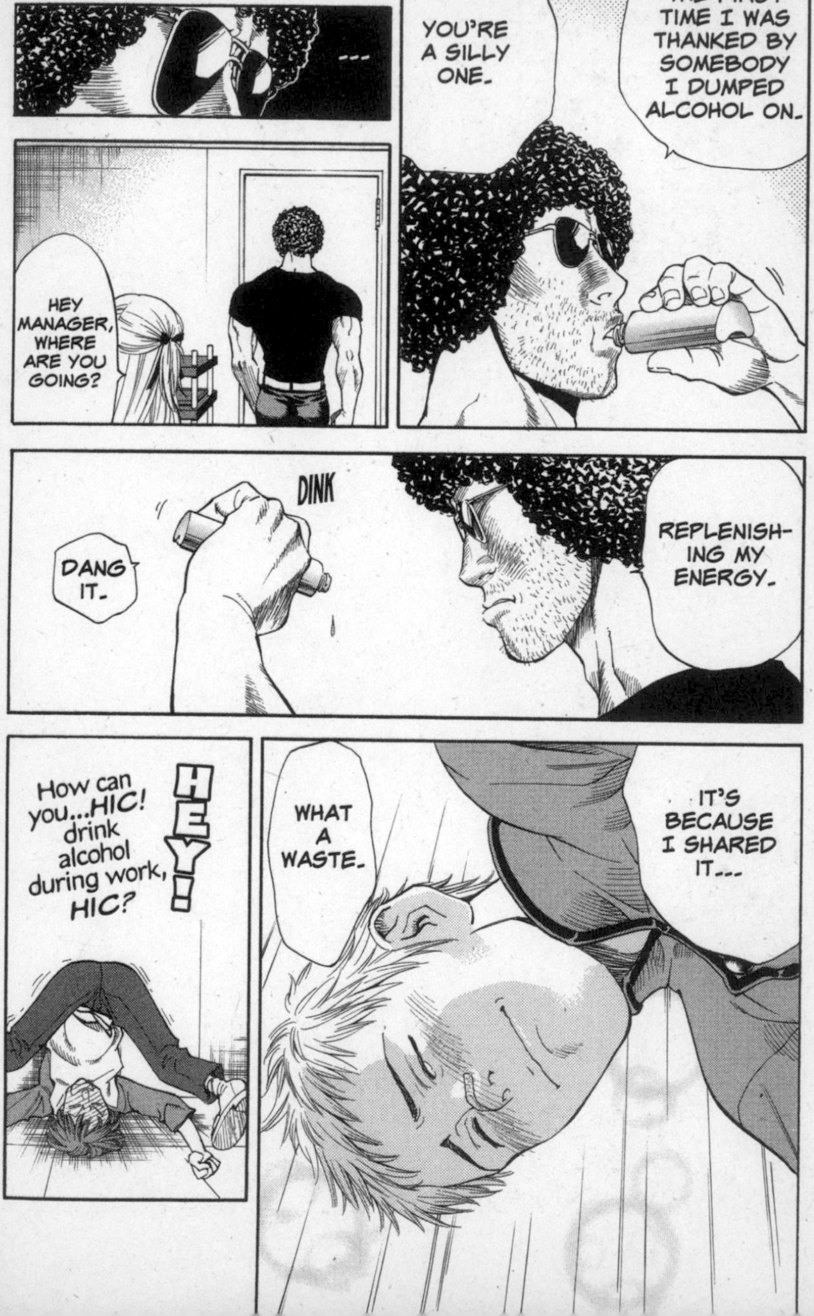

THIS IS THE FIRST TIME I WAS THANKED BY SOMEBODY I DUMPED ALCOHOL ON.
YOU'RE A SILLY ONE.
...
HEY MANAGER, WHERE ARE YOU GOING?
REPLENISHING MY ENERGY.
DINK
DANG IT.
IT'S BECAUSE I SHARED IT...
WHAT A WASTE.
HEY!
How can you...HIC! drink alcohol during work, HIC?

Story 18: A True Rival

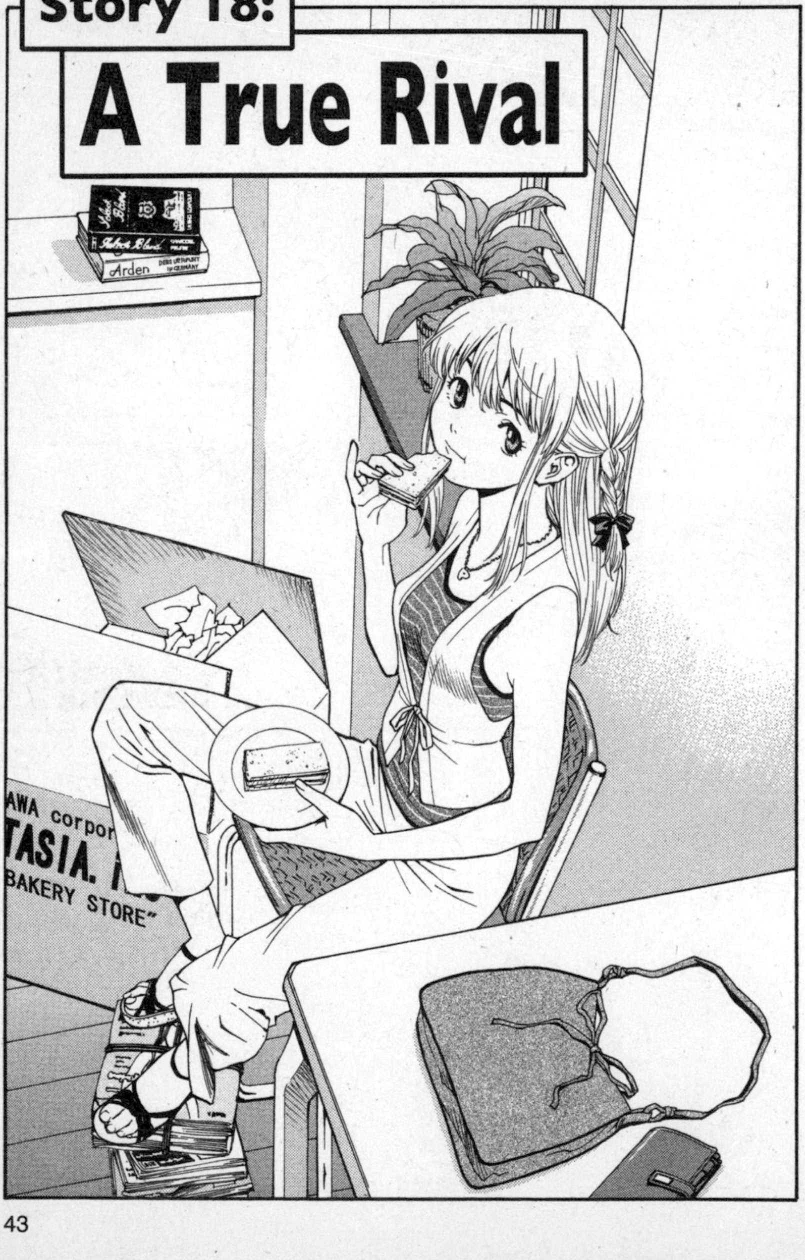
Arden
AWA corpor
TASIA.
BAKERY STORE"

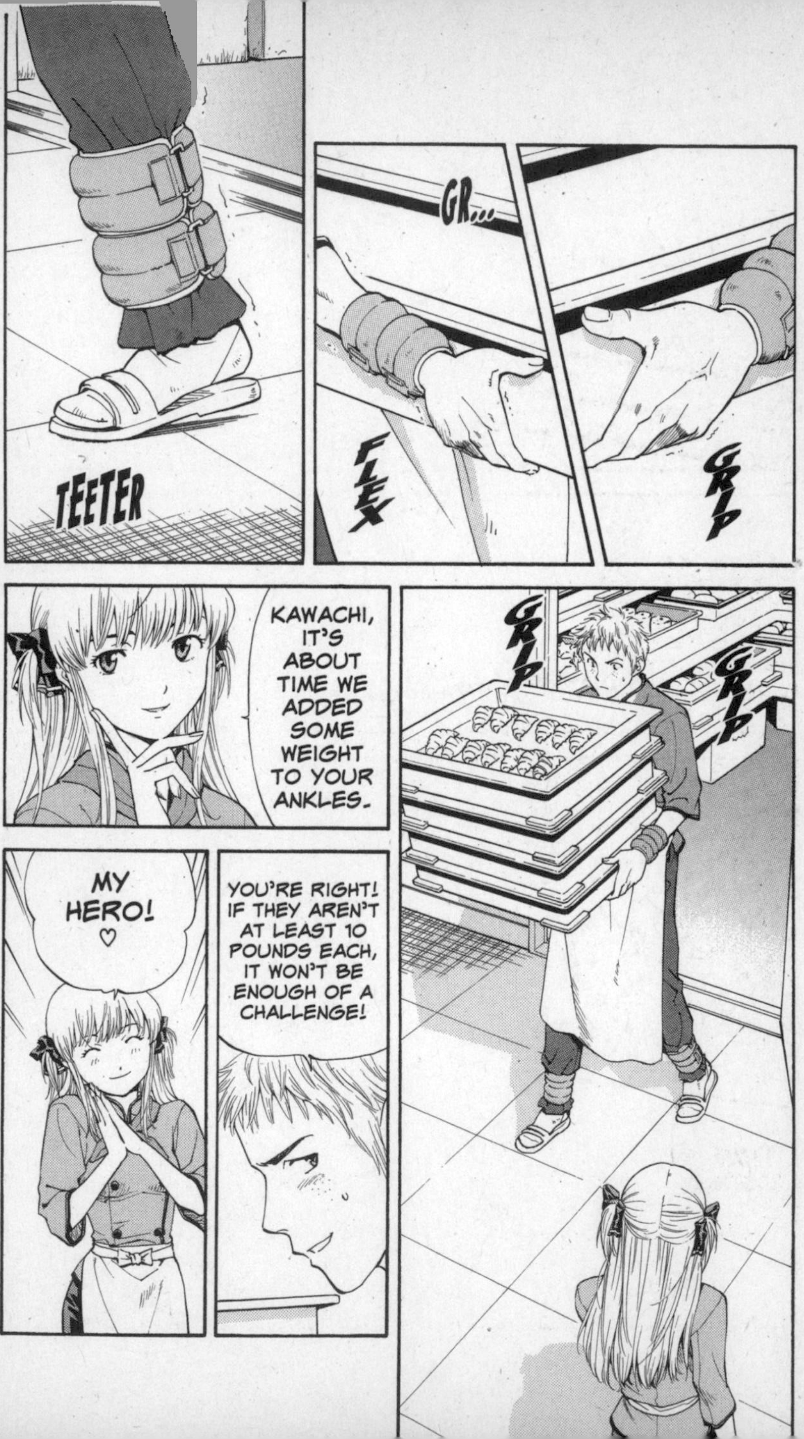
GRIP
GR...
FLEX
TEETER
GRIP
GRIP
KAWACHI, IT'S ABOUT TIME WE ADDED SOME WEIGHT TO YOUR ANKLES.
YOU'RE RIGHT! IF THEY AREN'T AT LEAST 10 POUNDS EACH, IT WON'T BE ENOUGH OF A CHALLENGE!
MY HERO! ♡

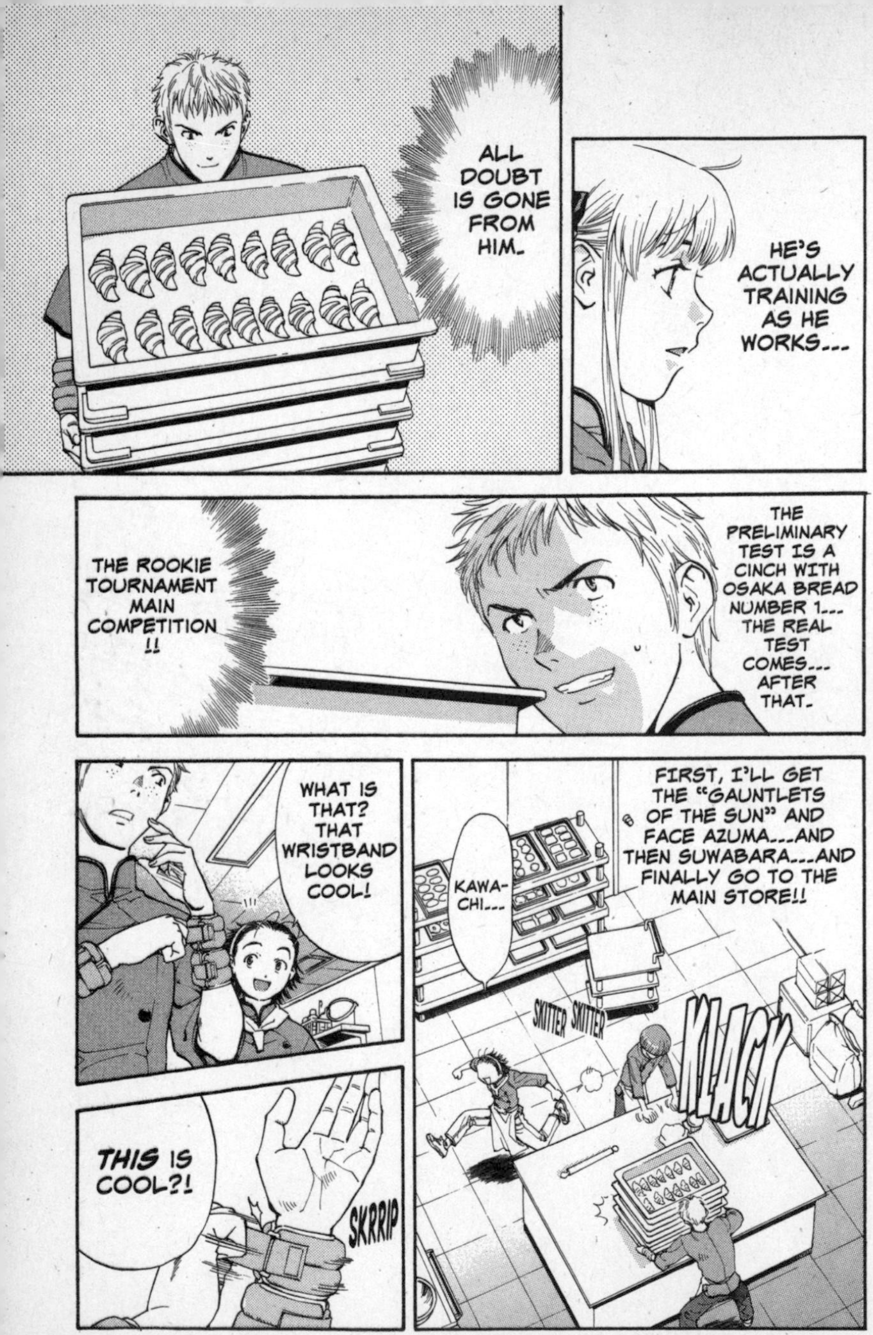
HE'S ACTUALLY TRAINING AS HE WORKS...
ALL DOUBT IS GONE FROM HIM.
THE PRELIMINARY TEST IS A CINCH WITH OSAKA BREAD NUMBER 1... THE REAL TEST COMES... AFTER THAT.
THE ROOKIE TOURNAMENT MAIN COMPETITION !!
FIRST, I'LL GET THE "GAUNTLETS OF THE SUN" AND FACE AZUMA...AND THEN SUWABARA...AND FINALLY GO TO THE MAIN STORE!!
KAWA-CHI...
SKITTER SKITTER
KLACK
WHAT IS THAT? THAT WRISTBAND LOOKS COOL!
THIS IS COOL?!
SKRRIP

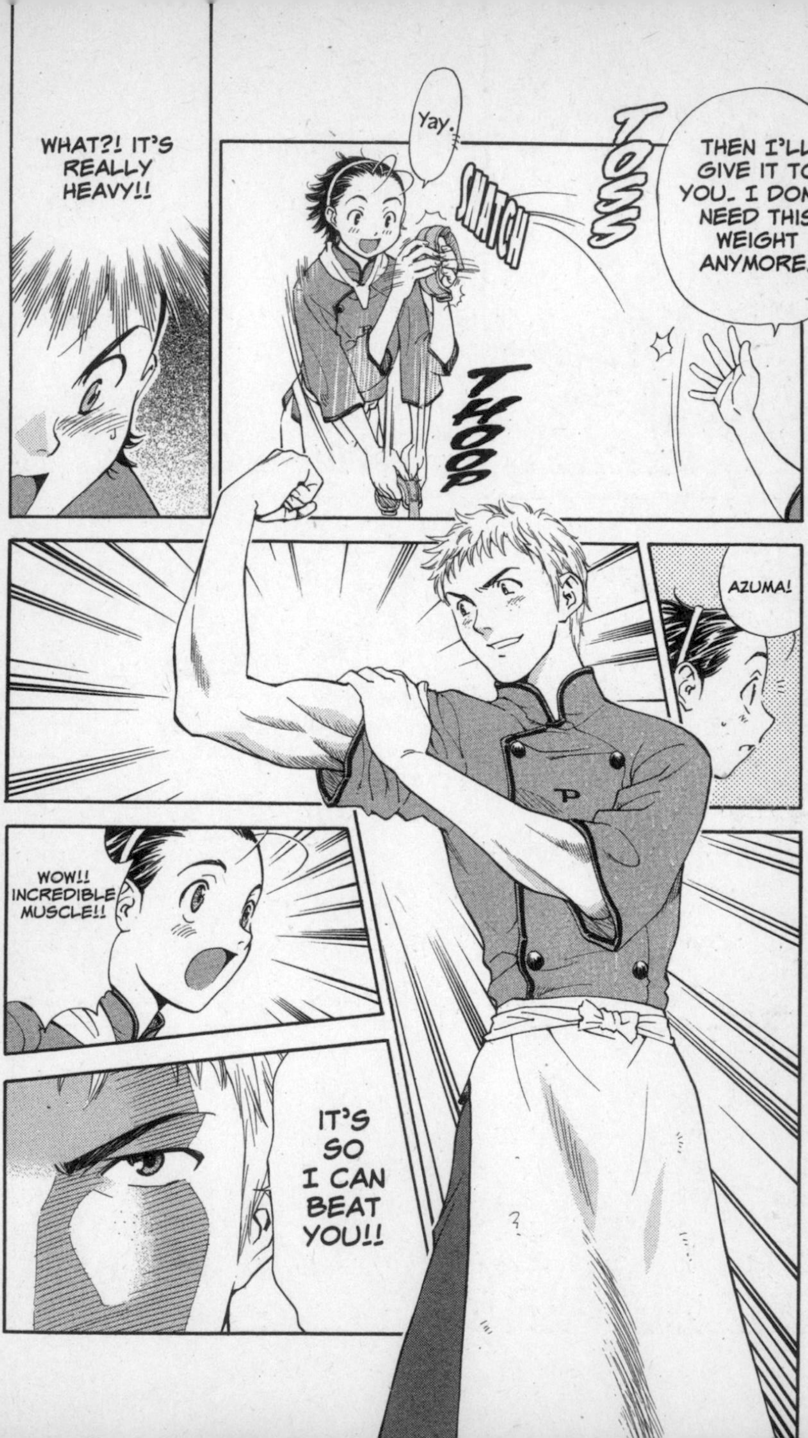
THEN I'LL GIVE IT TO YOU. I DON'T NEED THIS WEIGHT ANYMORE.
TOSS
SNATCH
Yay.
THOOP
WHAT?! IT'S REALLY HEAVY!!
AZUMA!
WOW!! INCREDIBLE MUSCLE!!
IT'S SO I CAN BEAT YOU!!

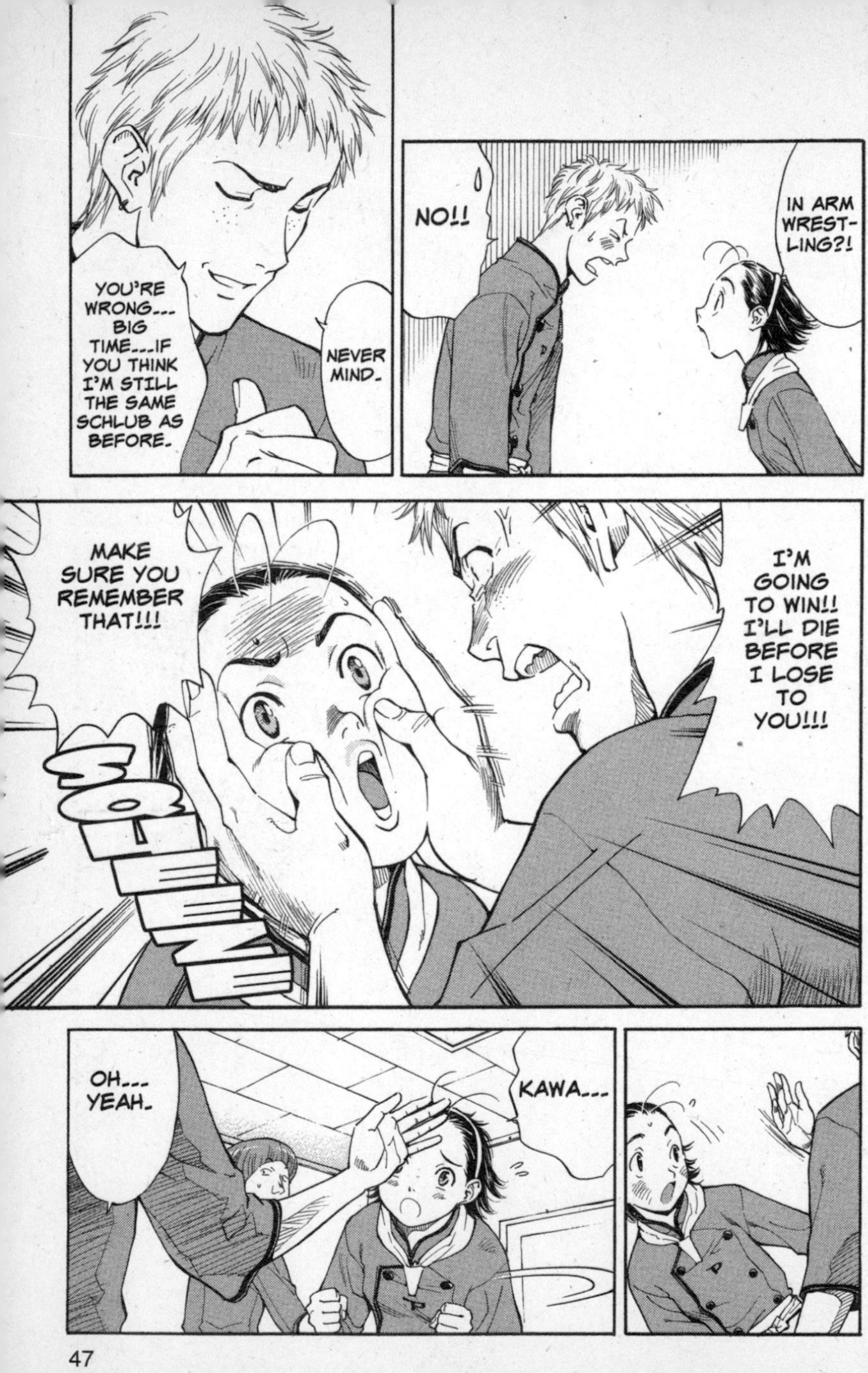
IN ARM WREST-LING?!
NO!!
NEVER MIND.
YOU'RE WRONG... BIG TIME...IF YOU THINK I'M STILL THE SAME SCHLUB AS BEFORE.
I'M GOING TO WIN!! I'LL DIE BEFORE I LOSE TO YOU!!!
MAKE SURE YOU REMEMBER THAT!!!
KAWA...
OH... YEAH.

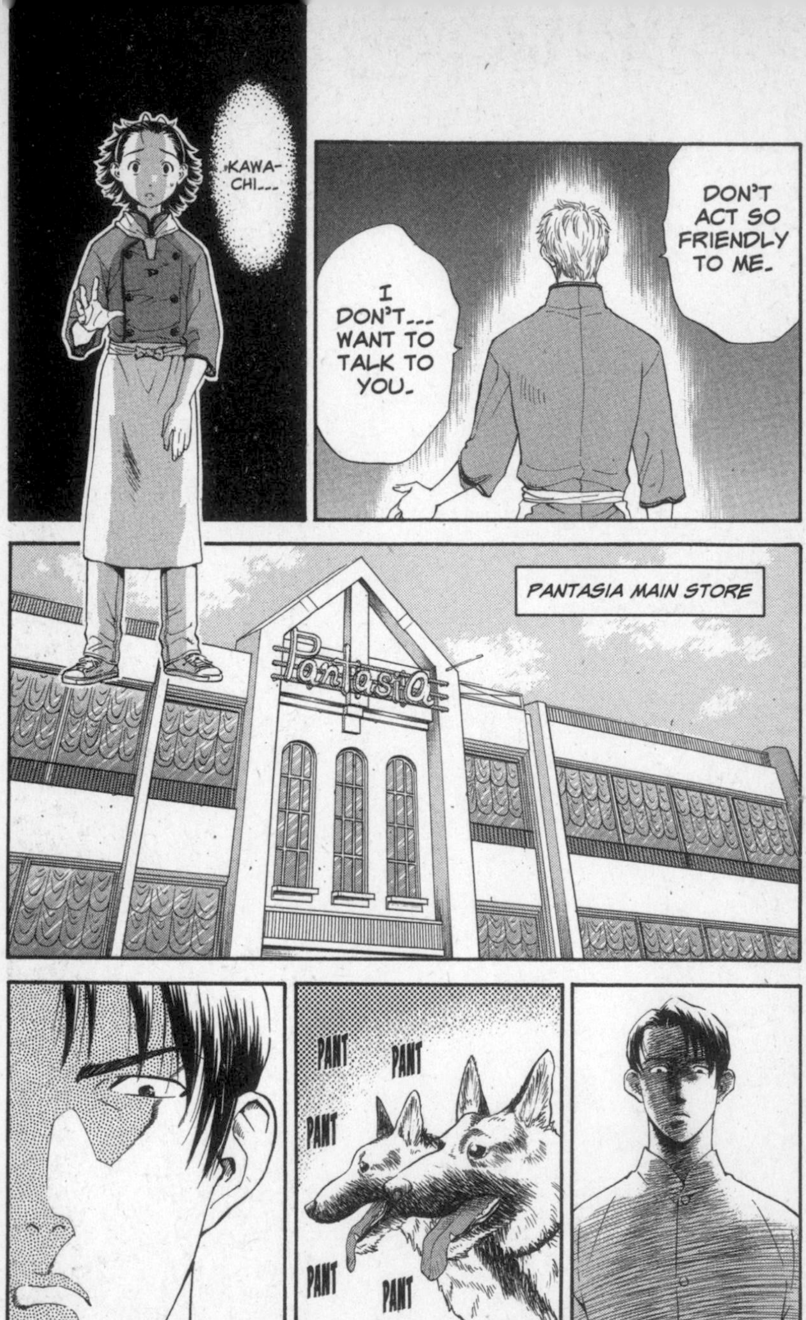
DON'T ACT SO FRIENDLY TO ME.
I DON'T... WANT TO TALK TO YOU.
KAWACHI...
PANTASIA MAIN STORE
Pantasia
PANT PANT PANT PANT PANT

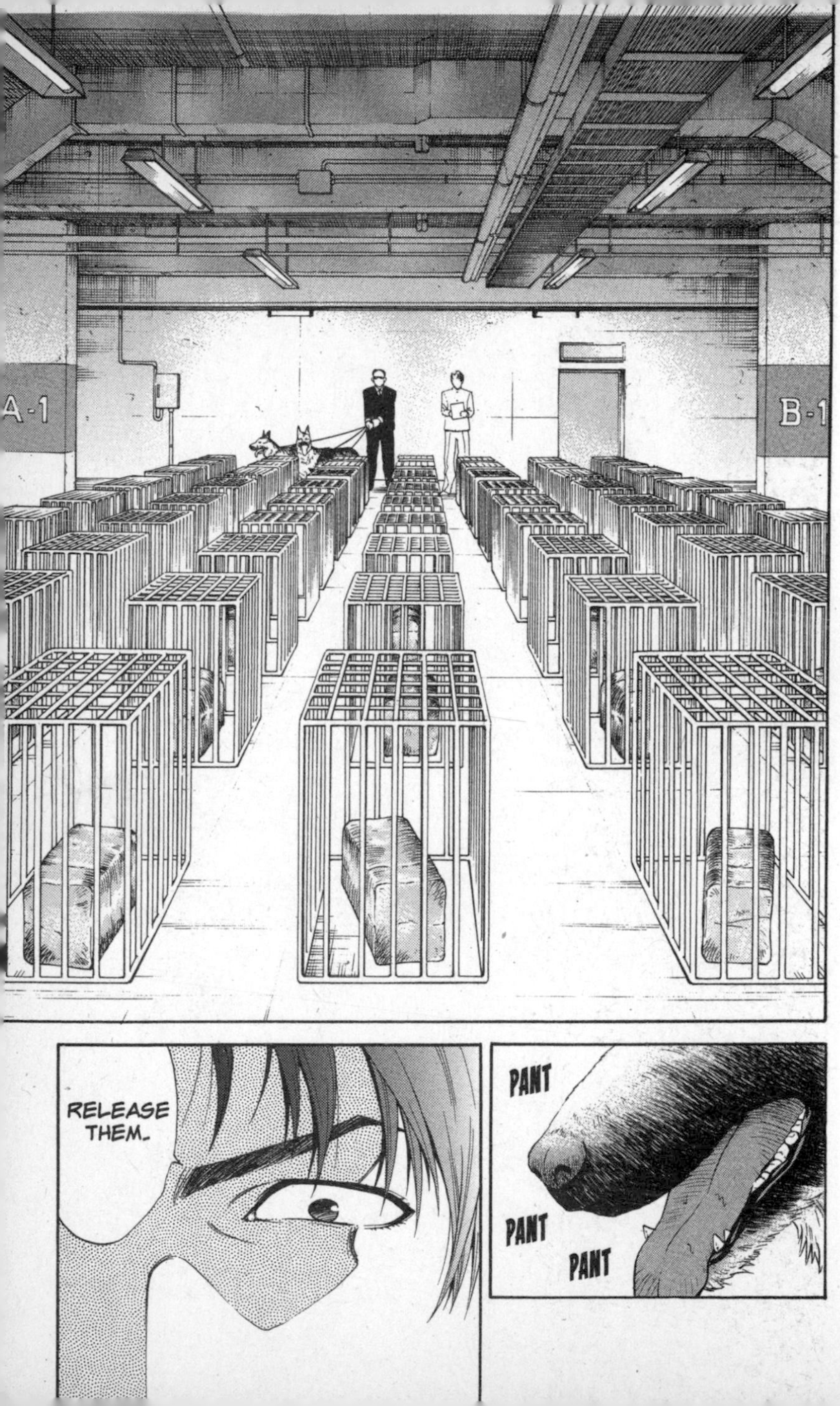
B-1
A-1
PANT
PANT
PANT
RELEASE THEM...

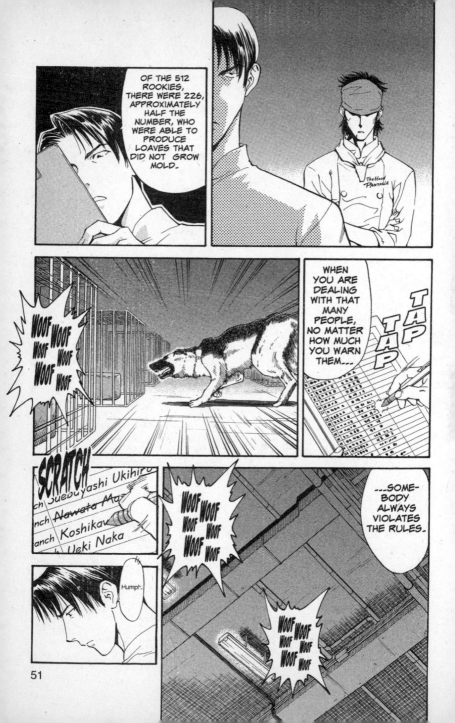

OF THE 512 ROOKIES, THERE WERE 226, APPROXIMATELY HALF THE NUMBER, WHO WERE ABLE TO PRODUCE LOAVES THAT DID NOT GROW MOLD.

WHEN YOU ARE DEALING WITH THAT MANY PEOPLE, NO MATTER HOW MUCH YOU WARN THEM...

...SOMEBODY ALWAYS VIOLATES THE RULES.

WOOF WOOF WOOF WOOF WOOF WOOF WOOF WOOF

TAP TAP

SCRATCH

ch Suebuyashi Ukihiro
nch Nawata Aa
anch Koshikav
h Ueki Naka

Humph.

WOOF WOOF WOOF WOOF WOOF WOOF

WOOF WOOF WOOF WOOF WOOF WOOF

51

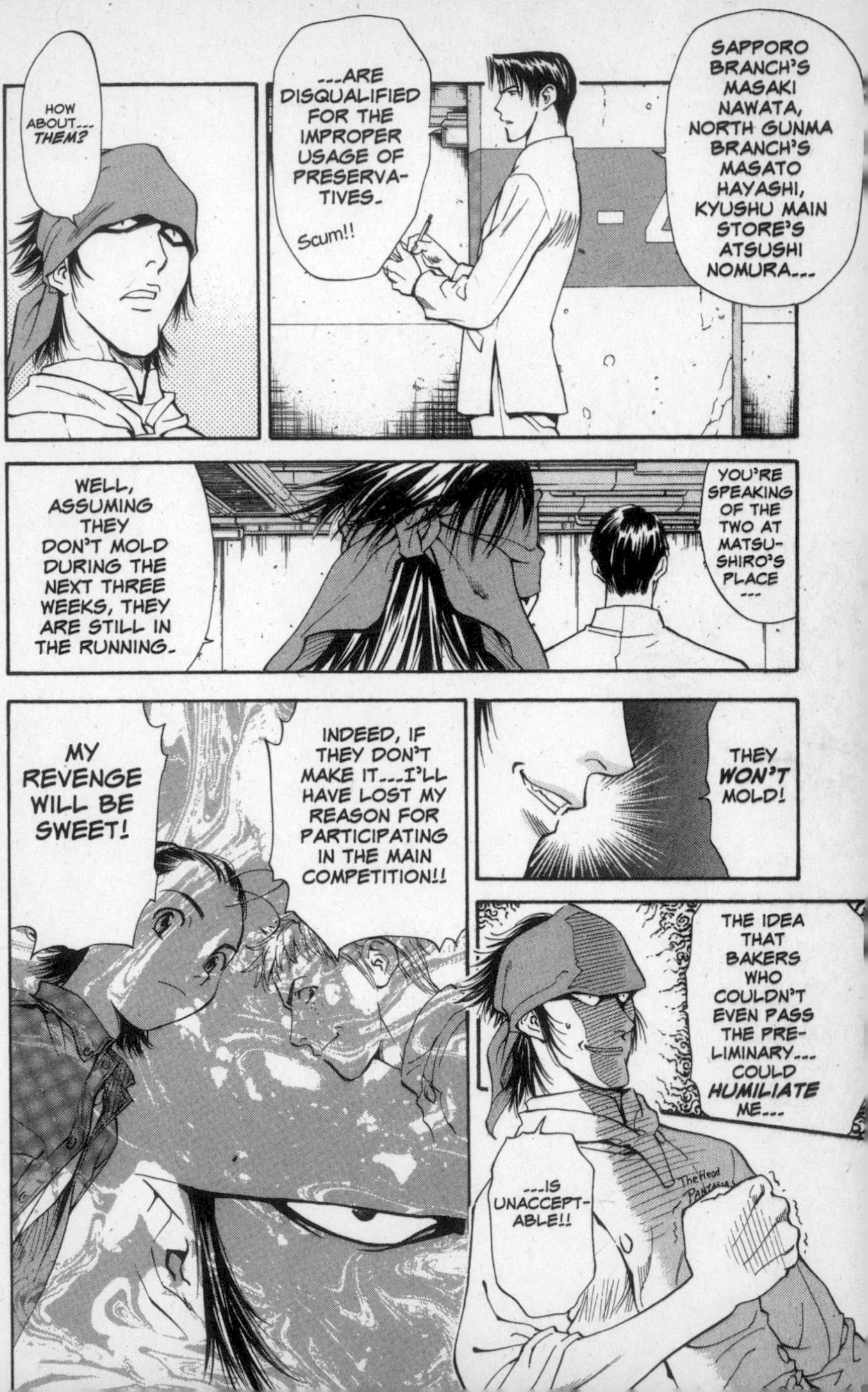
SAPPORO BRANCH'S MASAKI NAWATA, NORTH GUNMA BRANCH'S MASATO HAYASHI, KYUSHU MAIN STORE'S ATSUSHI NOMURA...
...ARE DISQUALIFIED FOR THE IMPROPER USAGE OF PRESERVA-TIVES.
Scum!!
HOW ABOUT... *THEM?*
YOU'RE SPEAKING OF THE TWO AT MATSU-SHIRO'S PLACE ...
WELL, ASSUMING THEY DON'T MOLD DURING THE NEXT THREE WEEKS, THEY ARE STILL IN THE RUNNING.
THEY ***WON'T*** MOLD!
THE IDEA THAT BAKERS WHO COULDN'T EVEN PASS THE PRE-LIMINARY... COULD ***HUMILIATE*** ME...
...IS UNACCEPT-ABLE!!
The Head
INDEED, IF THEY DON'T MAKE IT...I'LL HAVE LOST MY REASON FOR PARTICIPATING IN THE MAIN COMPETITION!!
MY REVENGE WILL BE SWEET!

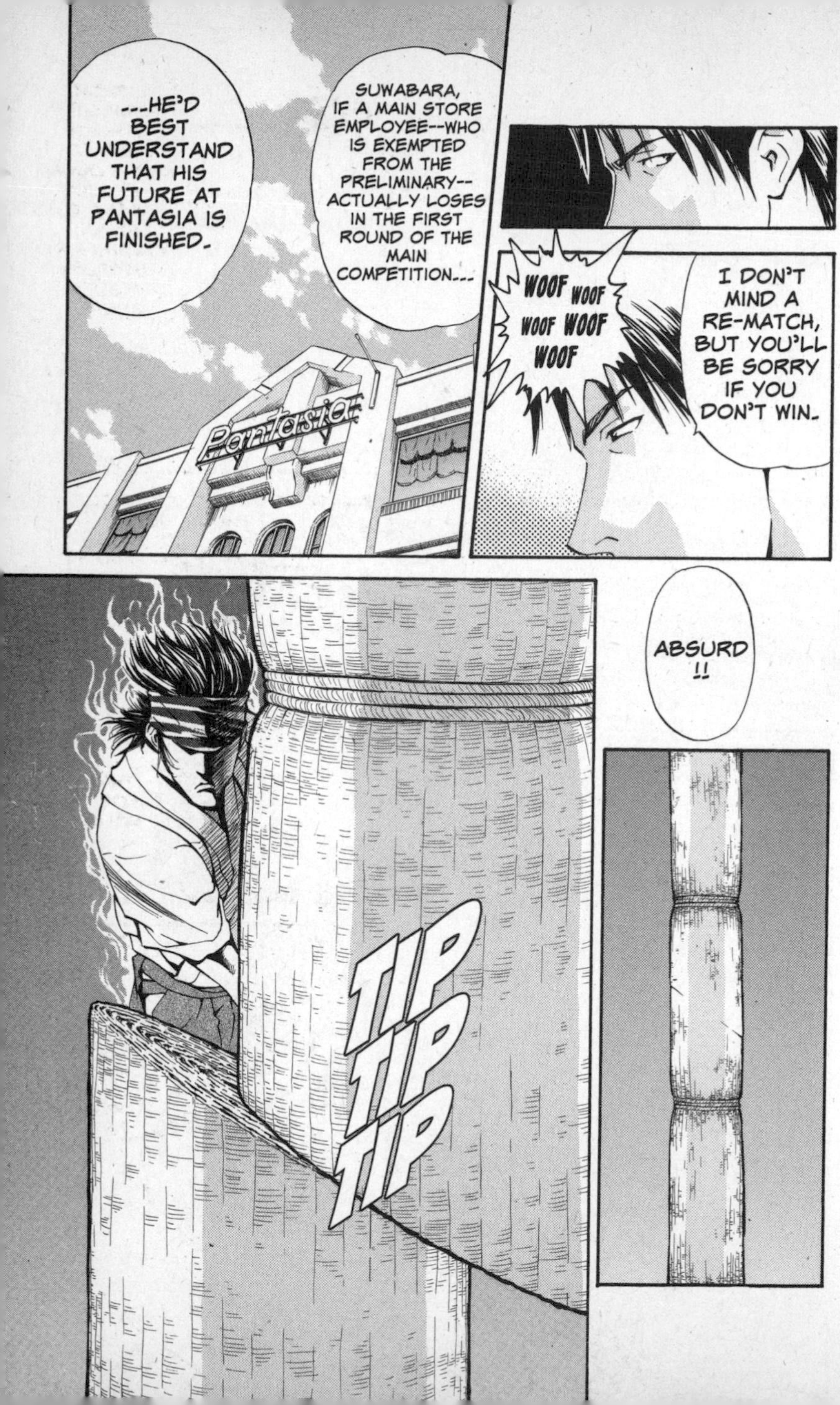

WOOF WOOF WOOF WOOF WOOF
I DON'T MIND A RE-MATCH, BUT YOU'LL BE SORRY IF YOU DON'T WIN.
SUWABARA, IF A MAIN STORE EMPLOYEE--WHO IS EXEMPTED FROM THE PRELIMINARY--ACTUALLY LOSES IN THE FIRST ROUND OF THE MAIN COMPETITION...
...HE'D BEST UNDERSTAND THAT HIS FUTURE AT PANTASIA IS FINISHED.
Pantasia
ABSURD !!
TIP TIP TIP

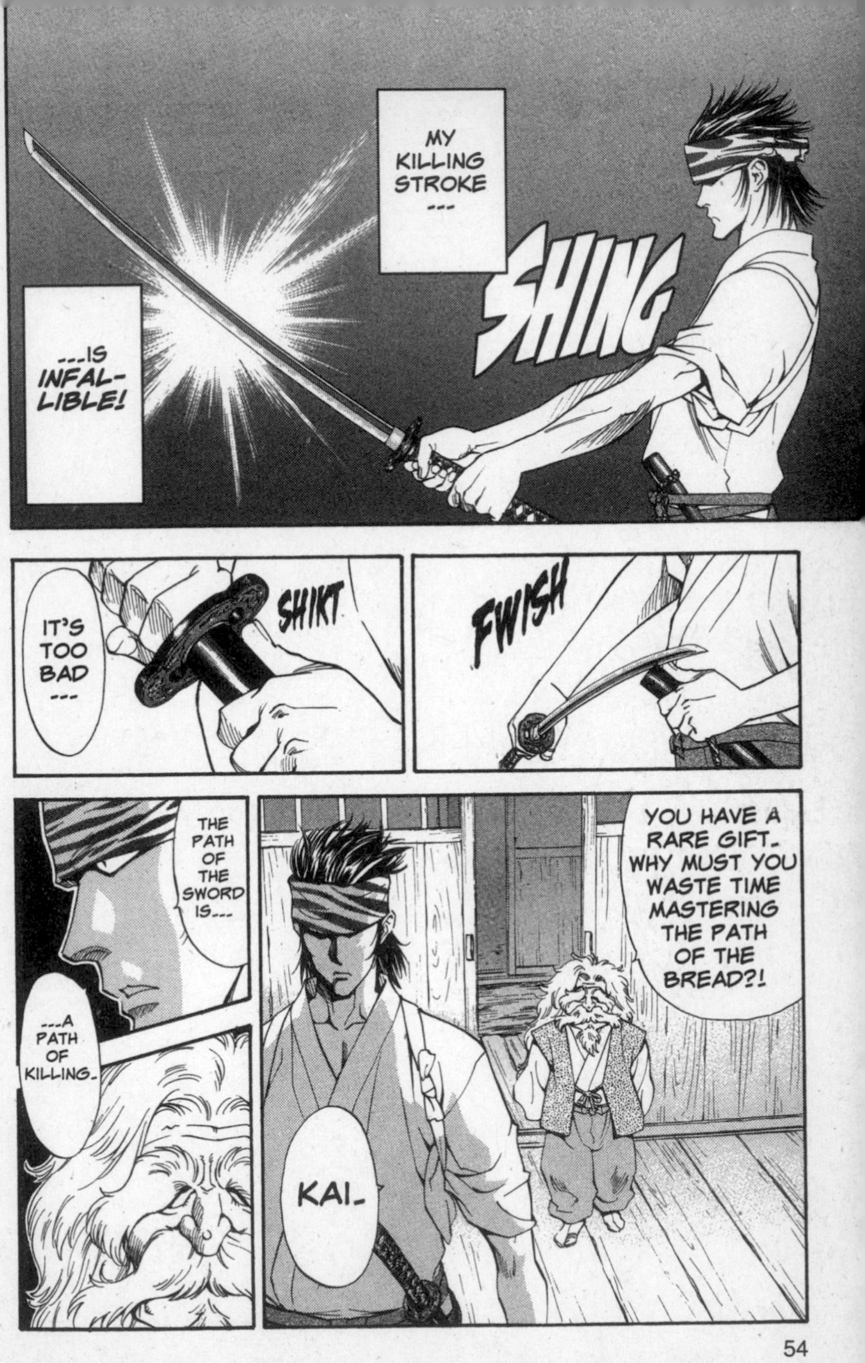
MY KILLING STROKE ---
SHING
---IS INFAL-LIBLE!
FWISH
IT'S TOO BAD ---
SHIKT
YOU HAVE A RARE GIFT. WHY MUST YOU WASTE TIME MASTERING THE PATH OF THE BREAD?!
KAI.
THE PATH OF THE SWORD IS---
---A PATH OF KILLING.

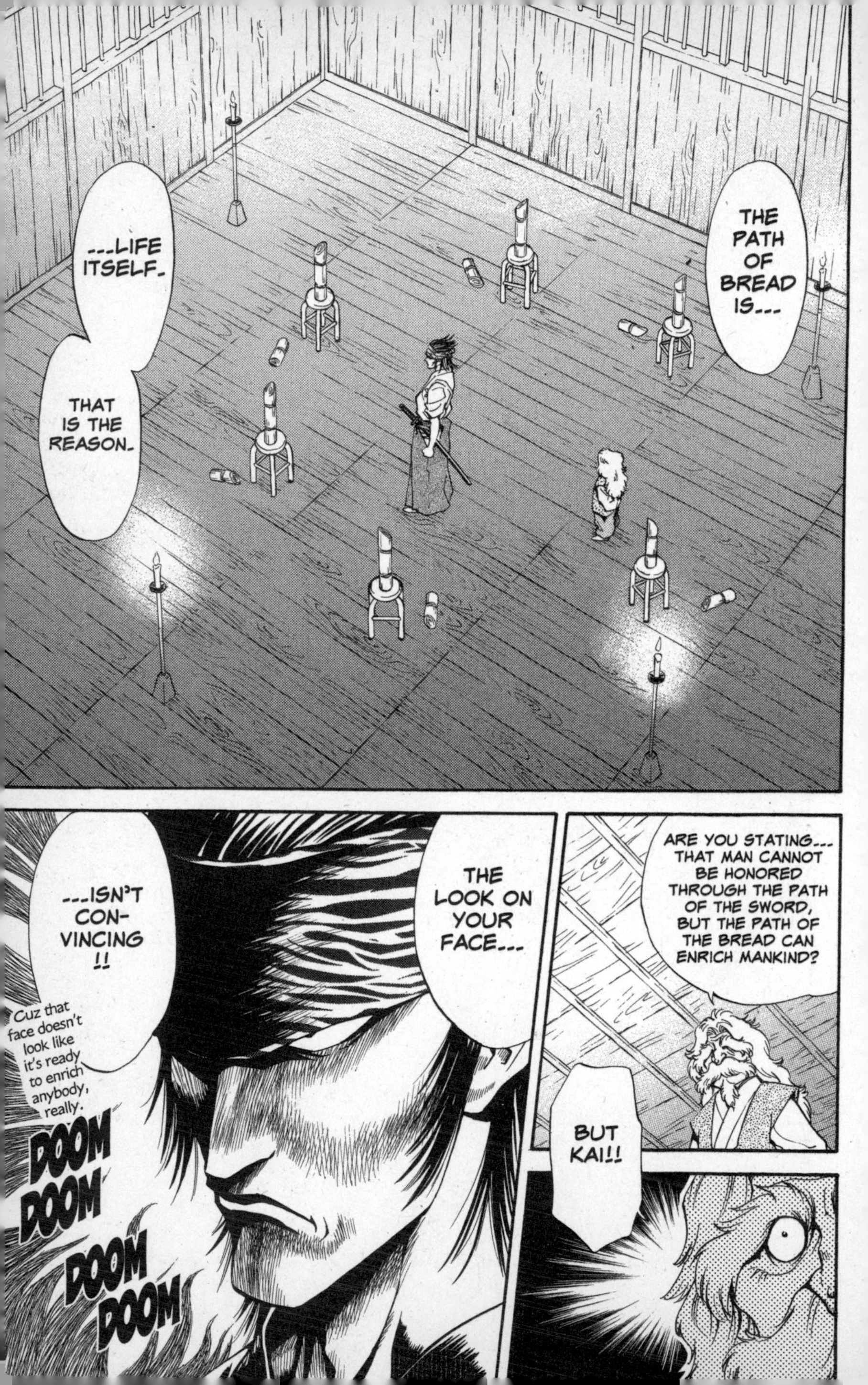
THE PATH OF BREAD IS---
---LIFE ITSELF.
THAT IS THE REASON.
ARE YOU STATING--- THAT MAN CANNOT BE HONORED THROUGH THE PATH OF THE SWORD, BUT THE PATH OF THE BREAD CAN ENRICH MANKIND?
BUT KAI!!
THE LOOK ON YOUR FACE---
---ISN'T CON-VINCING !!
Cuz that face doesn't look like it's ready to enrich anybody, really.
DOOM DOOM
DOOM DOOM

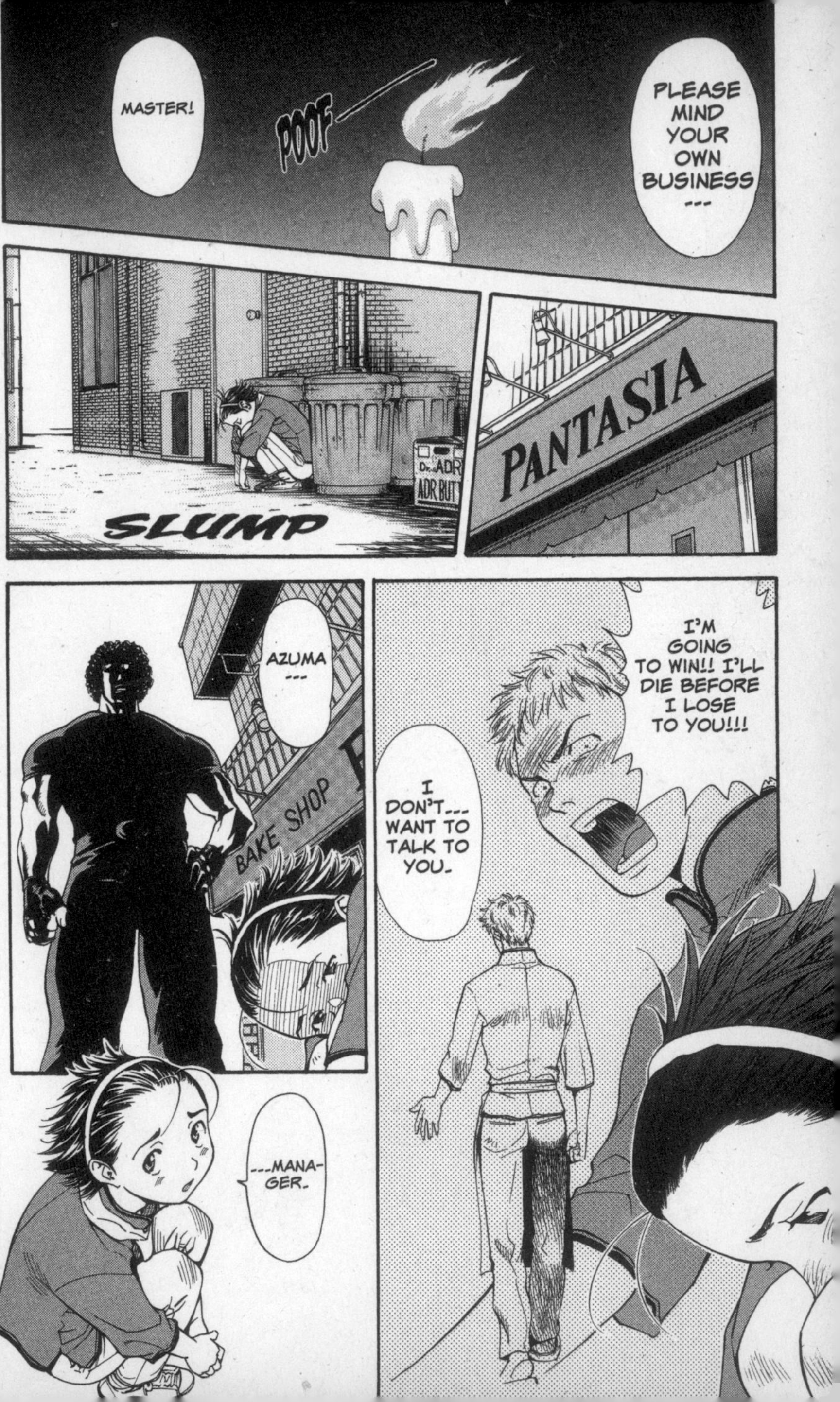
PLEASE MIND YOUR OWN BUSINESS ---
POOF
MASTER!
PANTASIA
SLUMP
I'M GOING TO WIN!! I'LL DIE BEFORE I LOSE TO YOU!!!
I DON'T--- WANT TO TALK TO YOU.
AZUMA ---
BAKE SHOP
---MANA-GER.

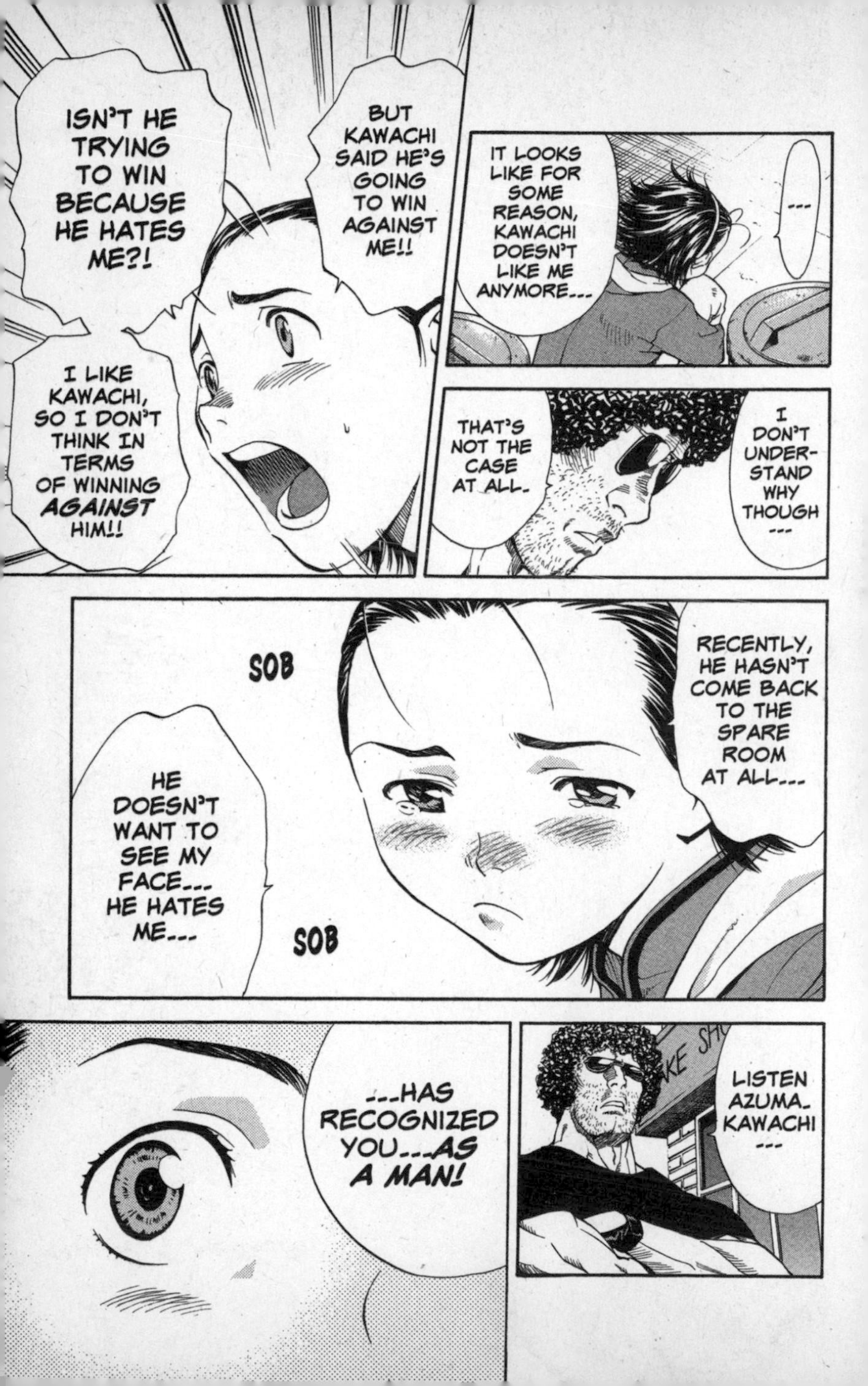
...
IT LOOKS LIKE FOR SOME REASON, KAWACHI DOESN'T LIKE ME ANYMORE...
I DON'T UNDERSTAND WHY THOUGH...
THAT'S NOT THE CASE AT ALL.
BUT KAWACHI SAID HE'S GOING TO WIN AGAINST ME!!
ISN'T HE TRYING TO WIN BECAUSE HE HATES ME?!
I LIKE KAWACHI, SO I DON'T THINK IN TERMS OF WINNING *AGAINST* HIM!!
RECENTLY, HE HASN'T COME BACK TO THE SPARE ROOM AT ALL...
SOB
HE DOESN'T WANT TO SEE MY FACE... HE HATES ME...
SOB
LISTEN AZUMA. KAWACHI...
...HAS RECOGNIZED YOU...*AS A MAN!*

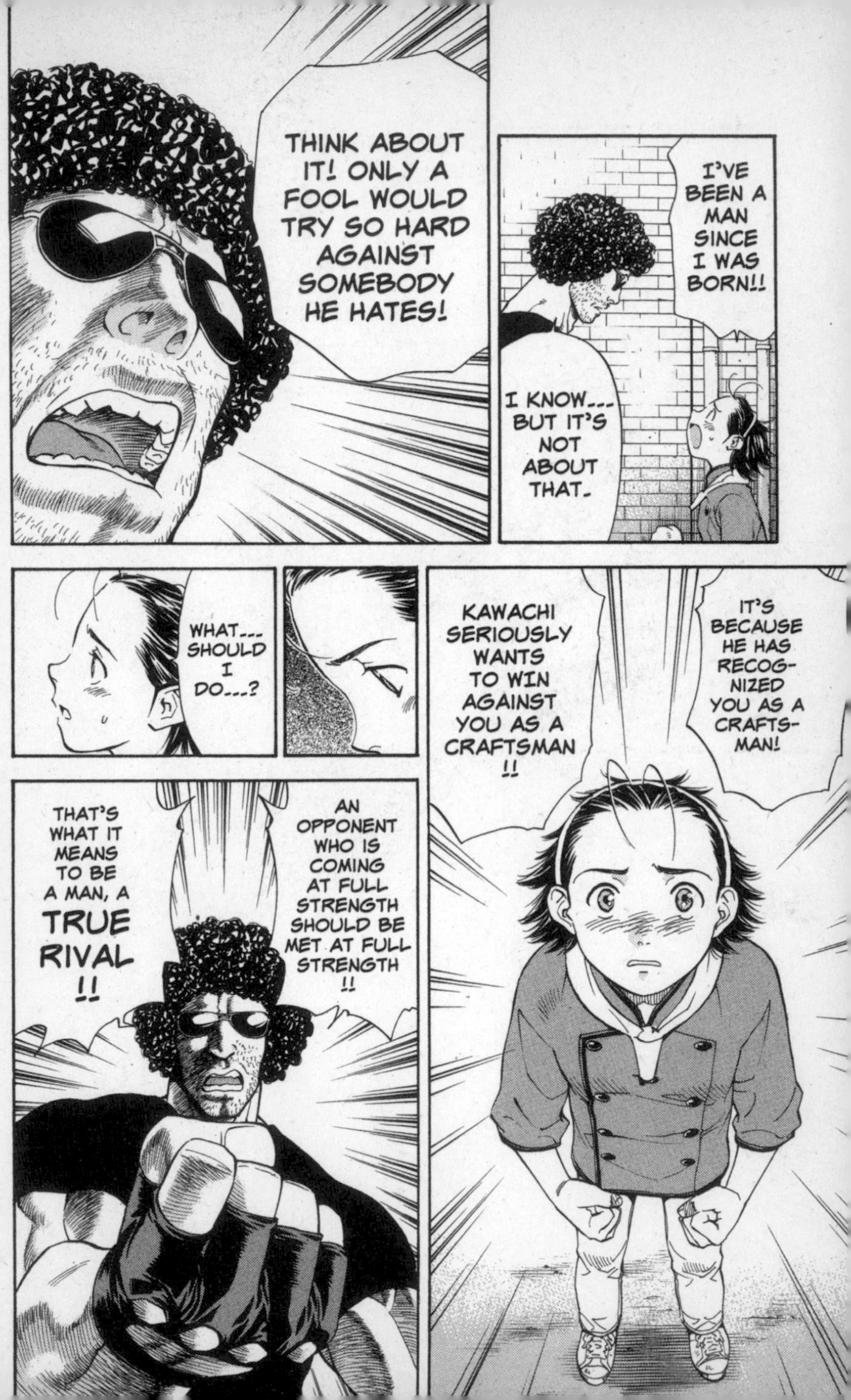
I'VE BEEN A MAN SINCE I WAS BORN!!
I KNOW... BUT IT'S NOT ABOUT THAT.
THINK ABOUT IT! ONLY A FOOL WOULD TRY SO HARD AGAINST SOMEBODY HE HATES!
IT'S BECAUSE HE HAS RECOGNIZED YOU AS A CRAFTSMAN!
KAWACHI SERIOUSLY WANTS TO WIN AGAINST YOU AS A CRAFTSMAN!!
WHAT... SHOULD I DO...?
AN OPPONENT WHO IS COMING AT FULL STRENGTH SHOULD BE MET AT FULL STRENGTH!!
THAT'S WHAT IT MEANS TO BE A MAN, A TRUE RIVAL!!

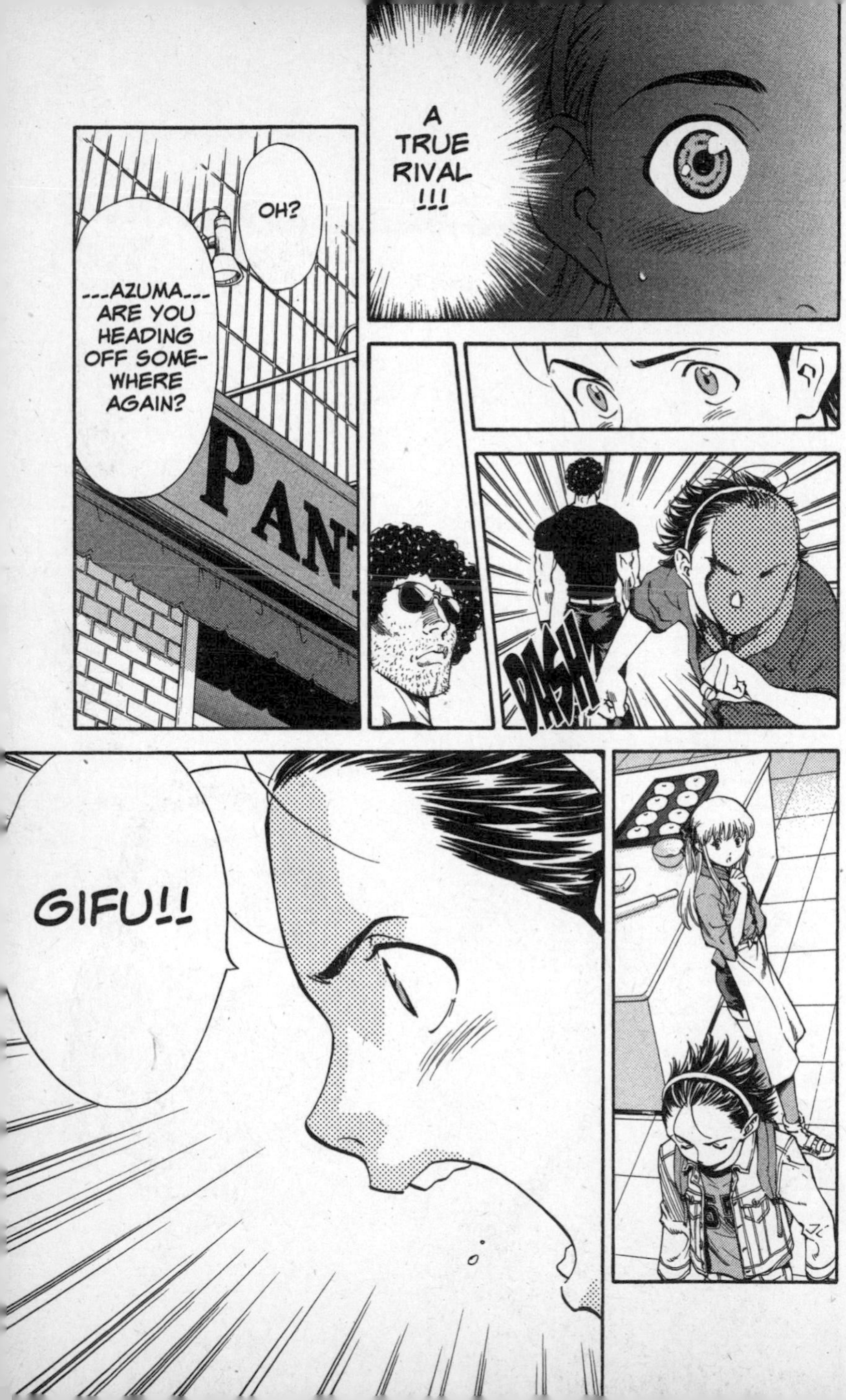
A TRUE RIVAL!!!
DASH
OH?
---AZUMA--- ARE YOU HEADING OFF SOME-WHERE AGAIN?
PAN
GIFU!!

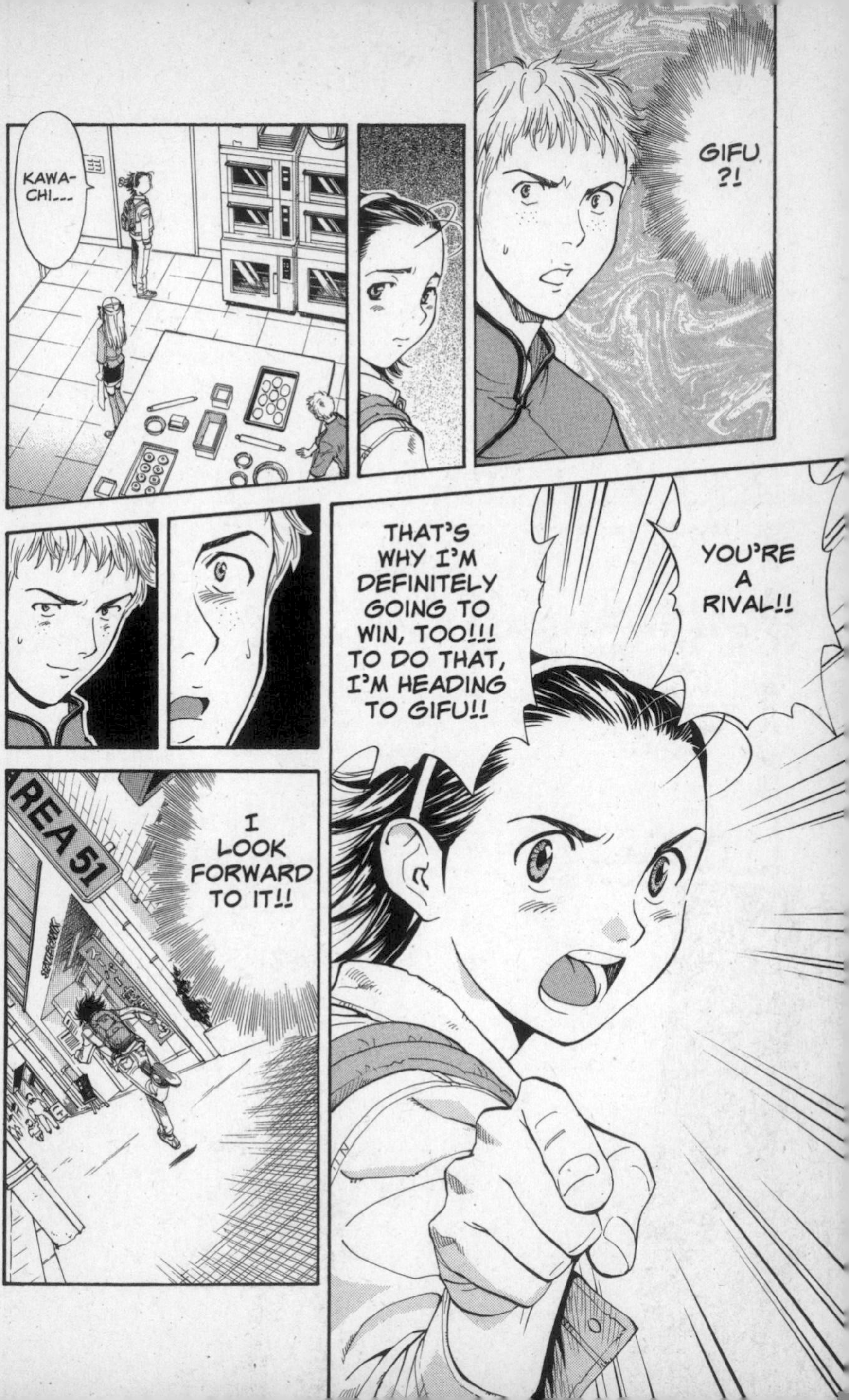
GIFU ?!
KAWA-CHI...
YOU'RE A RIVAL!!
THAT'S WHY I'M DEFINITELY GOING TO WIN, TOO!!! TO DO THAT, I'M HEADING TO GIFU!!
REA 51
I LOOK FORWARD TO IT!!

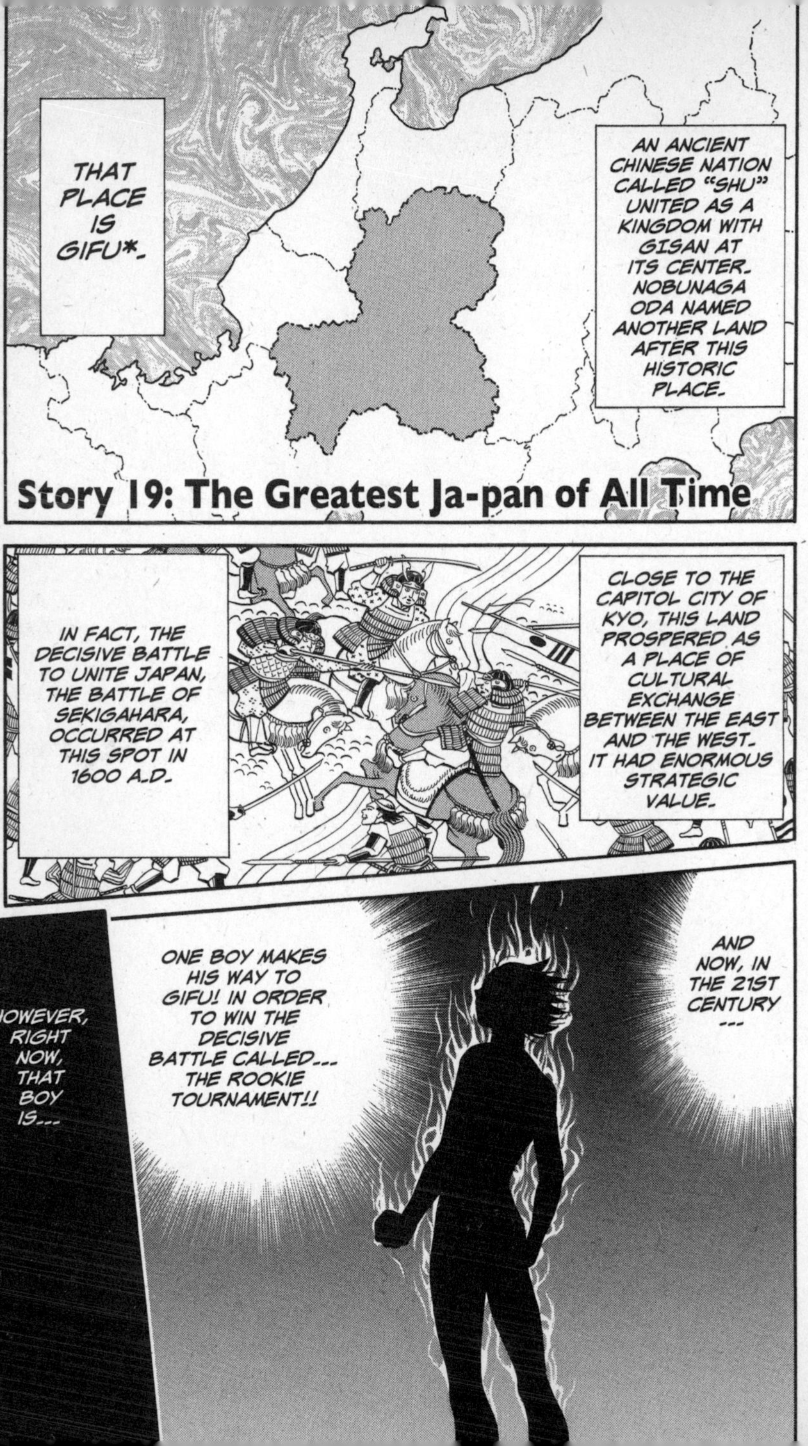
AN ANCIENT CHINESE NATION CALLED "SHU" UNITED AS A KINGDOM WITH GISAN AT ITS CENTER. NOBUNAGA ODA NAMED ANOTHER LAND AFTER THIS HISTORIC PLACE.
THAT PLACE IS GIFU*.
Story 19: The Greatest Ja-pan of All Time
CLOSE TO THE CAPITOL CITY OF KYO, THIS LAND PROSPERED AS A PLACE OF CULTURAL EXCHANGE BETWEEN THE EAST AND THE WEST. IT HAD ENORMOUS STRATEGIC VALUE.
IN FACT, THE DECISIVE BATTLE TO UNITE JAPAN, THE BATTLE OF SEKIGAHARA, OCCURRED AT THIS SPOT IN 1600 A.D.
AND NOW, IN THE 21ST CENTURY ...
ONE BOY MAKES HIS WAY TO GIFU! IN ORDER TO WIN THE DECISIVE BATTLE CALLED... THE ROOKIE TOURNAMENT!!
HOWEVER, RIGHT NOW, THAT BOY IS...

*GIFU: "GI" IS FROM THE GI OF GISAN. "FU" MEANS AT THE BOTTOM OF A HILL.

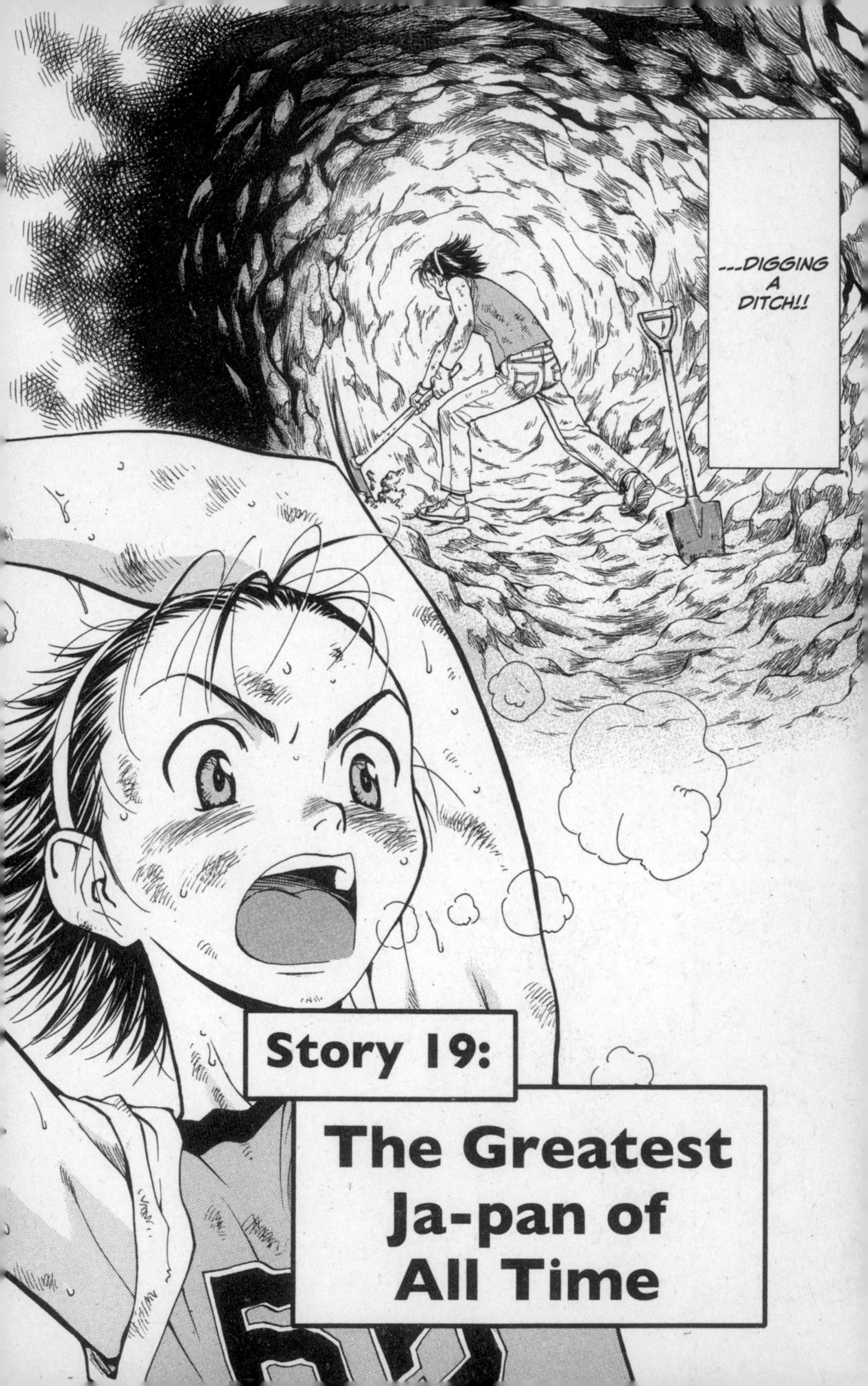
...DIGGING A DITCH!!
Story 19:
The Greatest Ja-pan of All Time

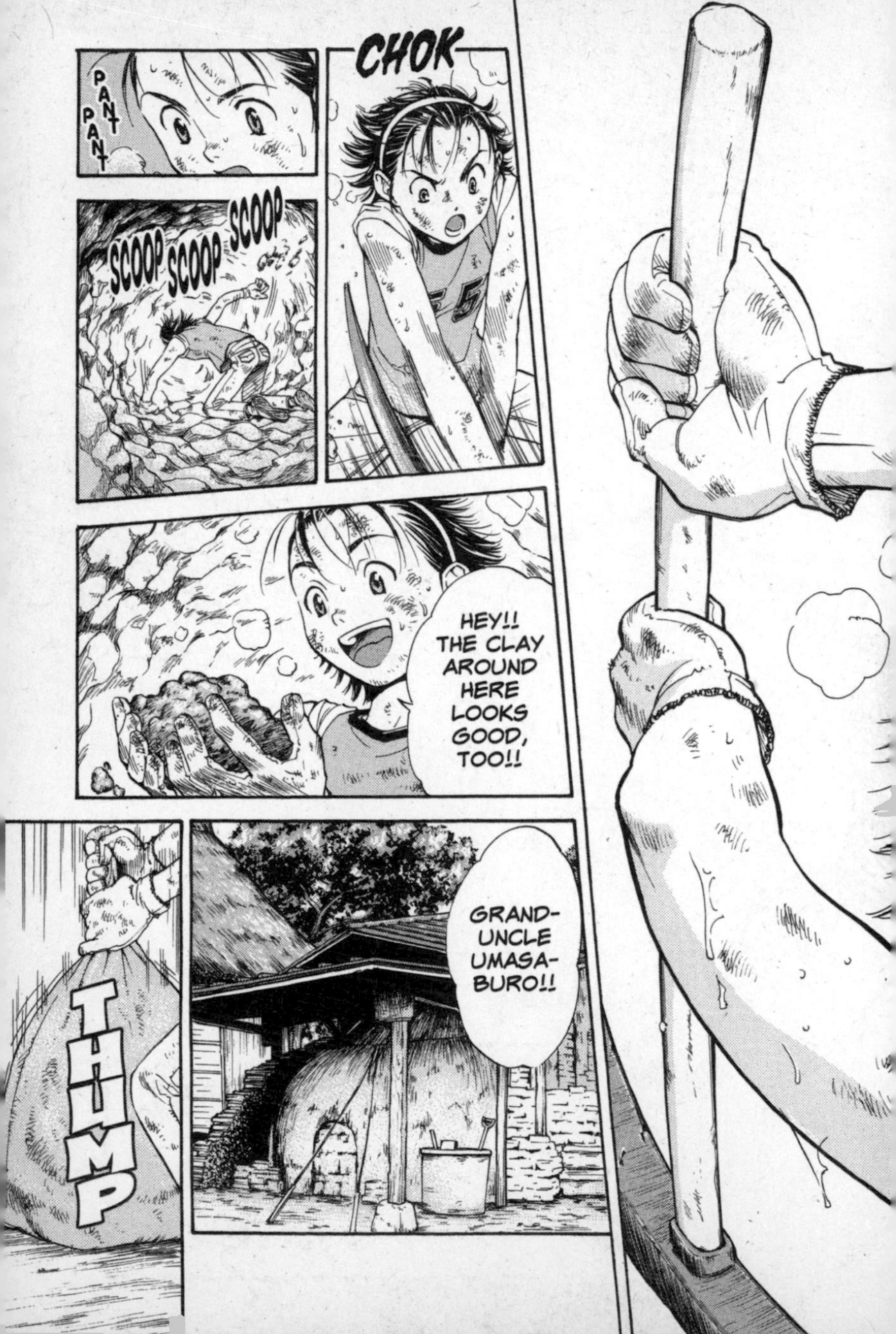
CHOK
PANT PANT
SCOOP SCOOP SCOOP
HEY!! THE CLAY AROUND HERE LOOKS GOOD, TOO!!
GRAND-UNCLE UMASA-BURO!!
THUMP

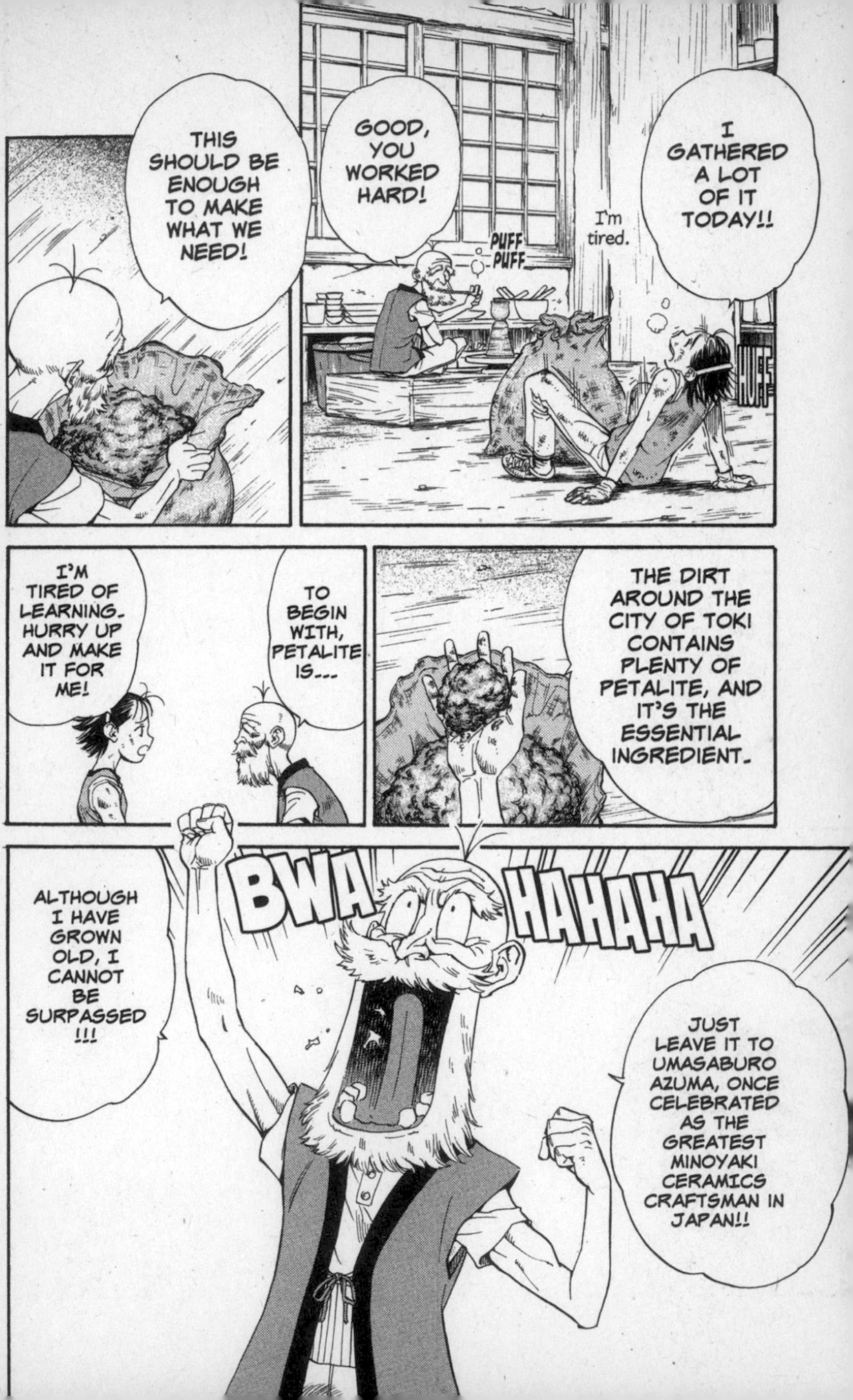

I GATHERED A LOT OF IT TODAY!!
HUFF
I'm tired.
GOOD, YOU WORKED HARD!
PUFF PUFF
THIS SHOULD BE ENOUGH TO MAKE WHAT WE NEED!
THE DIRT AROUND THE CITY OF TOKI CONTAINS PLENTY OF PETALITE, AND IT'S THE ESSENTIAL INGREDIENT.
TO BEGIN WITH, PETALITE IS...
I'M TIRED OF LEARNING. HURRY UP AND MAKE IT FOR ME!
BWA HAHAHA
JUST LEAVE IT TO UMASABURO AZUMA, ONCE CELEBRATED AS THE GREATEST MINOYAKI CERAMICS CRAFTSMAN IN JAPAN!!
ALTHOUGH I HAVE GROWN OLD, I CANNOT BE SURPASSED!!!

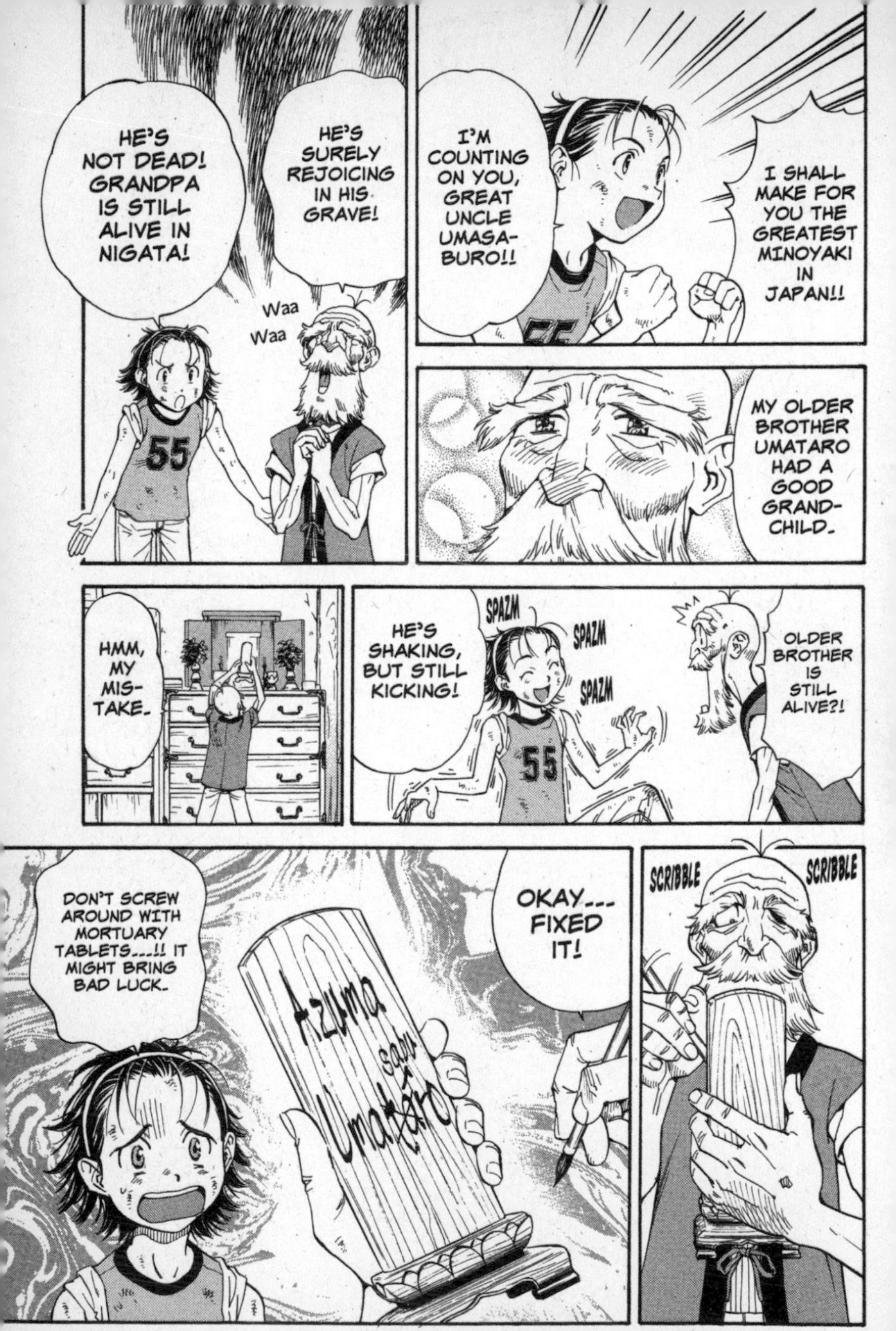
I SHALL MAKE FOR YOU THE GREATEST MINOYAKI IN JAPAN!!
I'M COUNTING ON YOU, GREAT UNCLE UMASA-BURO!!
MY OLDER BROTHER UMATARO HAD A GOOD GRAND-CHILD.
HE'S SURELY REJOICING IN HIS GRAVE!
HE'S NOT DEAD! GRANDPA IS STILL ALIVE IN NIGATA!
Waa
Waa
OLDER BROTHER IS STILL ALIVE?!
SPAZM
SPAZM
SPAZM
HE'S SHAKING, BUT STILL KICKING!
HMM, MY MIS-TAKE.
SCRIBBLE
SCRIBBLE
OKAY... FIXED IT!
DON'T SCREW AROUND WITH MORTUARY TABLETS...!! IT MIGHT BRING BAD LUCK.
Azuma
sabu
Umataro

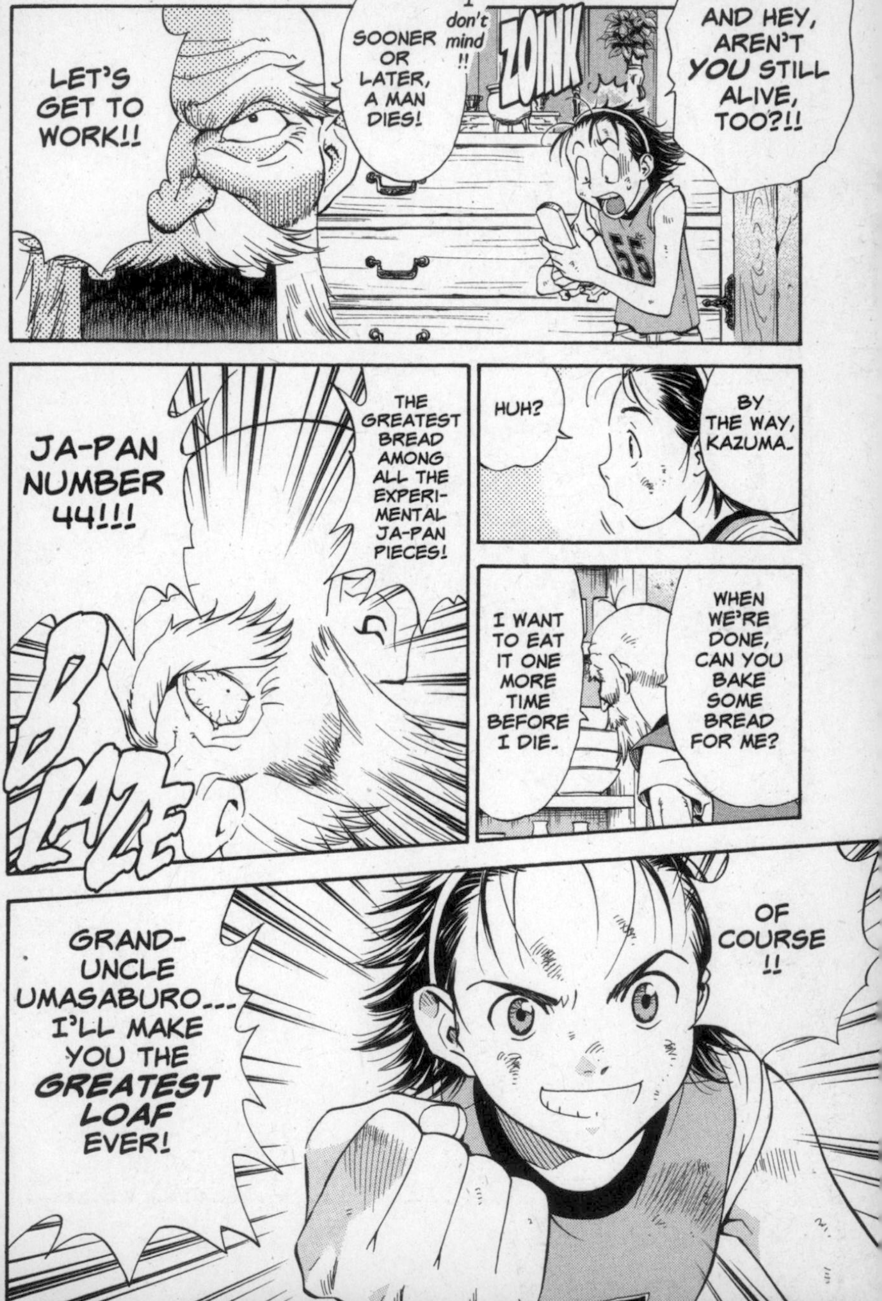
AND HEY, AREN'T YOU STILL ALIVE, TOO?!!
ZOINK
I don't mind !!
SOONER OR LATER, A MAN DIES!
LET'S GET TO WORK!!
BY THE WAY, KAZUMA.
HUH?
WHEN WE'RE DONE, CAN YOU BAKE SOME BREAD FOR ME?
I WANT TO EAT IT ONE MORE TIME BEFORE I DIE.
THE GREATEST BREAD AMONG ALL THE EXPERIMENTAL JA-PAN PIECES!
JA-PAN NUMBER 44!!!
BLAZE
OF COURSE !!
GRAND-UNCLE UMASABURO... I'LL MAKE YOU THE GREATEST LOAF EVER!

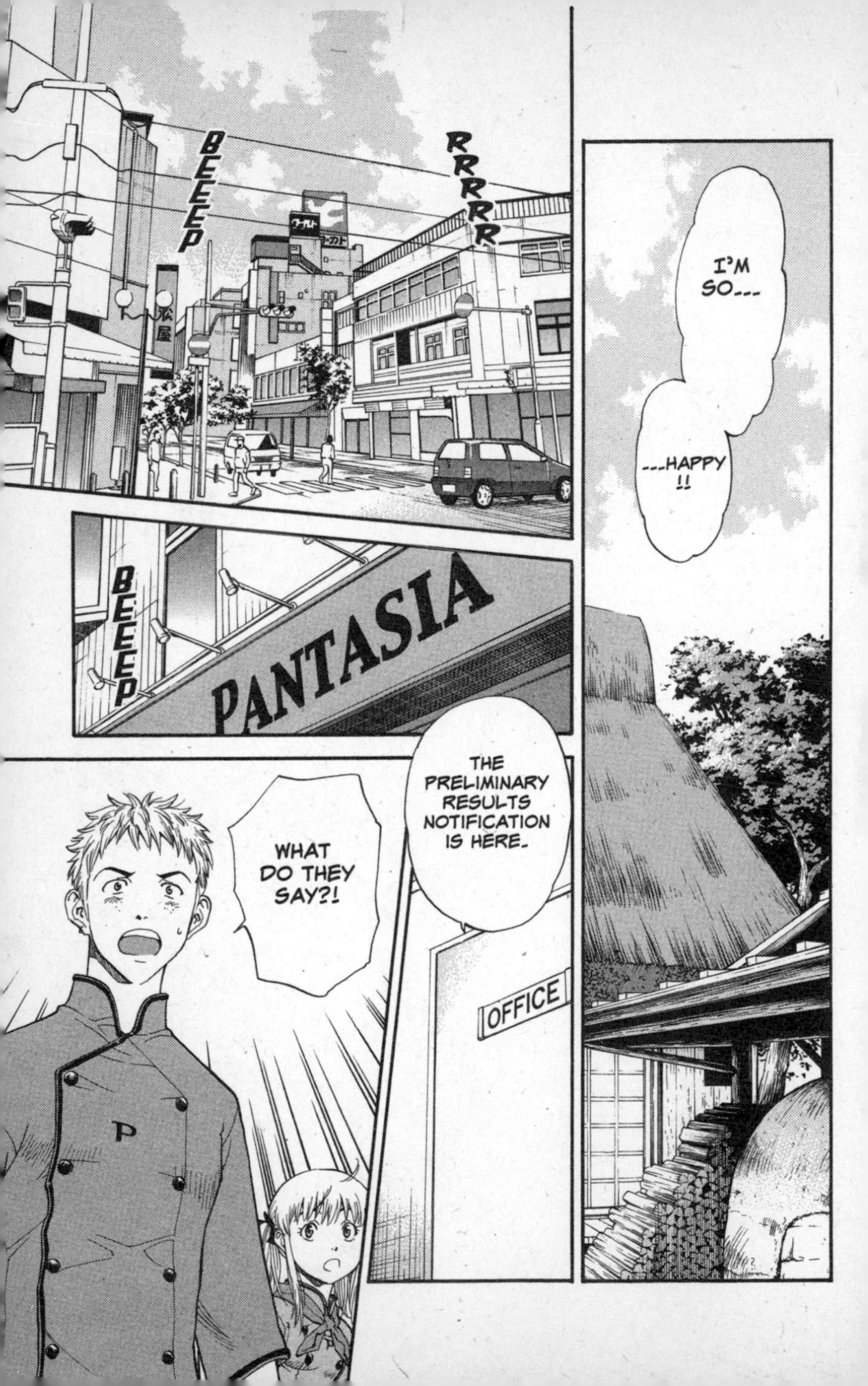
I'M SO...
...HAPPY!!
RRRRR
BEEEEP
BEEEEP
PANTASIA
THE PRELIMINARY RESULTS NOTIFICATION IS HERE.
OFFICE
WHAT DO THEY SAY?!

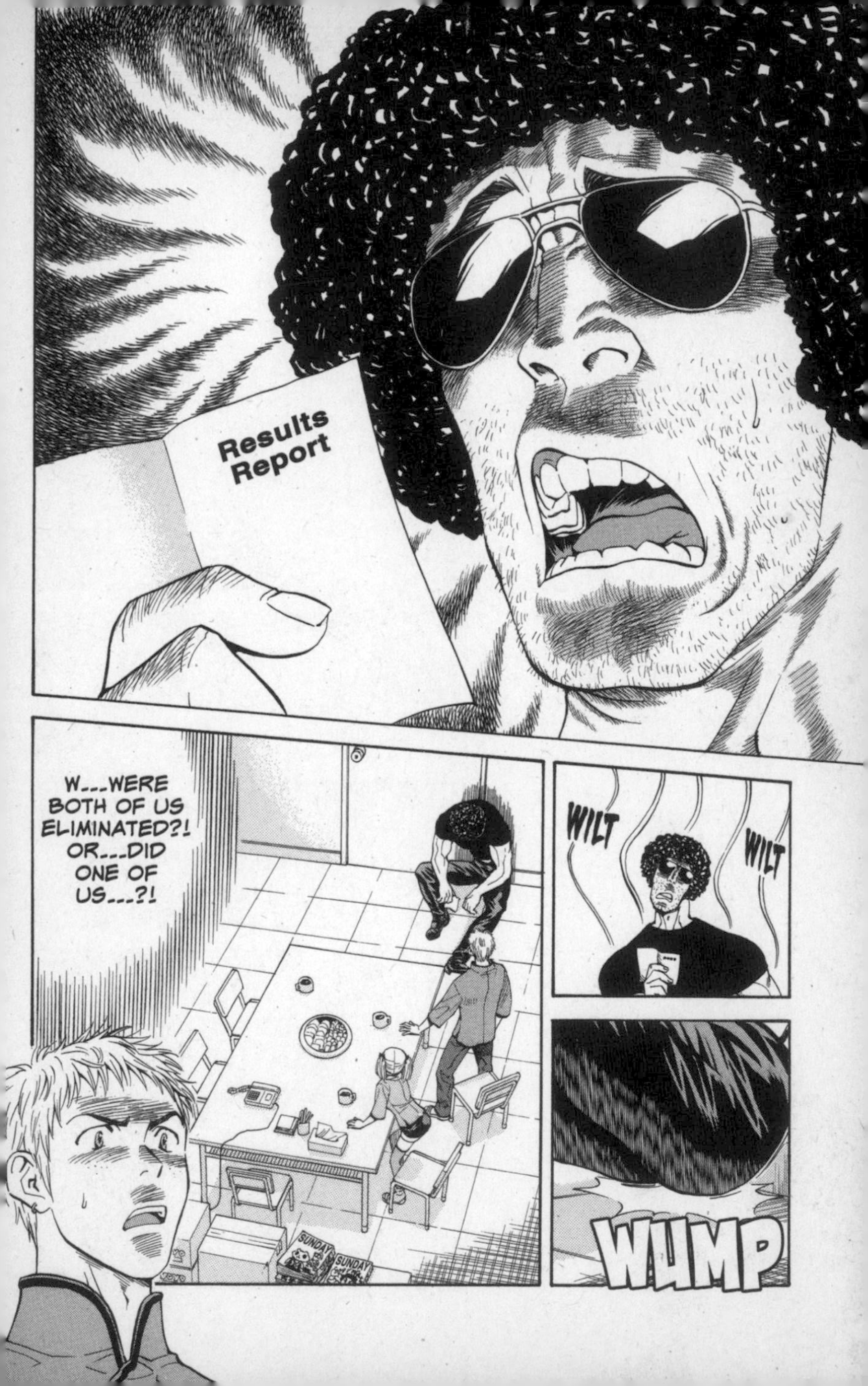
Results Report
WILT
WILT
WUMP
W---WERE BOTH OF US ELIMINATED?! OR---DID ONE OF US---?!
SUNDAY
SUNDAY

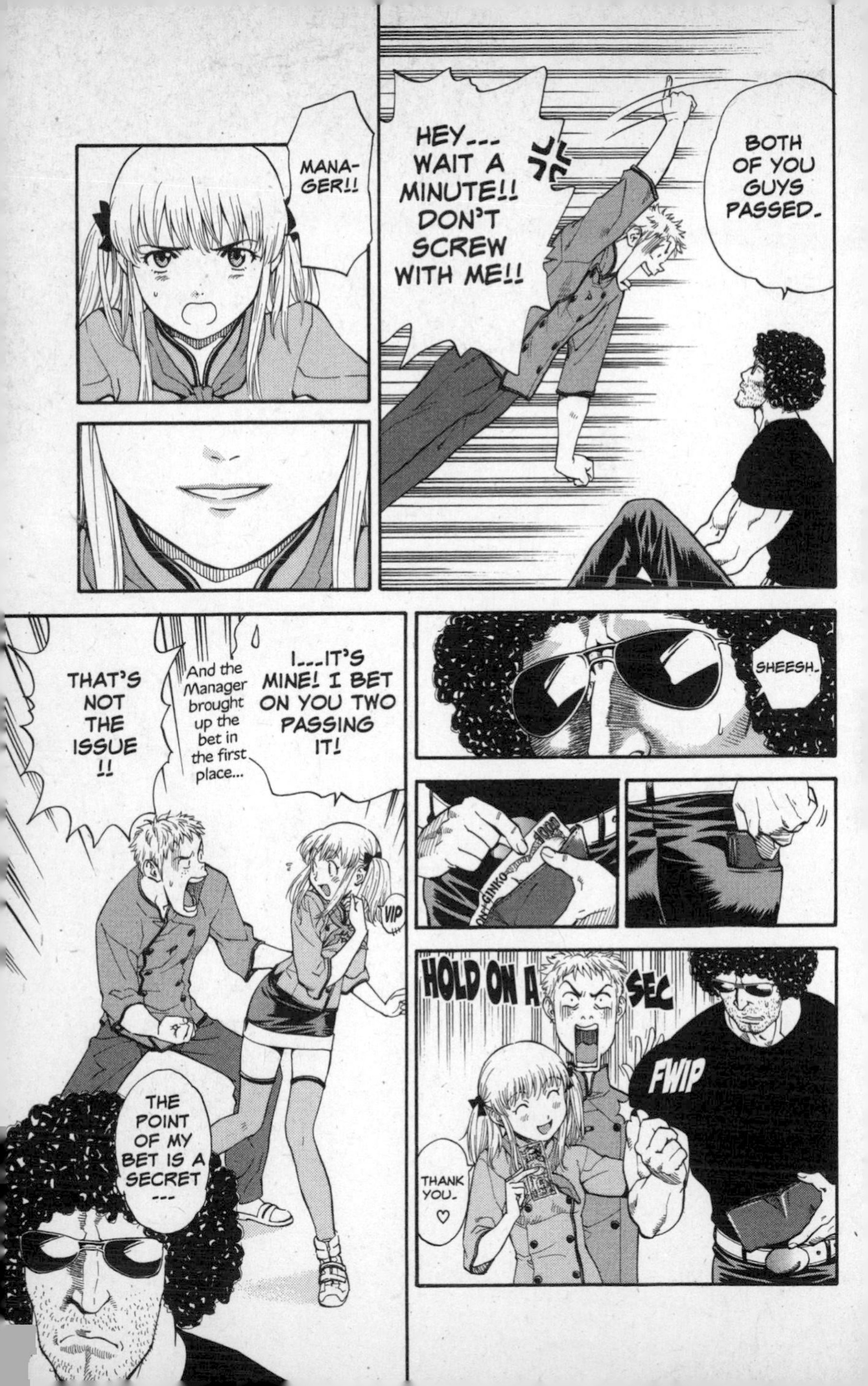
BOTH OF YOU GUYS PASSED.
HEY... WAIT A MINUTE!! DON'T SCREW WITH ME!!
MANA-GER!!
SHEESH.
HOLD ON A SEC
FWIP
THANK YOU. ♡
I...IT'S MINE! I BET ON YOU TWO PASSING IT!
And the Manager brought up the bet in the first place...
THAT'S NOT THE ISSUE!!
VIP
THE POINT OF MY BET IS A SECRET...

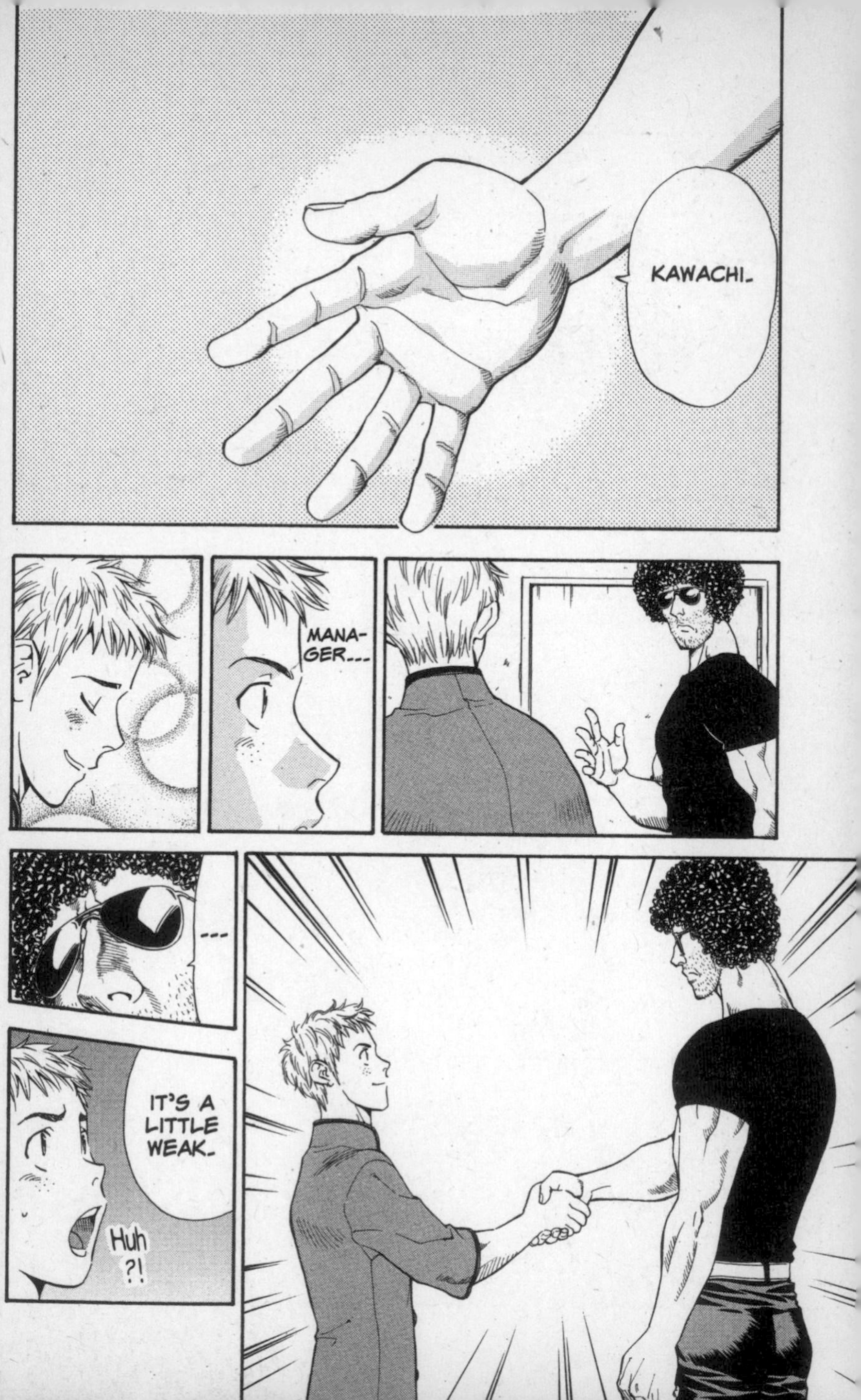
KAWACHI.
MANAGER...
...
IT'S A LITTLE WEAK.
Huh?!

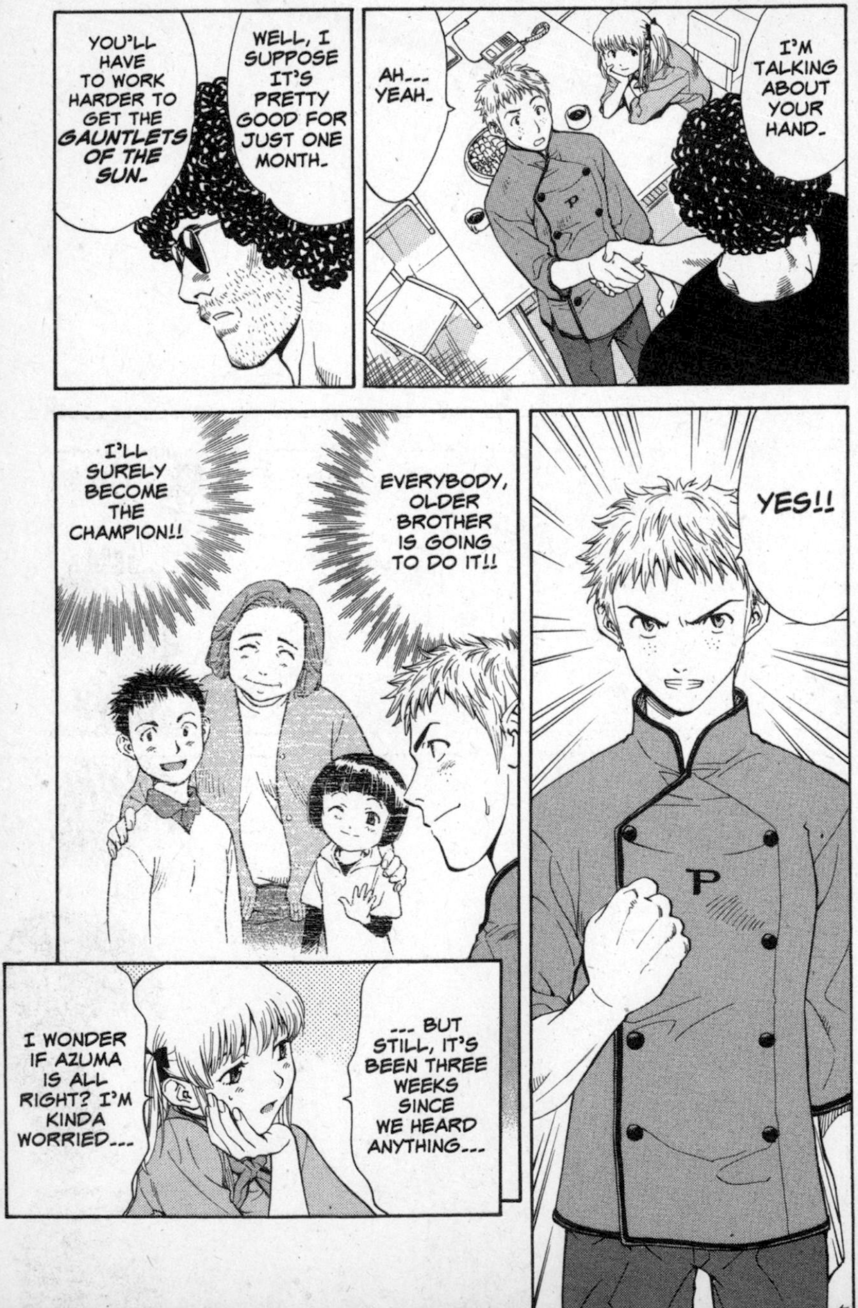
I'M TALKING ABOUT YOUR HAND.
AH... YEAH.
WELL, I SUPPOSE IT'S PRETTY GOOD FOR JUST ONE MONTH.
YOU'LL HAVE TO WORK HARDER TO GET THE GAUNTLETS OF THE SUN.
YES!!
EVERYBODY, OLDER BROTHER IS GOING TO DO IT!!
I'LL SURELY BECOME THE CHAMPION!!
... BUT STILL, IT'S BEEN THREE WEEKS SINCE WE HEARD ANYTHING...
I WONDER IF AZUMA IS ALL RIGHT? I'M KINDA WORRIED...

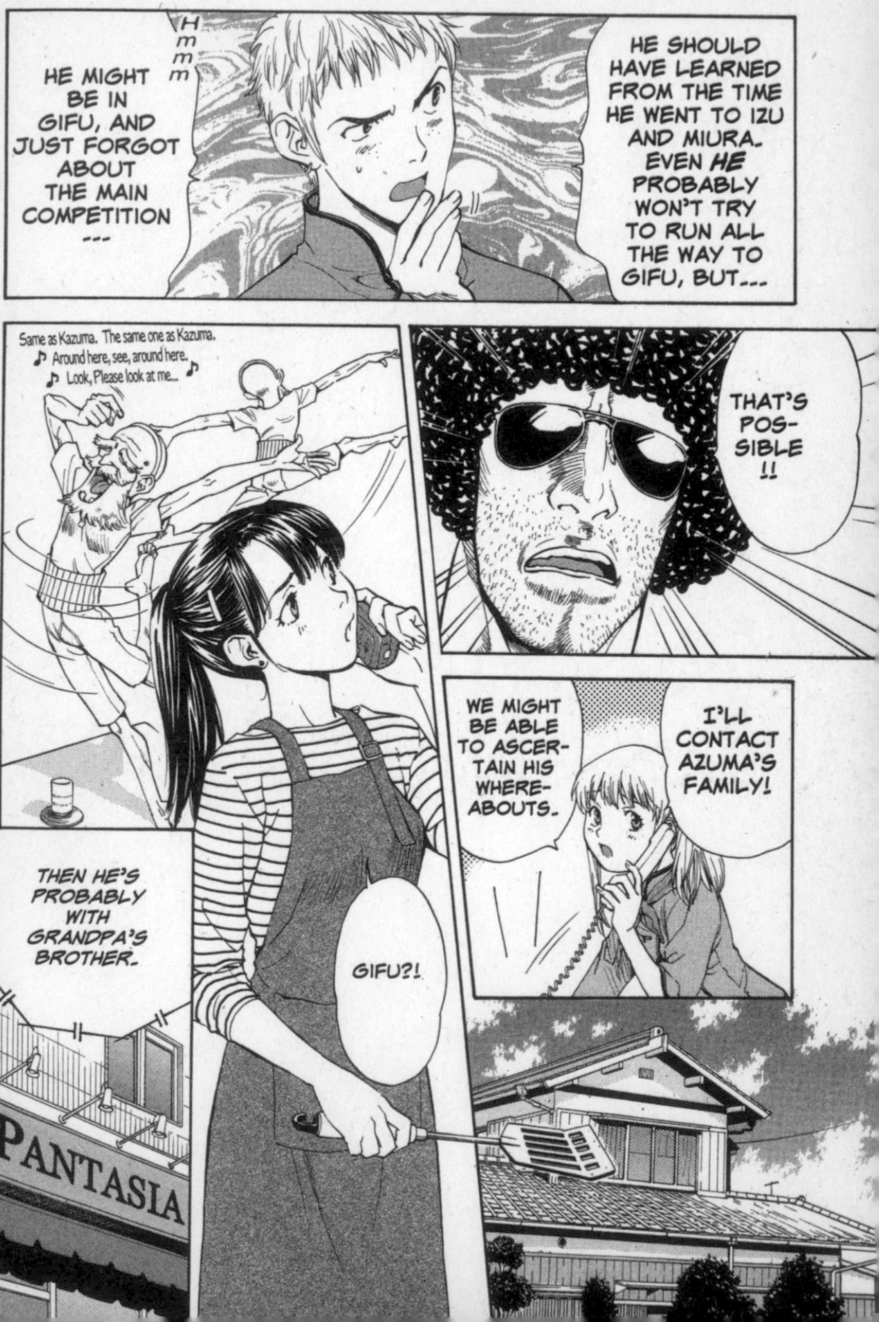
HE SHOULD HAVE LEARNED FROM THE TIME HE WENT TO IZU AND MIURA. EVEN *HE* PROBABLY WON'T TRY TO RUN ALL THE WAY TO GIFU, BUT...
Hmmm
HE MIGHT BE IN GIFU, AND JUST FORGOT ABOUT THE MAIN COMPETITION ---
THAT'S POS-SIBLE !!
I'LL CONTACT AZUMA'S FAMILY!
WE MIGHT BE ABLE TO ASCER-TAIN HIS WHERE-ABOUTS.
Same as Kazuma. The same one as Kazuma.
♪ Around here, see, around here.
♪ Look, Please look at me... ♪
GIFU?!
THEN HE'S PROBABLY WITH GRANDPA'S BROTHER.
PANTASIA

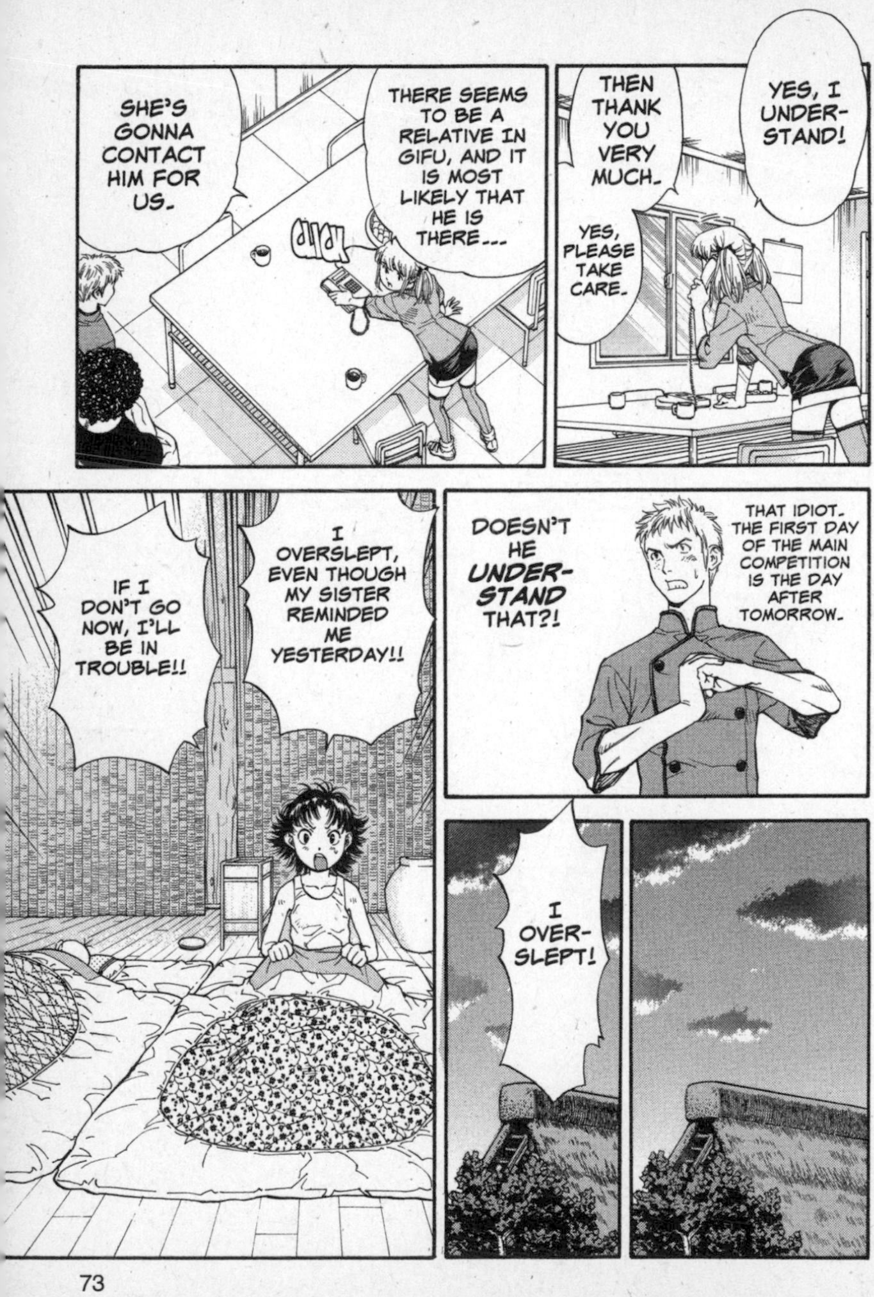
YES, I UNDER-STAND!
THEN THANK YOU VERY MUCH.
YES, PLEASE TAKE CARE.
THERE SEEMS TO BE A RELATIVE IN GIFU, AND IT IS MOST LIKELY THAT HE IS THERE...
SHE'S GONNA CONTACT HIM FOR US.
THAT IDIOT. THE FIRST DAY OF THE MAIN COMPETITION IS THE DAY AFTER TOMORROW.
DOESN'T HE *UNDER-STAND* THAT?!
I OVER-SLEPT!
I OVERSLEPT, EVEN THOUGH MY SISTER REMINDED ME YESTERDAY!!
IF I DON'T GO NOW, I'LL BE IN TROUBLE!!

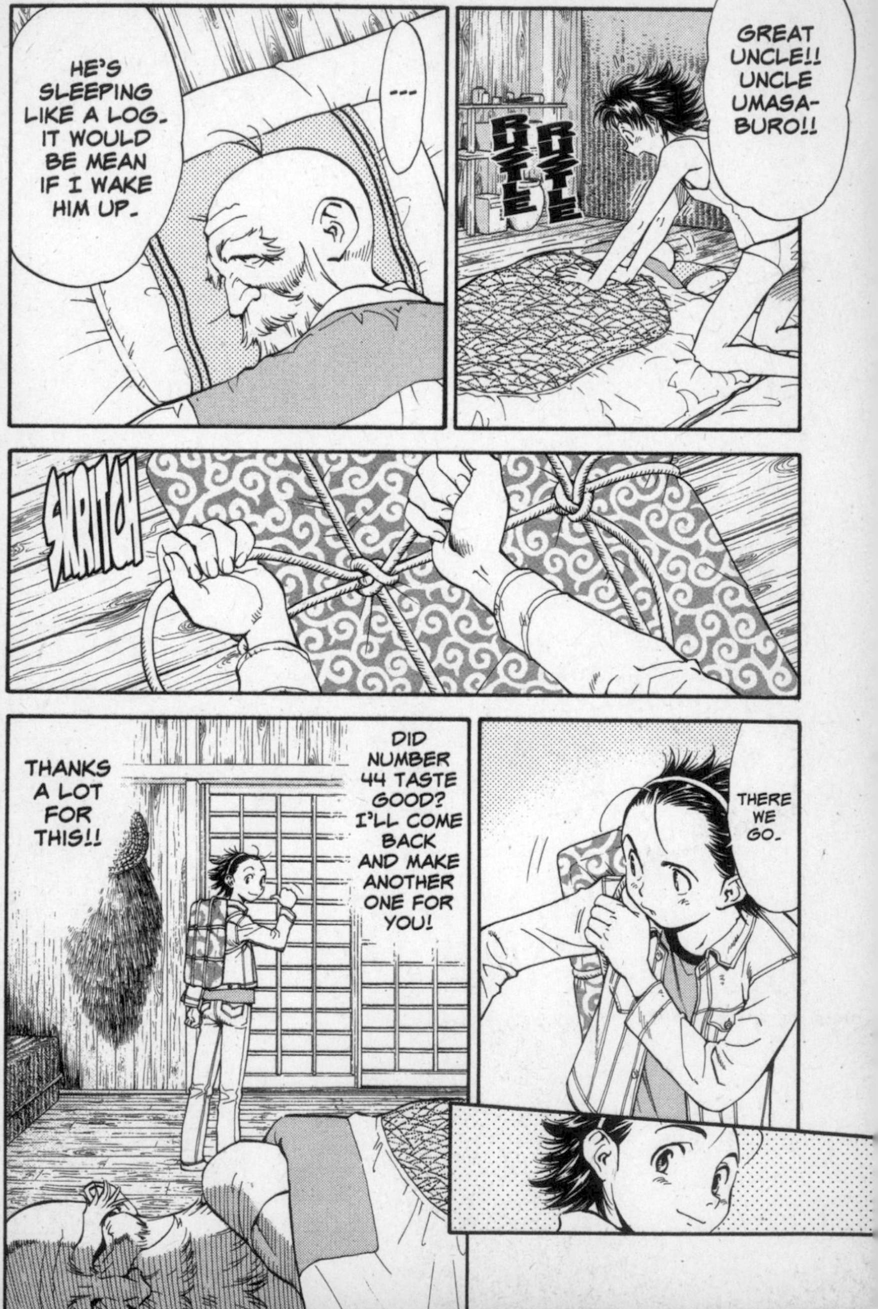
GREAT UNCLE!! UNCLE UMASABURO!!

HE'S SLEEPING LIKE A LOG. IT WOULD BE MEAN IF I WAKE HIM UP.
SKRITCH
THERE WE GO.
DID NUMBER 44 TASTE GOOD? I'LL COME BACK AND MAKE ANOTHER ONE FOR YOU!
THANKS A LOT FOR THIS!!

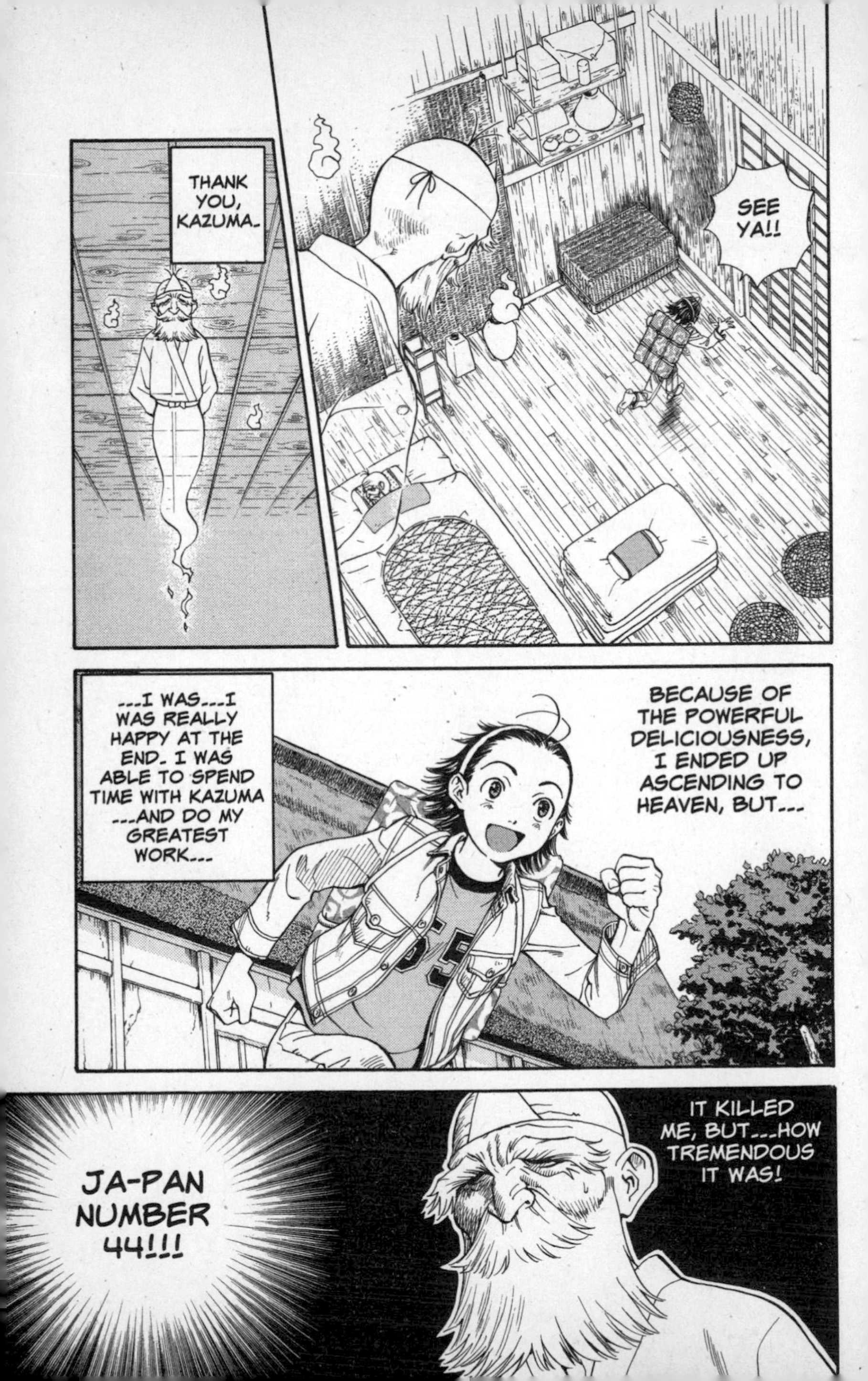
SEE YA!!
THANK YOU, KAZUMA.
BECAUSE OF THE POWERFUL DELICIOUSNESS, I ENDED UP ASCENDING TO HEAVEN, BUT...
...I WAS...I WAS REALLY HAPPY AT THE END. I WAS ABLE TO SPEND TIME WITH KAZUMA ...AND DO MY GREATEST WORK...
IT KILLED ME, BUT...HOW TREMENDOUS IT WAS!
JA-PAN NUMBER 44!!!

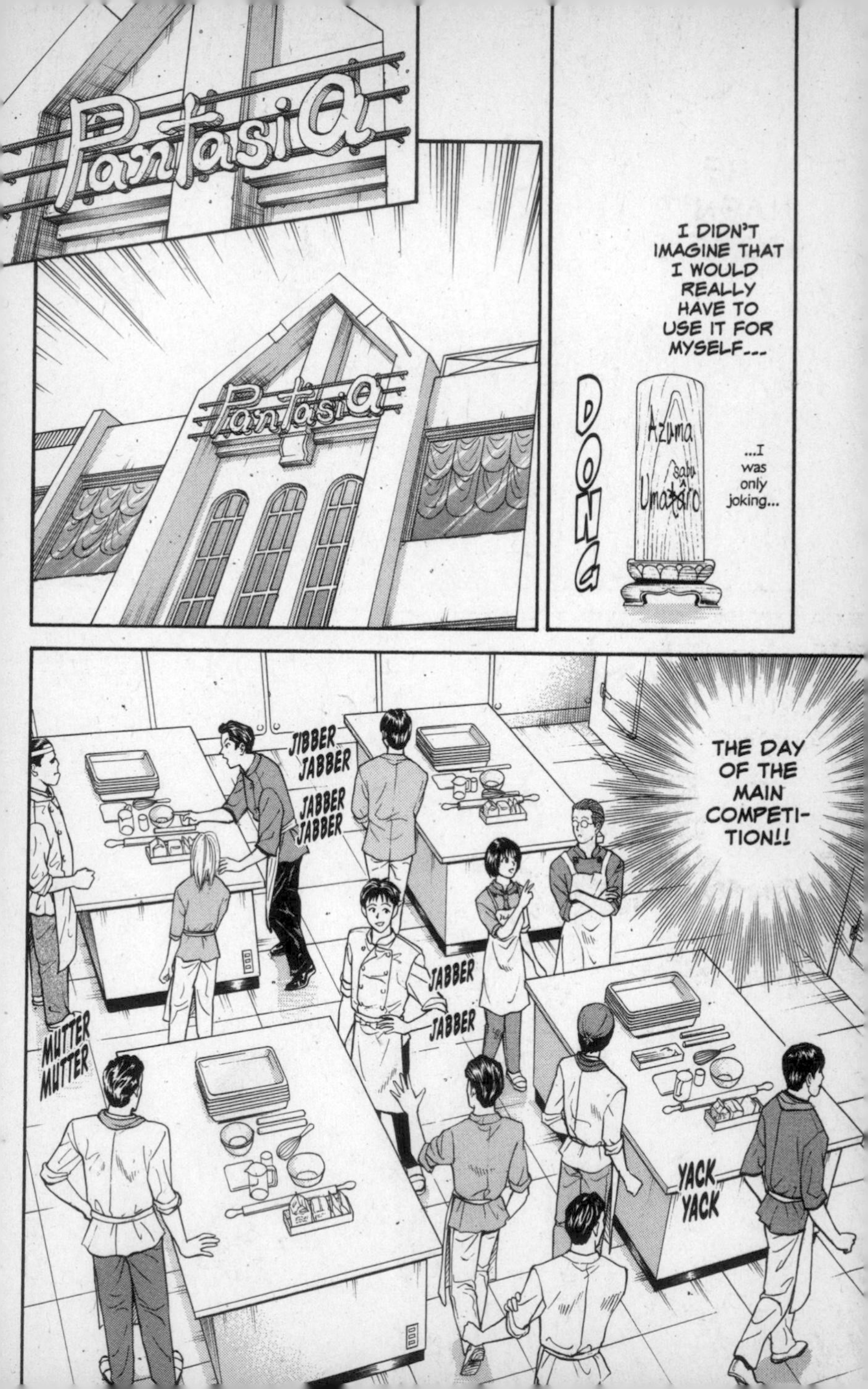
I DIDN'T IMAGINE THAT I WOULD REALLY HAVE TO USE IT FOR MYSELF...
DONG
Azuma
sabu
Umatâro
...I was only joking...
PantasiA
PantasiA
THE DAY OF THE MAIN COMPETI-TION!!
JIBBER JABBER
JABBER JABBER
JABBER JABBER
YACK YACK
MUTTER MUTTER

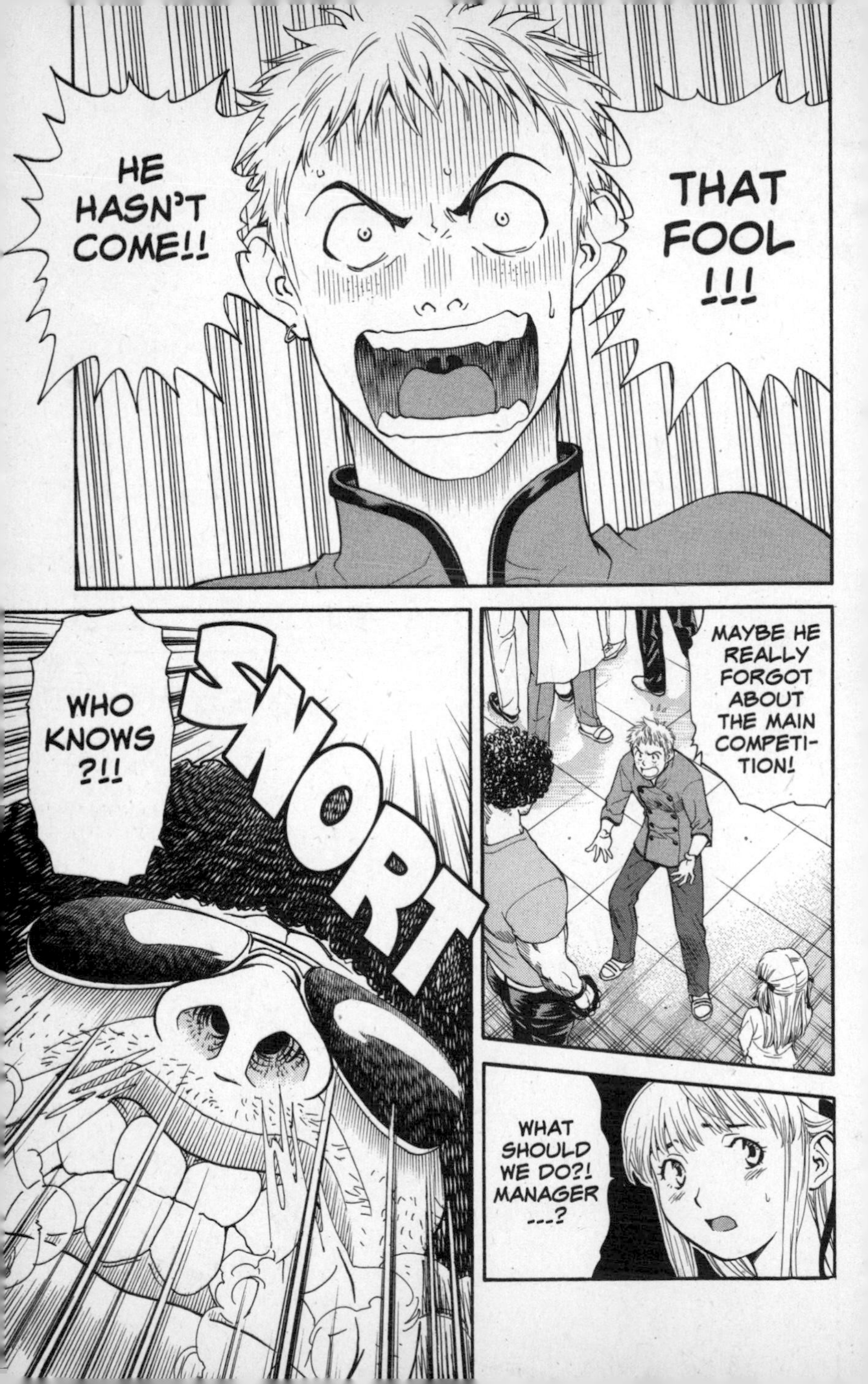
THAT FOOL!!!
HE HASN'T COME!!
MAYBE HE REALLY FORGOT ABOUT THE MAIN COMPETI-TION!
WHAT SHOULD WE DO?! MANAGER ---?
SNORT
WHO KNOWS?!!

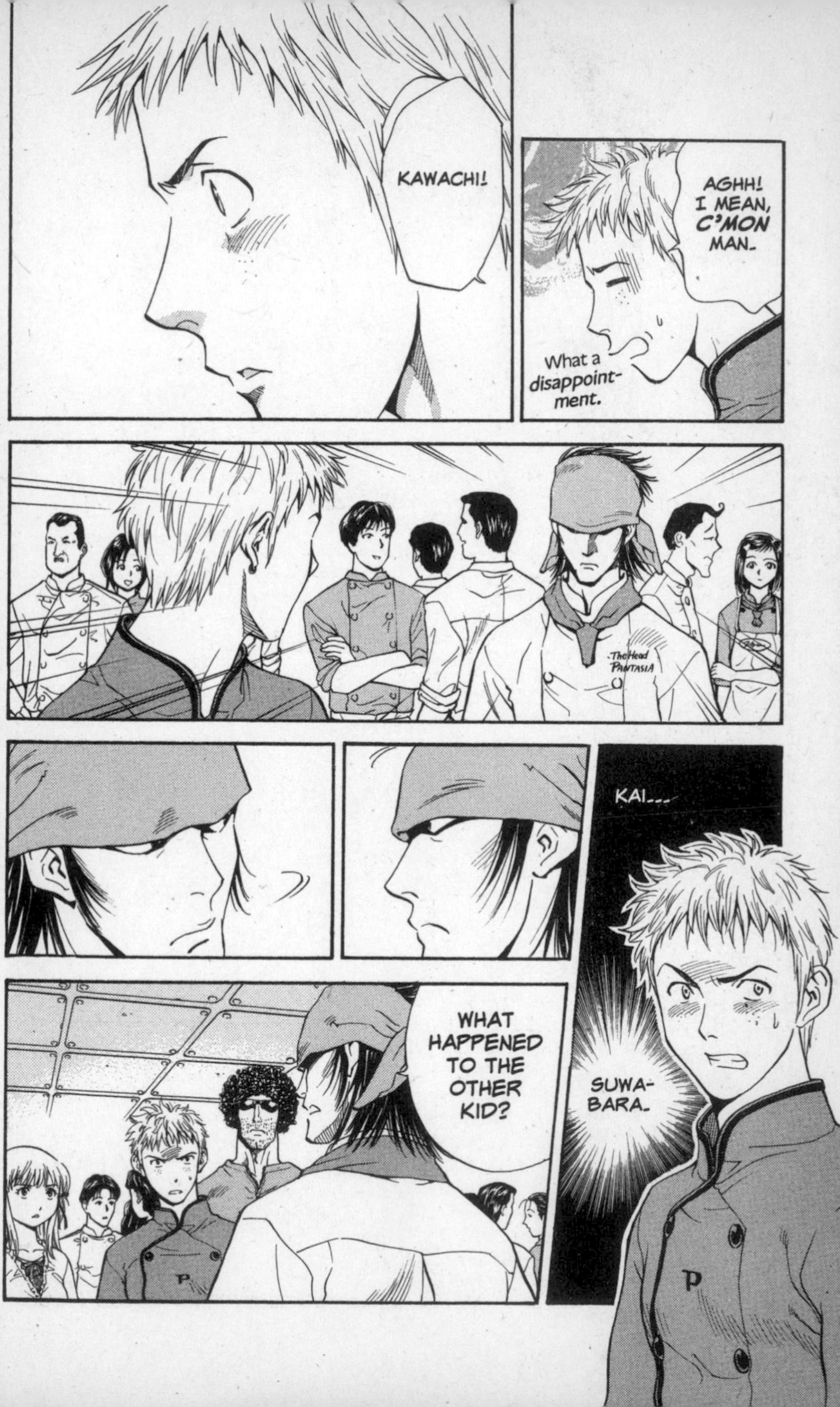
AGHH! I MEAN, C'MON MAN...
What a disappointment.
KAWACHI!
KAI...
SUWA-BARA...
WHAT HAPPENED TO THE OTHER KID?
The Head PANTASIA

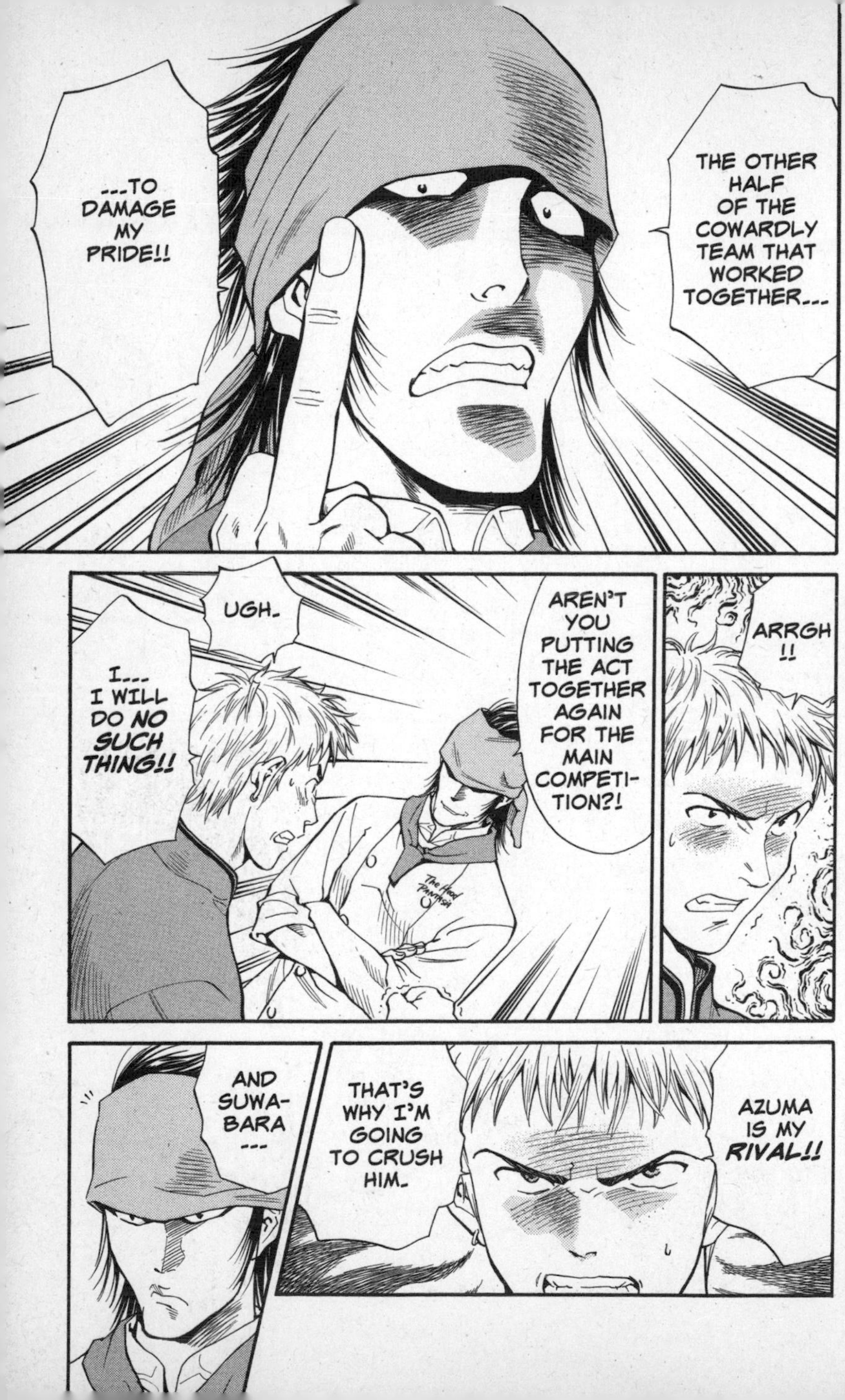
THE OTHER HALF OF THE COWARDLY TEAM THAT WORKED TOGETHER...
...TO DAMAGE MY PRIDE!!
ARRGH!!
AREN'T YOU PUTTING THE ACT TOGETHER AGAIN FOR THE MAIN COMPETITION?!
UGH.
I... I WILL DO NO SUCH THING!!
AZUMA IS MY RIVAL!!
THAT'S WHY I'M GOING TO CRUSH HIM.
AND SUWABARA ...

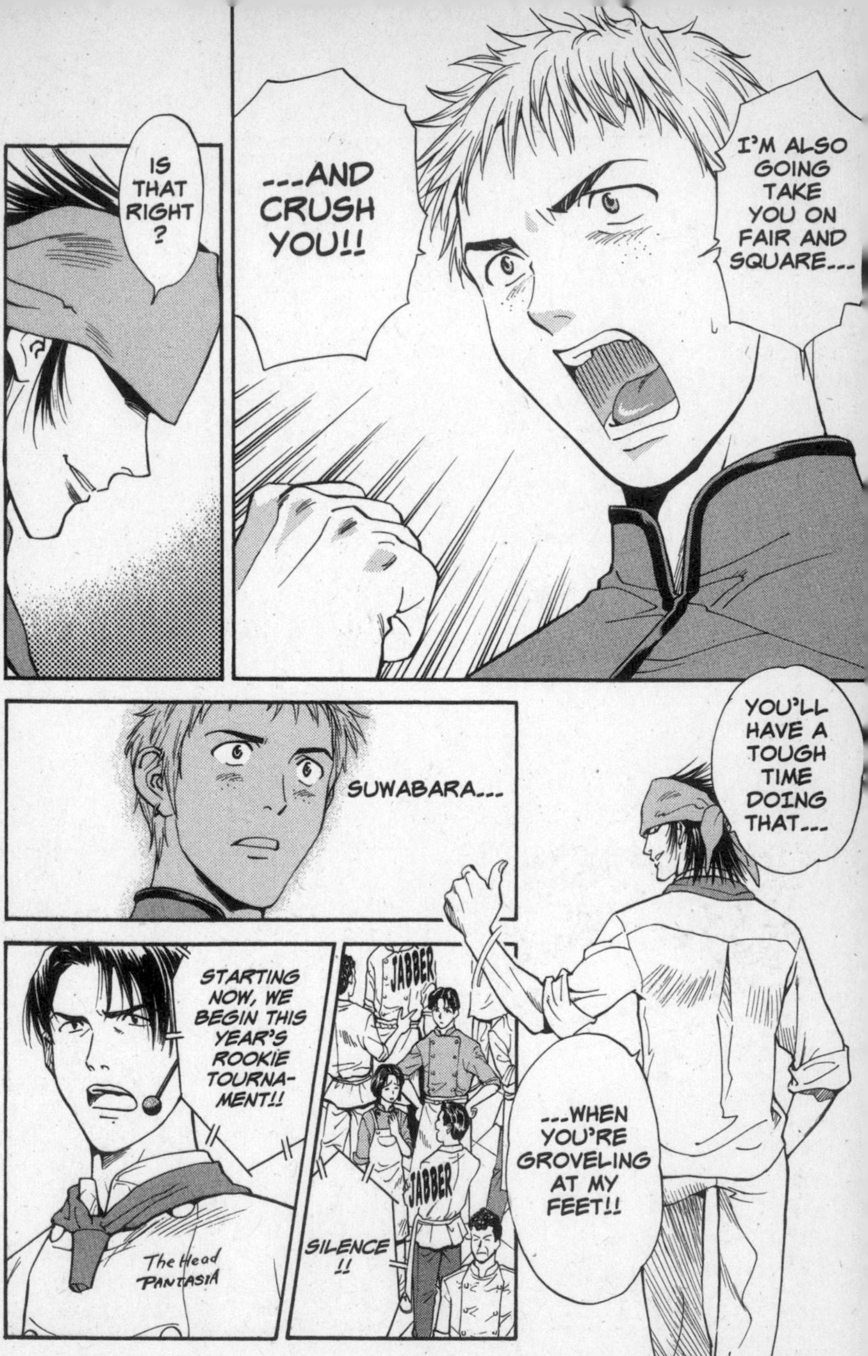

I'M ALSO GOING TAKE YOU ON FAIR AND SQUARE...
---AND CRUSH YOU!!
IS THAT RIGHT?
YOU'LL HAVE A TOUGH TIME DOING THAT...
---WHEN YOU'RE GROVELING AT MY FEET!!
SUWABARA...
JABBER
JABBER
SILENCE!!
STARTING NOW, WE BEGIN THIS YEAR'S ROOKIE TOURNAMENT!!
The Head PANTASIA

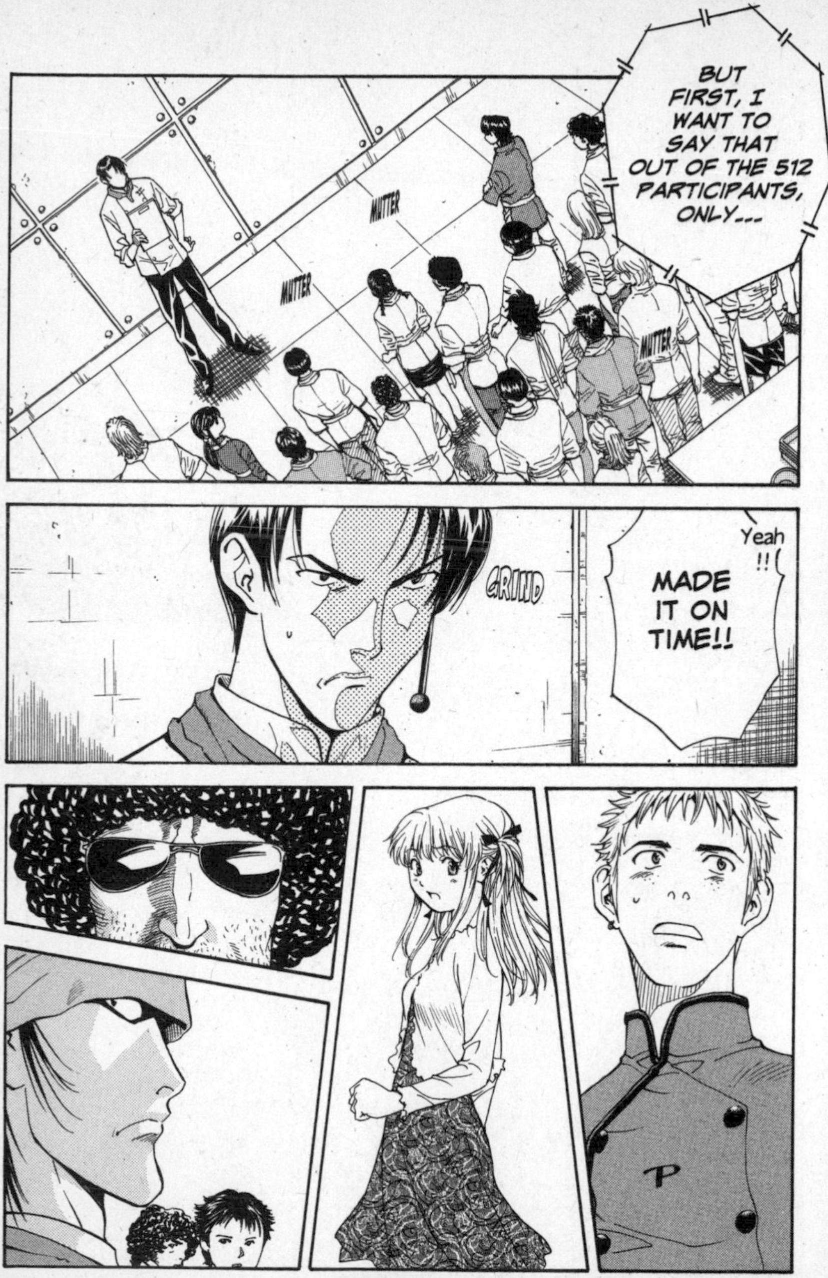
BUT FIRST, I WANT TO SAY THAT OUT OF THE 512 PARTICIPANTS, ONLY...
MUTTER
MUTTER
MUTTER
Yeah !!
MADE IT ON TIME!!
GRIND

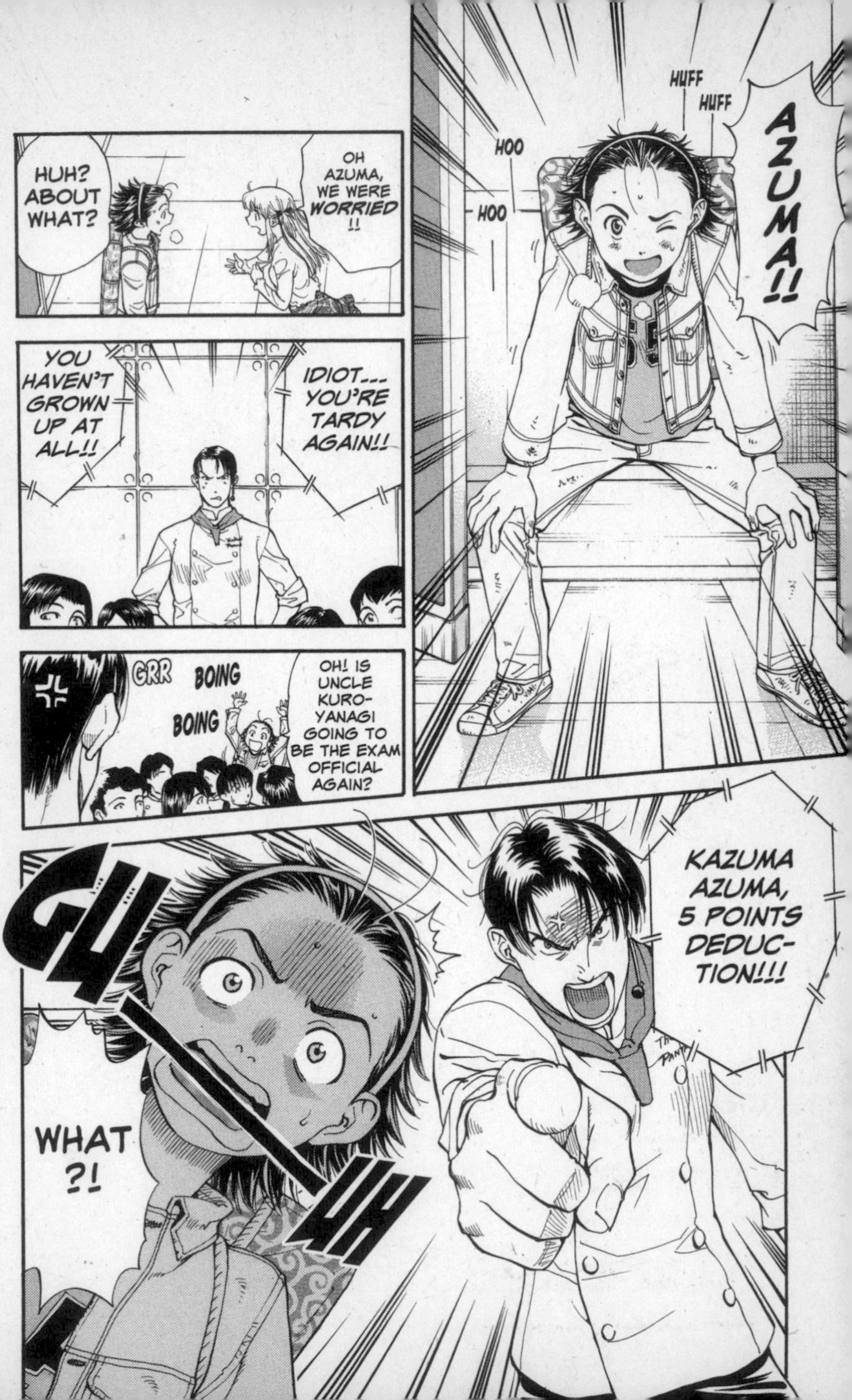
AZUMA!!
HUFF
HUFF
HOO
HOO
OH AZUMA, WE WERE WORRIED!!
HUH? ABOUT WHAT?
IDIOT... YOU'RE TARDY AGAIN!!
YOU HAVEN'T GROWN UP AT ALL!!
OH! IS UNCLE KURO-YANAGI GOING TO BE THE EXAM OFFICIAL AGAIN?
BOING
BOING
GRR
KAZUMA AZUMA, 5 POINTS DEDUC-TION!!!
WHAT ?!

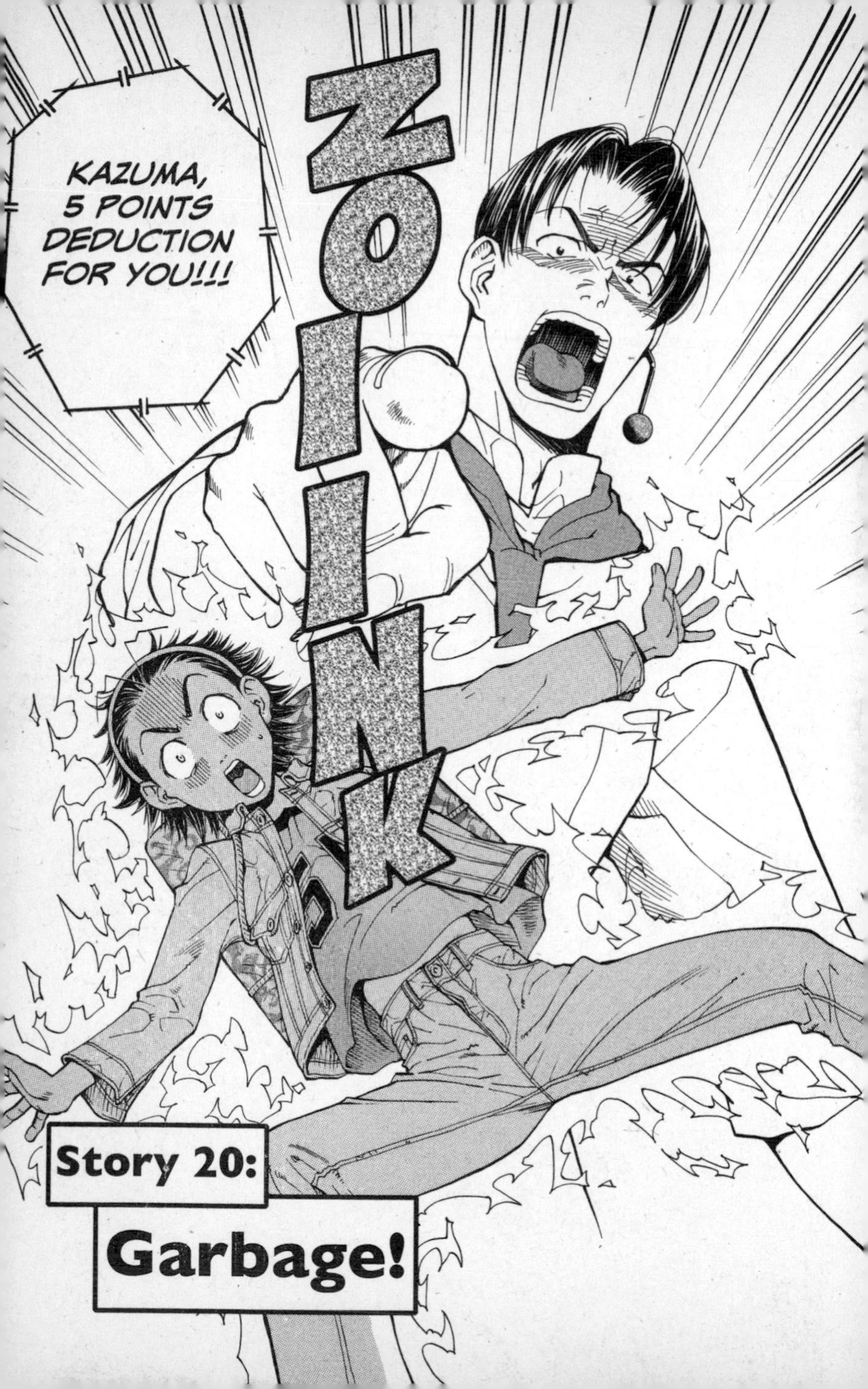
KAZUMA, 5 POINTS DEDUCTION FOR YOU!!!
ZOINK
Story 20:
Garbage!

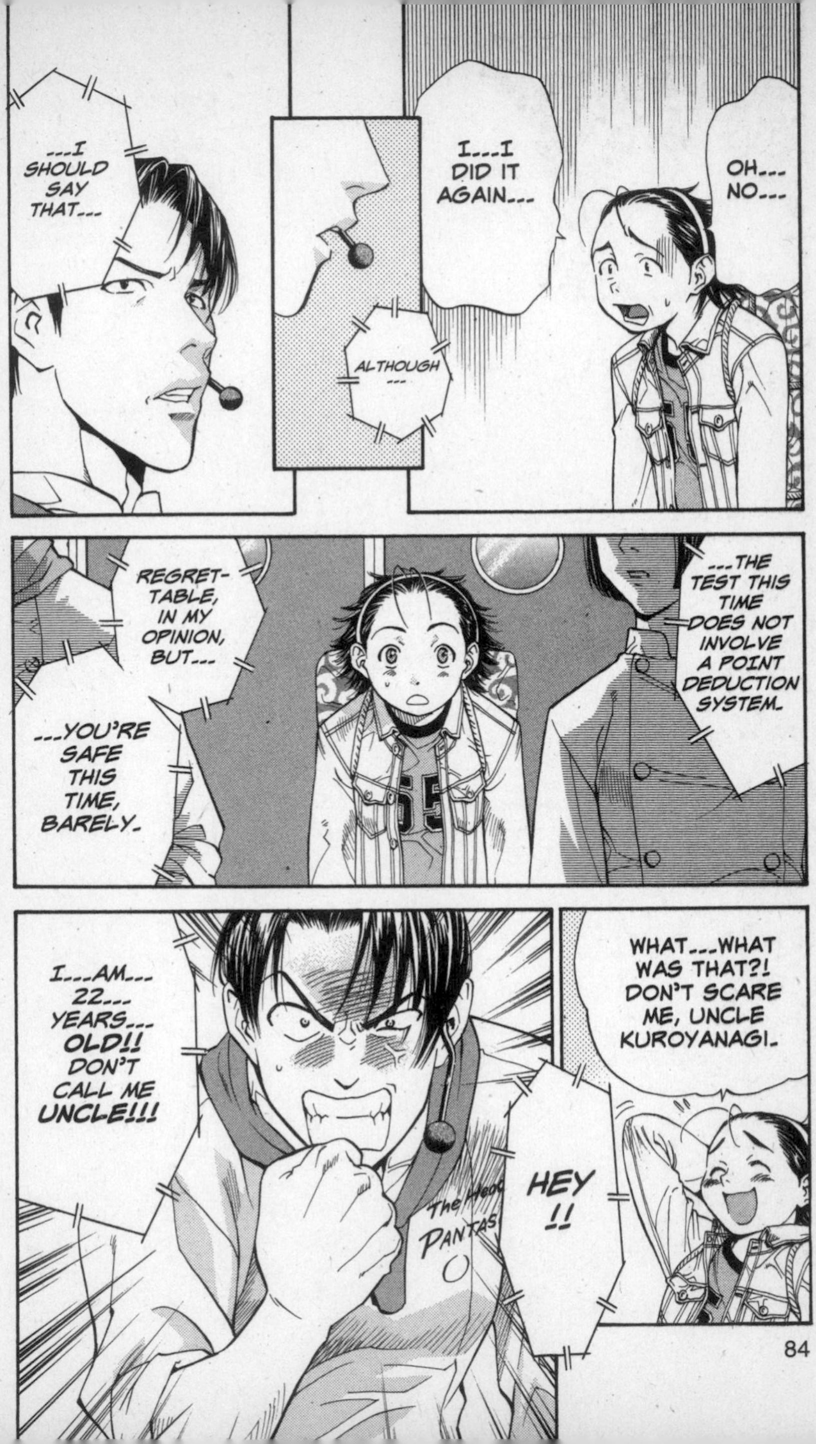
OH... NO...
I...I DID IT AGAIN...
ALTHOUGH ---
---I SHOULD SAY THAT---
---THE TEST THIS TIME DOES NOT INVOLVE A POINT DEDUCTION SYSTEM.
REGRETTABLE, IN MY OPINION, BUT---
---YOU'RE SAFE THIS TIME, BARELY.
WHAT---WHAT WAS THAT?! DON'T SCARE ME, UNCLE KUROYANAGI.
HEY!!
The Head PANTAS
I---AM--- 22--- YEARS--- OLD!! DON'T CALL ME UNCLE!!!

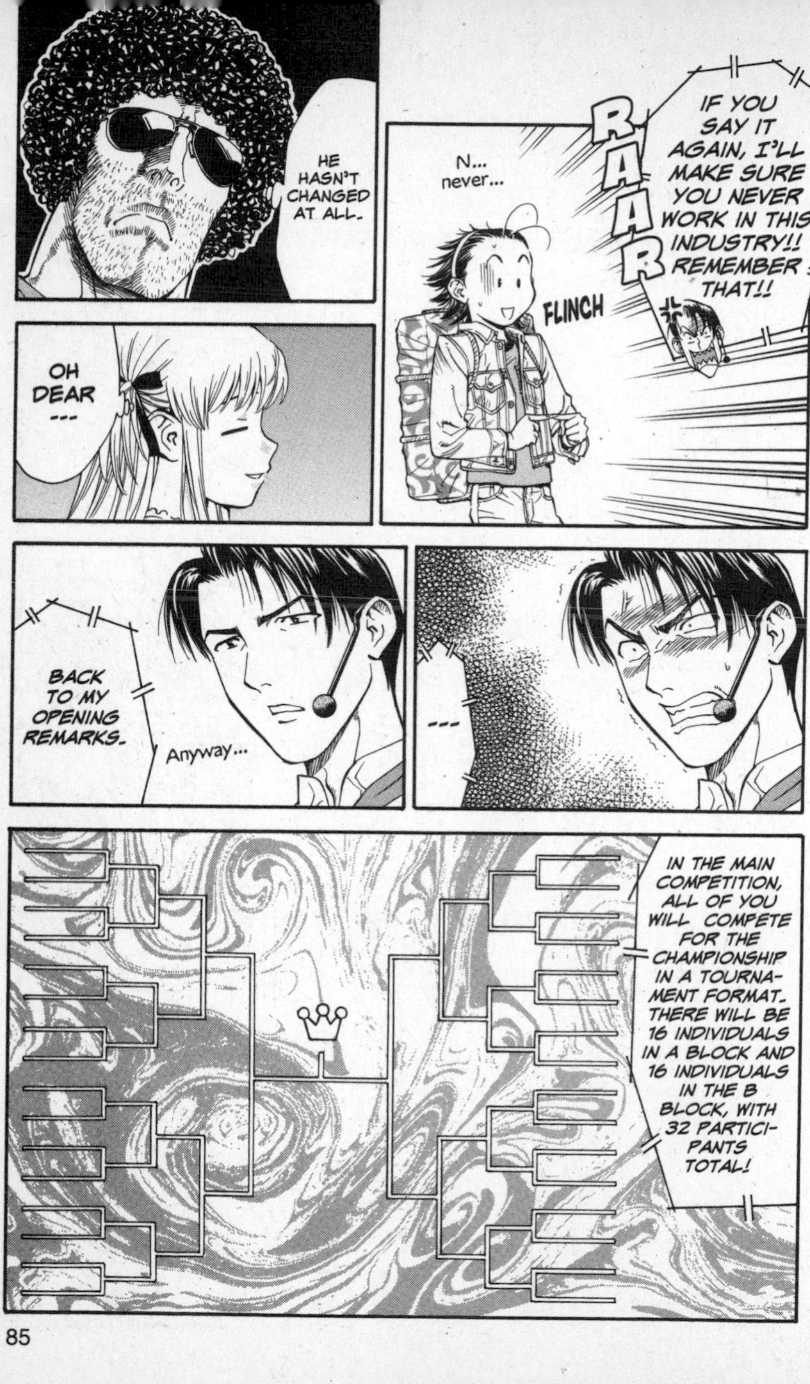

IF YOU SAY IT AGAIN, I'LL MAKE SURE YOU NEVER WORK IN THIS INDUSTRY!! REMEMBER THAT!!
RAAR
N... never...
FLINCH
HE HASN'T CHANGED AT ALL.
OH DEAR ---

Anyway...
BACK TO MY OPENING REMARKS.
IN THE MAIN COMPETITION, ALL OF YOU WILL COMPETE FOR THE CHAMPIONSHIP IN A TOURNAMENT FORMAT. THERE WILL BE 16 INDIVIDUALS IN A BLOCK AND 16 INDIVIDUALS IN THE B BLOCK, WITH 32 PARTICIPANTS TOTAL!

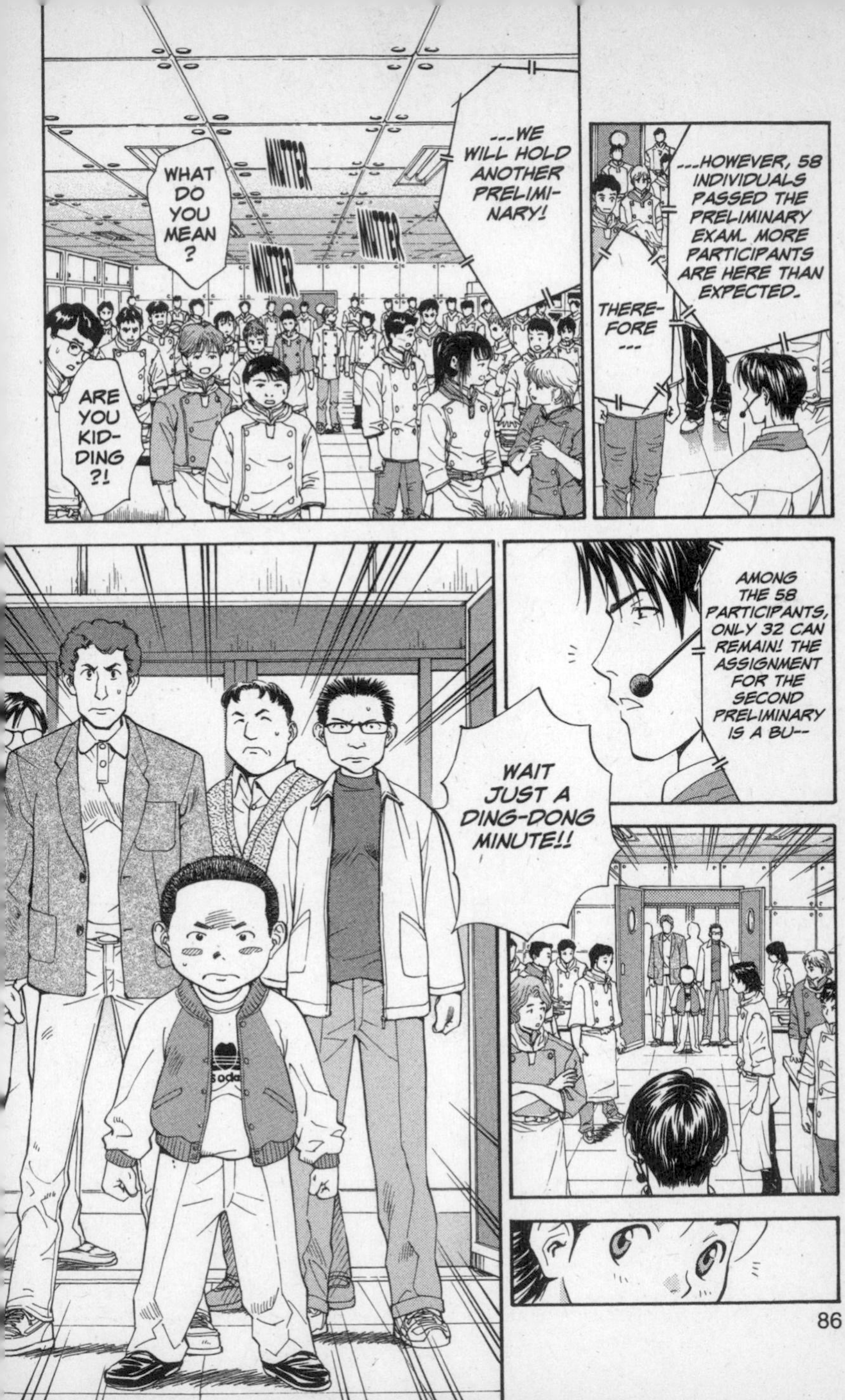
---HOWEVER, 58 INDIVIDUALS PASSED THE PRELIMINARY EXAM. MORE PARTICIPANTS ARE HERE THAN EXPECTED.
THEREFORE ---
---WE WILL HOLD ANOTHER PRELIMINARY!
NATTER
NATTER
NATTER
WHAT DO YOU MEAN?
ARE YOU KIDDING?!
AMONG THE 58 PARTICIPANTS, ONLY 32 CAN REMAIN! THE ASSIGNMENT FOR THE SECOND PRELIMINARY IS A BU--
WAIT JUST A DING-DONG MINUTE!!

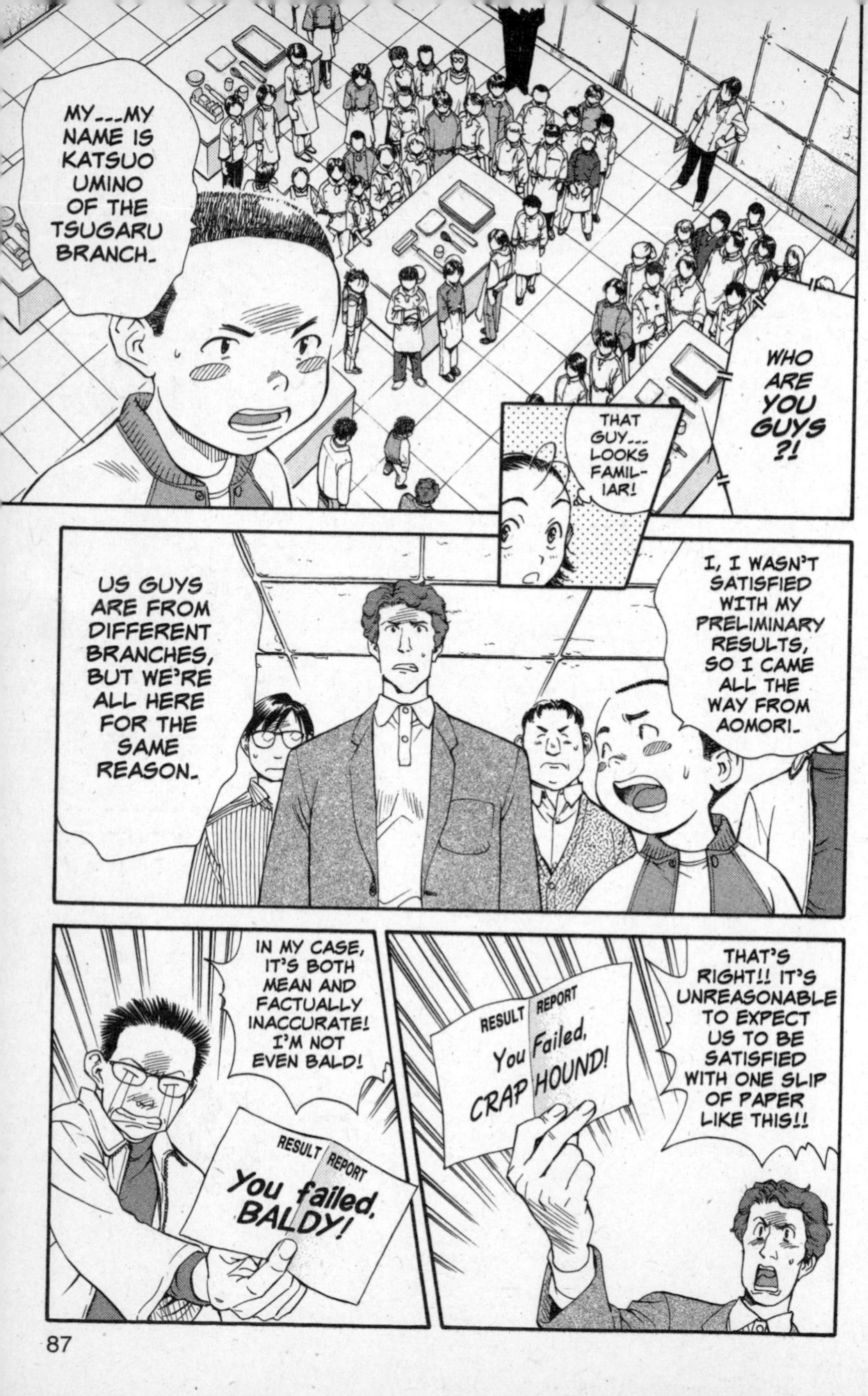
WHO ARE YOU GUYS?!
MY...MY NAME IS KATSUO UMINO OF THE TSUGARU BRANCH.
THAT GUY... LOOKS FAMIL-IAR!
I, I WASN'T SATISFIED WITH MY PRELIMINARY RESULTS, SO I CAME ALL THE WAY FROM AOMORI.
US GUYS ARE FROM DIFFERENT BRANCHES, BUT WE'RE ALL HERE FOR THE SAME REASON.
THAT'S RIGHT!! IT'S UNREASONABLE TO EXPECT US TO BE SATISFIED WITH ONE SLIP OF PAPER LIKE THIS!!
RESULT REPORT
You Failed, CRAP HOUND!
IN MY CASE, IT'S BOTH MEAN AND FACTUALLY INACCURATE! I'M NOT EVEN BALD!
RESULT REPORT
You failed. BALDY!

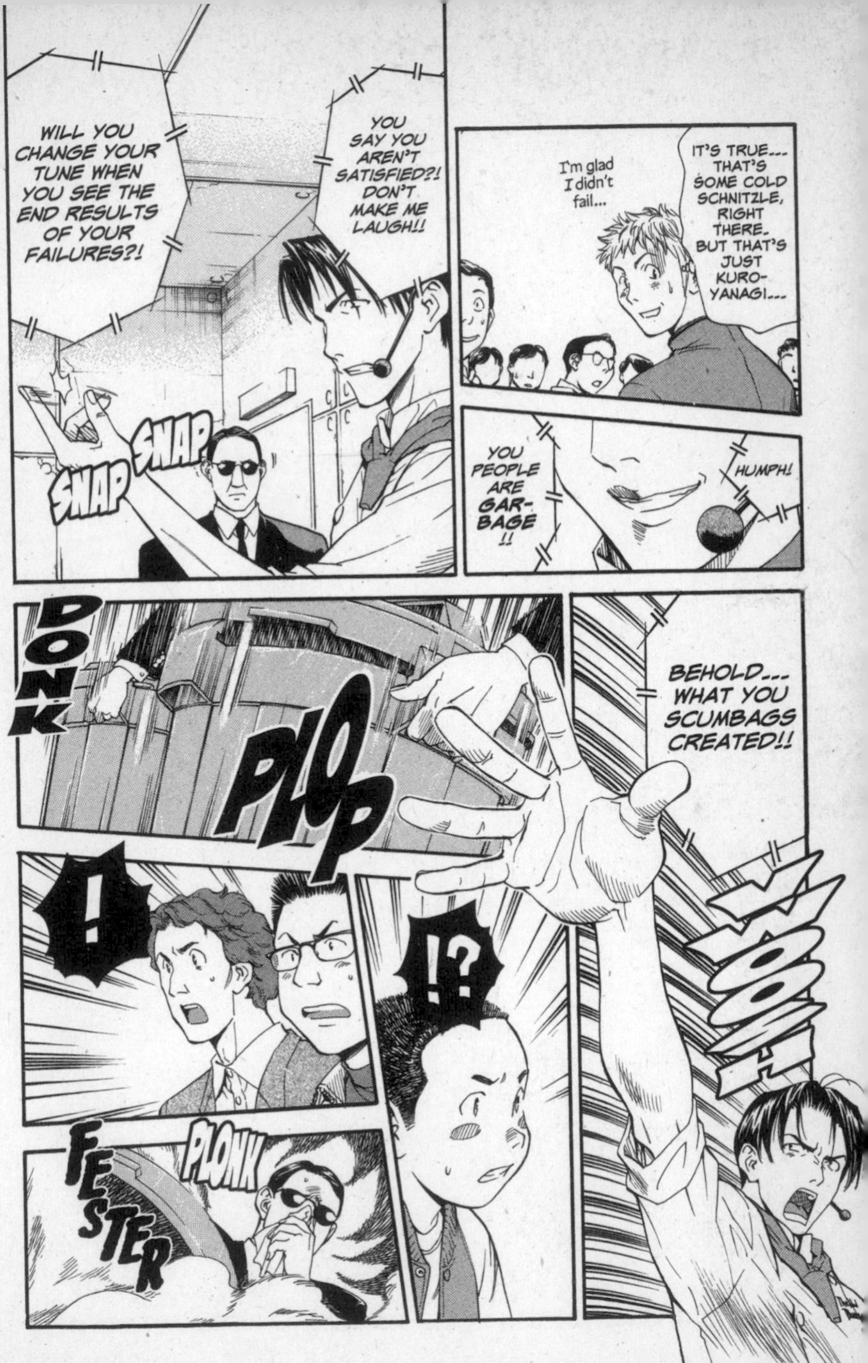
IT'S TRUE... THAT'S SOME COLD SCHNITZLE, RIGHT THERE. BUT THAT'S JUST KURO-YANAGI...
I'm glad I didn't fail...
HUMPH!
YOU PEOPLE ARE GAR-BAGE!!
YOU SAY YOU AREN'T SATISFIED?! DON'T MAKE ME LAUGH!!
WILL YOU CHANGE YOUR TUNE WHEN YOU SEE THE END RESULTS OF YOUR FAILURES?!
SNAP
SNAP
BEHOLD... WHAT YOU SCUMBAGS CREATED!!
WHOOSH
PLOP
DONK
!?
!
PLONK
FESTER

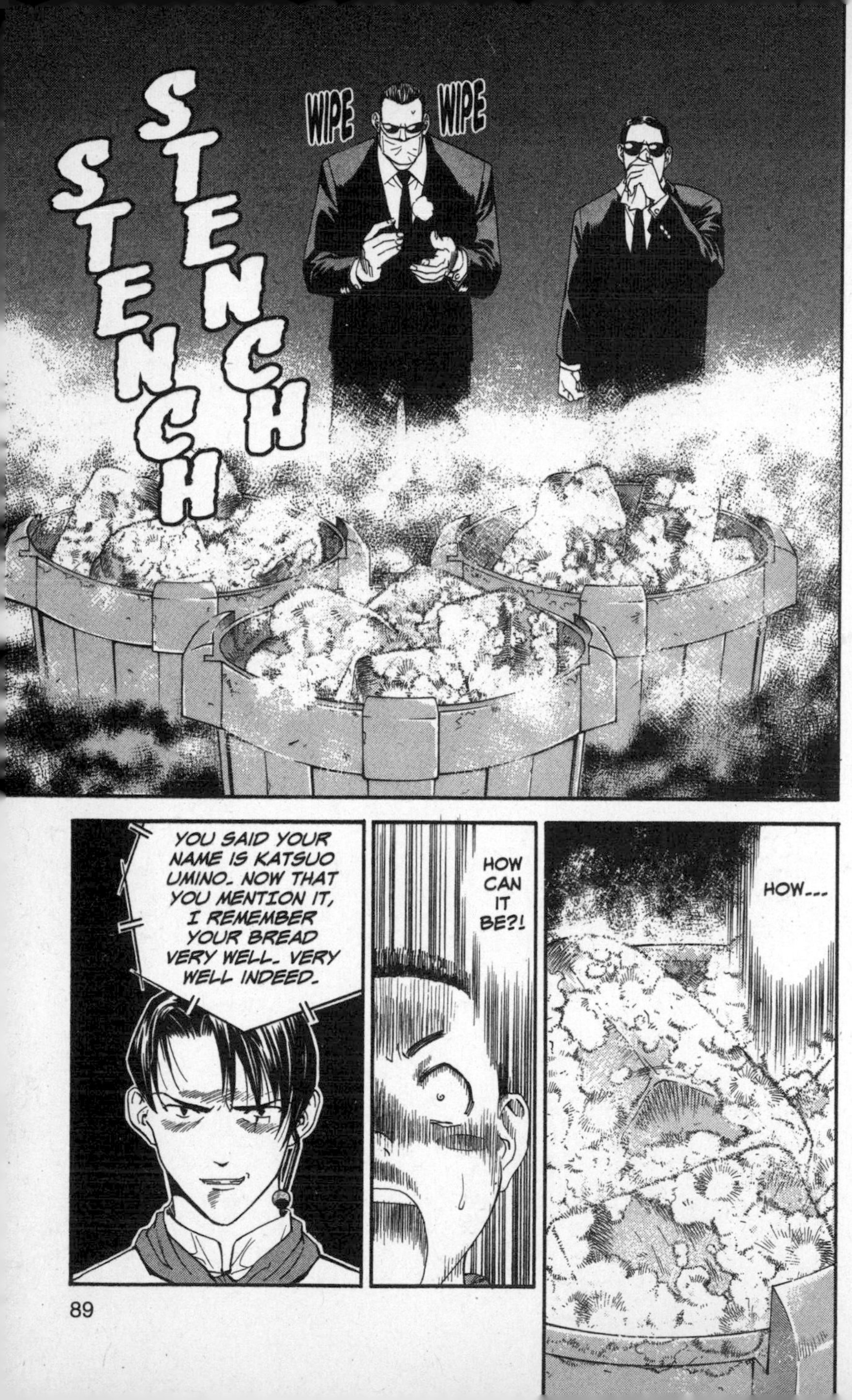
WIPE WIPE
STENCH STENCH
HOW...
HOW CAN IT BE?!
YOU SAID YOUR NAME IS KATSUO UMINO. NOW THAT YOU MENTION IT, I REMEMBER YOUR BREAD VERY WELL. VERY WELL INDEED.

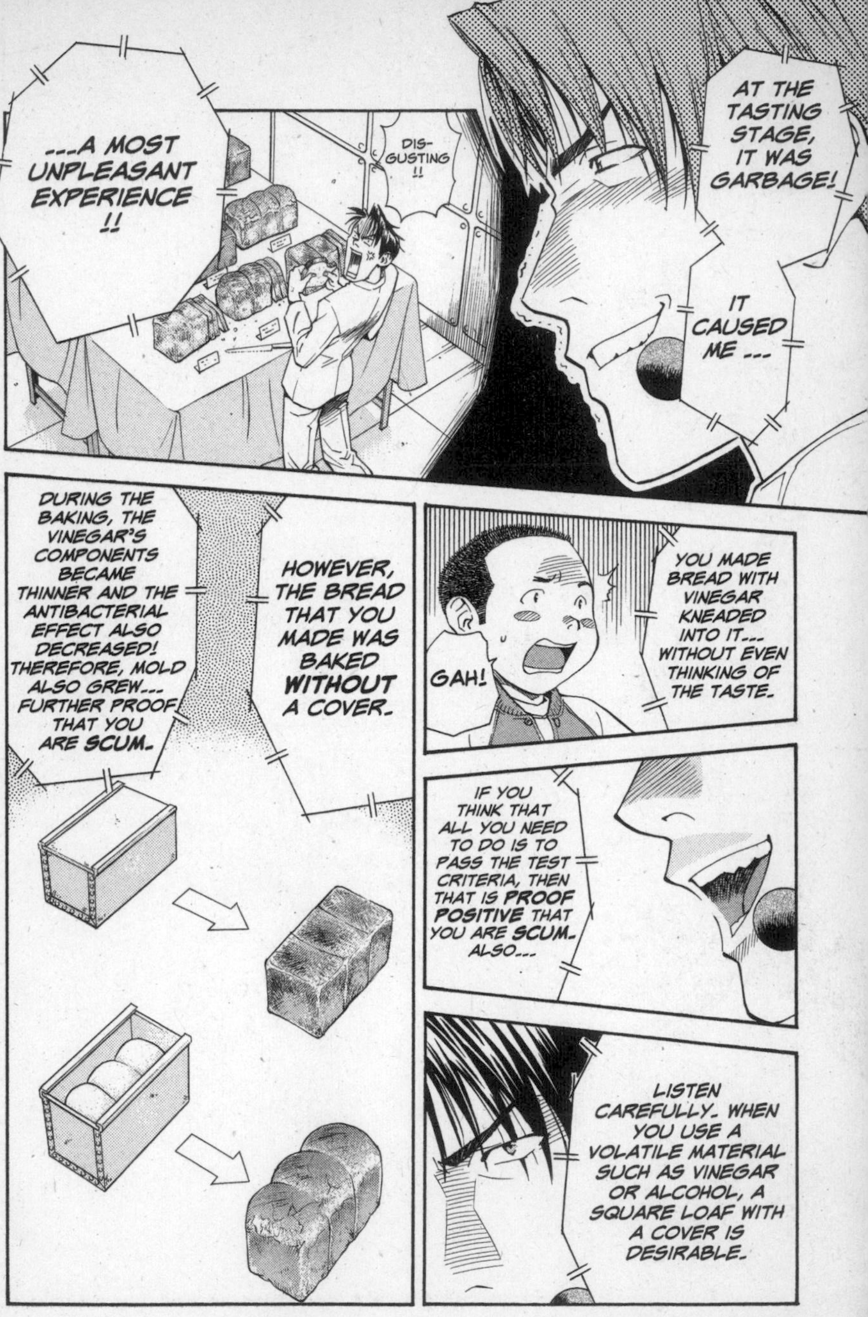
AT THE TASTING STAGE, IT WAS GARBAGE!
IT CAUSED ME ---
---A MOST UNPLEASANT EXPERIENCE !!
DIS-GUSTING !!
YOU MADE BREAD WITH VINEGAR KNEADED INTO IT... WITHOUT EVEN THINKING OF THE TASTE.
GAH!
IF YOU THINK THAT ALL YOU NEED TO DO IS TO PASS THE TEST CRITERIA, THEN THAT IS PROOF POSITIVE THAT YOU ARE SCUM. ALSO...
LISTEN CAREFULLY. WHEN YOU USE A VOLATILE MATERIAL SUCH AS VINEGAR OR ALCOHOL, A SQUARE LOAF WITH A COVER IS DESIRABLE.
HOWEVER, THE BREAD THAT YOU MADE WAS BAKED WITHOUT A COVER.
DURING THE BAKING, THE VINEGAR'S COMPONENTS BECAME THINNER AND THE ANTIBACTERIAL EFFECT ALSO DECREASED! THEREFORE, MOLD ALSO GREW... FURTHER PROOF THAT YOU ARE SCUM.

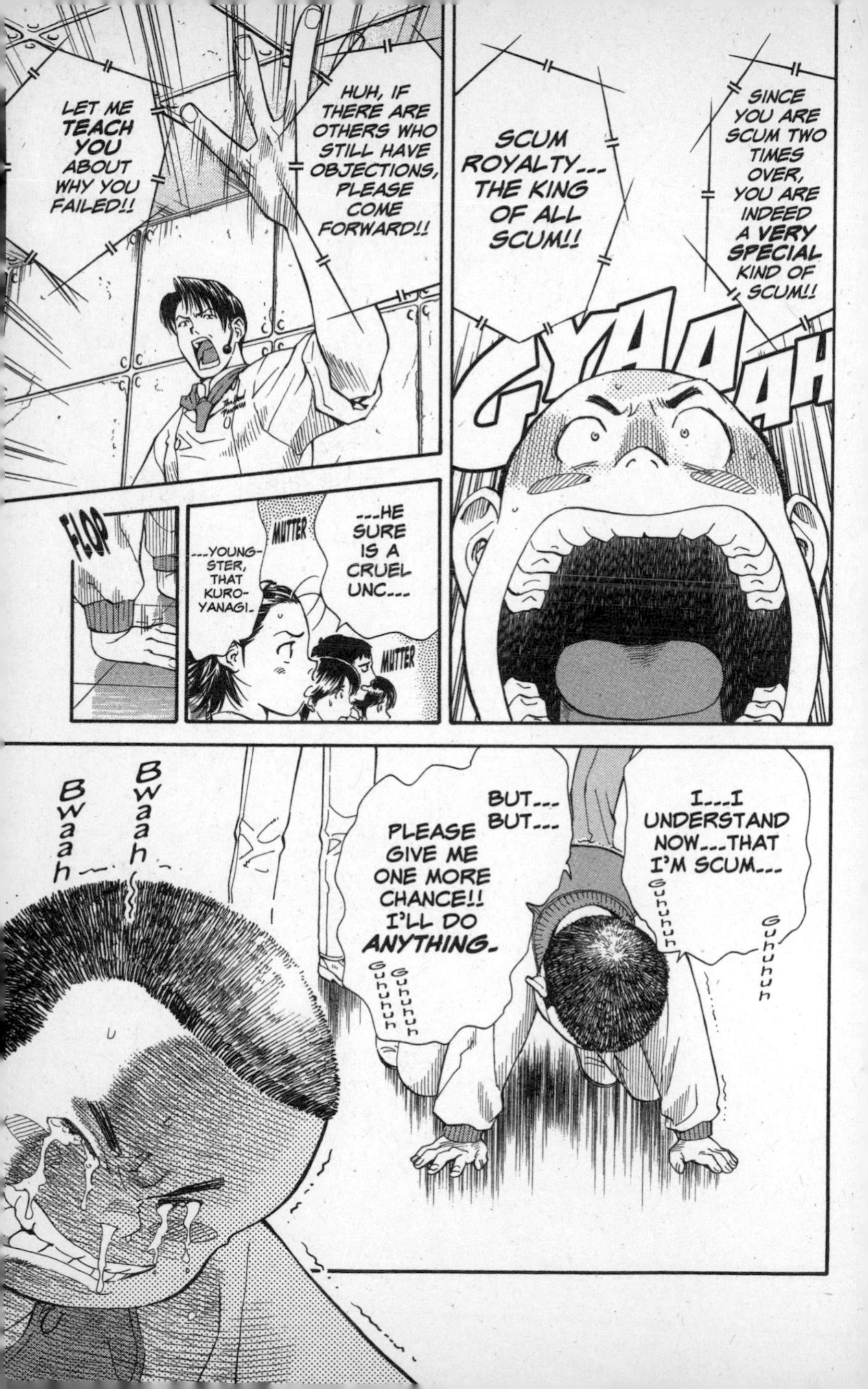
SINCE YOU ARE SCUM TWO TIMES OVER, YOU ARE INDEED A VERY SPECIAL KIND OF SCUM!!
SCUM ROYALTY... THE KING OF ALL SCUM!!
YAAAH
HUH, IF THERE ARE OTHERS WHO STILL HAVE OBJECTIONS, PLEASE COME FORWARD!!
LET ME TEACH YOU ABOUT WHY YOU FAILED!!
...HE SURE IS A CRUEL UNC...
MUTTER
...YOUNGSTER, THAT KUROYANAGI.
MUTTER
FLOP
I...I UNDERSTAND NOW...THAT I'M SCUM...
Guhuhuh
Guhuhuh
BUT... BUT...
PLEASE GIVE ME ONE MORE CHANCE!! I'LL DO ANYTHING.
Guhuhuh
Guhuhuh
Bwaah
Bwaah

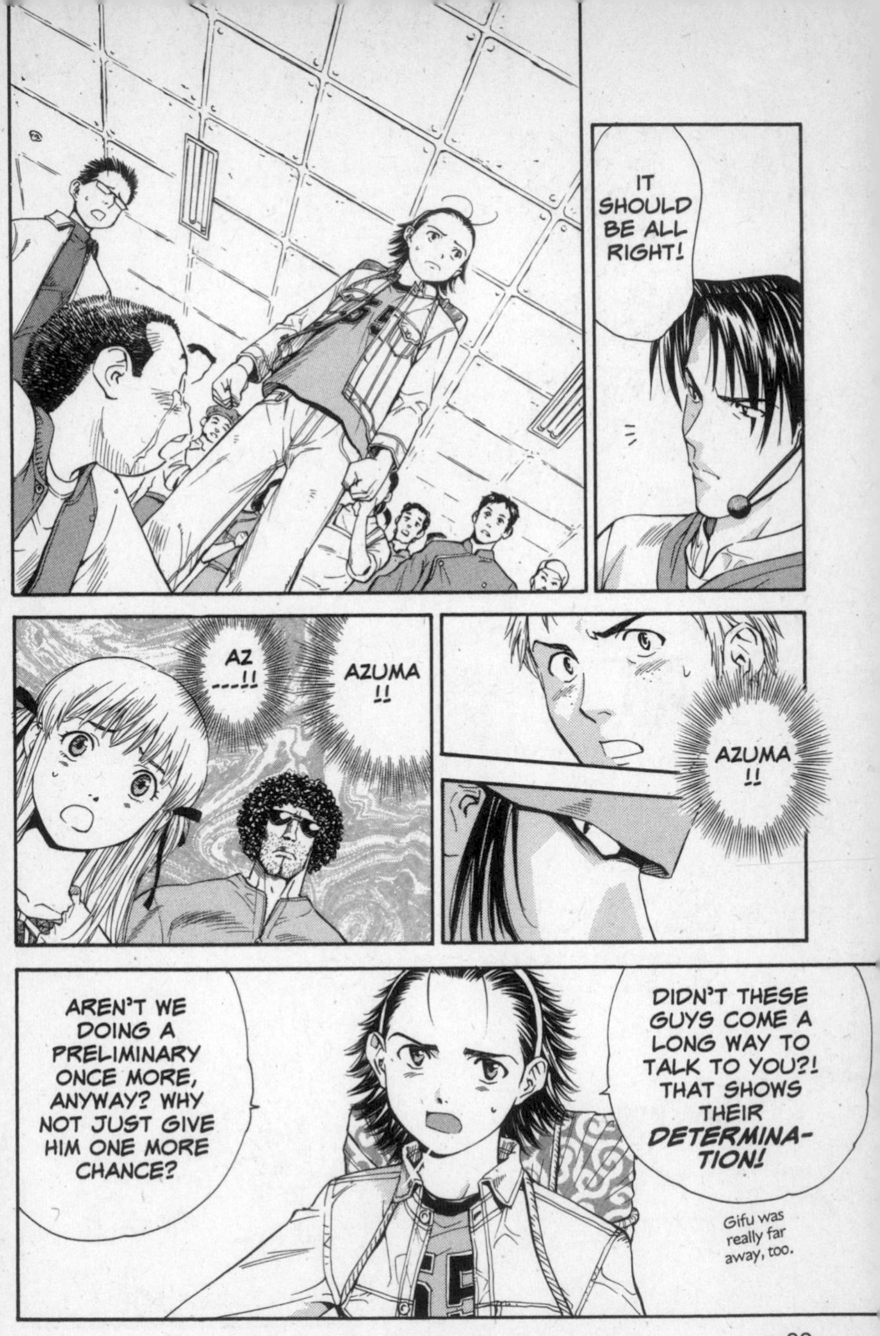
IT SHOULD BE ALL RIGHT!
AZUMA!!
AZUMA!!
AZ---!!
DIDN'T THESE GUYS COME A LONG WAY TO TALK TO YOU?! THAT SHOWS THEIR DETERMINATION!
Gifu was really far away, too.
AREN'T WE DOING A PRELIMINARY ONCE MORE, ANYWAY? WHY NOT JUST GIVE HIM ONE MORE CHANCE?

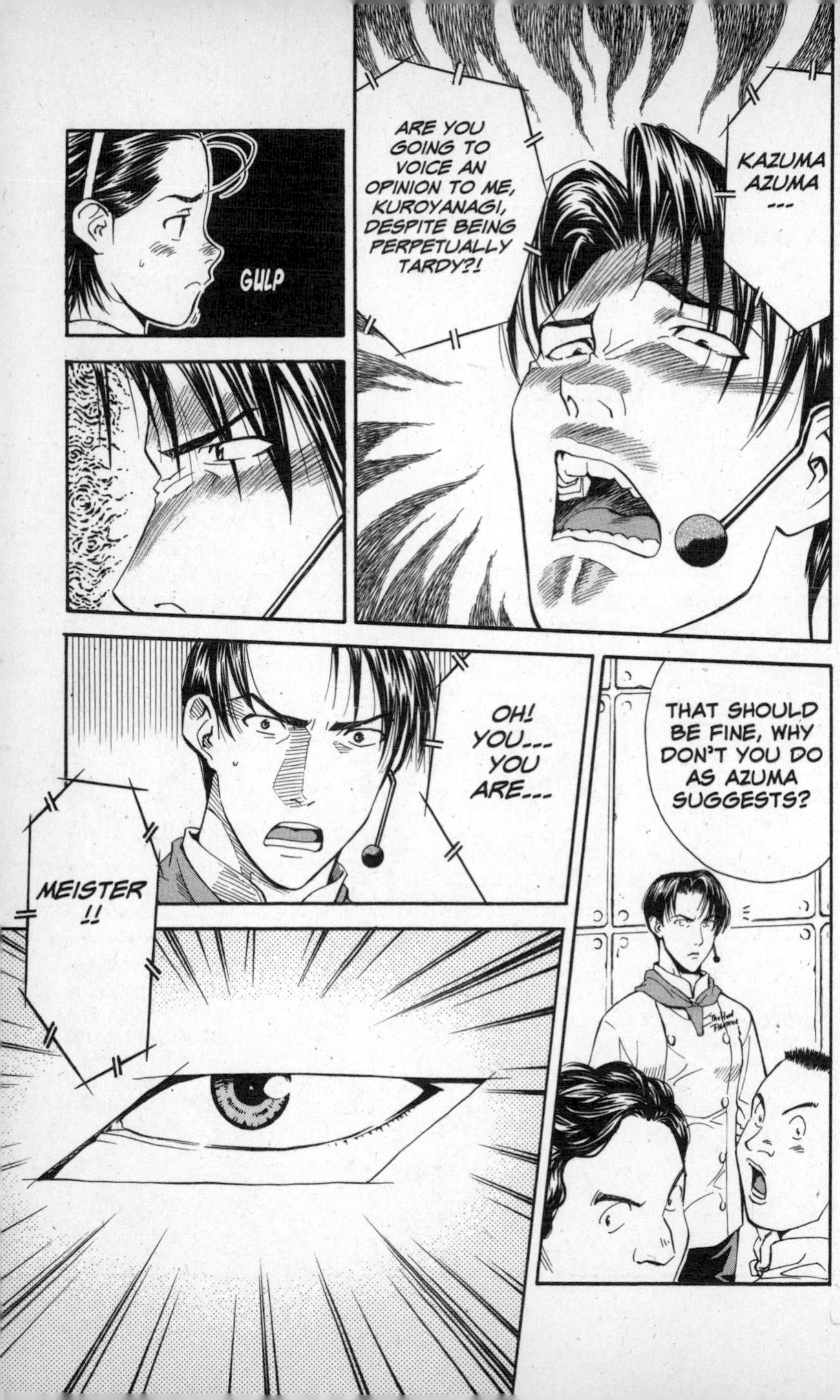
KAZUMA AZUMA ---
ARE YOU GOING TO VOICE AN OPINION TO ME, KUROYANAGI, DESPITE BEING PERPETUALLY TARDY?!
GULP
THAT SHOULD BE FINE, WHY DON'T YOU DO AS AZUMA SUGGESTS?
OH! YOU... YOU ARE...
MEISTER !!

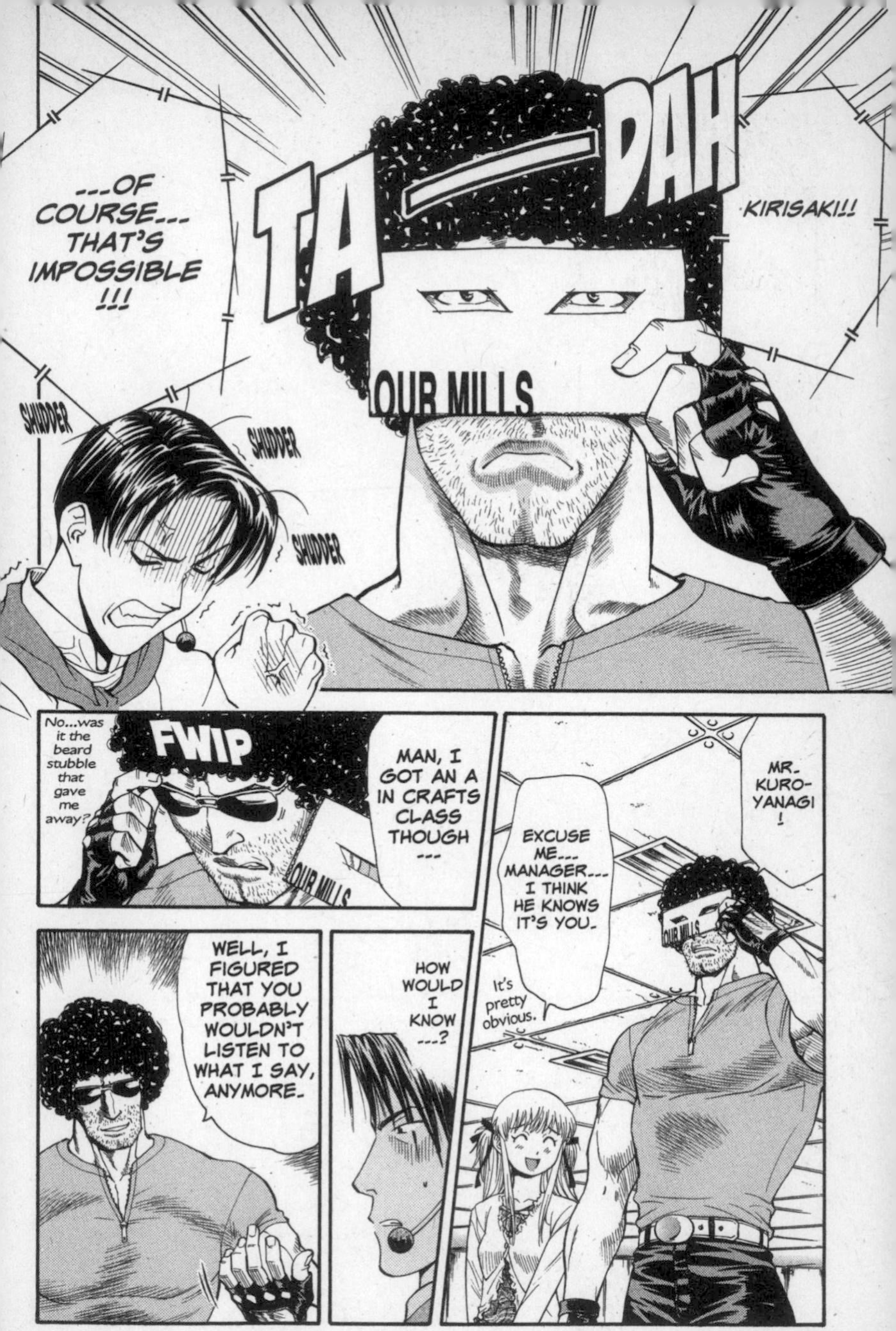
KIRISAKI!!
TA—DAH
---OF COURSE--- THAT'S IMPOSSIBLE !!!
OUR MILLS
SHUDDER
SHUDDER
SHUDDER
MR. KURO-YANAGI!
EXCUSE ME--- MANAGER--- I THINK HE KNOWS IT'S YOU.
It's pretty obvious.
OUR MILLS
MAN, I GOT AN A IN CRAFTS CLASS THOUGH ---
FWIP
No...was it the beard stubble that gave me away?
OUR MILLS
HOW WOULD I KNOW ---?
WELL, I FIGURED THAT YOU PROBABLY WOULDN'T LISTEN TO WHAT I SAY, ANYMORE.

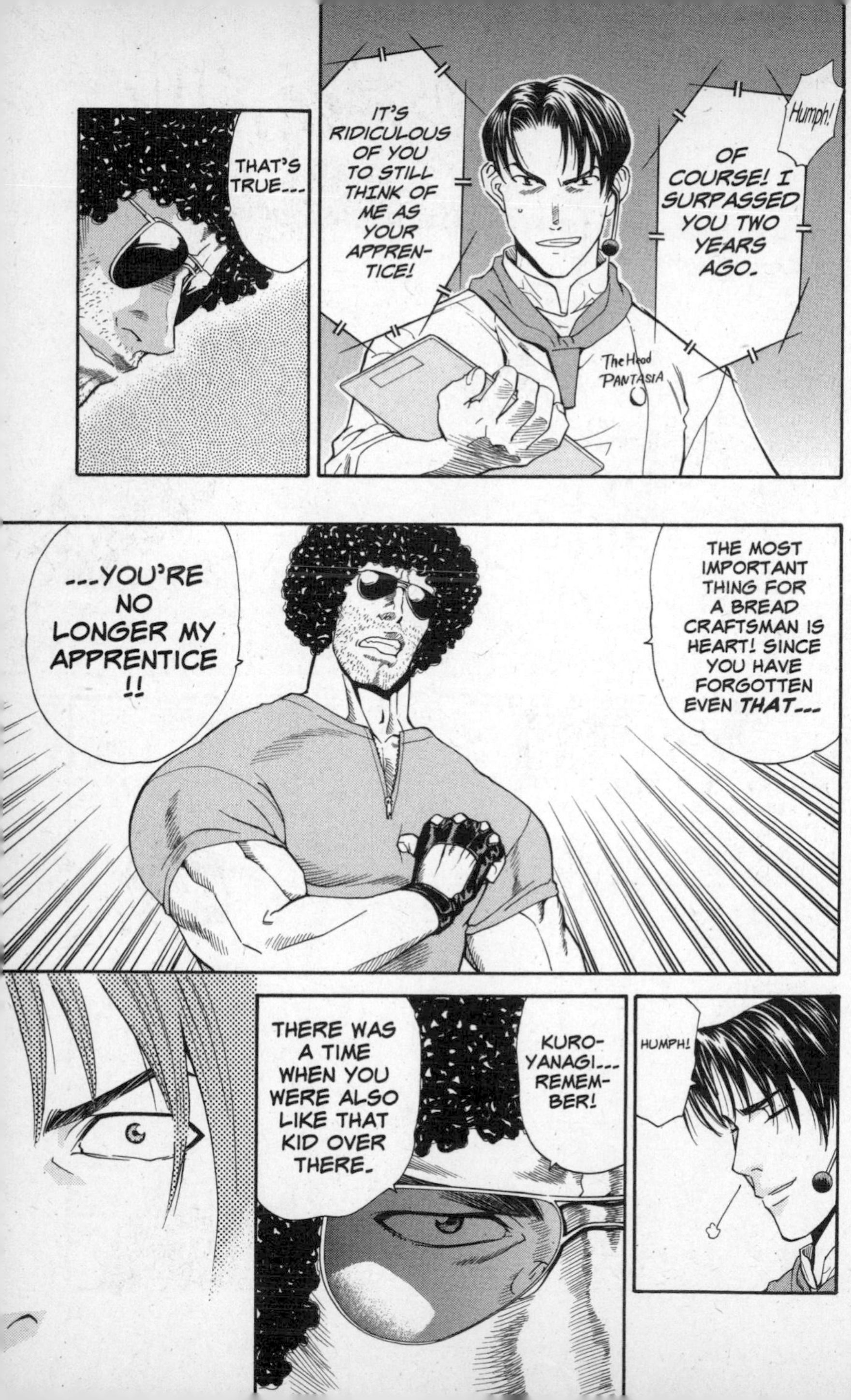
Humph!
OF COURSE! I SURPASSED YOU TWO YEARS AGO.
IT'S RIDICULOUS OF YOU TO STILL THINK OF ME AS YOUR APPRENTICE!
The Head PANTASIA
THAT'S TRUE...
THE MOST IMPORTANT THING FOR A BREAD CRAFTSMAN IS HEART! SINCE YOU HAVE FORGOTTEN EVEN THAT...
...YOU'RE NO LONGER MY APPRENTICE !!
HUMPH!
KURO-YANAGI... REMEMBER!
THERE WAS A TIME WHEN YOU WERE ALSO LIKE THAT KID OVER THERE.

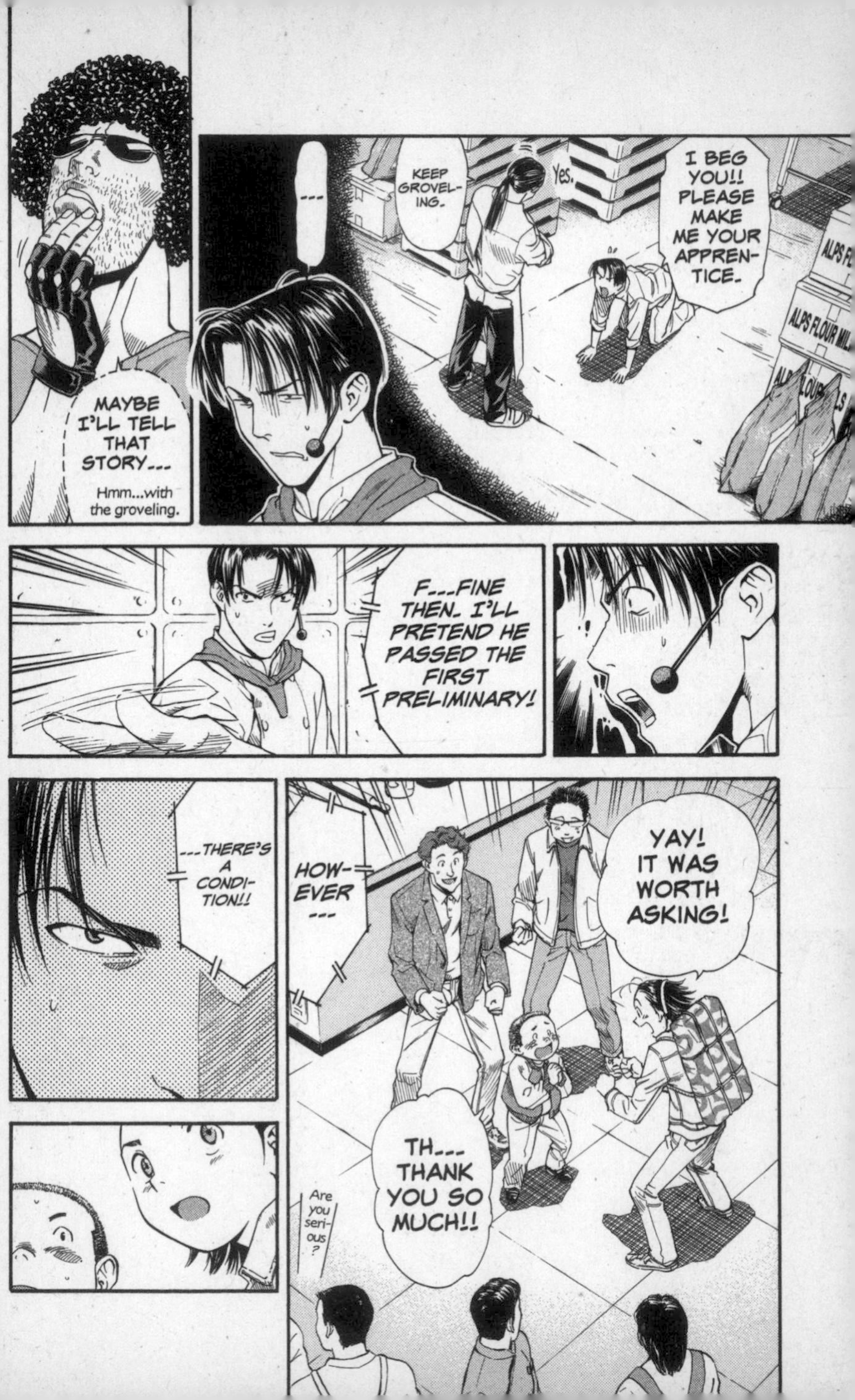
I BEG YOU!! PLEASE MAKE ME YOUR APPRENTICE.
Yes.
KEEP GROVELING.
...
MAYBE I'LL TELL THAT STORY...
Hmm...with the groveling.
F...FINE THEN. I'LL PRETEND HE PASSED THE FIRST PRELIMINARY!
YAY! IT WAS WORTH ASKING!
HOWEVER...
TH... THANK YOU SO MUCH!!
Are you serious?
...THERE'S A CONDITION!!

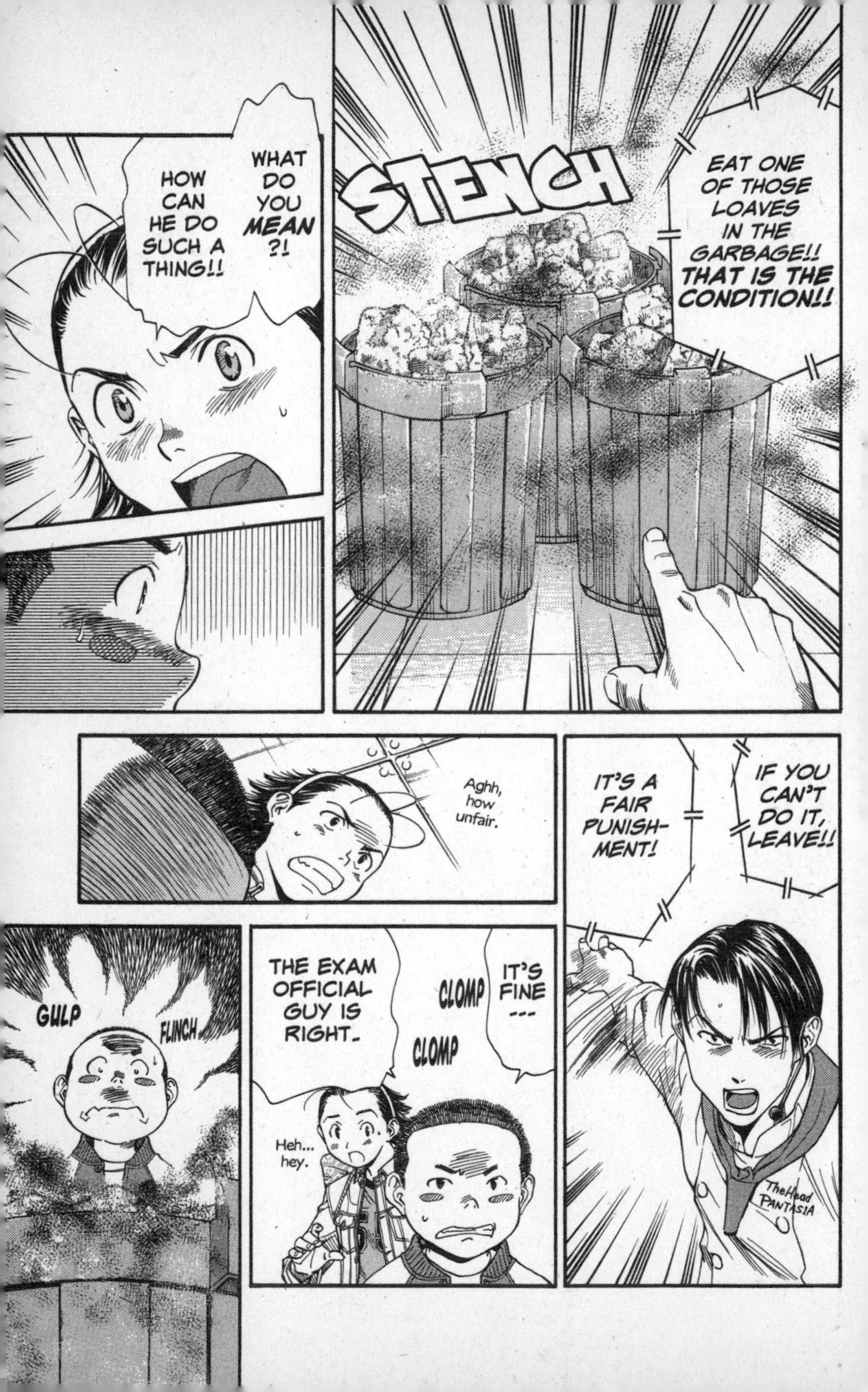
STENCH
EAT ONE OF THOSE LOAVES IN THE GARBAGE!! THAT IS THE CONDITION!!
WHAT DO YOU MEAN ?!
HOW CAN HE DO SUCH A THING!!
IF YOU CAN'T DO IT, LEAVE!!
IT'S A FAIR PUNISH-MENT!
The Head PANTASIA
Aghh, how unfair.
IT'S FINE ---
CLOMP
THE EXAM OFFICIAL GUY IS RIGHT.
CLOMP
Heh... hey.
FLINCH
GULP

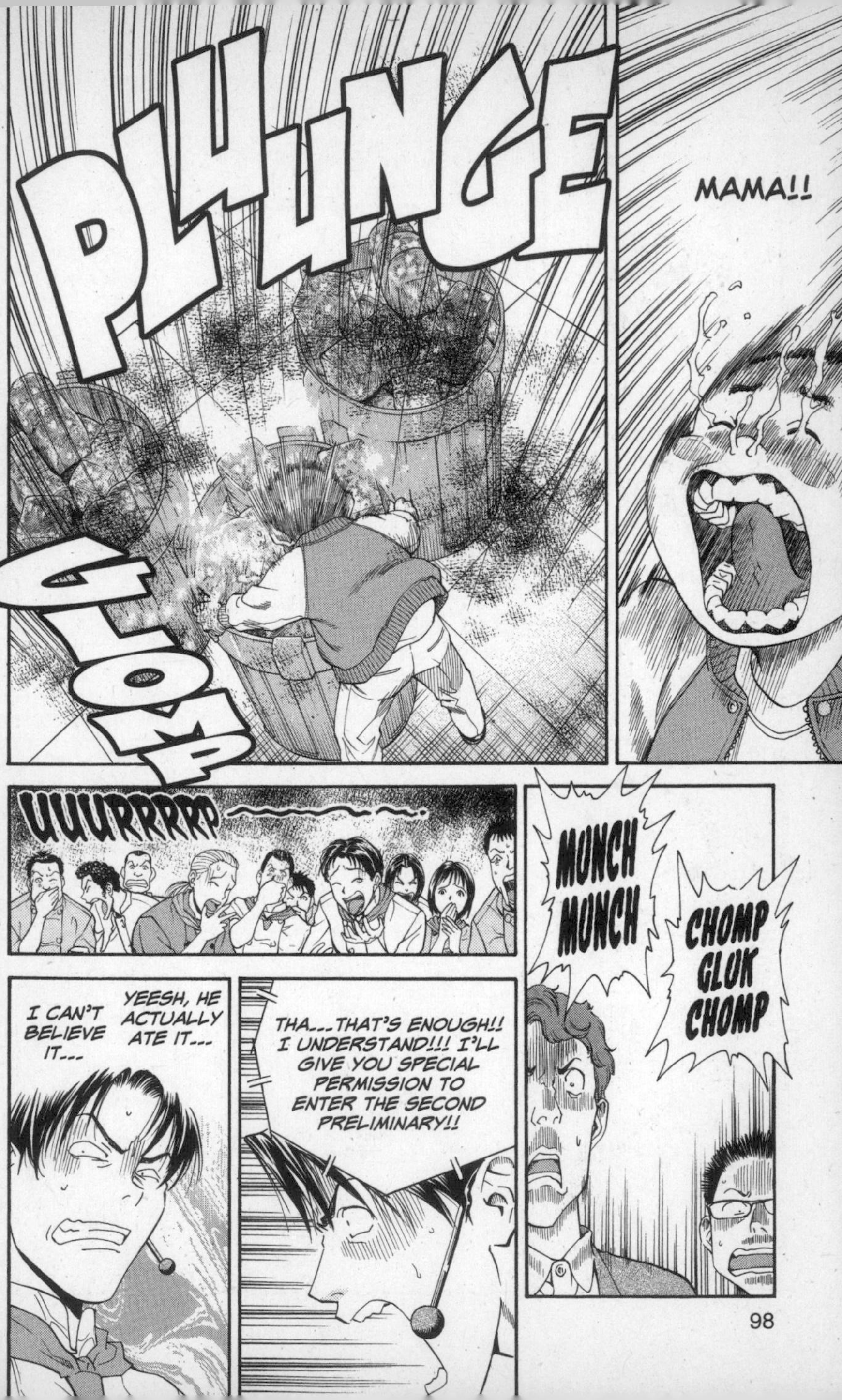
MAMA!!
PLHUNGE
GLOMP
MUNCH MUNCH
CHOMP GLUK CHOMP
UUURRRP
THA...THAT'S ENOUGH!! I UNDERSTAND!!! I'LL GIVE YOU SPECIAL PERMISSION TO ENTER THE SECOND PRELIMINARY!!
YEESH, HE ACTUALLY ATE IT...
I CAN'T BELIEVE IT...

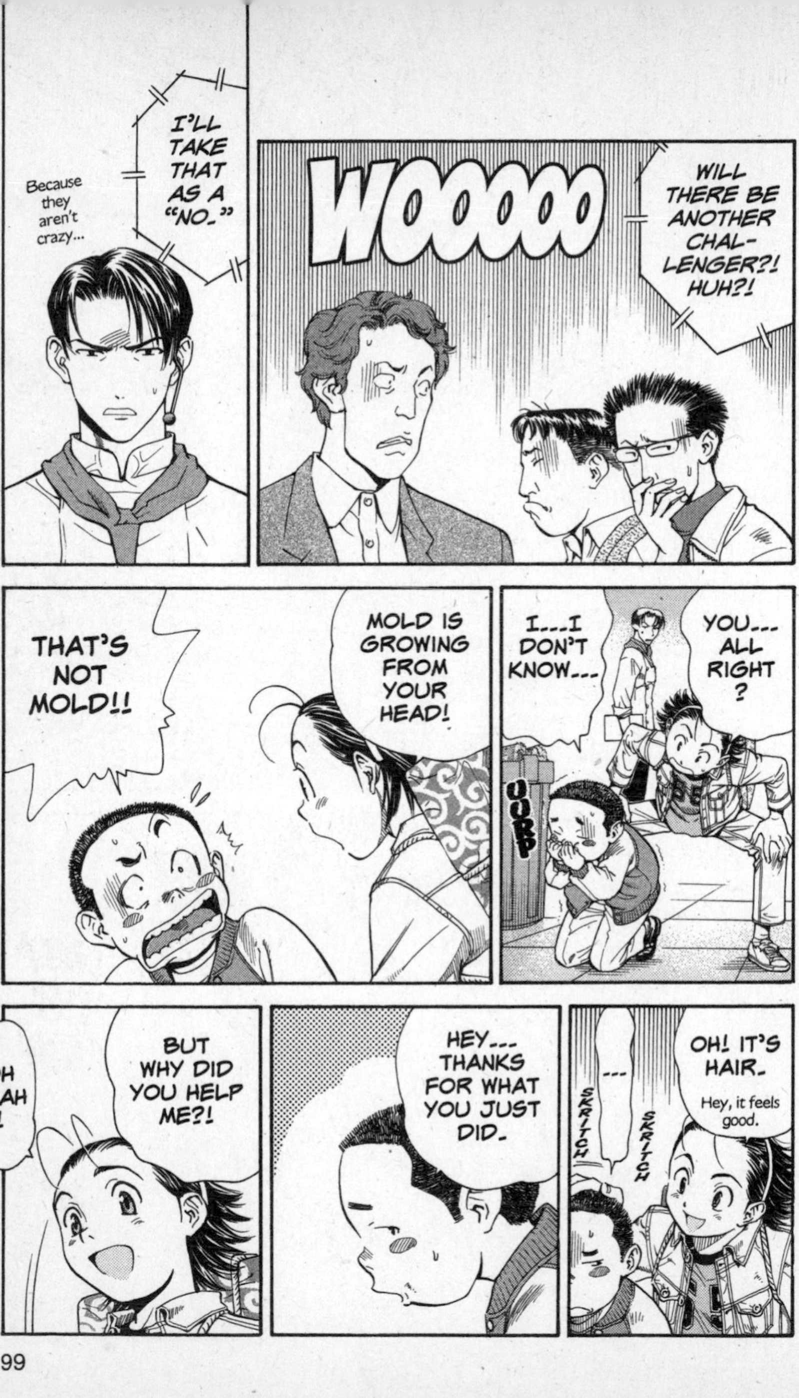
WILL THERE BE ANOTHER CHALLENGER?! HUH?!
WOOOOO
I'LL TAKE THAT AS A "NO."
Because they aren't crazy...
YOU... ALL RIGHT?
I...I DON'T KNOW...
UURP
MOLD IS GROWING FROM YOUR HEAD!
THAT'S NOT MOLD!!
OH! IT'S HAIR.
Hey, it feels good.
...
SKRITCH
SKRITCH
HEY... THANKS FOR WHAT YOU JUST DID.
BUT WHY DID YOU HELP ME?!
OH YEAH!

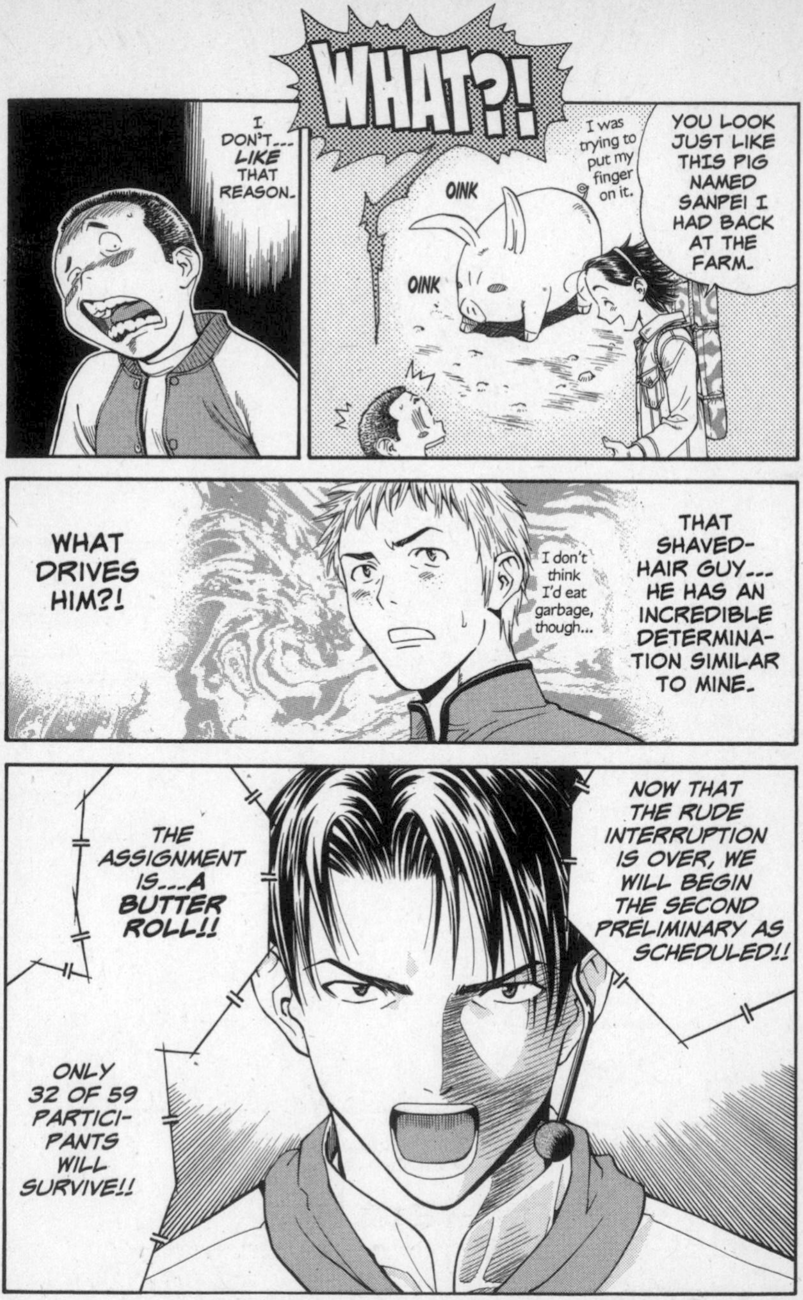
YOU LOOK JUST LIKE THIS PIG NAMED SANPEI I HAD BACK AT THE FARM.
I was trying to put my finger on it.
OINK
OINK
WHAT?!
I DON'T... LIKE THAT REASON.
THAT SHAVED-HAIR GUY... HE HAS AN INCREDIBLE DETERMINATION SIMILAR TO MINE.
I don't think I'd eat garbage, though...
WHAT DRIVES HIM?!
NOW THAT THE RUDE INTERRUPTION IS OVER, WE WILL BEGIN THE SECOND PRELIMINARY AS SCHEDULED!!
THE ASSIGNMENT IS...A BUTTER ROLL!!
ONLY 32 OF 59 PARTICIPANTS WILL SURVIVE!!

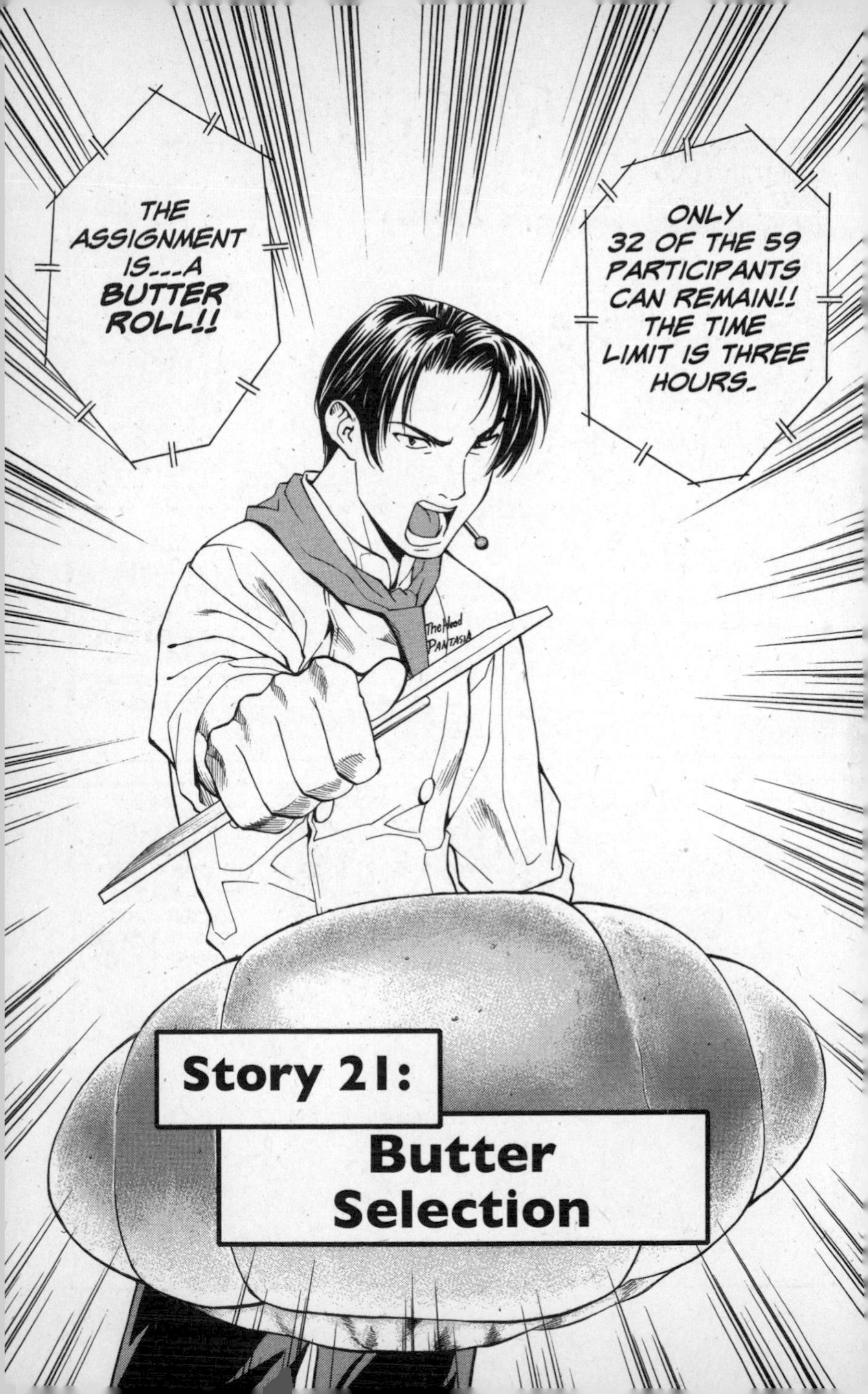
ONLY 32 OF THE 59 PARTICIPANTS CAN REMAIN!! THE TIME LIMIT IS THREE HOURS.
THE ASSIGNMENT IS...A BUTTER ROLL!!
The Head PANTASIA
Story 21:
Butter Selection

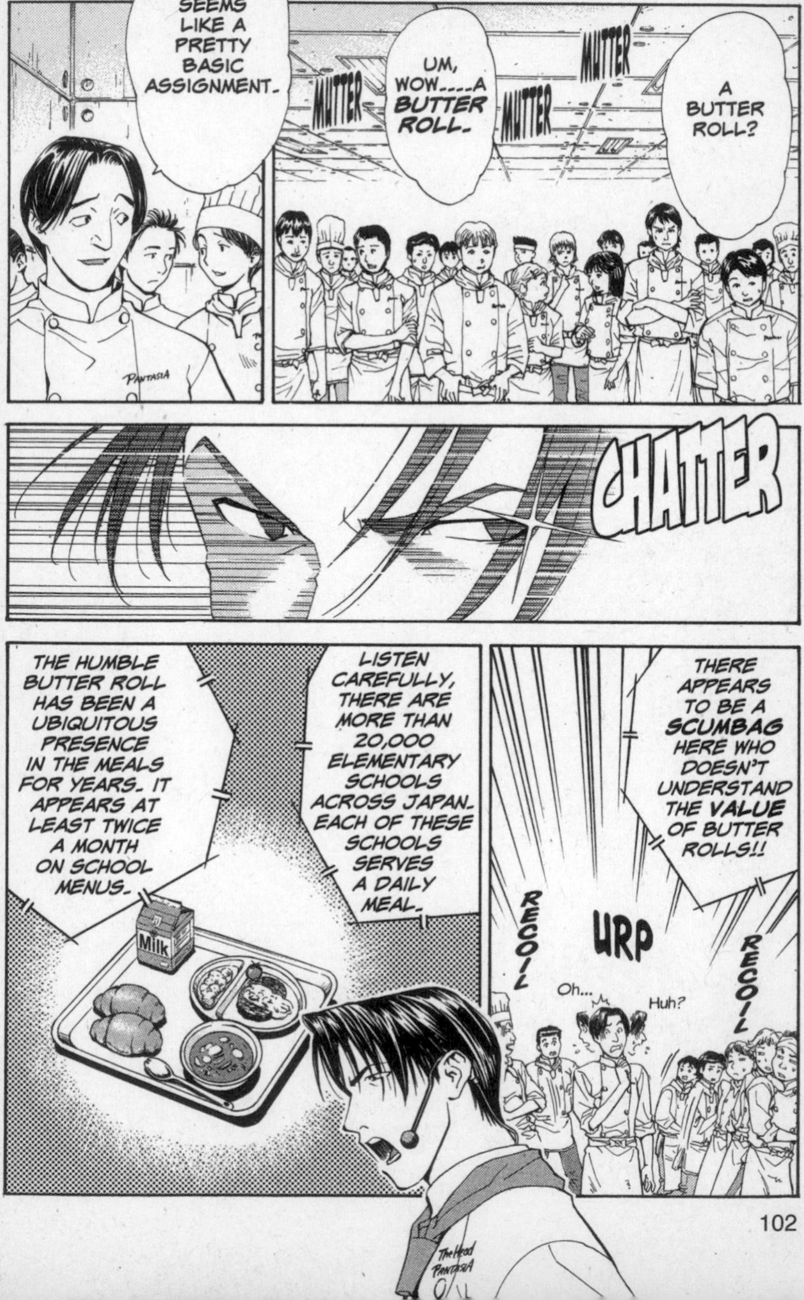
A BUTTER ROLL?
MUTTER
MUTTER
MUTTER
UM, WOW.... A BUTTER ROLL.
SEEMS LIKE A PRETTY BASIC ASSIGNMENT.
PANTASIA
CHATTER
THERE APPEARS TO BE A SCUMBAG HERE WHO DOESN'T UNDERSTAND THE VALUE OF BUTTER ROLLS!!
RECOIL
URP
RECOIL
Oh...
Huh?
LISTEN CAREFULLY, THERE ARE MORE THAN 20,000 ELEMENTARY SCHOOLS ACROSS JAPAN. EACH OF THESE SCHOOLS SERVES A DAILY MEAL.
THE HUMBLE BUTTER ROLL HAS BEEN A UBIQUITOUS PRESENCE IN THE MEALS FOR YEARS. IT APPEARS AT LEAST TWICE A MONTH ON SCHOOL MENUS.
Milk
The Head
PANTASIA

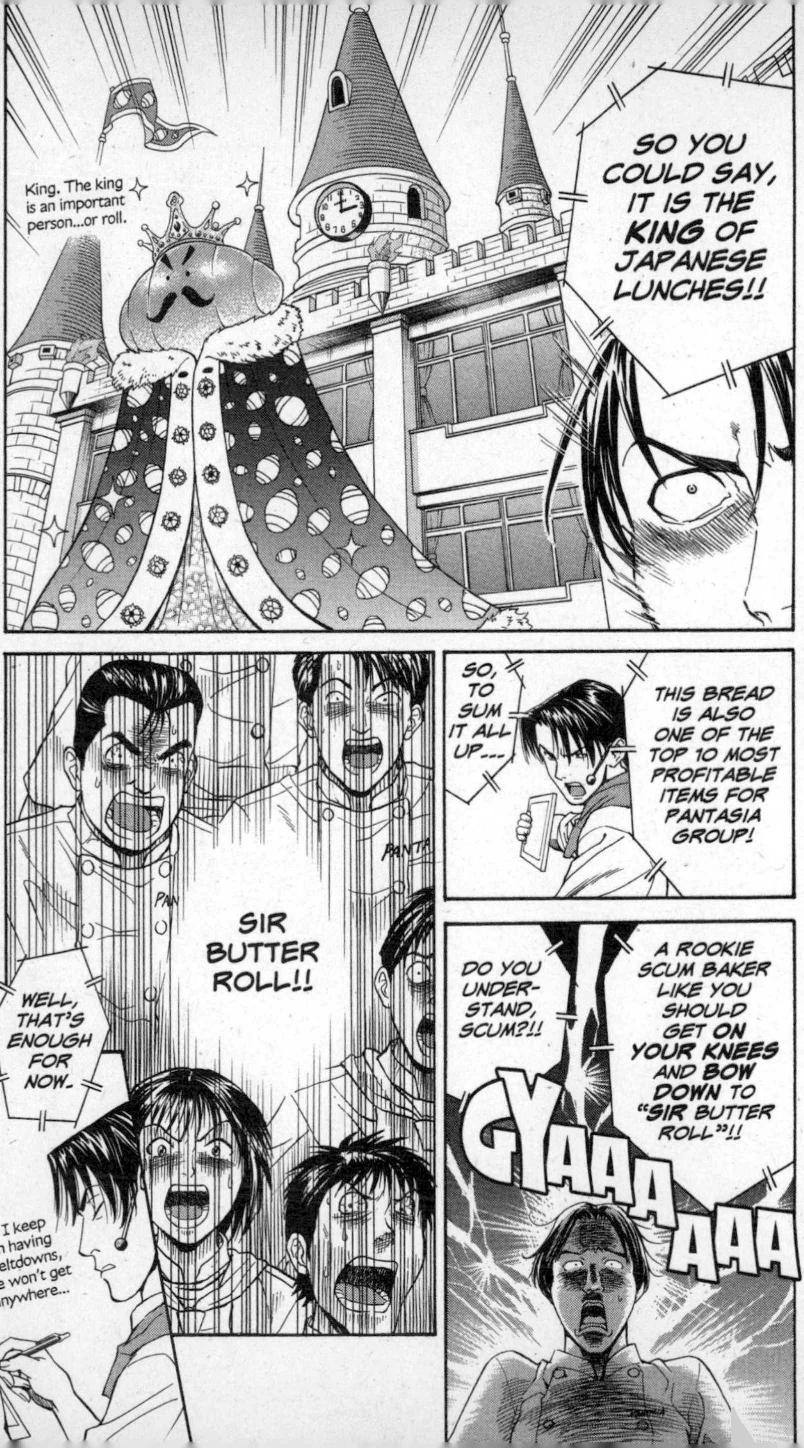
SO YOU COULD SAY, IT IS THE **KING** OF JAPANESE LUNCHES!!
King. The king is an important person...or roll.
SO, TO SUM IT ALL UP...
THIS BREAD IS ALSO ONE OF THE TOP 10 MOST PROFITABLE ITEMS FOR PANTASIA GROUP!
A ROOKIE SCUM BAKER LIKE YOU SHOULD GET **ON YOUR KNEES** AND **BOW DOWN** TO "SIR BUTTER ROLL"!!
DO YOU UNDERSTAND, SCUM?!!
GYAAAAAA
SIR BUTTER ROLL!!
PANTA
PAN
WELL, THAT'S ENOUGH FOR NOW.
If I keep on having meltdowns, we won't get anywhere...

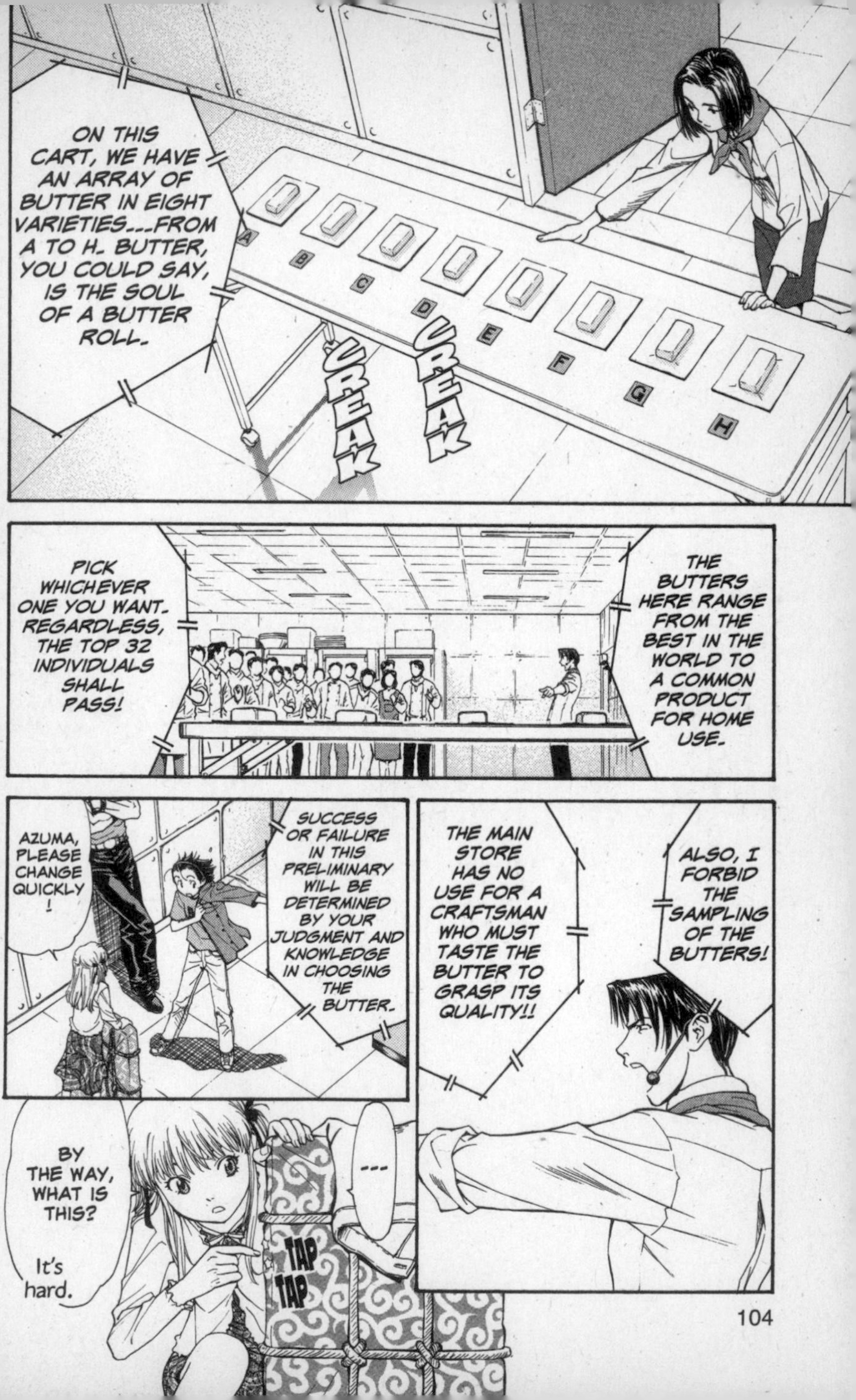
ON THIS CART, WE HAVE AN ARRAY OF EIGHT BUTTER IN EIGHT VARIETIES...FROM A TO H. BUTTER, YOU COULD SAY, IS THE SOUL OF A BUTTER ROLL.
A
B
C
D
E
F
G
H
CREAK
CREAK
THE BUTTERS HERE RANGE FROM THE BEST IN THE WORLD TO A COMMON PRODUCT FOR HOME USE.
PICK WHICHEVER ONE YOU WANT. REGARDLESS, THE TOP 32 INDIVIDUALS SHALL PASS!
ALSO, I FORBID THE SAMPLING OF THE BUTTERS!
THE MAIN STORE HAS NO USE FOR A CRAFTSMAN WHO MUST TASTE THE BUTTER TO GRASP ITS QUALITY!!
SUCCESS OR FAILURE IN THIS PRELIMINARY WILL BE DETERMINED BY YOUR JUDGMENT AND KNOWLEDGE IN CHOOSING THE BUTTER.
AZUMA, PLEASE CHANGE QUICKLY!
...
BY THE WAY, WHAT IS THIS?
It's hard.
TAP TAP

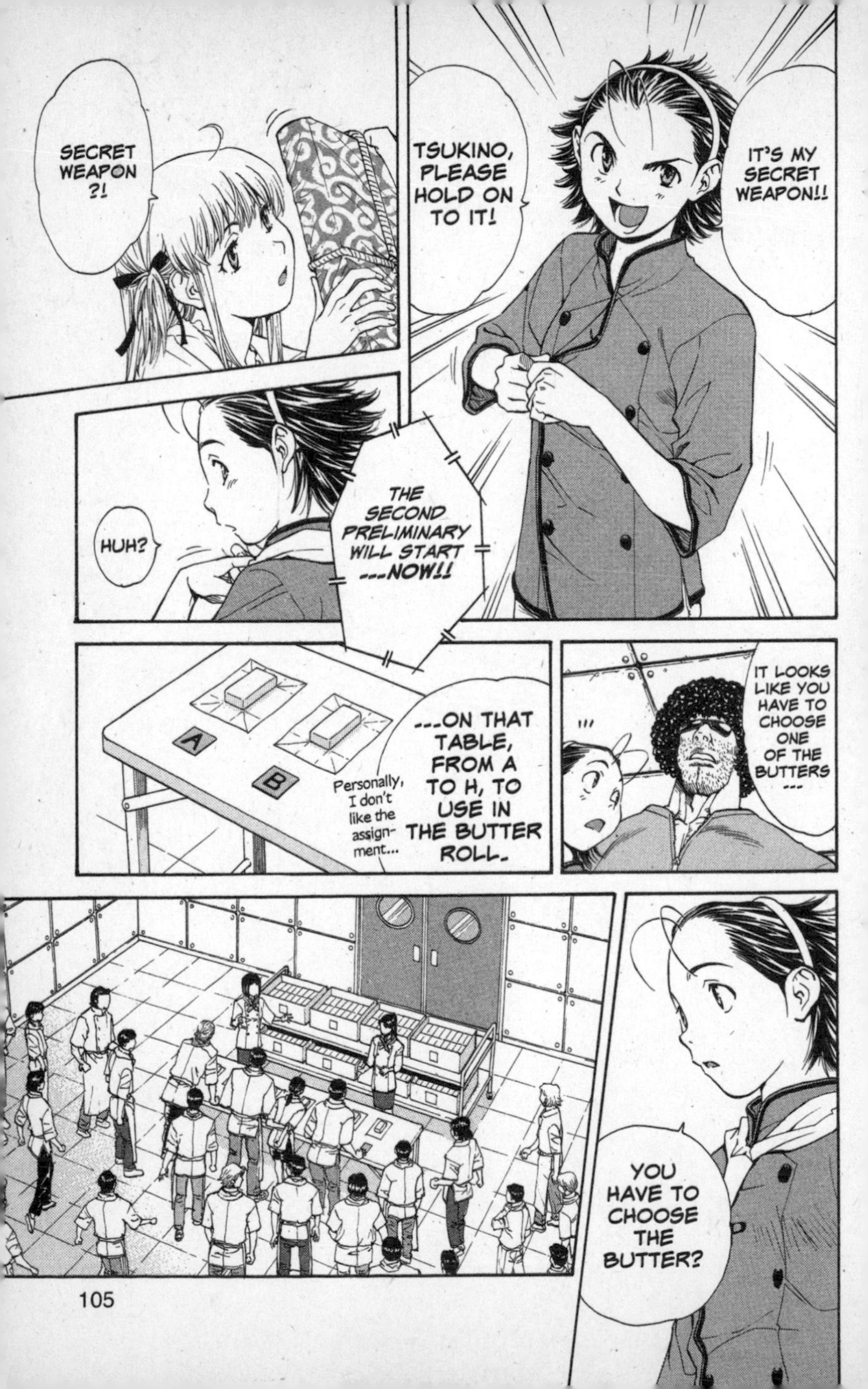
IT'S MY SECRET WEAPON!!
TSUKINO, PLEASE HOLD ON TO IT!
SECRET WEAPON ?!
HUH?
THE SECOND PRELIMINARY WILL START ---NOW!!
IT LOOKS LIKE YOU HAVE TO CHOOSE ONE OF THE BUTTERS ---
---ON THAT TABLE, FROM A TO H, TO USE IN THE BUTTER ROLL.
Personally, I don't like the assignment...
A
B
YOU HAVE TO CHOOSE THE BUTTER?

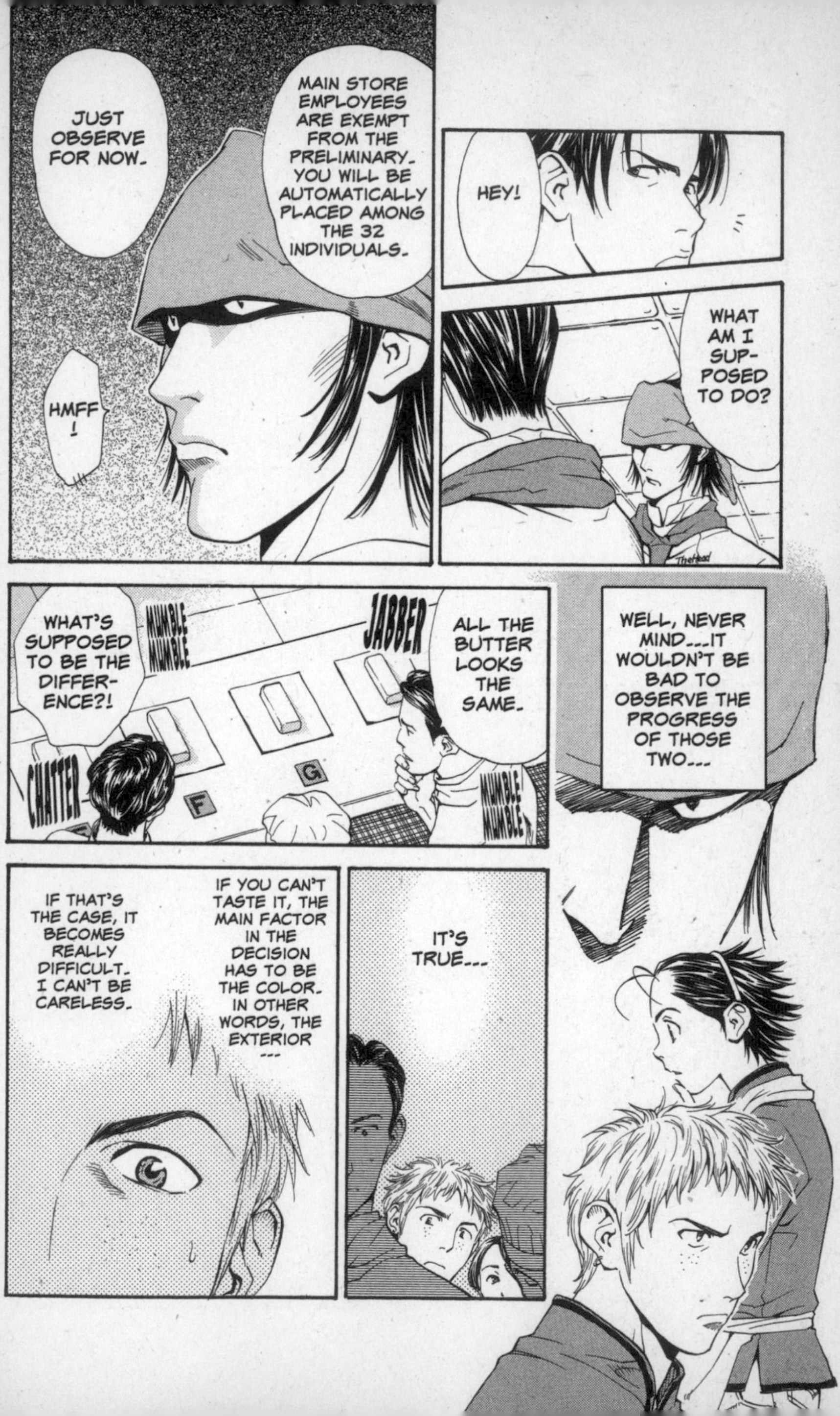
HEY!
WHAT AM I SUP-POSED TO DO?
MAIN STORE EMPLOYEES ARE EXEMPT FROM THE PRELIMINARY. YOU WILL BE AUTOMATICALLY PLACED AMONG THE 32 INDIVIDUALS.
JUST OBSERVE FOR NOW.
HMFF!
WELL, NEVER MIND...IT WOULDN'T BE BAD TO OBSERVE THE PROGRESS OF THOSE TWO...
JABBER
ALL THE BUTTER LOOKS THE SAME.
MUMBLE MUMBLE
WHAT'S SUPPOSED TO BE THE DIFFER-ENCE?!
MUMBLE MUMBLE
G
F
CHATTER
IT'S TRUE...
IF YOU CAN'T TASTE IT, THE MAIN FACTOR IN THE DECISION HAS TO BE THE COLOR. IN OTHER WORDS, THE EXTERIOR ...
IF THAT'S THE CASE, IT BECOMES REALLY DIFFICULT. I CAN'T BE CARELESS.

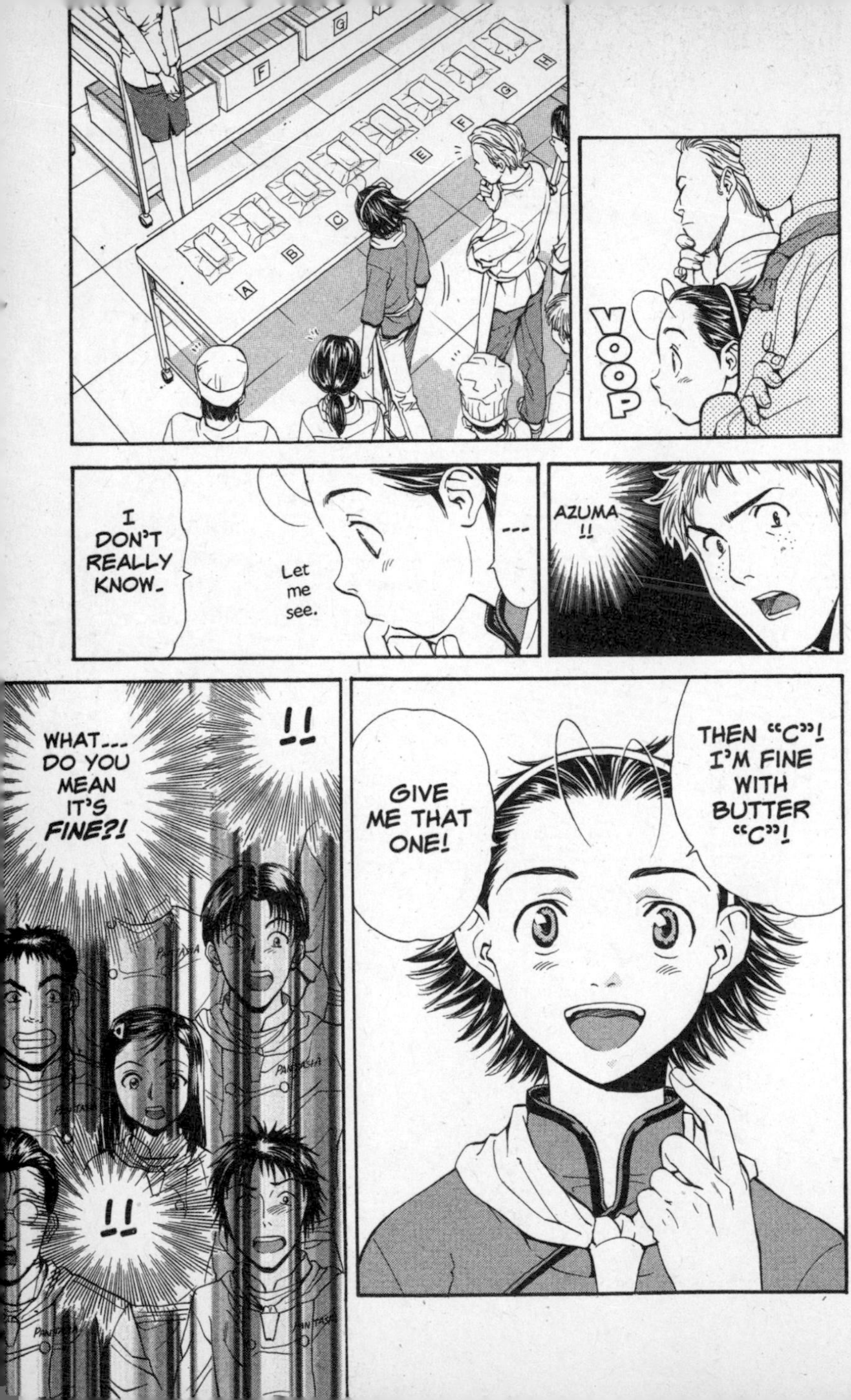
VOOP
AZUMA!!
...
Let me see.
I DON'T REALLY KNOW...
THEN "C"! I'M FINE WITH BUTTER "C"!
GIVE ME THAT ONE!
!!
WHAT... DO YOU MEAN IT'S FINE?!
!!

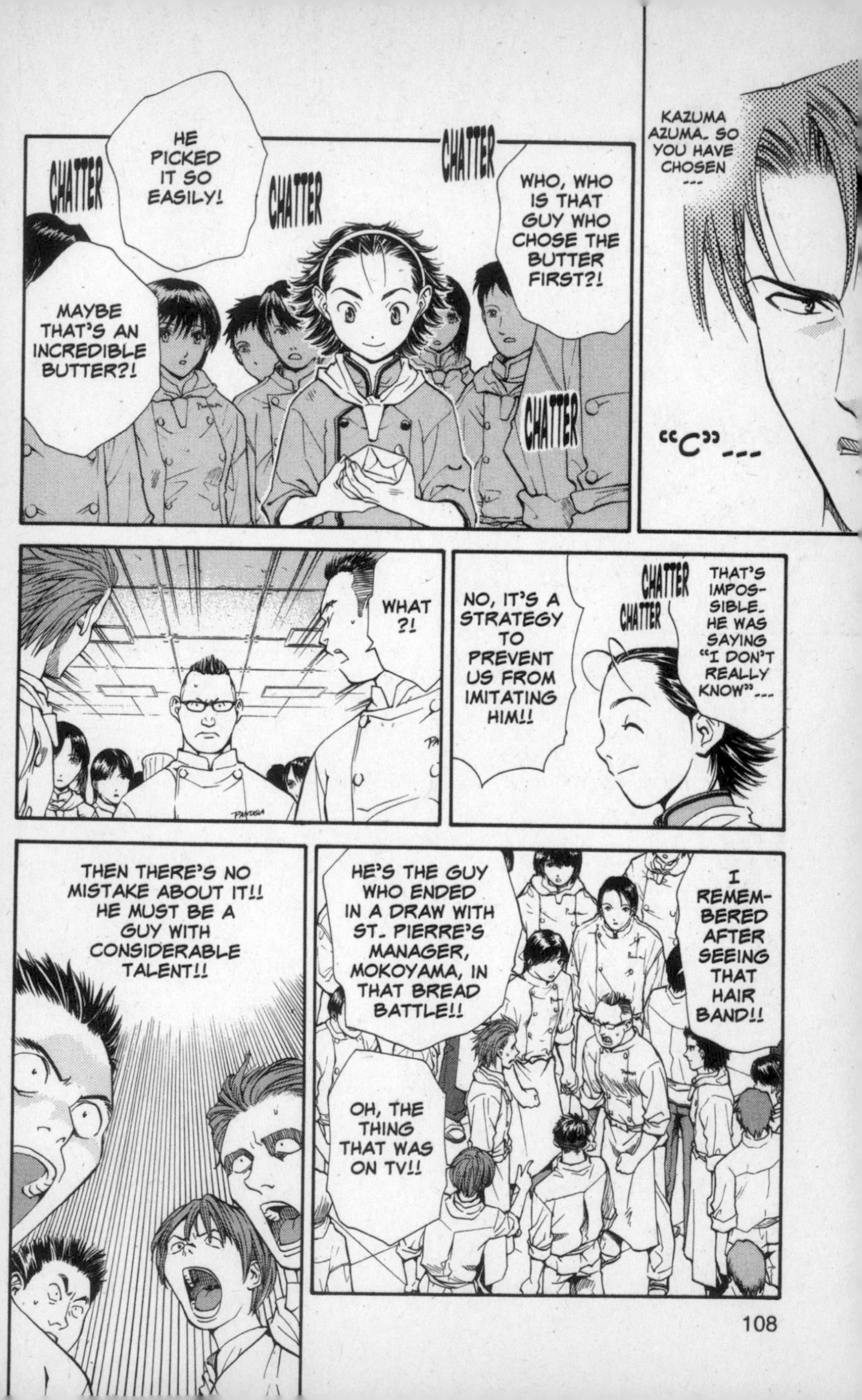
KAZUMA AZUMA. SO YOU HAVE CHOSEN ---
"C"---
CHATTER
WHO, WHO IS THAT GUY WHO CHOSE THE BUTTER FIRST?!
CHATTER
HE PICKED IT SO EASILY!
CHATTER
CHATTER
MAYBE THAT'S AN INCREDIBLE BUTTER?!
THAT'S IMPOSSIBLE. HE WAS SAYING "I DON'T REALLY KNOW"---
CHATTER
CHATTER
NO, IT'S A STRATEGY TO PREVENT US FROM IMITATING HIM!!
WHAT?!
I REMEMBERED AFTER SEEING THAT HAIR BAND!!
HE'S THE GUY WHO ENDED IN A DRAW WITH ST. PIERRE'S MANAGER, MOKOYAMA, IN THAT BREAD BATTLE!!
OH, THE THING THAT WAS ON TV!!
THEN THERE'S NO MISTAKE ABOUT IT!! HE MUST BE A GUY WITH CONSIDERABLE TALENT!!

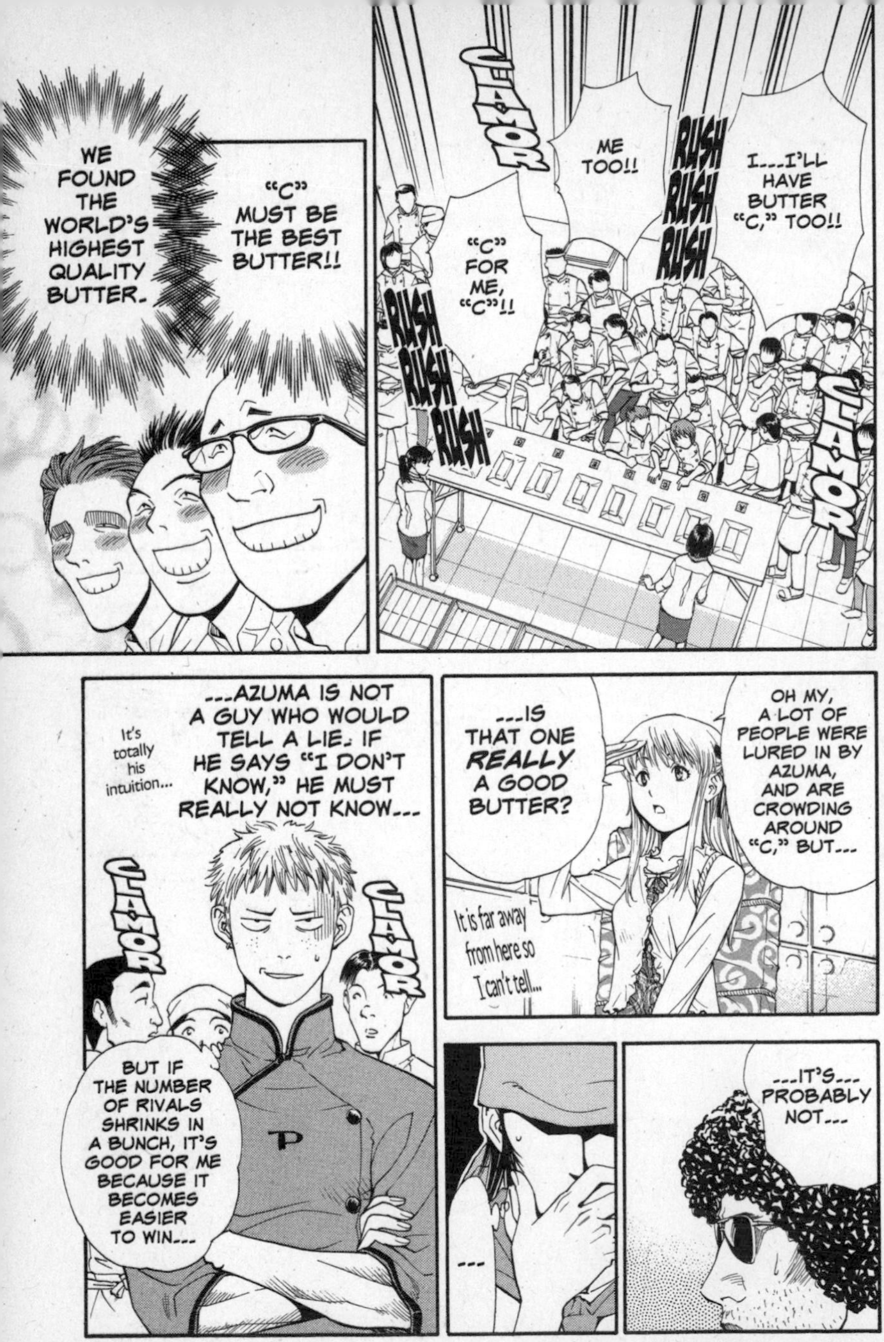
I...I'LL HAVE BUTTER "C," TOO!!
RUSH RUSH RUSH
ME TOO!!
CLAMOR
CLAMOR
"C" FOR ME, "C"!!
RUSH RUSH RUSH
"C" MUST BE THE BEST BUTTER!!
WE FOUND THE WORLD'S HIGHEST QUALITY BUTTER.
OH MY, A LOT OF PEOPLE WERE LURED IN BY AZUMA, AND ARE CROWDING AROUND "C," BUT...
...IS THAT ONE *REALLY* A GOOD BUTTER?
It is far away from here so I can't tell...
...IT'S... PROBABLY NOT...
...
...AZUMA IS NOT A GUY WHO WOULD TELL A LIE. IF HE SAYS "I DON'T KNOW," HE MUST REALLY NOT KNOW...
It's totally his intuition...
CLAMOR
CLAMOR
BUT IF THE NUMBER OF RIVALS SHRINKS IN A BUNCH, IT'S GOOD FOR ME BECAUSE IT BECOMES EASIER TO WIN...

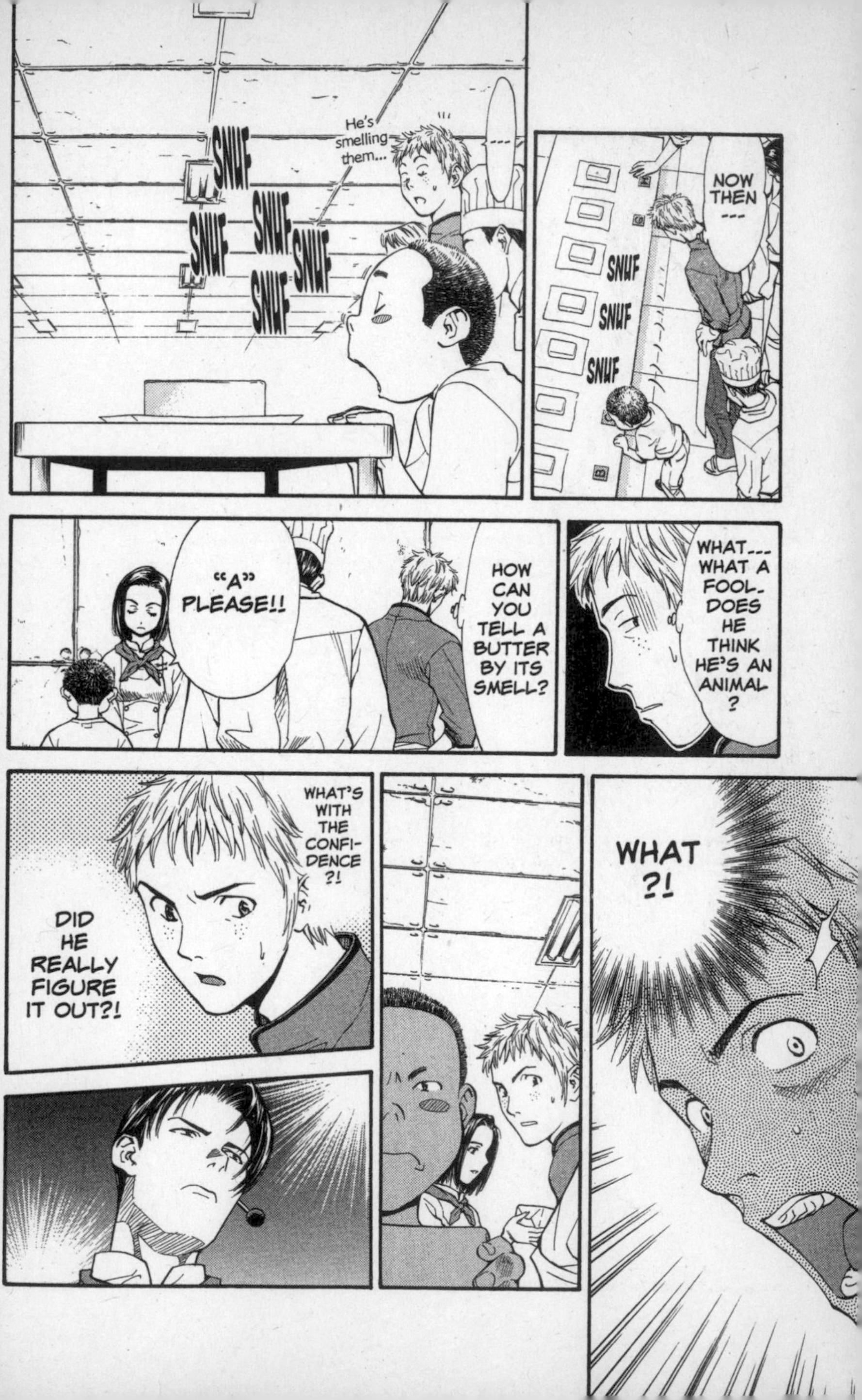
NOW THEN ---
SNUF
SNUF
SNUF

He's smelling them...
SNUF
SNUF
SNUF
SNUF
SNUF
WHAT... WHAT A FOOL. DOES HE THINK HE'S AN ANIMAL?
HOW CAN YOU TELL A BUTTER BY ITS SMELL?
"A" PLEASE!!
WHAT?!
WHAT'S WITH THE CONFIDENCE?!
DID HE REALLY FIGURE IT OUT?!

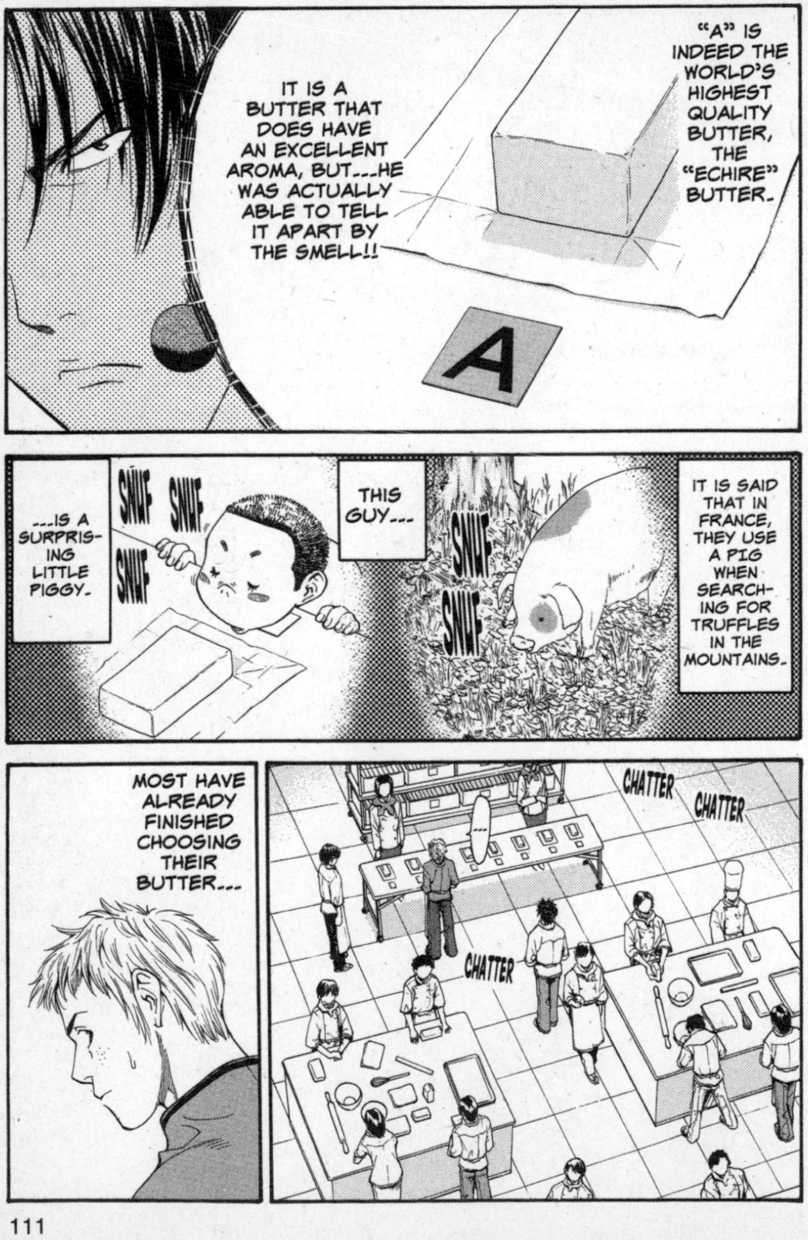
"A" IS INDEED THE WORLD'S HIGHEST QUALITY BUTTER, THE "ECHIRE" BUTTER.
IT IS A BUTTER THAT DOES HAVE AN EXCELLENT AROMA, BUT...HE WAS ACTUALLY ABLE TO TELL IT APART BY THE SMELL!!
A
IT IS SAID THAT IN FRANCE, THEY USE A PIG WHEN SEARCHING FOR TRUFFLES IN THE MOUNTAINS.
SNUF SNUF
THIS GUY...
SNUF SNUF SNUF
...IS A SURPRISING LITTLE PIGGY.
CHATTER CHATTER
...
CHATTER
MOST HAVE ALREADY FINISHED CHOOSING THEIR BUTTER...

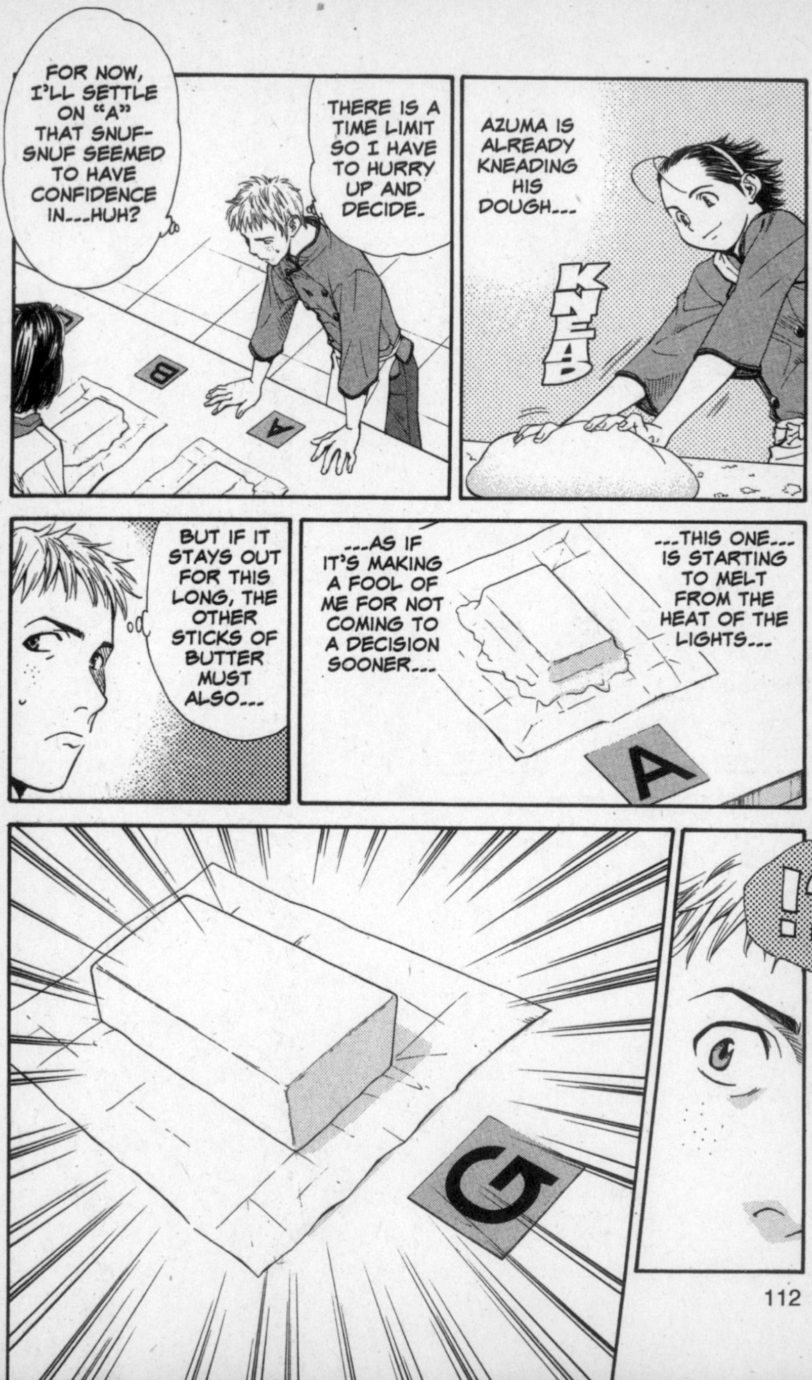

AZUMA IS ALREADY KNEADING HIS DOUGH...
KNEAD
THERE IS A TIME LIMIT SO I HAVE TO HURRY UP AND DECIDE.
FOR NOW, I'LL SETTLE ON "A" THAT SNUF-SNUF SEEMED TO HAVE CONFIDENCE IN...HUH?
...THIS ONE... IS STARTING TO MELT FROM THE HEAT OF THE LIGHTS...
...AS IF IT'S MAKING A FOOL OF ME FOR NOT COMING TO A DECISION SOONER...
BUT IF IT STAYS OUT FOR THIS LONG, THE OTHER STICKS OF BUTTER MUST ALSO...
!?

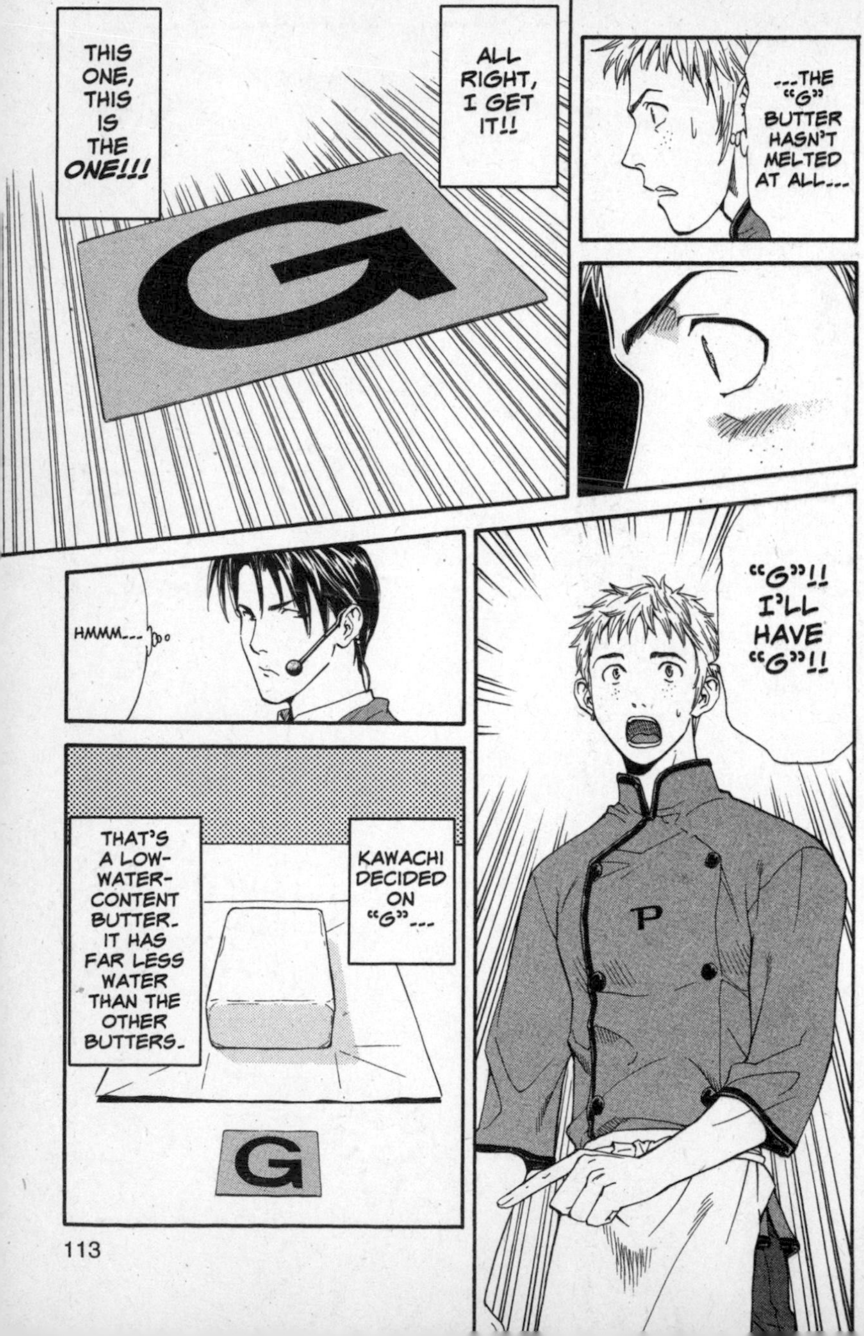
...THE "G" BUTTER HASN'T MELTED AT ALL...
ALL RIGHT, I GET IT!!
THIS ONE, THIS IS THE ONE!!!
"G"!! I'LL HAVE "G"!!
HMMM...
KAWACHI DECIDED ON "G"...
THAT'S A LOW-WATER-CONTENT BUTTER. IT HAS FAR LESS WATER THAN THE OTHER BUTTERS.

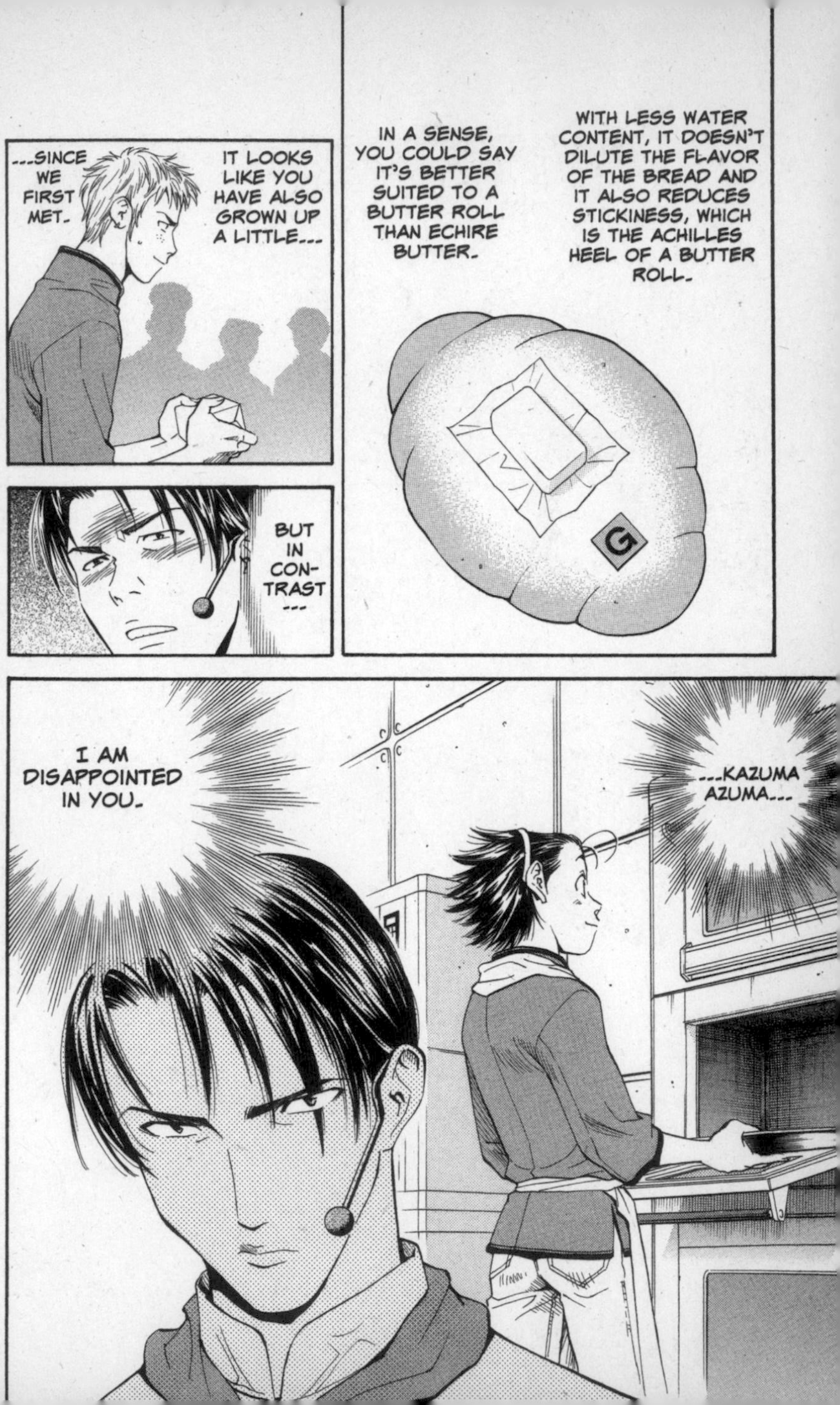
WITH LESS WATER CONTENT, IT DOESN'T DILUTE THE FLAVOR OF THE BREAD AND IT ALSO REDUCES STICKINESS, WHICH IS THE ACHILLES HEEL OF A BUTTER ROLL.
IN A SENSE, YOU COULD SAY IT'S BETTER SUITED TO A BUTTER ROLL THAN ECHIRE BUTTER.
G
IT LOOKS LIKE YOU HAVE ALSO GROWN UP A LITTLE...
...SINCE WE FIRST MET.
BUT IN CON-TRAST...
...KAZUMA AZUMA...
I AM DISAPPOINTED IN YOU.

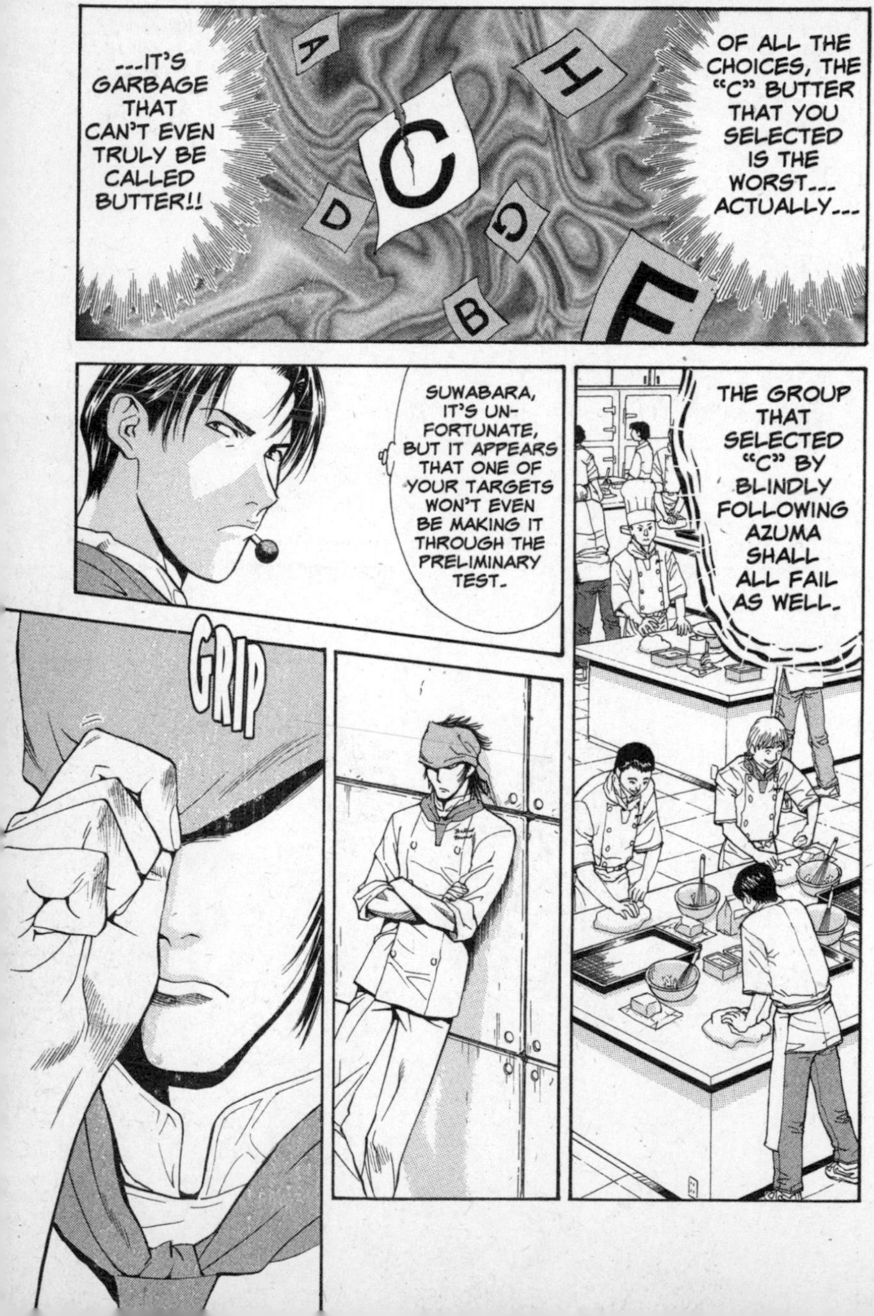
OF ALL THE CHOICES, THE "C" BUTTER THAT YOU SELECTED IS THE WORST... ACTUALLY...
...IT'S GARBAGE THAT CAN'T EVEN TRULY BE CALLED BUTTER!!
A
H
C
D
G
B
F
THE GROUP THAT SELECTED "C" BY BLINDLY FOLLOWING AZUMA SHALL ALL FAIL AS WELL.
SUWABARA, IT'S UN-FORTUNATE, BUT IT APPEARS THAT ONE OF YOUR TARGETS WON'T EVEN BE MAKING IT THROUGH THE PRELIMINARY TEST.
GRIP

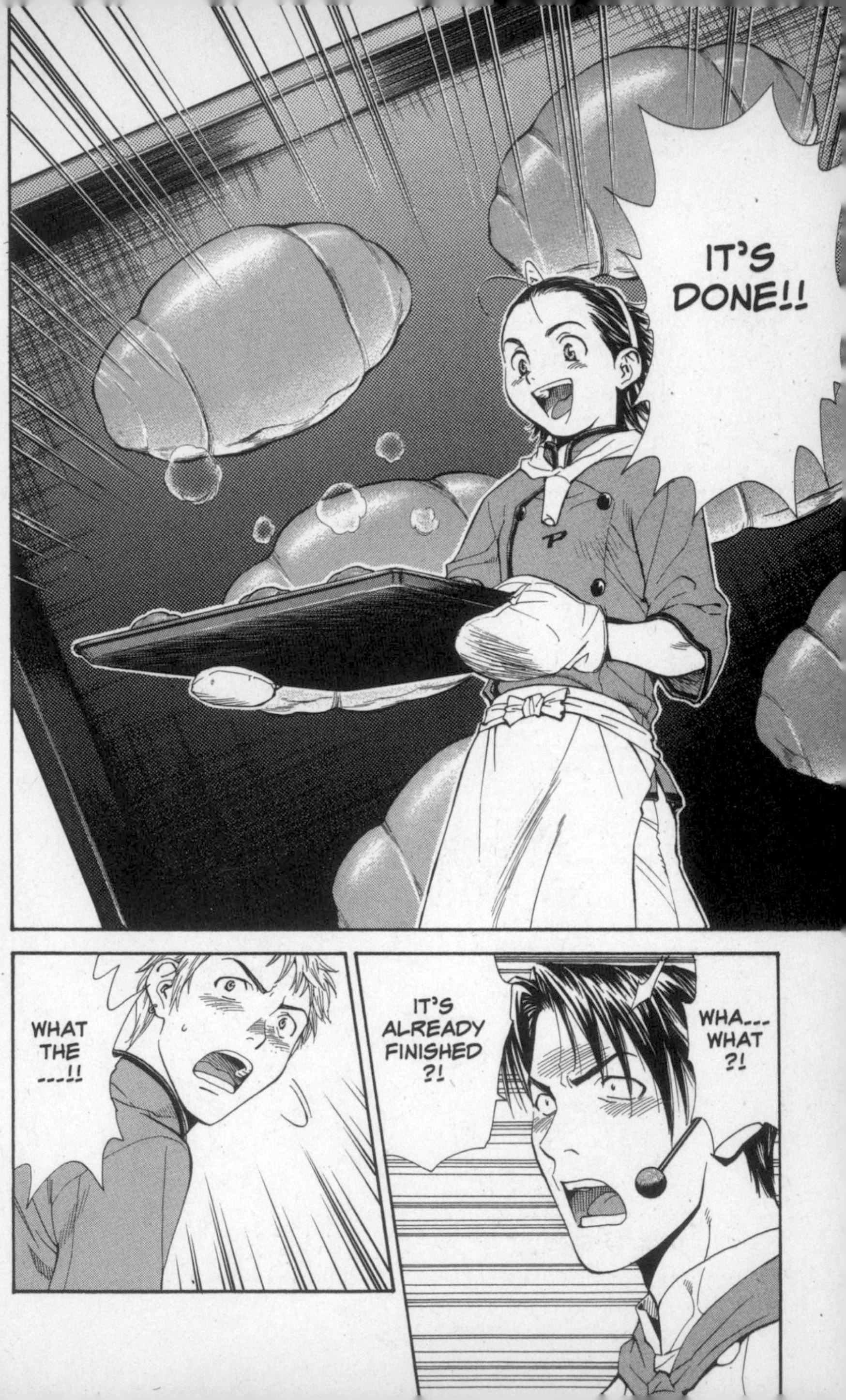
IT'S DONE!!
WHA... WHAT ?!
IT'S ALREADY FINISHED ?!
WHAT THE ---!!

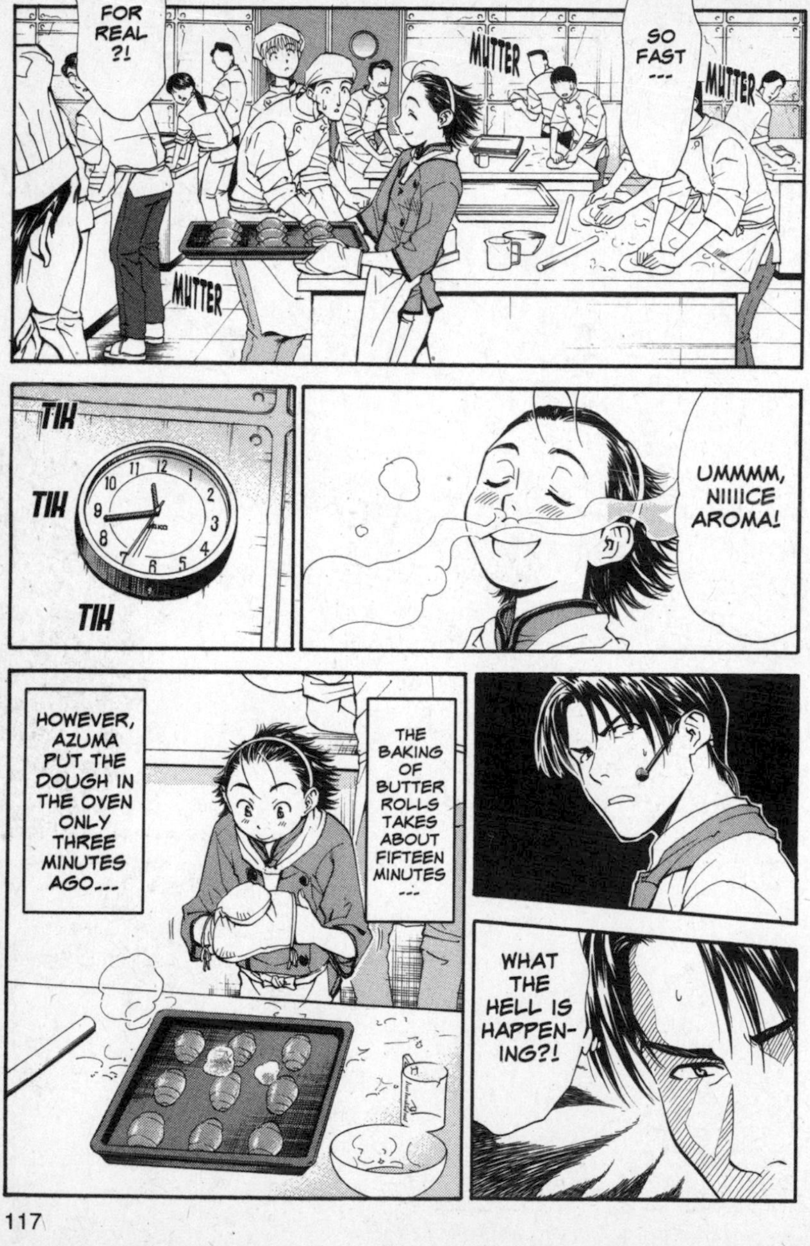
SO FAST ---
MUTTER
MUTTER
FOR REAL?!
MUTTER
UMMMM, NIIIICE AROMA!
TIK
TIK
TIK
WHAT THE HELL IS HAPPEN-ING?!
THE BAKING OF BUTTER ROLLS TAKES ABOUT FIFTEEN MINUTES ---
HOWEVER, AZUMA PUT THE DOUGH IN THE OVEN ONLY THREE MINUTES AGO---

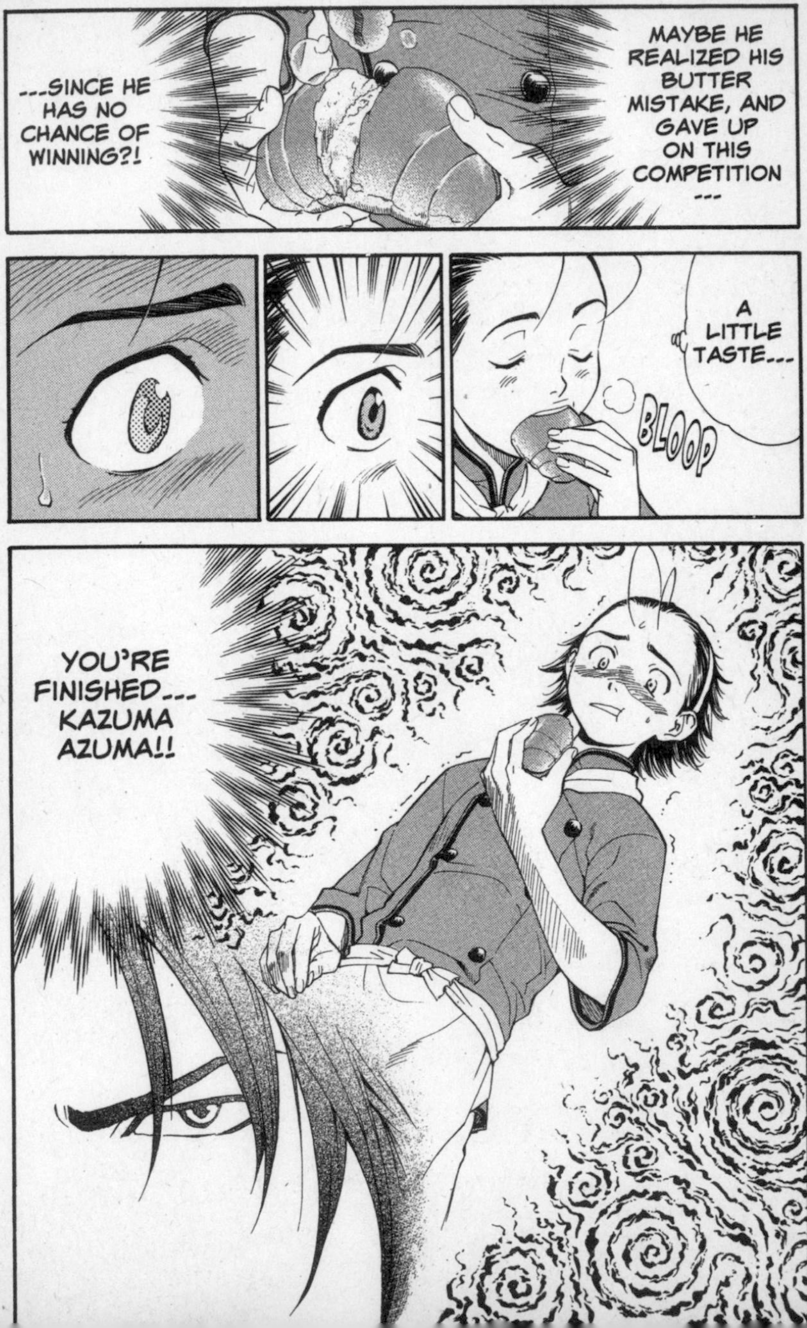
MAYBE HE REALIZED HIS BUTTER MISTAKE, AND GAVE UP ON THIS COMPETITION ...
...SINCE HE HAS NO CHANCE OF WINNING?!
A LITTLE TASTE...
BLOOP
YOU'RE FINISHED... KAZUMA AZUMA!!

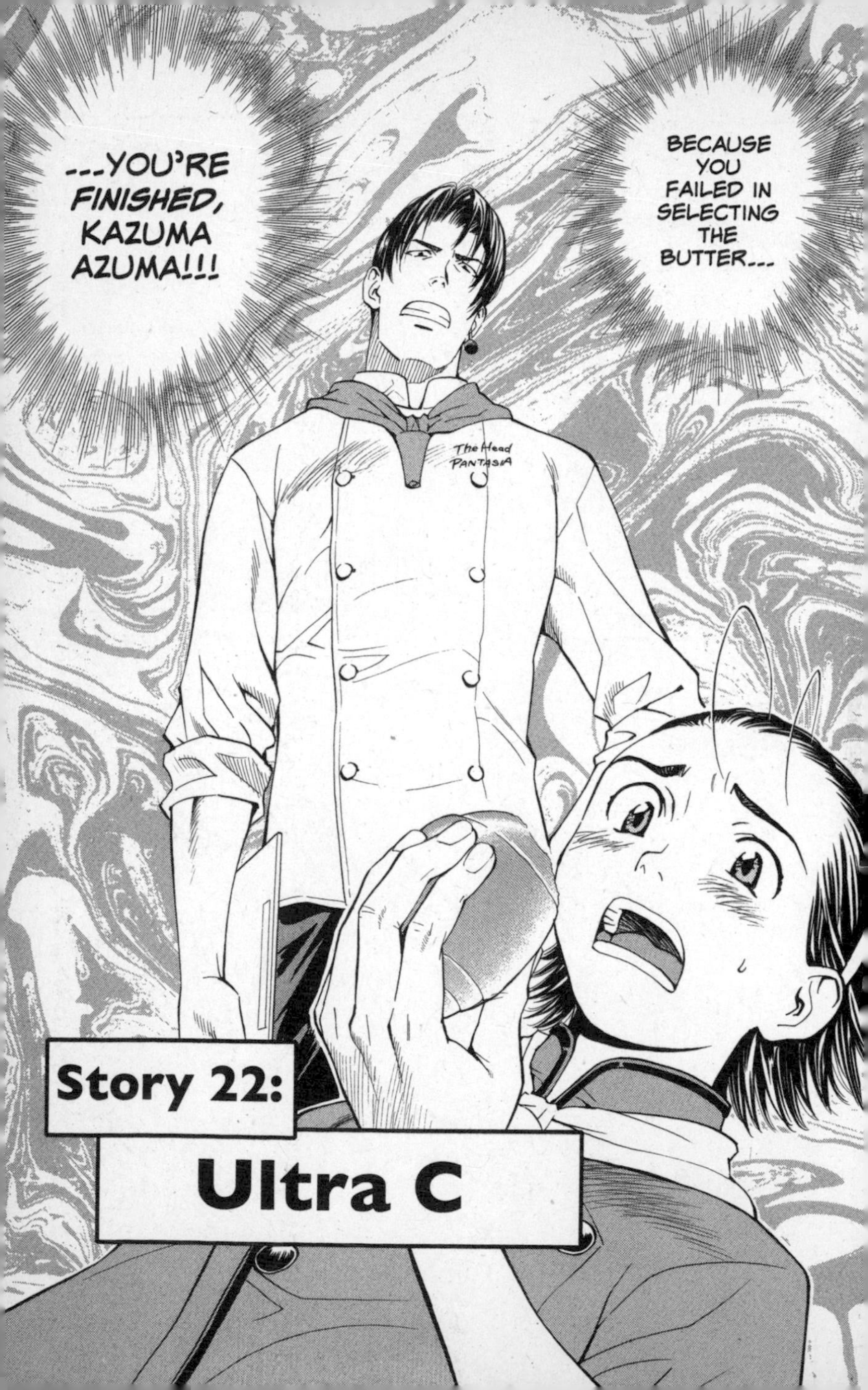
BECAUSE YOU FAILED IN SELECTING THE BUTTER...
...YOU'RE FINISHED, KAZUMA AZUMA!!!
The Head PANTASIA
Story 22:
Ultra C

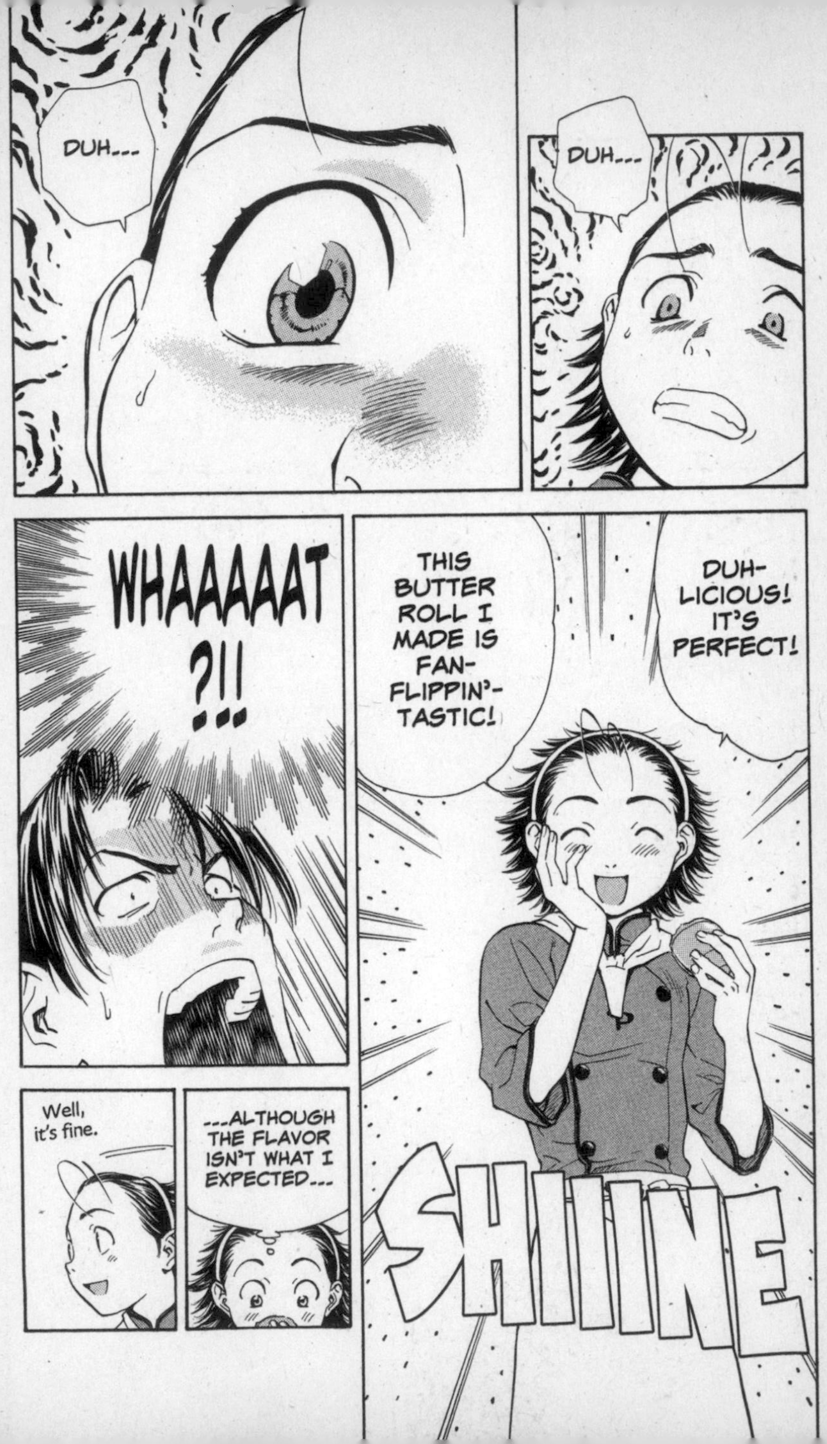
DUH...
DUH...
DUH-LICIOUS! IT'S PERFECT!
THIS BUTTER ROLL I MADE IS FAN-FLIPPIN'-TASTIC!
SHIIINE
WHAAAAAT?!!
...ALTHOUGH THE FLAVOR ISN'T WHAT I EXPECTED...
Well, it's fine.

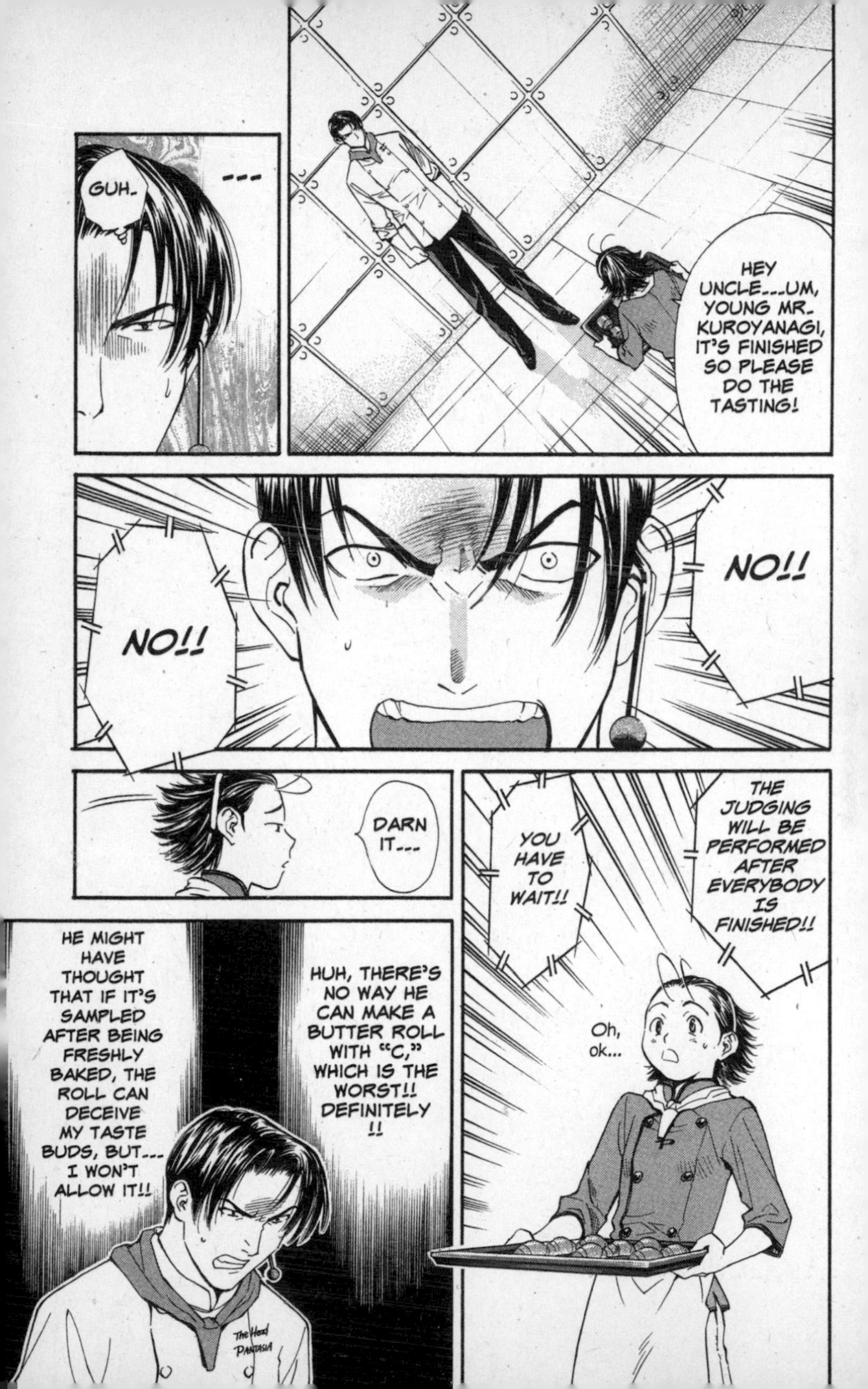
HEY UNCLE...UM, YOUNG MR. KUROYANAGI, IT'S FINISHED SO PLEASE DO THE TASTING!
...
GUH.
NO!!
NO!!
THE JUDGING WILL BE PERFORMED AFTER EVERYBODY IS FINISHED!!
YOU HAVE TO WAIT!!
Oh, ok...
DARN IT...
HUH, THERE'S NO WAY HE CAN MAKE A BUTTER ROLL WITH "C," WHICH IS THE WORST!! DEFINITELY!!
HE MIGHT HAVE THOUGHT THAT IF IT'S SAMPLED AFTER BEING FRESHLY BAKED, THE ROLL CAN DECEIVE MY TASTE BUDS, BUT... I WON'T ALLOW IT!!
The Head PANTASIA

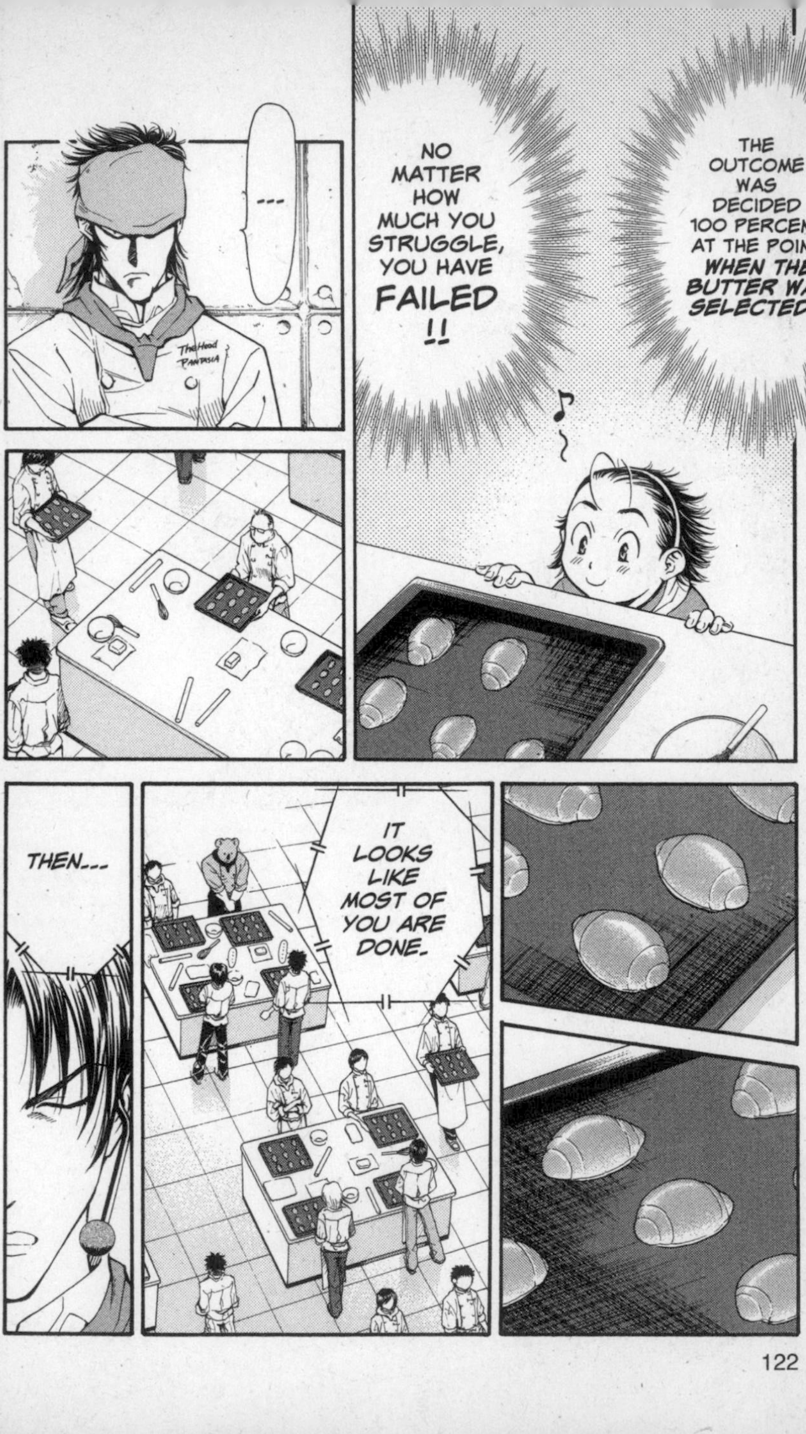
THE OUTCOME WAS DECIDED 100 PERCENT AT THE POINT WHEN THE BUTTER WAS SELECTED!!
NO MATTER HOW MUCH YOU STRUGGLE, YOU HAVE FAILED!!

The Head PANTASIA
IT LOOKS LIKE MOST OF YOU ARE DONE.
THEN...

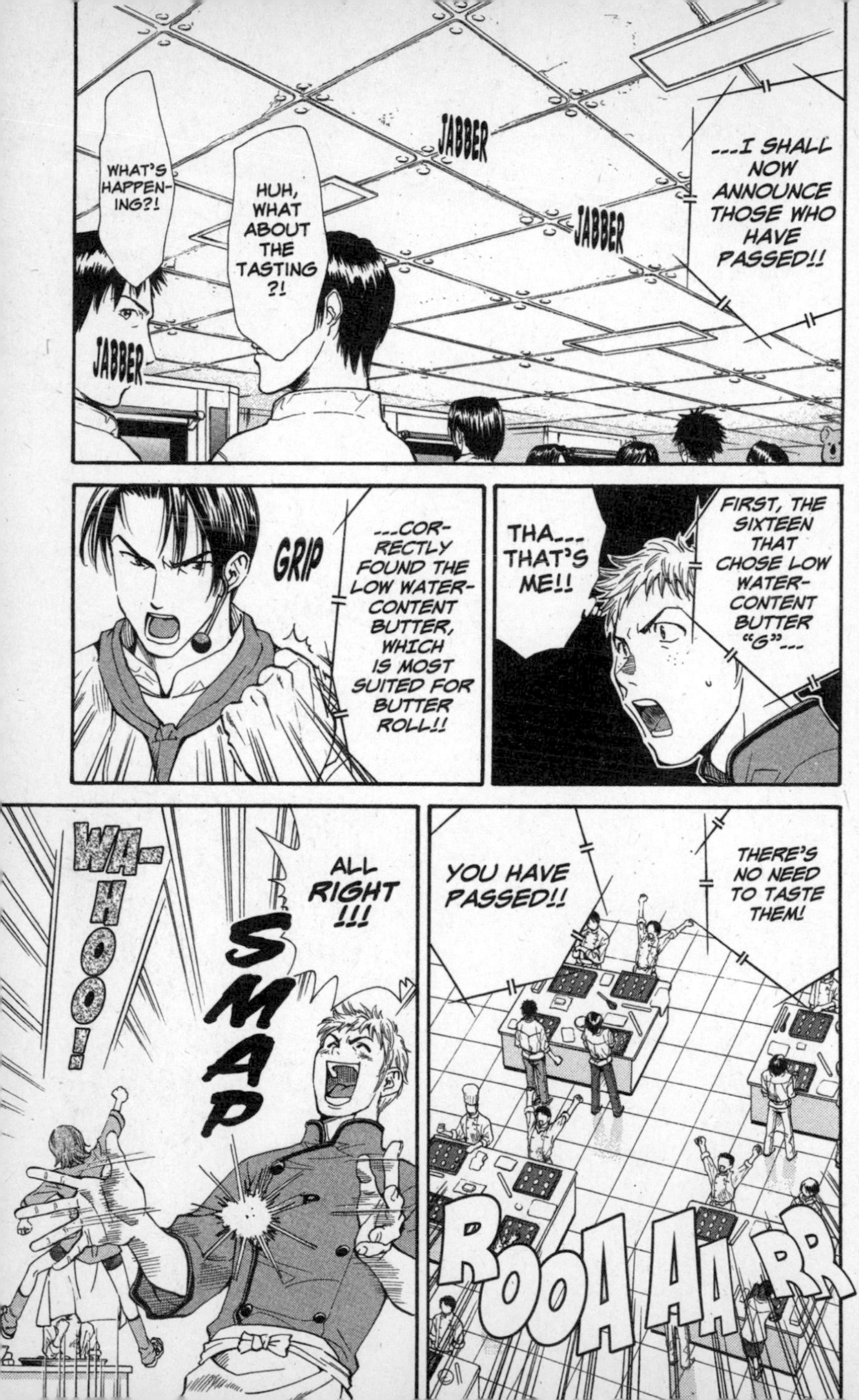
---I SHALL NOW ANNOUNCE THOSE WHO HAVE PASSED!!
JABBER
JABBER
HUH, WHAT ABOUT THE TASTING?!
WHAT'S HAPPENING?!
JABBER
FIRST, THE SIXTEEN THAT CHOSE LOW WATER-CONTENT BUTTER "G"---
THA--- THAT'S ME!!
---CORRECTLY FOUND THE LOW WATER-CONTENT BUTTER, WHICH IS MOST SUITED FOR BUTTER ROLL!!
GRIP
THERE'S NO NEED TO TASTE THEM!
YOU HAVE PASSED!!
ROOAAARR
ALL RIGHT!!!
SMAP
WA-HOOO!!

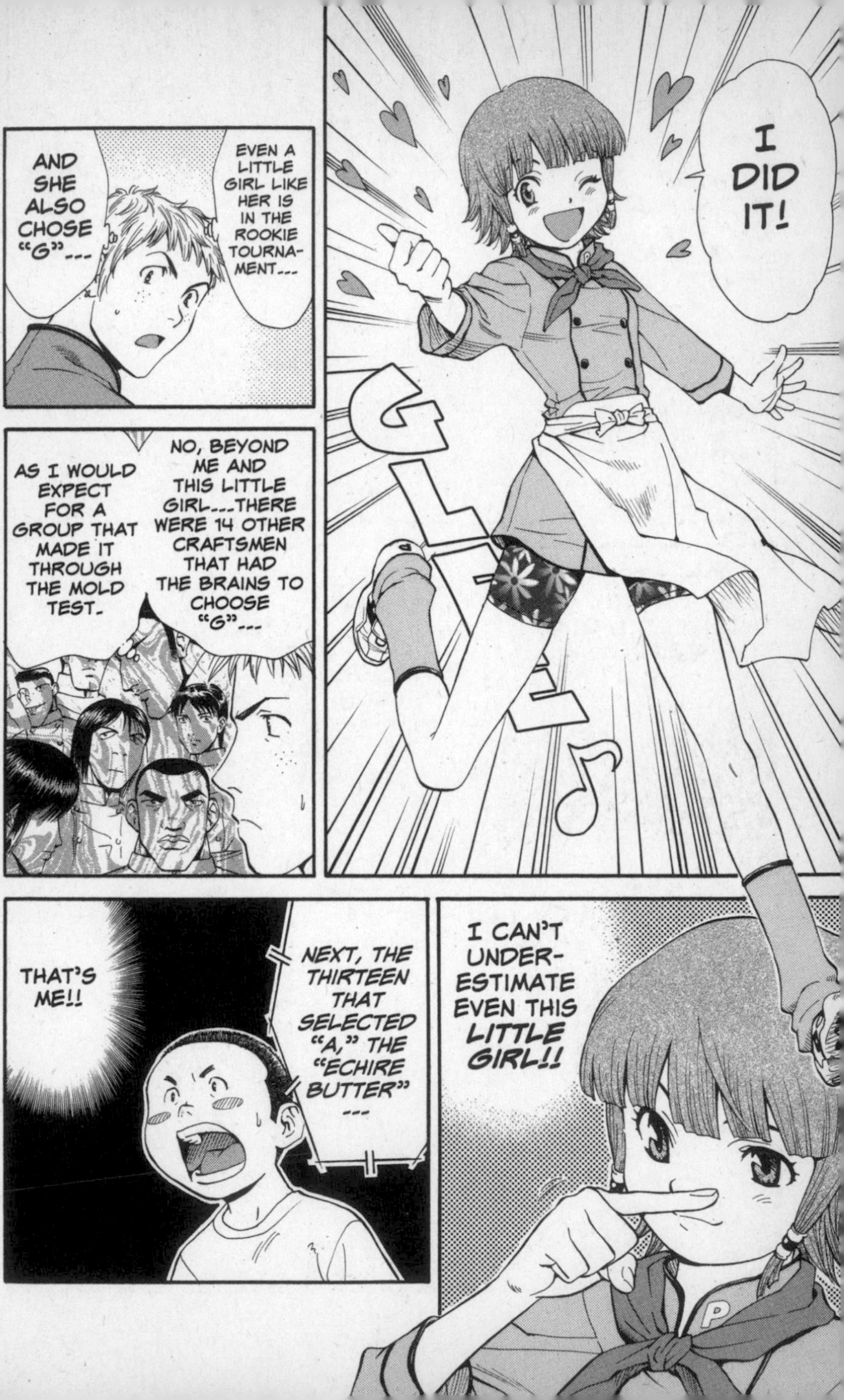
I DID IT!
EVEN A LITTLE GIRL LIKE HER IS IN THE ROOKIE TOURNAMENT...
AND SHE ALSO CHOSE "G"...
NO, BEYOND ME AND THIS LITTLE GIRL...THERE WERE 14 OTHER CRAFTSMEN THAT HAD THE BRAINS TO CHOOSE "G"...
AS I WOULD EXPECT FOR A GROUP THAT MADE IT THROUGH THE MOLD TEST.
I CAN'T UNDER-ESTIMATE EVEN THIS LITTLE GIRL!!
NEXT, THE THIRTEEN THAT SELECTED "A," THE "ECHIRE BUTTER"...
THAT'S ME!!

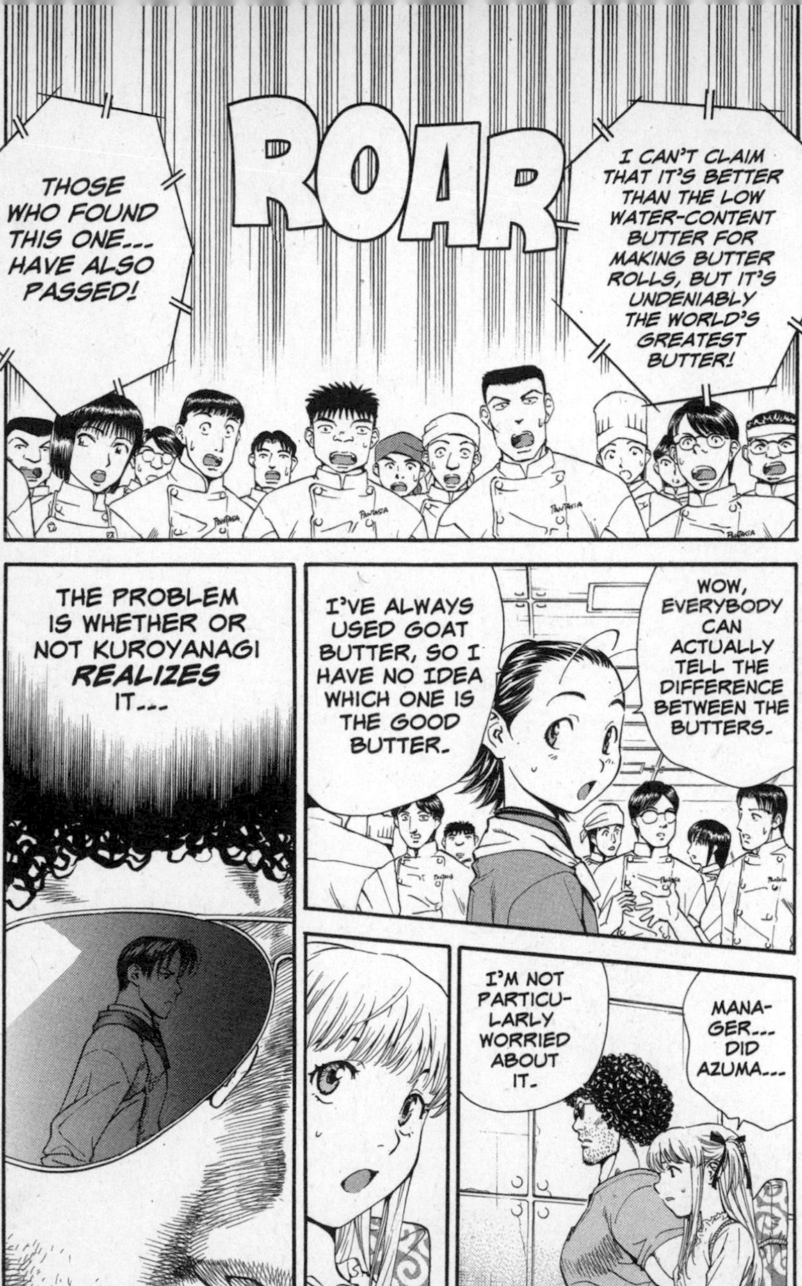
I CAN'T CLAIM THAT IT'S BETTER THAN THE LOW WATER-CONTENT BUTTER FOR MAKING BUTTER ROLLS, BUT IT'S UNDENIABLY THE WORLD'S GREATEST BUTTER!
ROAR
THOSE WHO FOUND THIS ONE... HAVE ALSO PASSED!
WOW, EVERYBODY CAN ACTUALLY TELL THE DIFFERENCE BETWEEN THE BUTTERS.
I'VE ALWAYS USED GOAT BUTTER, SO I HAVE NO IDEA WHICH ONE IS THE GOOD BUTTER.
MANAGER... DID AZUMA...
I'M NOT PARTICULARLY WORRIED ABOUT IT.
THE PROBLEM IS WHETHER OR NOT KUROYANAGI REALIZES IT...

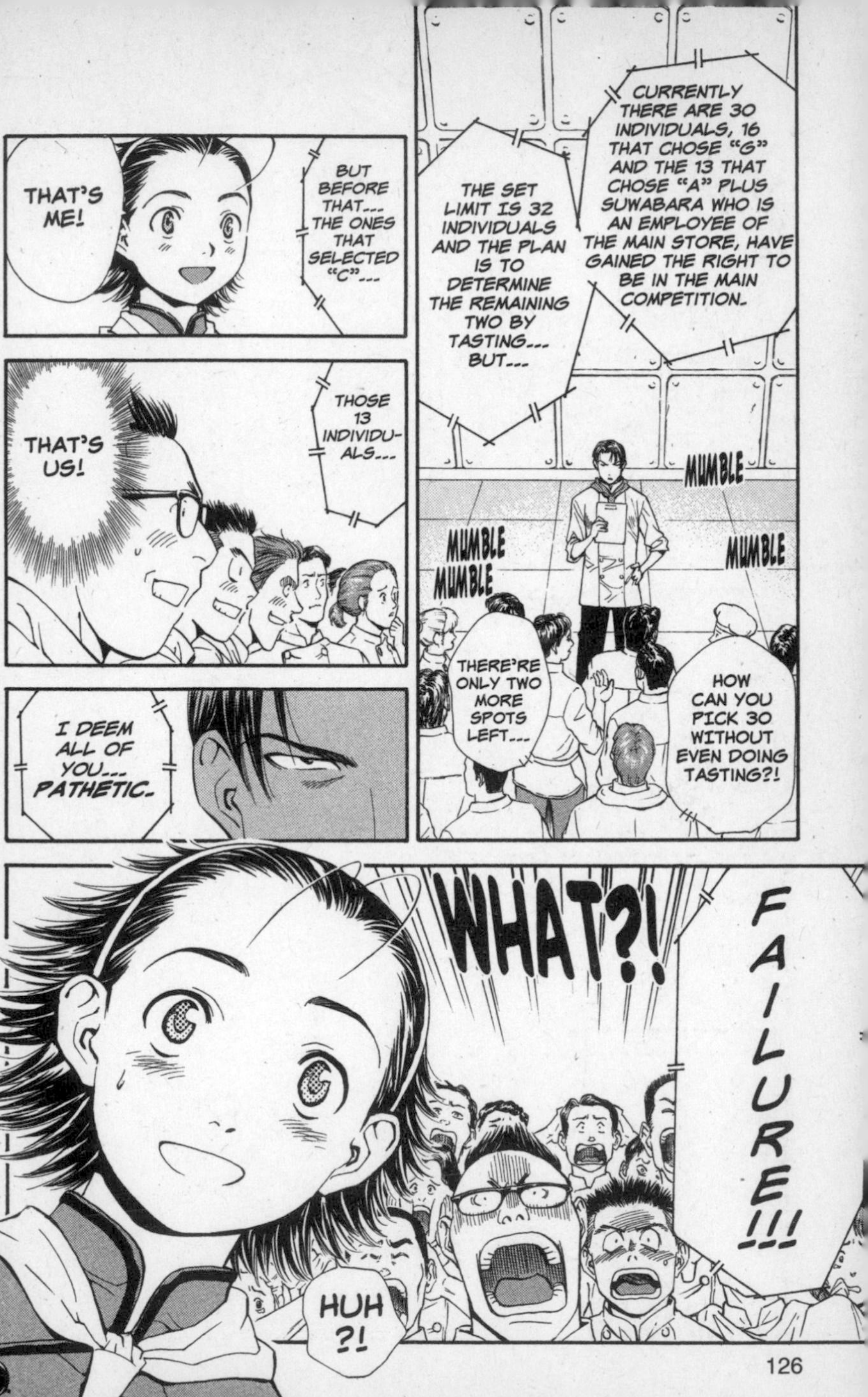
CURRENTLY THERE ARE 30 INDIVIDUALS, 16 THAT CHOSE "G" AND THE 13 THAT CHOSE "A" PLUS SUWABARA WHO IS AN EMPLOYEE OF THE MAIN STORE, HAVE GAINED THE RIGHT TO BE IN THE MAIN COMPETITION.
THE SET LIMIT IS 32 INDIVIDUALS AND THE PLAN IS TO DETERMINE THE REMAINING TWO BY TASTING... BUT...
MUMBLE
MUMBLE
MUMBLE MUMBLE
HOW CAN YOU PICK 30 WITHOUT EVEN DOING TASTING?!
THERE'RE ONLY TWO MORE SPOTS LEFT...
BUT BEFORE THAT... THE ONES THAT SELECTED "C"...
THAT'S ME!
THOSE 13 INDIVIDU-ALS...
THAT'S US!
I DEEM ALL OF YOU... PATHETIC.
FAILURE!!!
WHAT?!
HUH?!

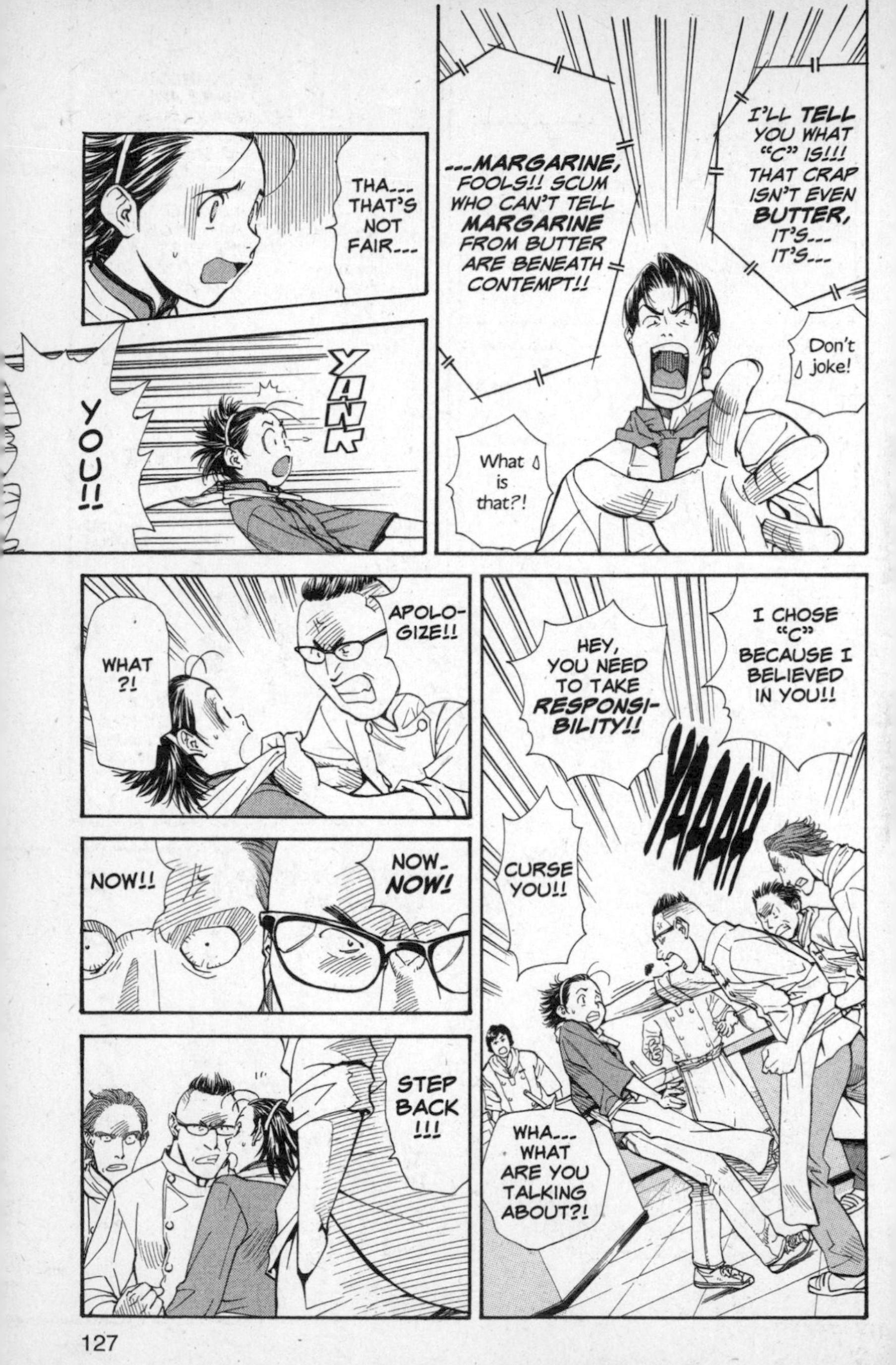
I'LL TELL YOU WHAT "C" IS!!! THAT CRAP ISN'T EVEN BUTTER, IT'S... IT'S...
---MARGARINE, FOOLS!! SCUM WHO CAN'T TELL MARGARINE FROM BUTTER ARE BENEATH CONTEMPT!!
Don't joke!
What is that?!
THA... THAT'S NOT FAIR...
YANK
YOU!!
I CHOSE "C" BECAUSE I BELIEVED IN YOU!!
HEY, YOU NEED TO TAKE RESPONSIBILITY!!
YAAAH
CURSE YOU!!
WHA... WHAT ARE YOU TALKING ABOUT?!
APOLOGIZE!!
WHAT?!
NOW. NOW!
NOW!!
STEP BACK!!!

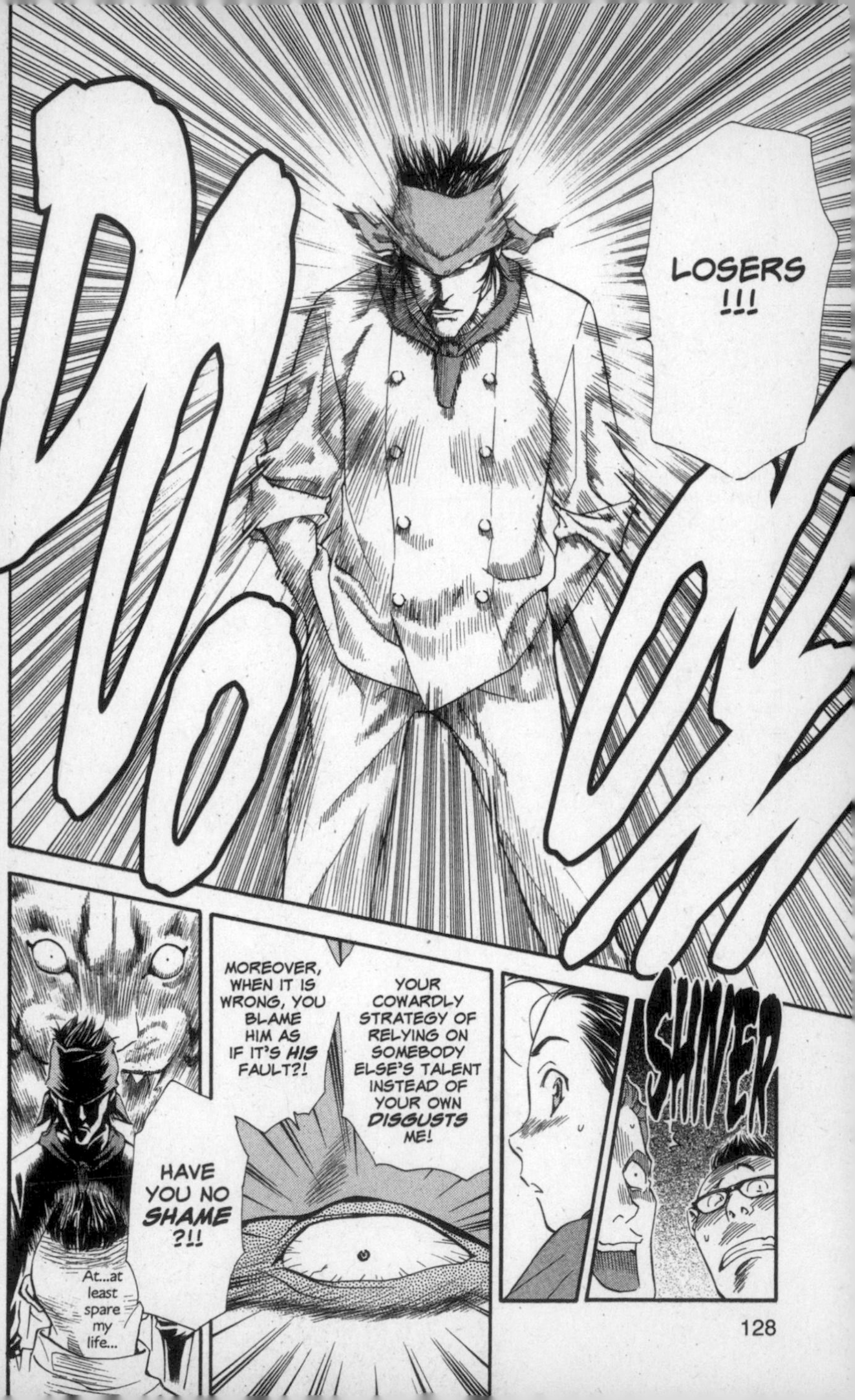
LOSERS !!!
SHIVER
YOUR COWARDLY STRATEGY OF RELYING ON SOMEBODY ELSE'S TALENT INSTEAD OF YOUR OWN DISGUSTS ME!
MOREOVER, WHEN IT IS WRONG, YOU BLAME HIM AS IF IT'S HIS FAULT?!
HAVE YOU NO SHAME ?!!
At...at least spare my life...

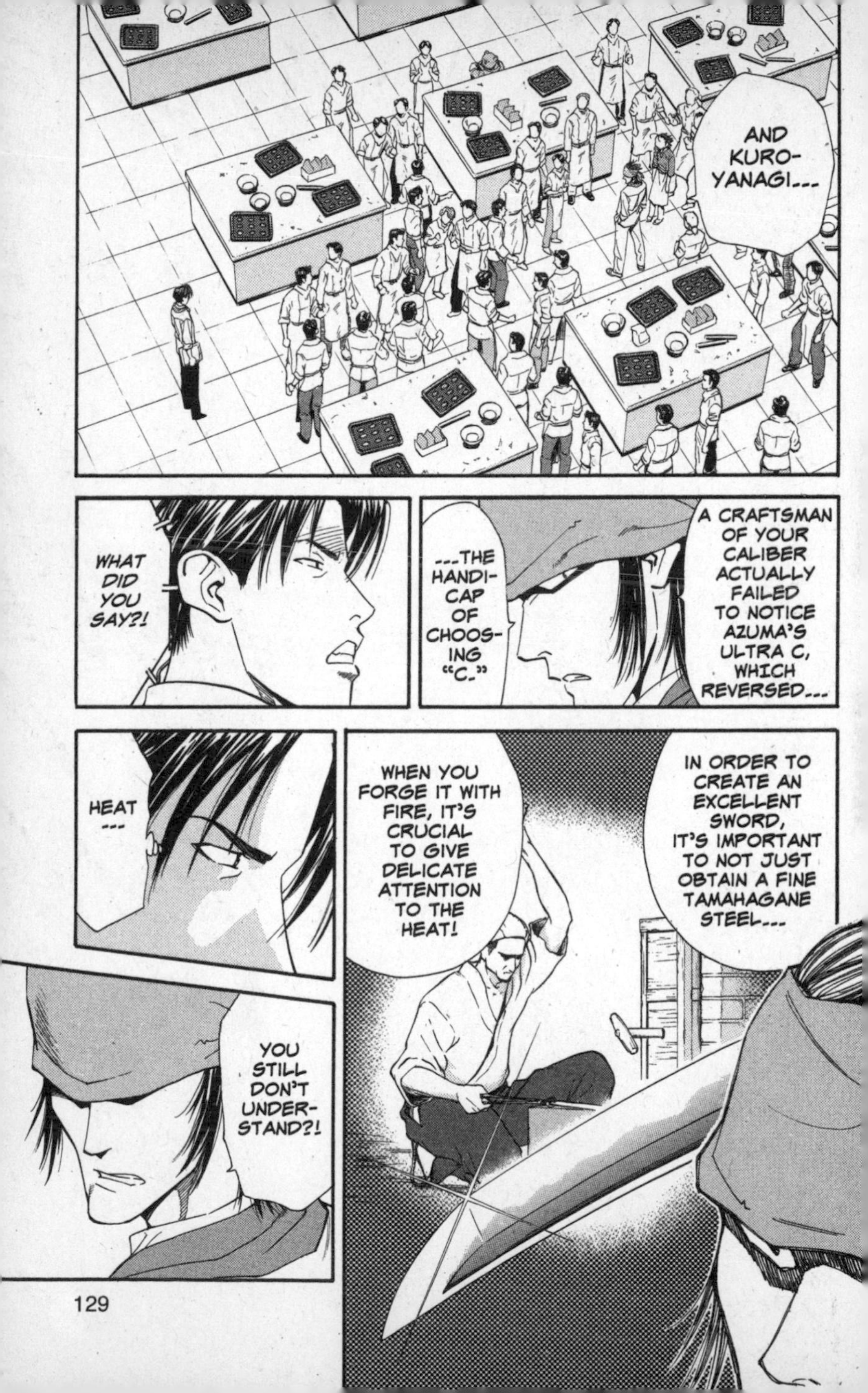
AND KURO-YANAGI...
A CRAFTSMAN OF YOUR CALIBER ACTUALLY FAILED TO NOTICE AZUMA'S ULTRA C, WHICH REVERSED...
...THE HANDICAP OF CHOOSING "C."
WHAT DID YOU SAY?!
IN ORDER TO CREATE AN EXCELLENT SWORD, IT'S IMPORTANT TO NOT JUST OBTAIN A FINE TAMAHAGANE STEEL...
WHEN YOU FORGE IT WITH FIRE, IT'S CRUCIAL TO GIVE DELICATE ATTENTION TO THE HEAT!
HEAT...
YOU STILL DON'T UNDERSTAND?!

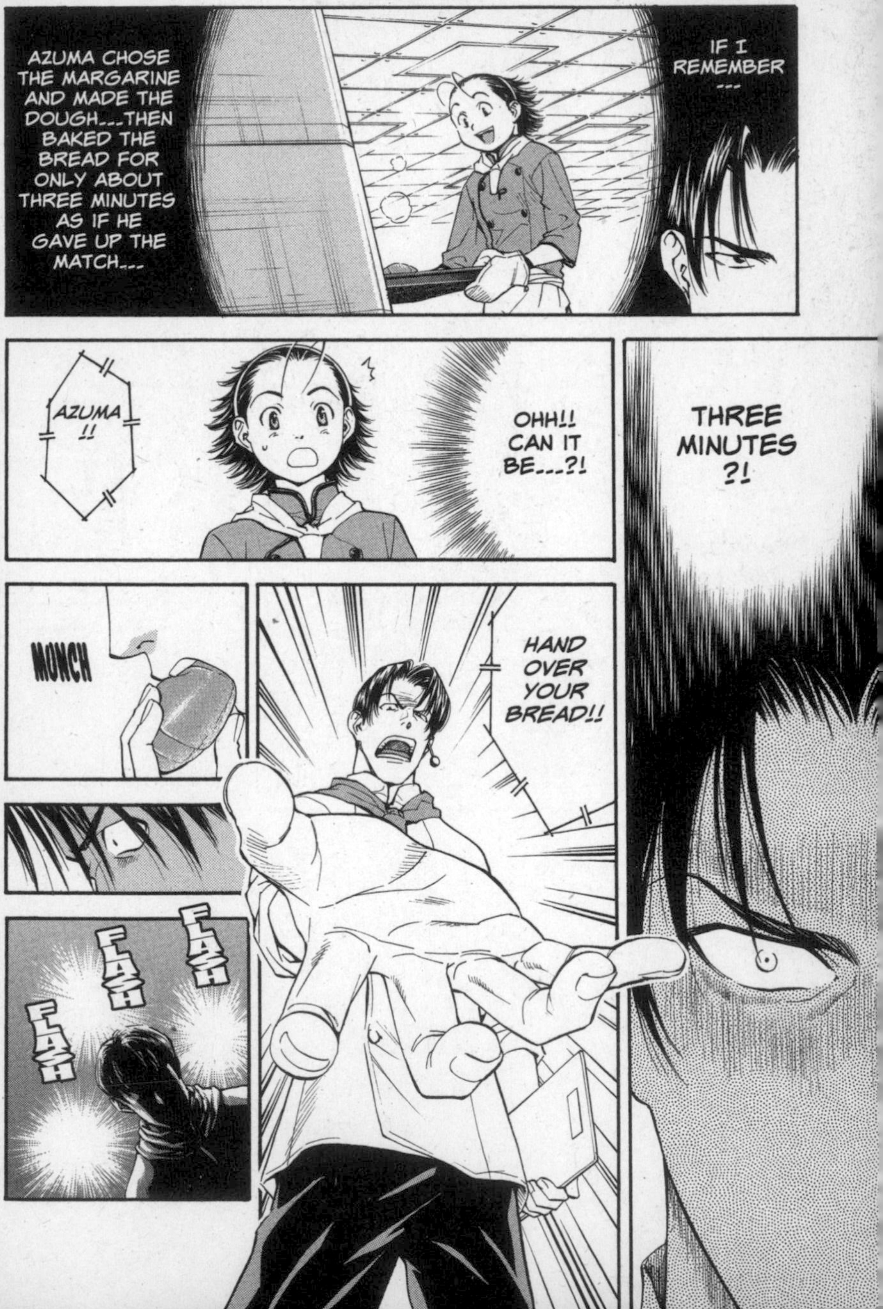
IF I REMEMBER ---
AZUMA CHOSE THE MARGARINE AND MADE THE DOUGH---THEN BAKED THE BREAD FOR ONLY ABOUT THREE MINUTES AS IF HE GAVE UP THE MATCH---
THREE MINUTES ?!
OHH!! CAN IT BE---?!
AZUMA !!
HAND OVER YOUR BREAD!!
MUNCH
FLASH
FLASH
FLASH

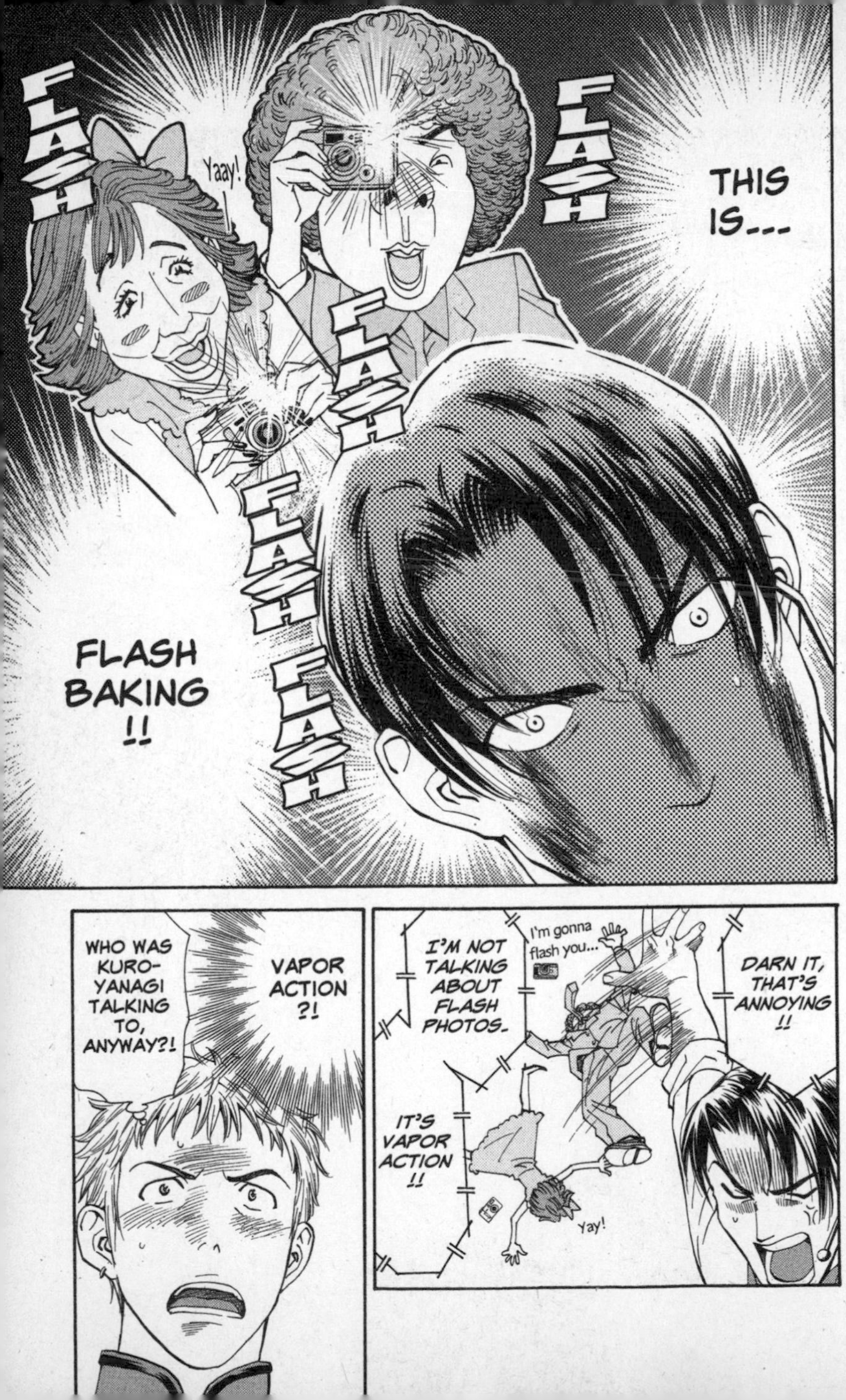
FLASH
THIS IS...
FLASH
Yaaay!
FLASH
FLASH
FLASH
FLASH BAKING !!
DARN IT, THAT'S ANNOYING !!
I'm gonna flash you...
I'M NOT TALKING ABOUT FLASH PHOTOS.
IT'S VAPOR ACTION !!
Yay!
VAPOR ACTION ?!
WHO WAS KURO-YANAGI TALKING TO, ANYWAY?!

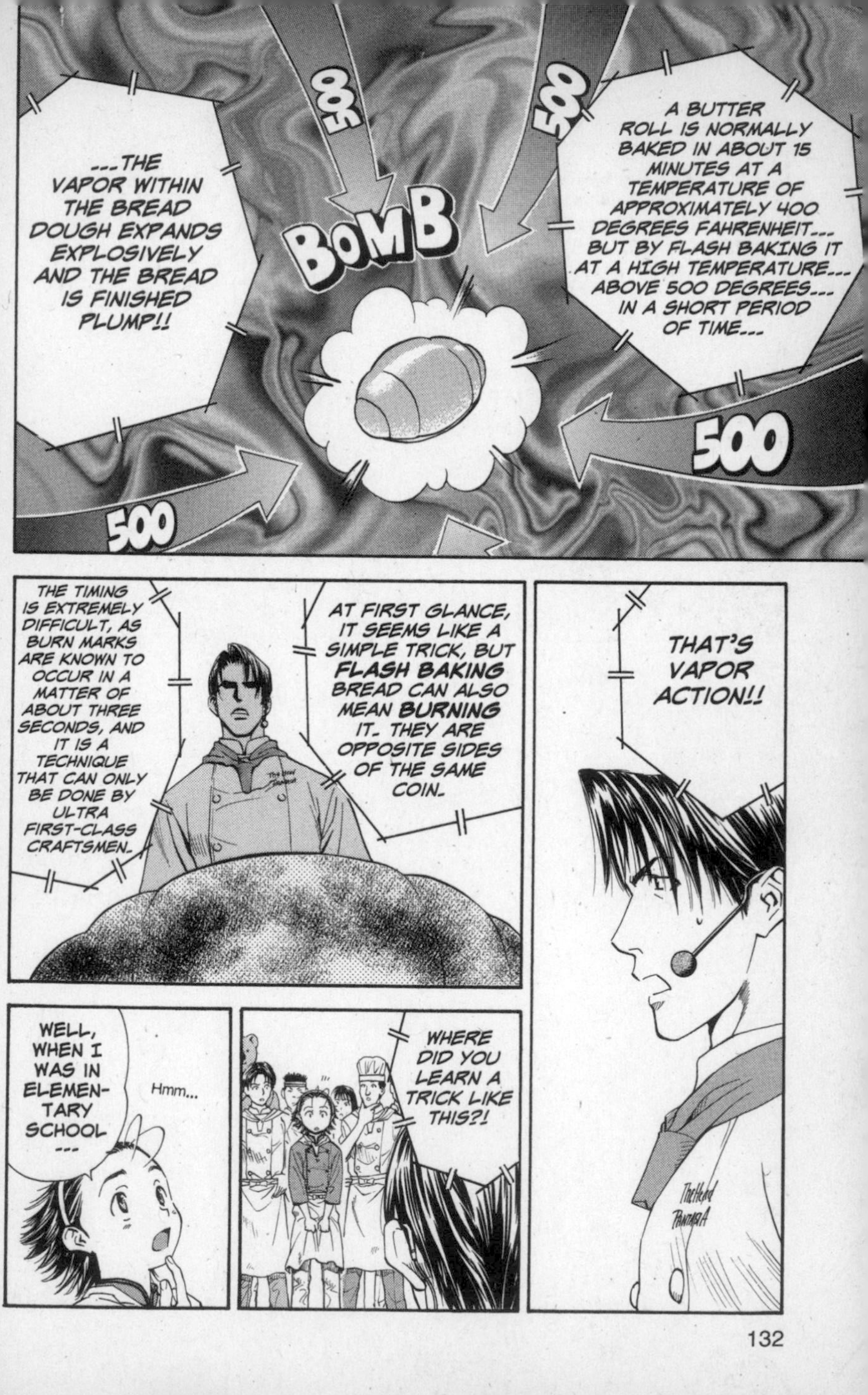

A BUTTER ROLL IS NORMALLY BAKED IN ABOUT 15 MINUTES AT A TEMPERATURE OF APPROXIMATELY 400 DEGREES FAHRENHEIT... BUT BY FLASH BAKING IT AT A HIGH TEMPERATURE... ABOVE 500 DEGREES... IN A SHORT PERIOD OF TIME...
500
500
BOMB
500
500
...THE VAPOR WITHIN THE BREAD DOUGH EXPANDS EXPLOSIVELY AND THE BREAD IS FINISHED PLUMP!!
THAT'S VAPOR ACTION!!
AT FIRST GLANCE, IT SEEMS LIKE A SIMPLE TRICK, BUT FLASH BAKING BREAD CAN ALSO MEAN BURNING IT. THEY ARE OPPOSITE SIDES OF THE SAME COIN.
THE TIMING IS EXTREMELY DIFFICULT, AS BURN MARKS ARE KNOWN TO OCCUR IN A MATTER OF ABOUT THREE SECONDS, AND IT IS A TECHNIQUE THAT CAN ONLY BE DONE BY ULTRA FIRST-CLASS CRAFTSMEN.
WHERE DID YOU LEARN A TRICK LIKE THIS?!
WELL, WHEN I WAS IN ELEMENTARY SCHOOL ...
Hmm...

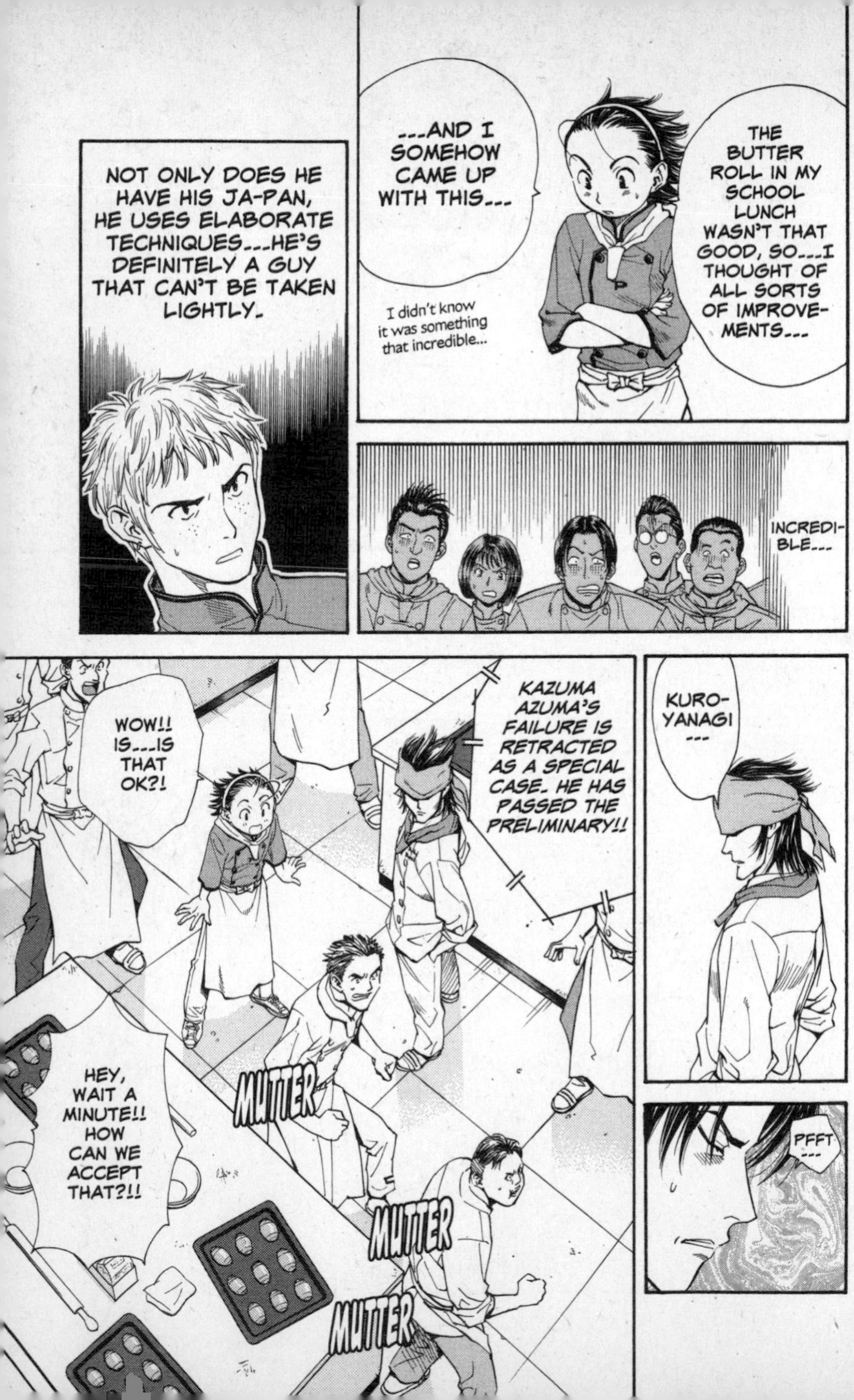
THE BUTTER ROLL IN MY SCHOOL LUNCH WASN'T THAT GOOD, SO...I THOUGHT OF ALL SORTS OF IMPROVE-MENTS...
...AND I SOMEHOW CAME UP WITH THIS...
I didn't know it was something that incredible...
INCREDI-BLE...
NOT ONLY DOES HE HAVE HIS JA-PAN, HE USES ELABORATE TECHNIQUES...HE'S DEFINITELY A GUY THAT CAN'T BE TAKEN LIGHTLY.
KURO-YANAGI...
PFFT...
KAZUMA AZUMA'S FAILURE IS RETRACTED AS A SPECIAL CASE. HE HAS PASSED THE PRELIMINARY!!
WOW!! IS...IS THAT OK?!
MUTTER
MUTTER
HEY, WAIT A MINUTE!! HOW CAN WE ACCEPT THAT?!!
MUTTER

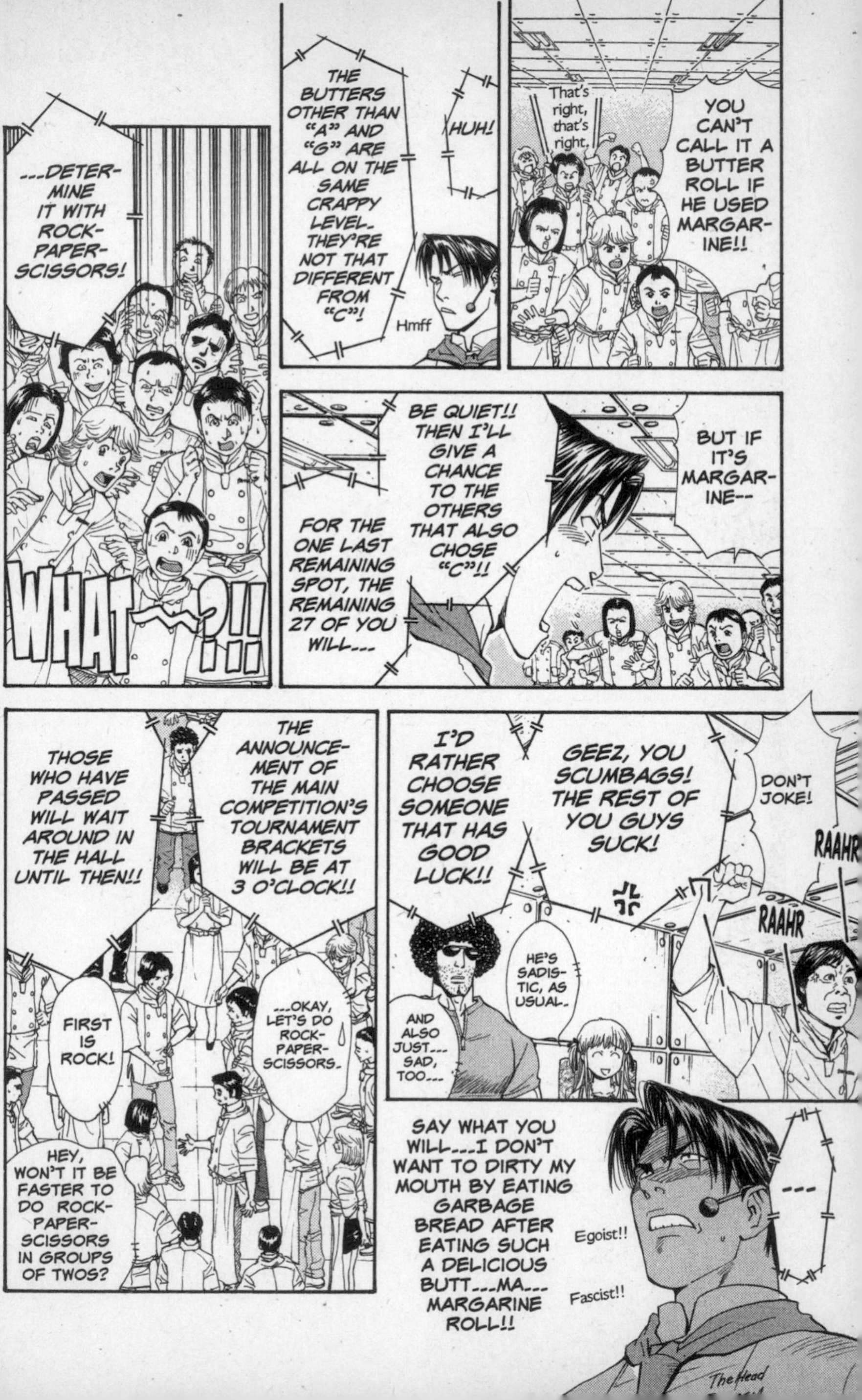
That's right, that's right.
YOU CAN'T CALL IT A BUTTER ROLL IF HE USED MARGARINE!!
HUH!
THE BUTTERS OTHER THAN "A" AND "G" ARE ALL ON THE SAME CRAPPY LEVEL. THEY'RE NOT THAT DIFFERENT FROM "C"!
Hmff
BUT IF IT'S MARGARINE--
BE QUIET!! THEN I'LL GIVE A CHANCE TO THE OTHERS THAT ALSO CHOSE "C"!!
FOR THE ONE LAST REMAINING SPOT, THE REMAINING 27 OF YOU WILL...
...DETERMINE IT WITH ROCK-PAPER-SCISSORS!
WHAT~~?!!
DON'T JOKE!
RAAHR
RAAHR
GEEZ, YOU SCUMBAGS! THE REST OF YOU GUYS SUCK!
I'D RATHER CHOOSE SOMEONE THAT HAS GOOD LUCK!!
HE'S SADISTIC, AS USUAL.
AND ALSO JUST... SAD, TOO...
...
SAY WHAT YOU WILL...I DON'T WANT TO DIRTY MY MOUTH BY EATING GARBAGE BREAD AFTER EATING SUCH A DELICIOUS BUTT...MA... MARGARINE ROLL!!
Egoist!!
Fascist!!
The Head
THE ANNOUNCEMENT OF THE MAIN COMPETITION'S TOURNAMENT BRACKETS WILL BE AT 3 O'CLOCK!!
THOSE WHO HAVE PASSED WILL WAIT AROUND IN THE HALL UNTIL THEN!!
...OKAY, LET'S DO ROCK-PAPER-SCISSORS.
FIRST IS ROCK!
HEY, WON'T IT BE FASTER TO DO ROCK-PAPER-SCISSORS IN GROUPS OF TWOS?

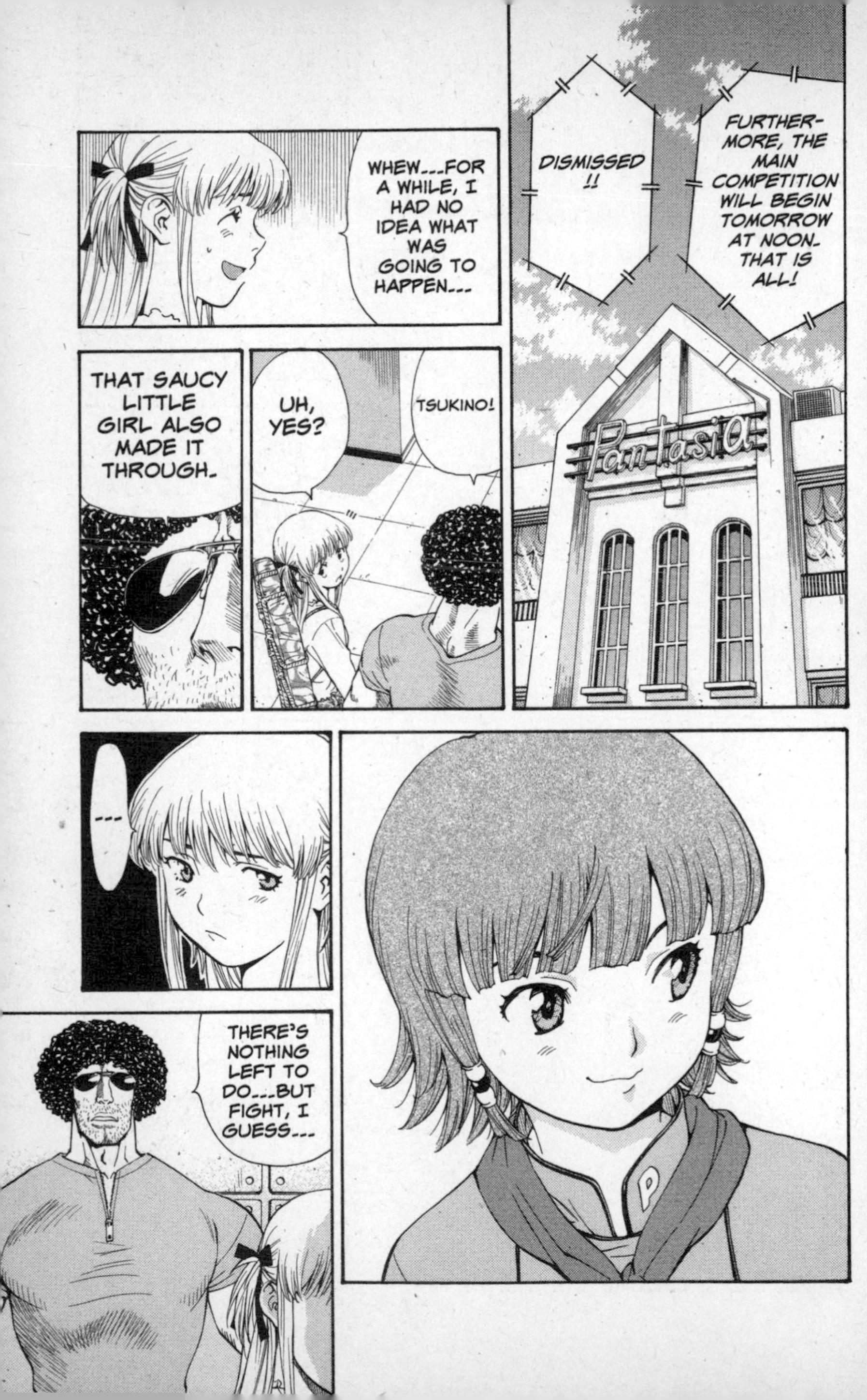
FURTHER-MORE, THE MAIN COMPETITION WILL BEGIN TOMORROW AT NOON. THAT IS ALL!
DISMISSED!!
Pantasia
WHEW...FOR A WHILE, I HAD NO IDEA WHAT WAS GOING TO HAPPEN...
TSUKINO!
UH, YES?
THAT SAUCY LITTLE GIRL ALSO MADE IT THROUGH.
...
THERE'S NOTHING LEFT TO DO...BUT FIGHT, I GUESS...

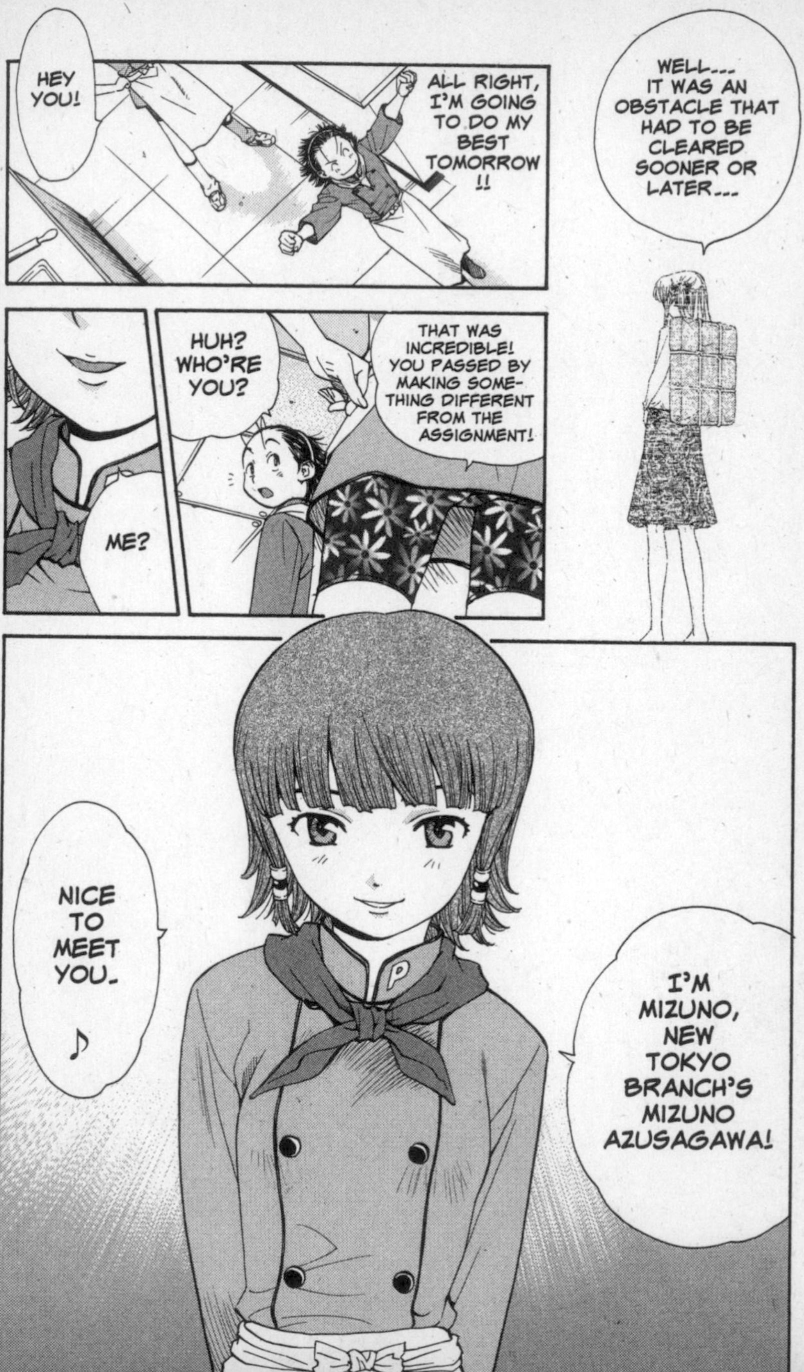
WELL... IT WAS AN OBSTACLE THAT HAD TO BE CLEARED SOONER OR LATER...
ALL RIGHT, I'M GOING TO DO MY BEST TOMORROW !!
HEY YOU!
THAT WAS INCREDIBLE! YOU PASSED BY MAKING SOME-THING DIFFERENT FROM THE ASSIGNMENT!
HUH? WHO'RE YOU?
ME?
I'M MIZUNO, NEW TOKYO BRANCH'S MIZUNO AZUSAGAWA!
NICE TO MEET YOU. ♪

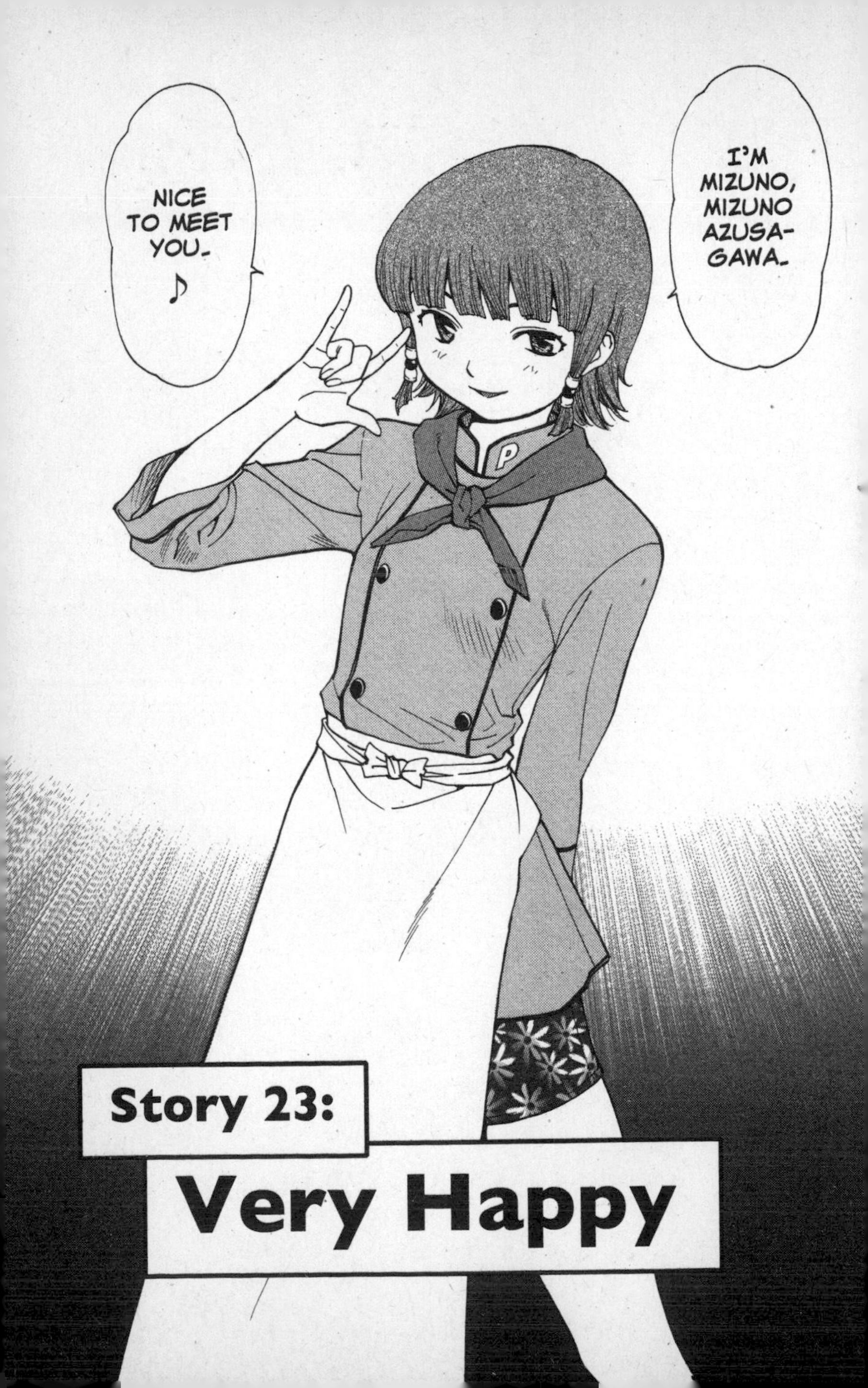
I'M MIZUNO, MIZUNO AZUSAGAWA.
NICE TO MEET YOU. ♪

Story 23: Very Happy

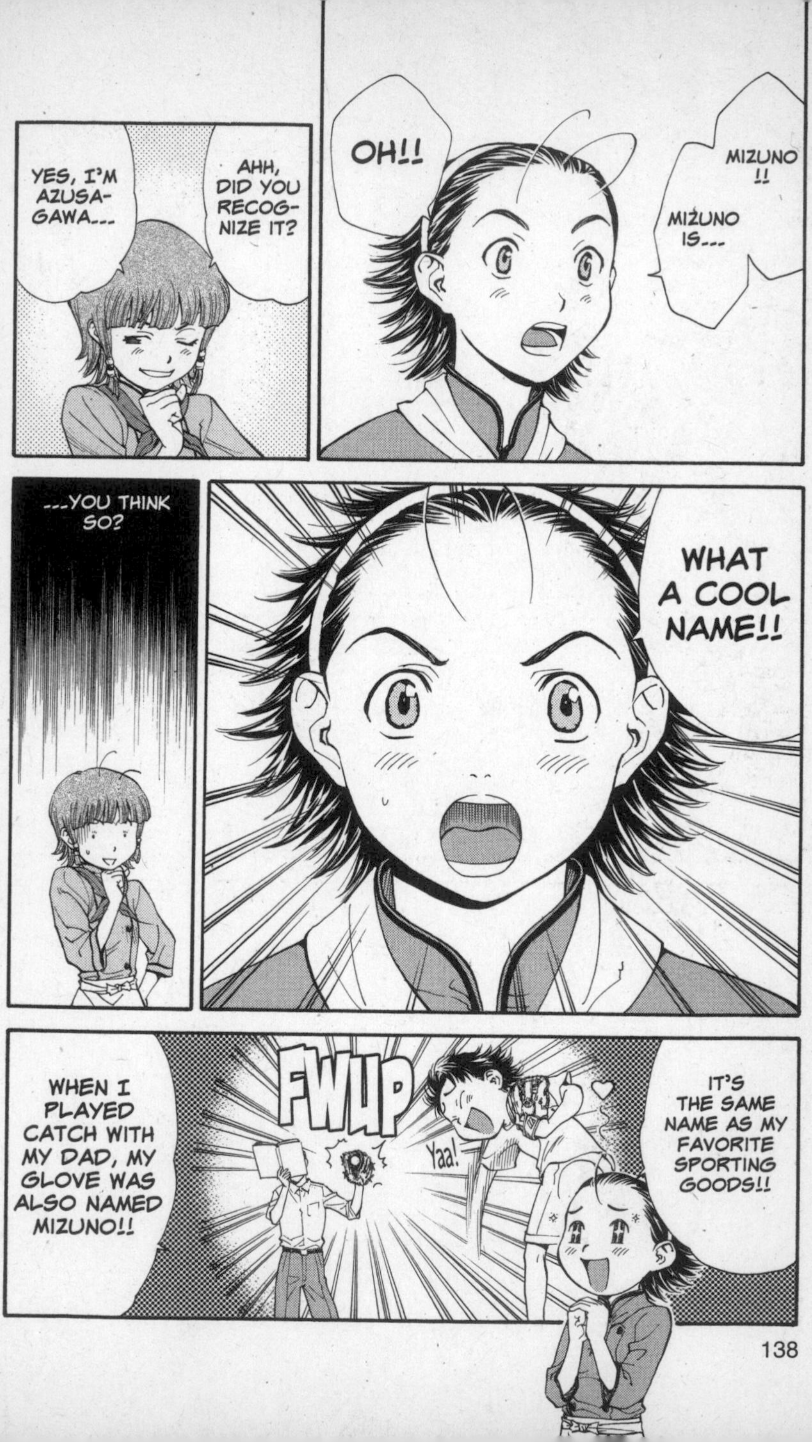

MIZUNO !!
MIZUNO IS...
OH!!
AHH, DID YOU RECOGNIZE IT?
YES, I'M AZUSAGAWA...
WHAT A COOL NAME!!
...YOU THINK SO?
IT'S THE SAME NAME AS MY FAVORITE SPORTING GOODS!!
FWUP
Yaa!
WHEN I PLAYED CATCH WITH MY DAD, MY GLOVE WAS ALSO NAMED MIZUNO!!

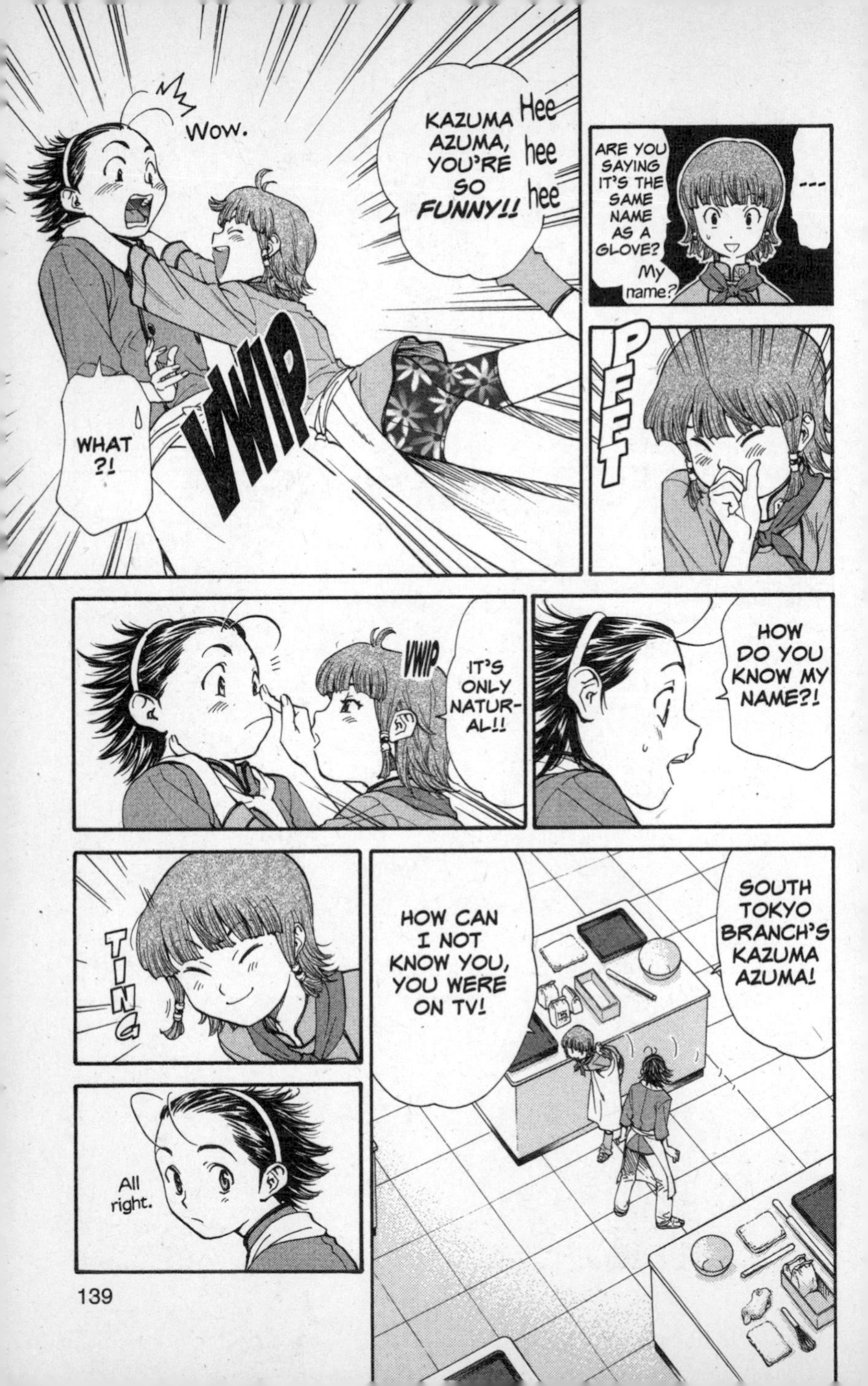

ARE YOU SAYING IT'S THE SAME NAME AS A GLOVE?
My name?
PFFT
Hee hee hee
KAZUMA AZUMA, YOU'RE SO FUNNY!!
Wow.
VWIP
WHAT?!
HOW DO YOU KNOW MY NAME?!
VWIP
IT'S ONLY NATURAL!!
SOUTH TOKYO BRANCH'S KAZUMA AZUMA!
HOW CAN I NOT KNOW YOU, YOU WERE ON TV!
TING
All right.

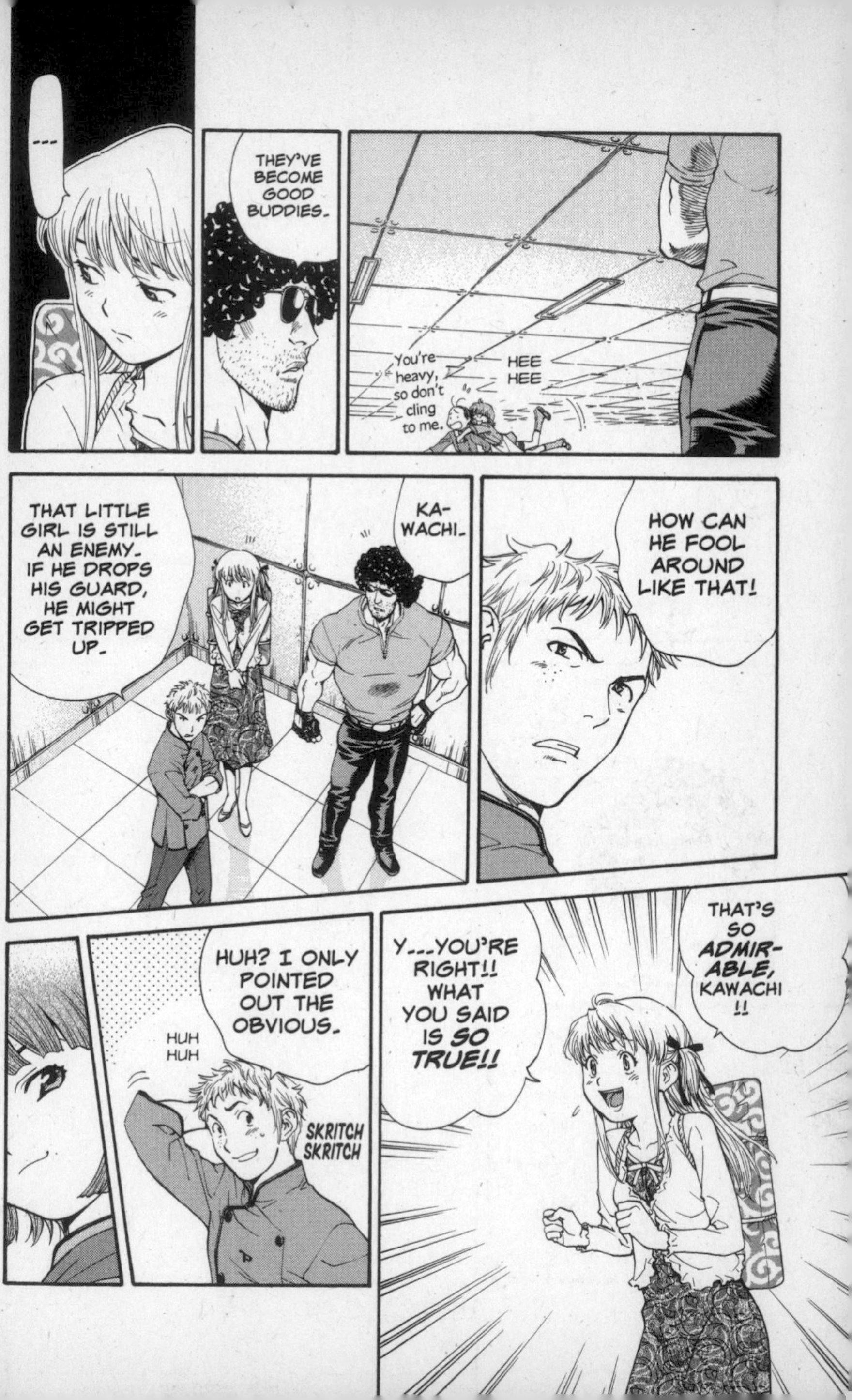
HEE HEE
You're heavy, so don't cling to me.
THEY'VE BECOME GOOD BUDDIES.
...
HOW CAN HE FOOL AROUND LIKE THAT!
KA-WACHI.
THAT LITTLE GIRL IS STILL AN ENEMY. IF HE DROPS HIS GUARD, HE MIGHT GET TRIPPED UP.
THAT'S SO ADMIRABLE, KAWACHI!!
Y...YOU'RE RIGHT!! WHAT YOU SAID IS SO TRUE!!
HUH? I ONLY POINTED OUT THE OBVIOUS.
SKRITCH SKRITCH
HUH HUH

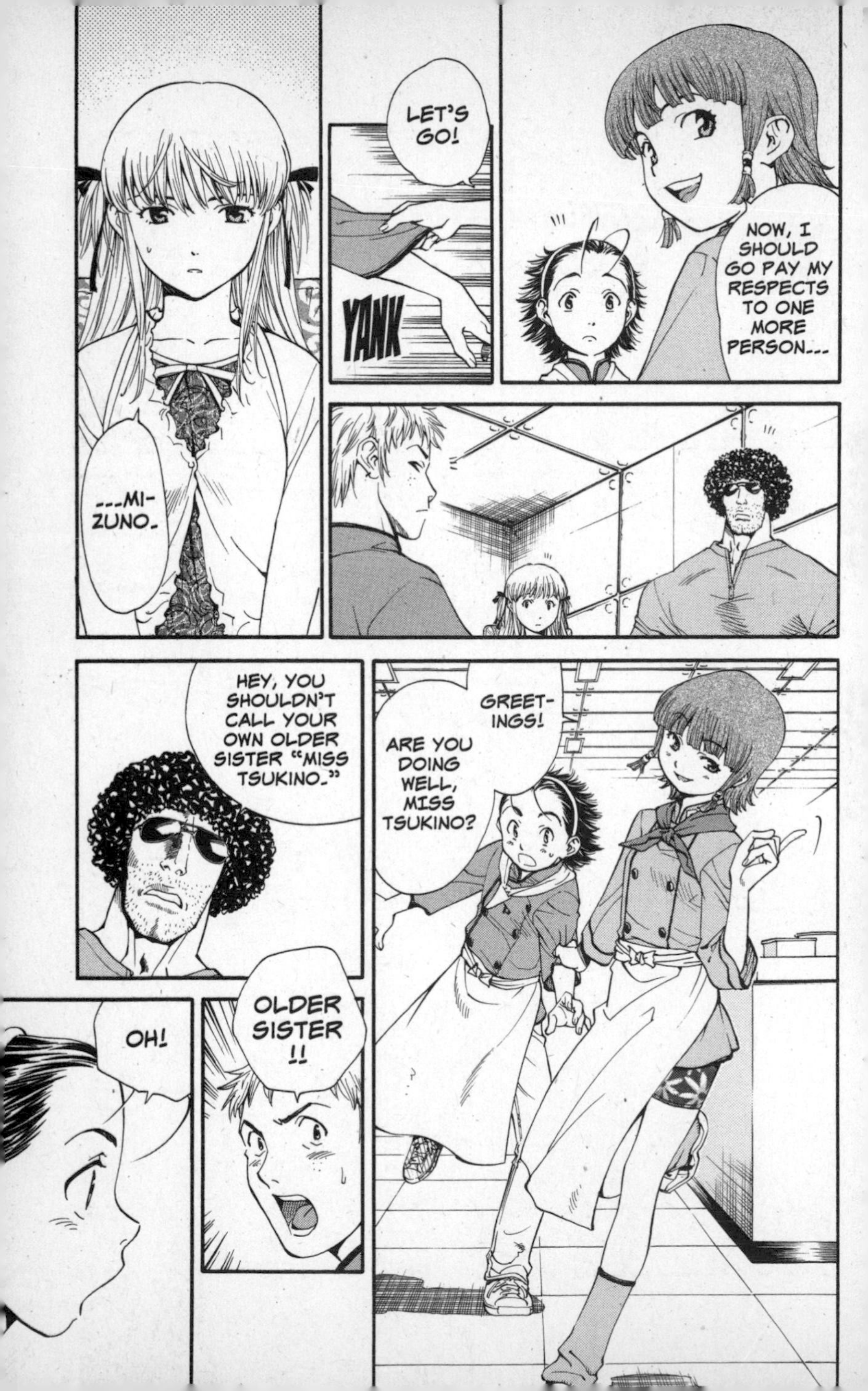
NOW, I SHOULD GO PAY MY RESPECTS TO ONE MORE PERSON...
LET'S GO!
YANK
...MI-ZUNO.
GREET-INGS!
ARE YOU DOING WELL, MISS TSUKINO?
HEY, YOU SHOULDN'T CALL YOUR OWN OLDER SISTER "MISS TSUKINO."
OLDER SISTER !!
OH!

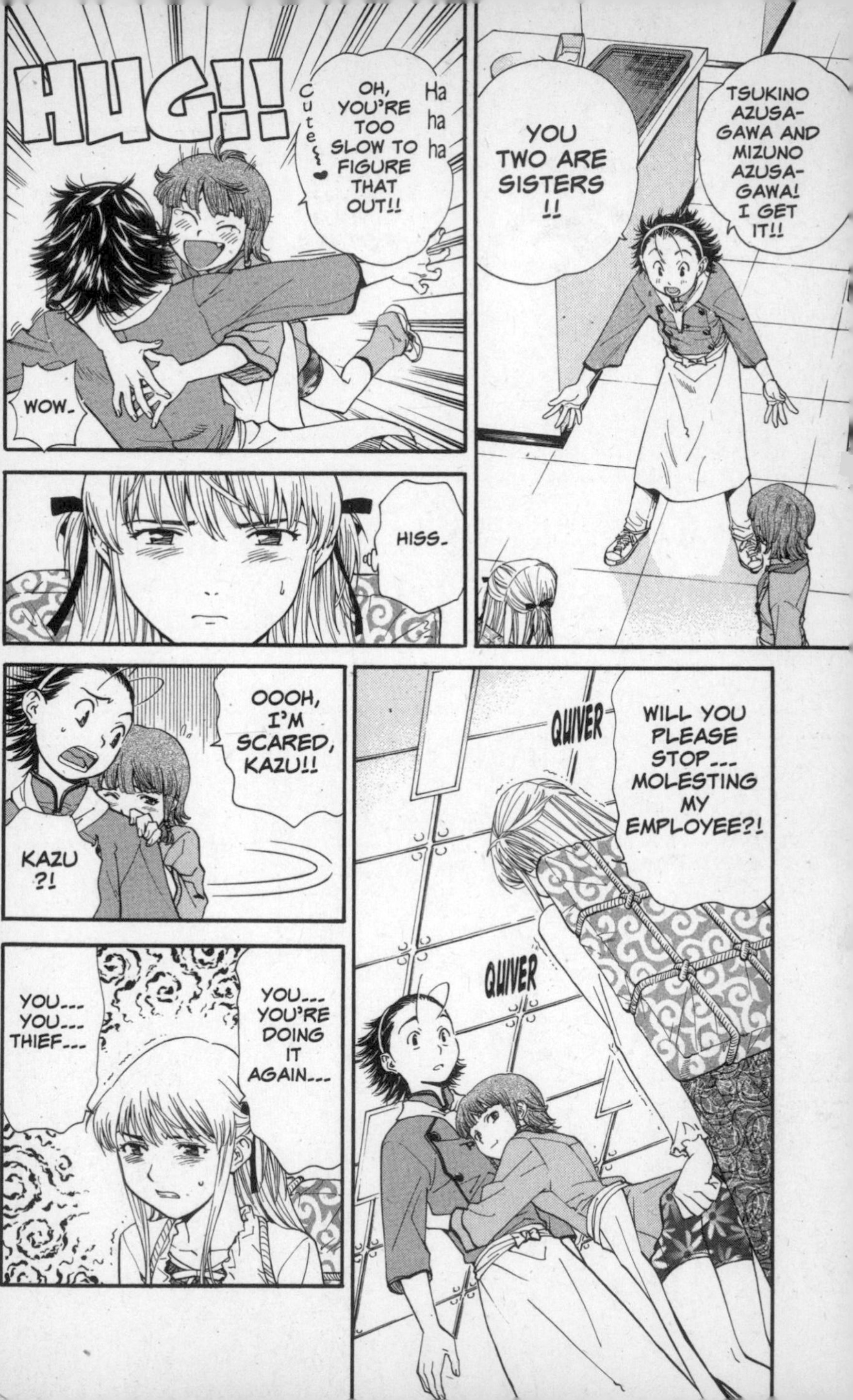
TSUKINO AZUSA-GAWA AND MIZUNO AZUSA-GAWA! I GET IT!!
YOU TWO ARE SISTERS!!
Ha ha ha
OH, YOU'RE TOO SLOW TO FIGURE THAT OUT!!
Cute~
HUG!!
WOW...
HISS...
WILL YOU PLEASE STOP... MOLESTING MY EMPLOYEE?!
QUIVER
QUIVER
OOOH, I'M SCARED, KAZU!!
KAZU?!
YOU... YOU'RE DOING IT AGAIN...
YOU... YOU... THIEF...

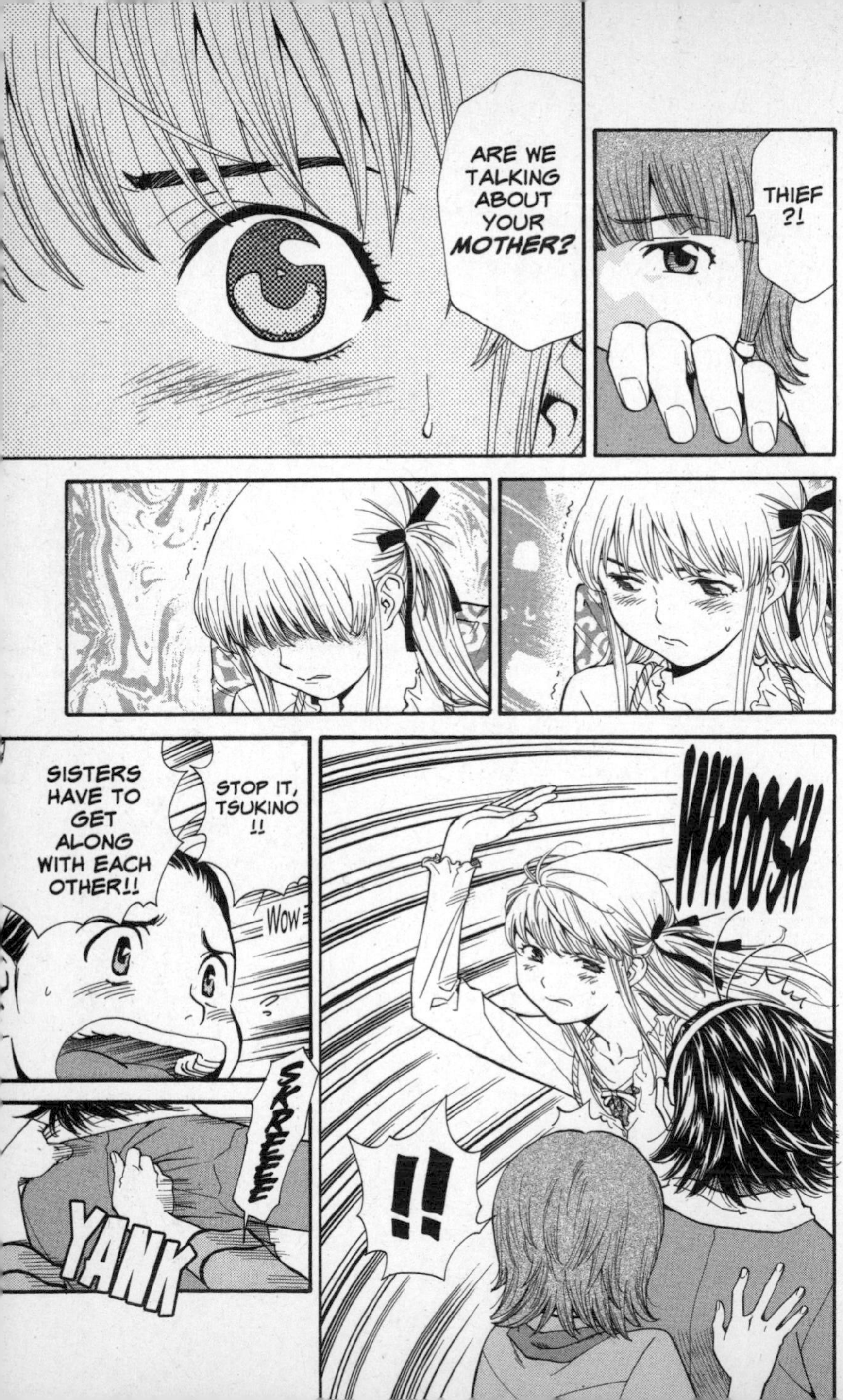
THIEF ?!
ARE WE TALKING ABOUT YOUR MOTHER?
WHOOSH
!!
STOP IT, TSUKINO !!
SISTERS HAVE TO GET ALONG WITH EACH OTHER!!
WOW
SKREEEEE
YANK

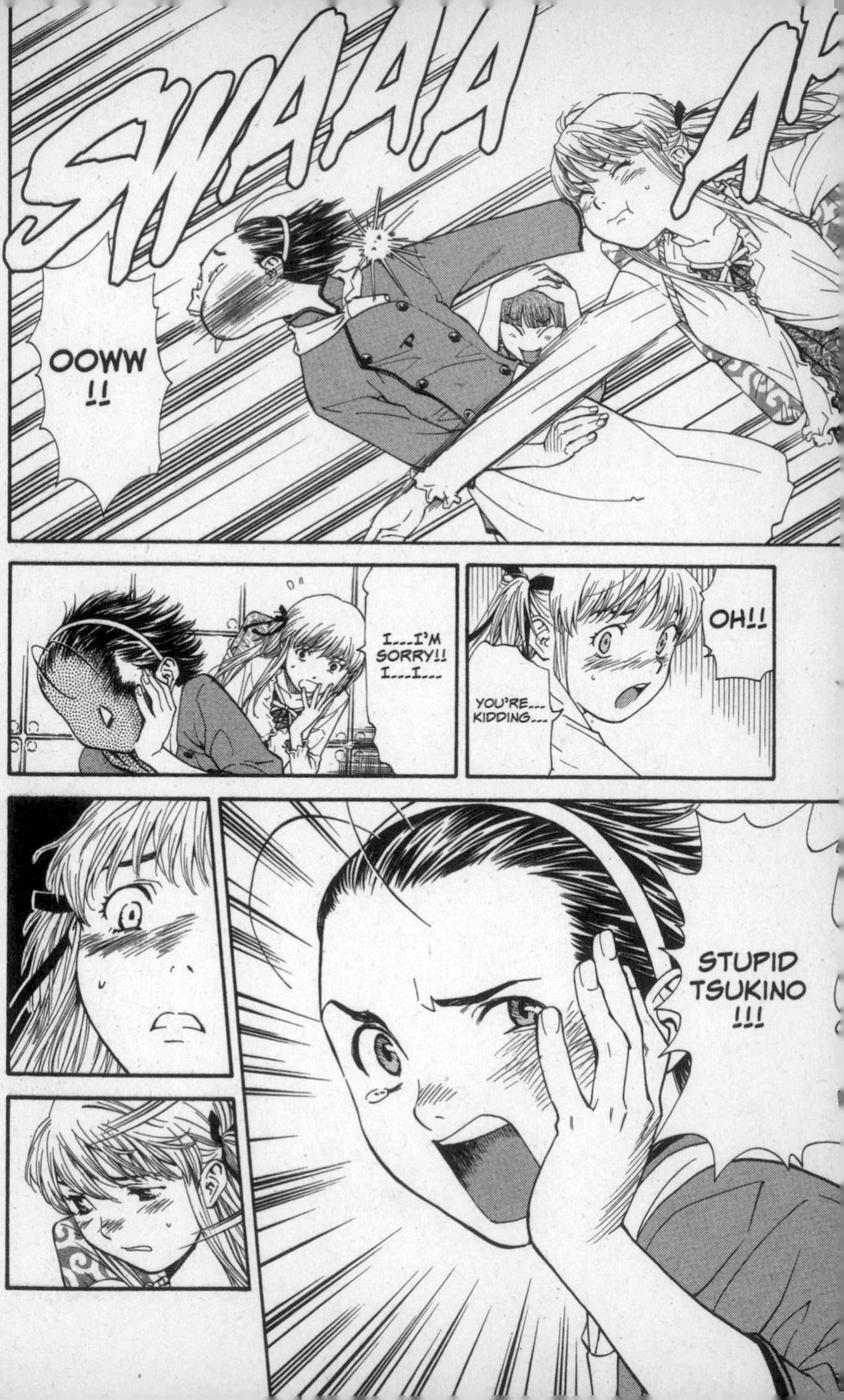
SWAAAA A
OOWW !!
OH!!
YOU'RE... KIDDING...
I...I'M SORRY!! I...I...
STUPID TSUKINO !!!

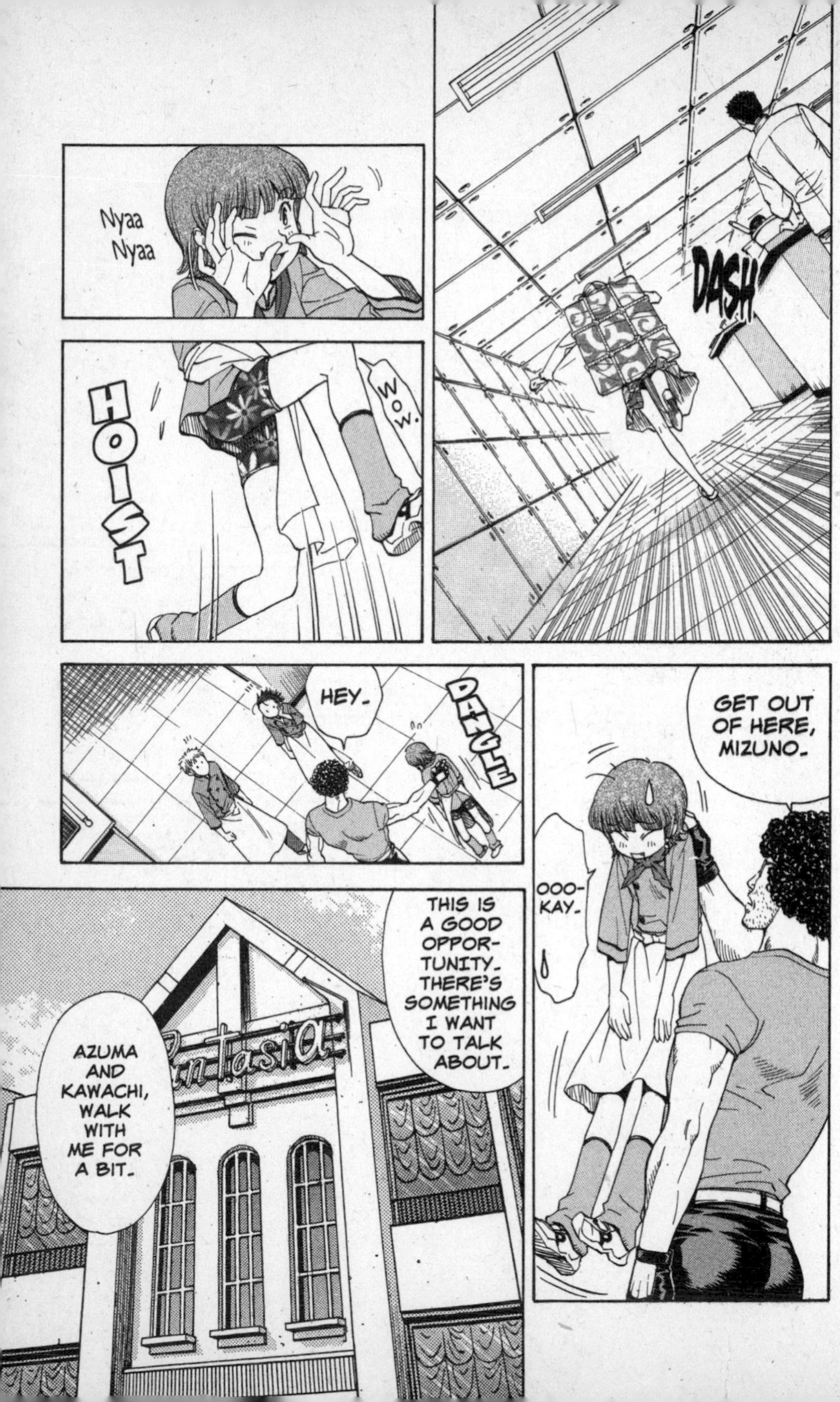
DASH
Nyaa Nyaa
WOW.
HOIST
GET OUT OF HERE, MIZUNO.
OOO-KAY.
HEY.
DANGLE
THIS IS A GOOD OPPOR-TUNITY. THERE'S SOMETHING I WANT TO TALK ABOUT.
AZUMA AND KAWACHI, WALK WITH ME FOR A BIT.

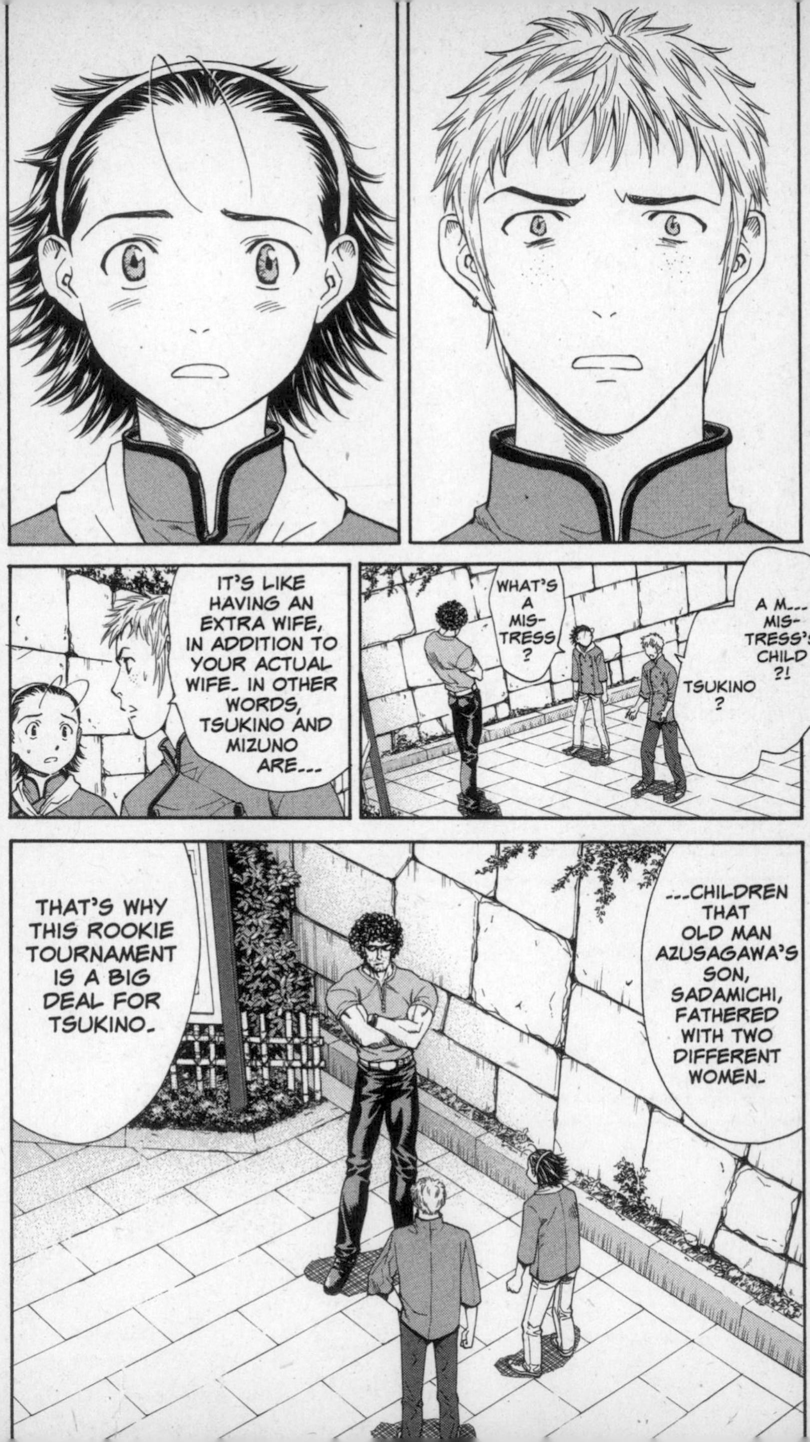
A M... MIS-TRESS'S CHILD ?!
TSUKINO ?
WHAT'S A MIS-TRESS ?
IT'S LIKE HAVING AN EXTRA WIFE, IN ADDITION TO YOUR ACTUAL WIFE. IN OTHER WORDS, TSUKINO AND MIZUNO ARE...
...CHILDREN THAT OLD MAN AZUSAGAWA'S SON, SADAMICHI, FATHERED WITH TWO DIFFERENT WOMEN.
THAT'S WHY THIS ROOKIE TOURNAMENT IS A BIG DEAL FOR TSUKINO.

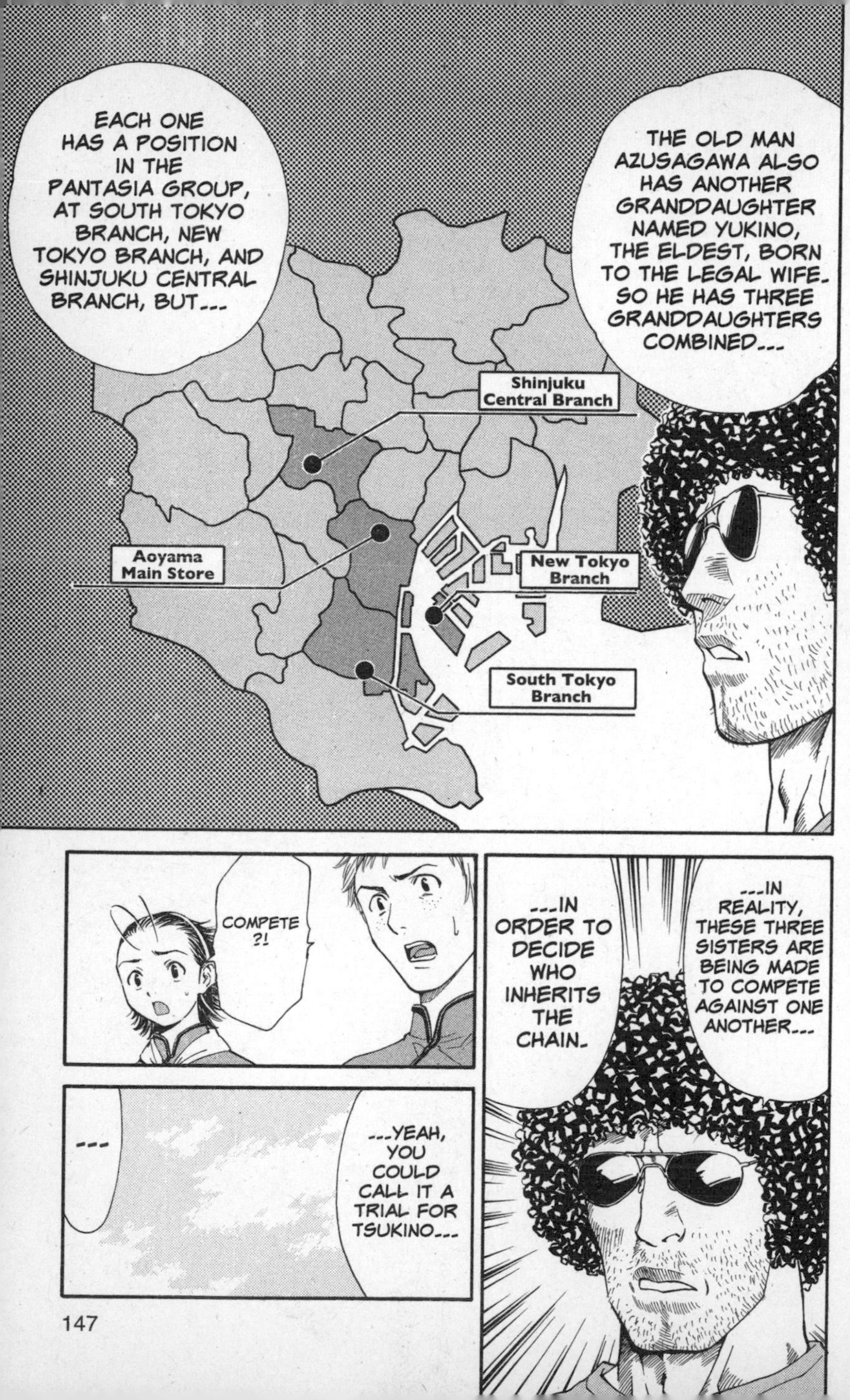
THE OLD MAN AZUSAGAWA ALSO HAS ANOTHER GRANDDAUGHTER NAMED YUKINO, THE ELDEST, BORN TO THE LEGAL WIFE. SO HE HAS THREE GRANDDAUGHTERS COMBINED...
EACH ONE HAS A POSITION IN THE PANTASIA GROUP, AT SOUTH TOKYO BRANCH, NEW TOKYO BRANCH, AND SHINJUKU CENTRAL BRANCH, BUT...
Shinjuku Central Branch
New Tokyo Branch
Aoyama Main Store
South Tokyo Branch
...IN REALITY, THESE THREE SISTERS ARE BEING MADE TO COMPETE AGAINST ONE ANOTHER...
...IN ORDER TO DECIDE WHO INHERITS THE CHAIN.
COMPETE ?!
...YEAH, YOU COULD CALL IT A TRIAL FOR TSUKINO...
...

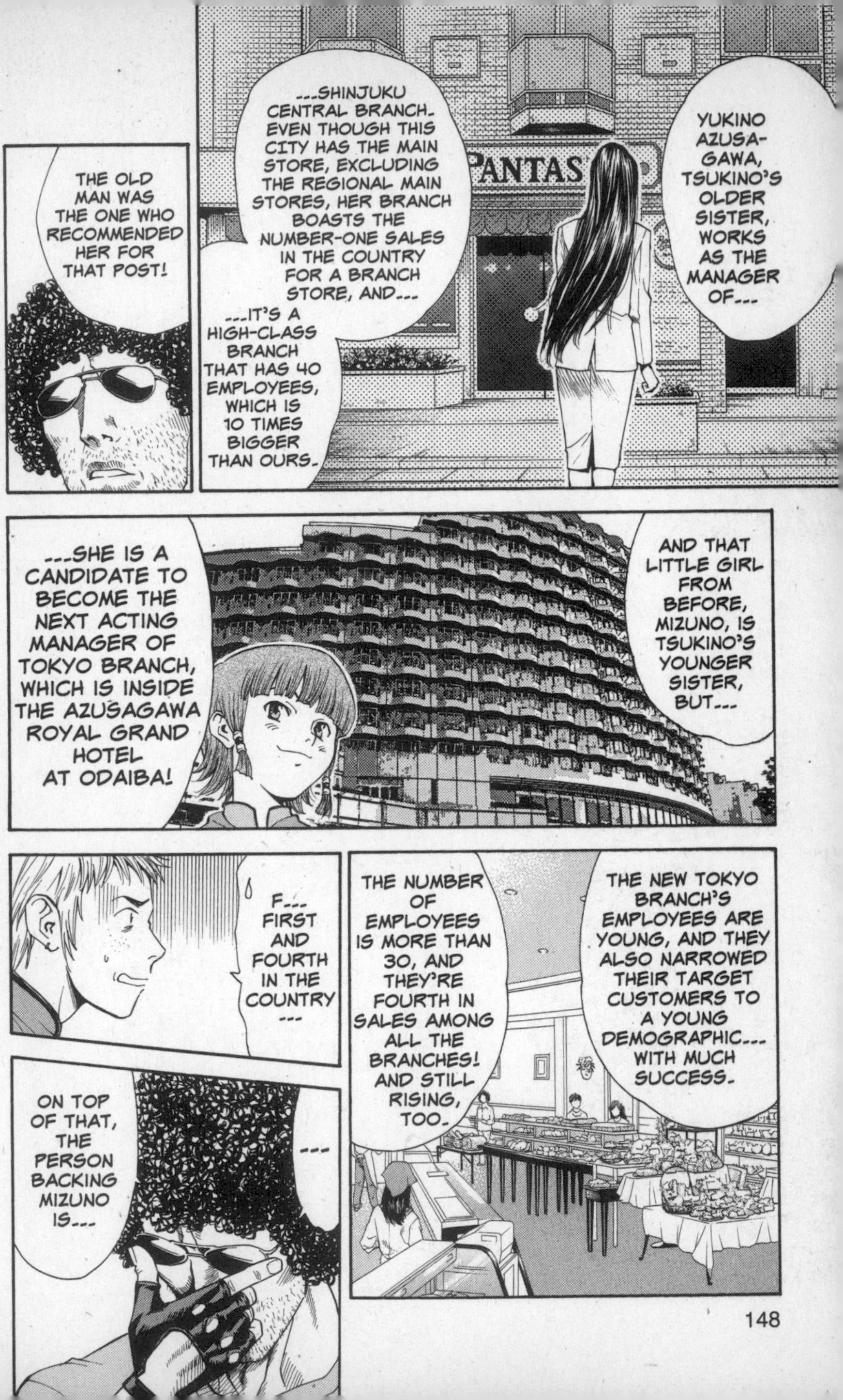
YUKINO AZUSAGAWA, TSUKINO'S OLDER SISTER, WORKS AS THE MANAGER OF---
---SHINJUKU CENTRAL BRANCH. EVEN THOUGH THIS CITY HAS THE MAIN STORE, EXCLUDING THE REGIONAL MAIN STORES, HER BRANCH BOASTS THE NUMBER-ONE SALES IN THE COUNTRY FOR A BRANCH STORE, AND---
---IT'S A HIGH-CLASS BRANCH THAT HAS 40 EMPLOYEES, WHICH IS 10 TIMES BIGGER THAN OURS.
PANTAS
THE OLD MAN WAS THE ONE WHO RECOMMENDED HER FOR THAT POST!
AND THAT LITTLE GIRL FROM BEFORE, MIZUNO, IS TSUKINO'S YOUNGER SISTER, BUT---
---SHE IS A CANDIDATE TO BECOME THE NEXT ACTING MANAGER OF TOKYO BRANCH, WHICH IS INSIDE THE AZUSAGAWA ROYAL GRAND HOTEL AT ODAIBA!
THE NEW TOKYO BRANCH'S EMPLOYEES ARE YOUNG, AND THEY ALSO NARROWED THEIR TARGET CUSTOMERS TO A YOUNG DEMOGRAPHIC--- WITH MUCH SUCCESS.
THE NUMBER OF EMPLOYEES IS MORE THAN 30, AND THEY'RE FOURTH IN SALES AMONG ALL THE BRANCHES! AND STILL RISING, TOO.
F--- FIRST AND FOURTH IN THE COUNTRY ---

ON TOP OF THAT, THE PERSON BACKING MIZUNO IS---

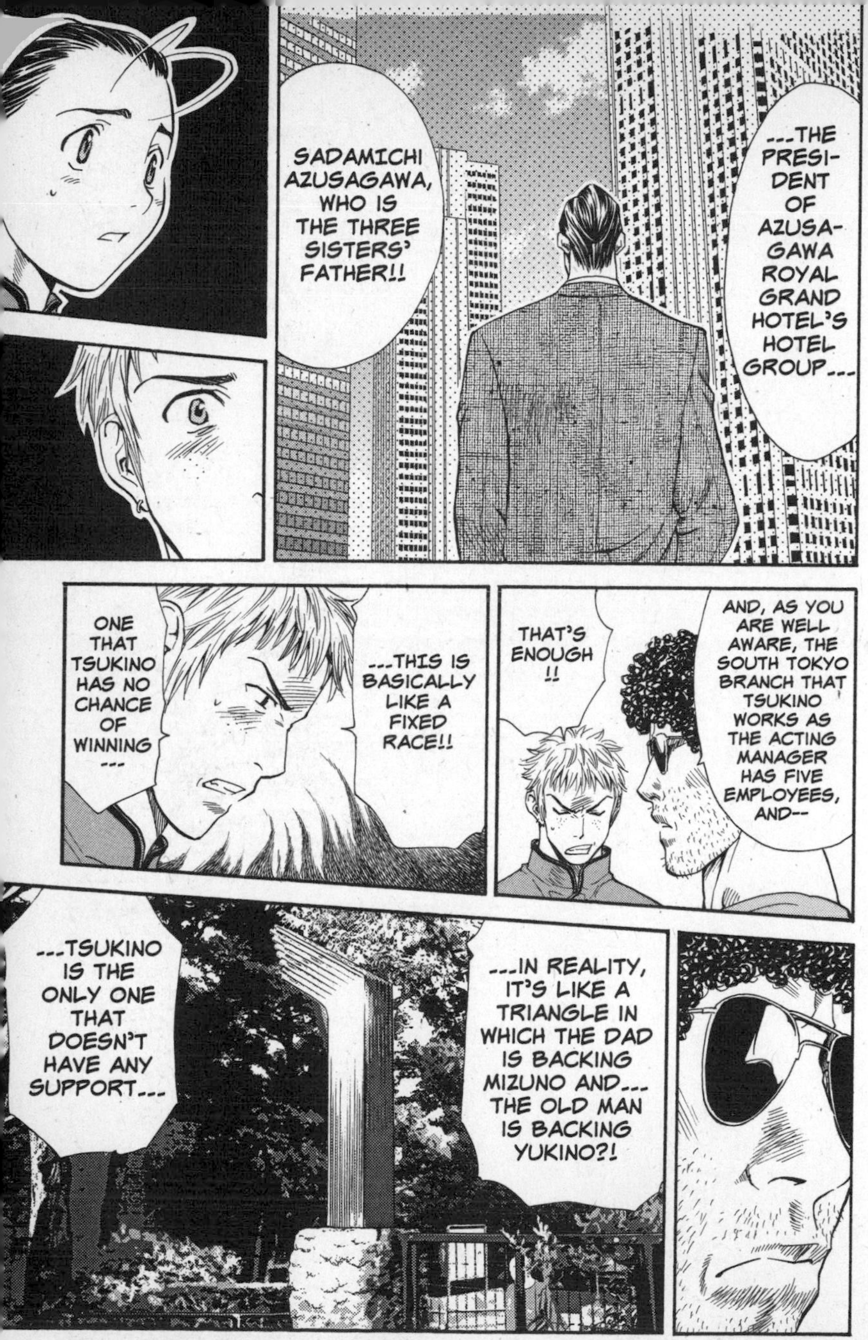
---THE PRESIDENT OF AZUSAGAWA ROYAL GRAND HOTEL'S HOTEL GROUP---
SADAMICHI AZUSAGAWA, WHO IS THE THREE SISTERS' FATHER!!
AND, AS YOU ARE WELL AWARE, THE SOUTH TOKYO BRANCH THAT TSUKINO WORKS AS THE ACTING MANAGER HAS FIVE EMPLOYEES, AND--
THAT'S ENOUGH!!
---THIS IS BASICALLY LIKE A FIXED RACE!!
ONE THAT TSUKINO HAS NO CHANCE OF WINNING---
---IN REALITY, IT'S LIKE A TRIANGLE IN WHICH THE DAD IS BACKING MIZUNO AND--- THE OLD MAN IS BACKING YUKINO?!
---TSUKINO IS THE ONLY ONE THAT DOESN'T HAVE ANY SUPPORT---

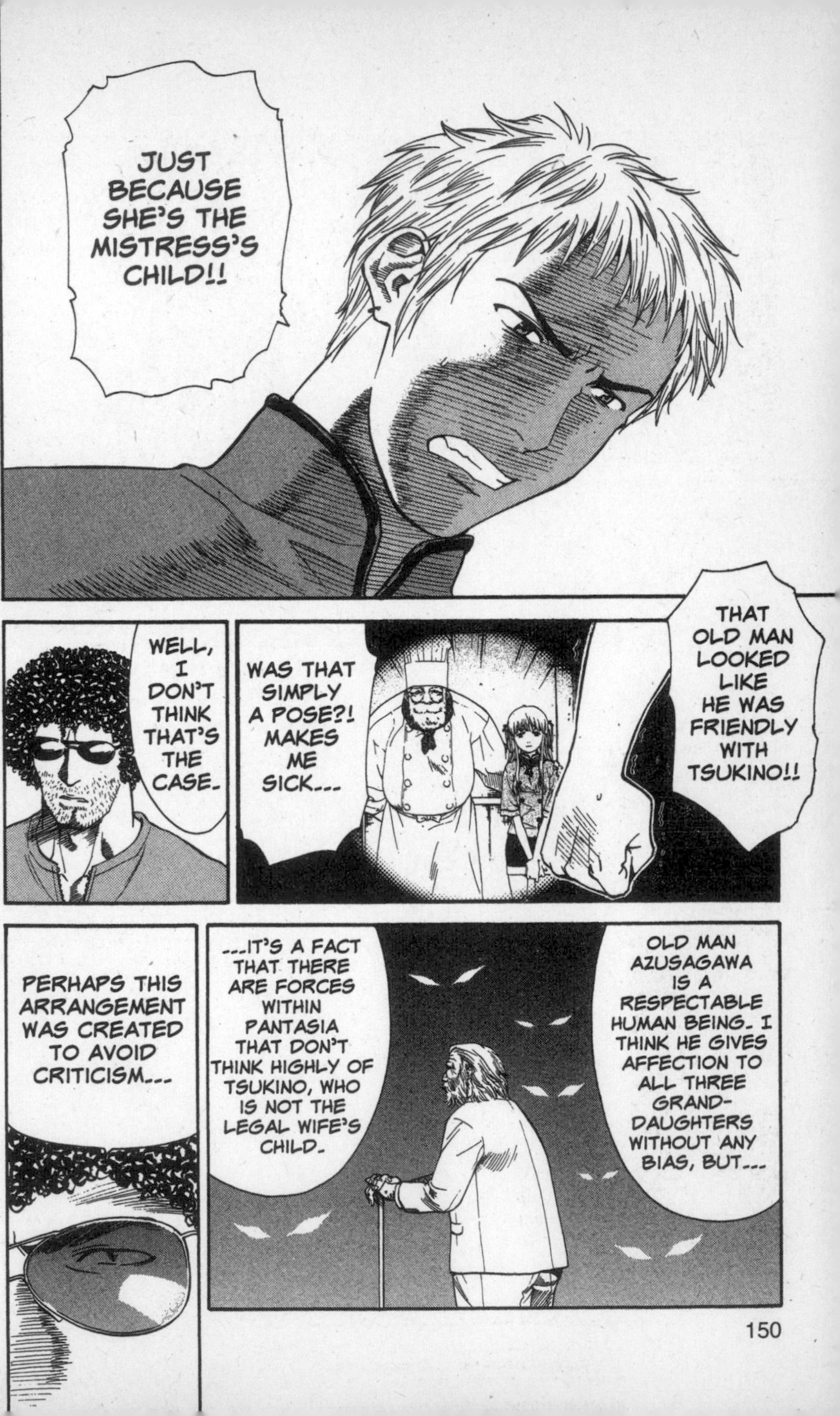
JUST BECAUSE SHE'S THE MISTRESS'S CHILD!!
THAT OLD MAN LOOKED LIKE HE WAS FRIENDLY WITH TSUKINO!!
WAS THAT SIMPLY A POSE?! MAKES ME SICK...
WELL, I DON'T THINK THAT'S THE CASE.
OLD MAN AZUSAGAWA IS A RESPECTABLE HUMAN BEING. I THINK HE GIVES AFFECTION TO ALL THREE GRAND-DAUGHTERS WITHOUT ANY BIAS, BUT...
...IT'S A FACT THAT THERE ARE FORCES WITHIN PANTASIA THAT DON'T THINK HIGHLY OF TSUKINO, WHO IS NOT THE LEGAL WIFE'S CHILD.
PERHAPS THIS ARRANGEMENT WAS CREATED TO AVOID CRITICISM...

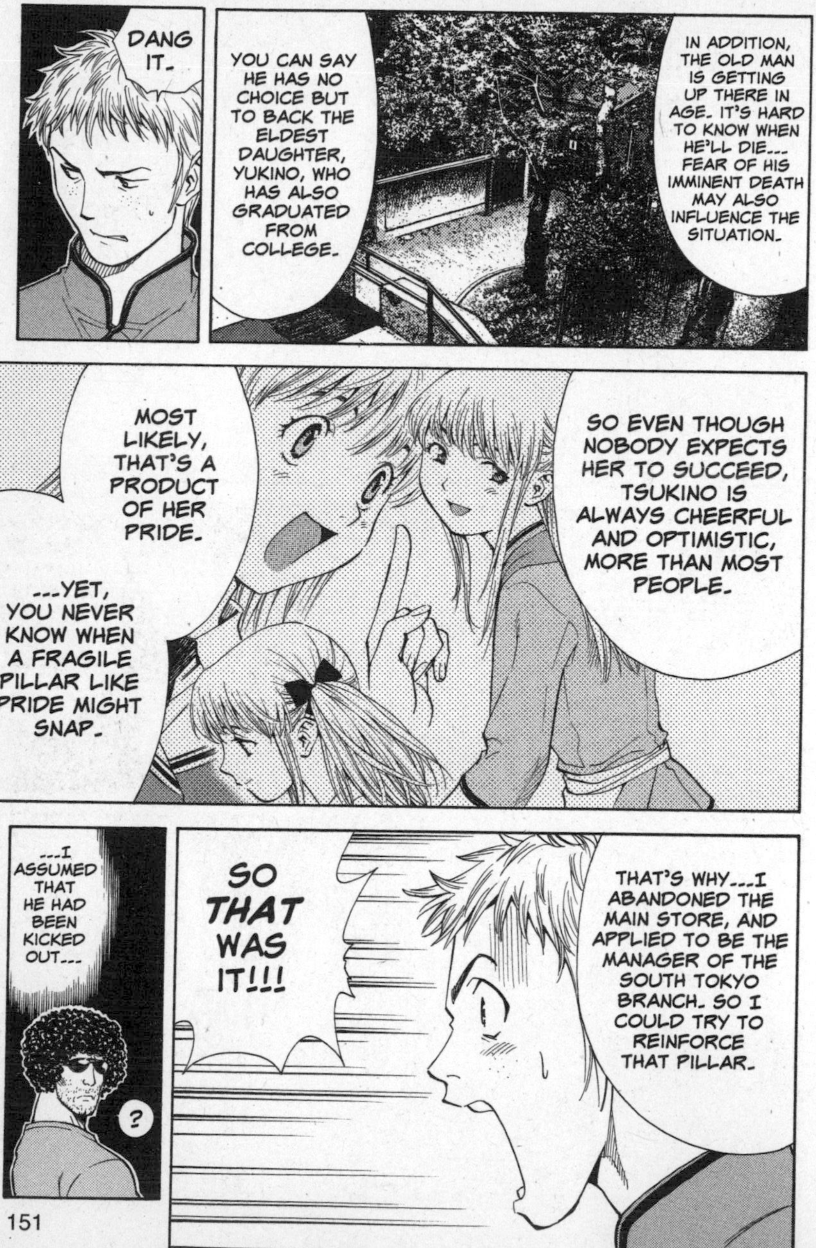
IN ADDITION, THE OLD MAN IS GETTING UP THERE IN AGE. IT'S HARD TO KNOW WHEN HE'LL DIE... FEAR OF HIS IMMINENT DEATH MAY ALSO INFLUENCE THE SITUATION.
YOU CAN SAY HE HAS NO CHOICE BUT TO BACK THE ELDEST DAUGHTER, YUKINO, WHO HAS ALSO GRADUATED FROM COLLEGE.
DANG IT.
SO EVEN THOUGH NOBODY EXPECTS HER TO SUCCEED, TSUKINO IS ALWAYS CHEERFUL AND OPTIMISTIC, MORE THAN MOST PEOPLE.
MOST LIKELY, THAT'S A PRODUCT OF HER PRIDE.
...YET, YOU NEVER KNOW WHEN A FRAGILE PILLAR LIKE PRIDE MIGHT SNAP.
THAT'S WHY...I ABANDONED THE MAIN STORE, AND APPLIED TO BE THE MANAGER OF THE SOUTH TOKYO BRANCH. SO I COULD TRY TO REINFORCE THAT PILLAR.
SO THAT WAS IT!!!
...I ASSUMED THAT HE HAD BEEN KICKED OUT...
?

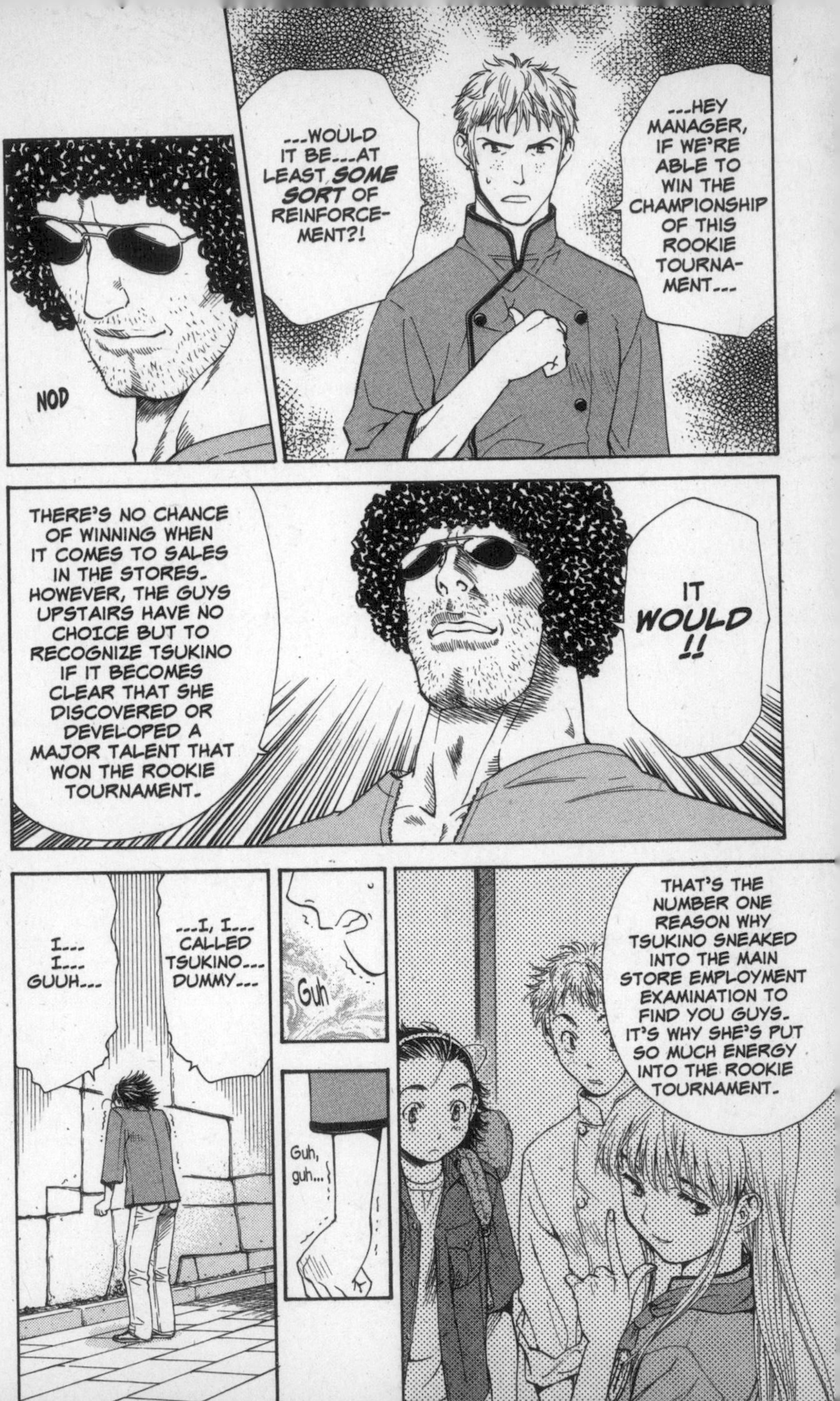
...HEY MANAGER, IF WE'RE ABLE TO WIN THE CHAMPIONSHIP OF THIS ROOKIE TOURNAMENT...
...WOULD IT BE...AT LEAST SOME SORT OF REINFORCEMENT?!
NOD
IT WOULD!!
THERE'S NO CHANCE OF WINNING WHEN IT COMES TO SALES IN THE STORES. HOWEVER, THE GUYS UPSTAIRS HAVE NO CHOICE BUT TO RECOGNIZE TSUKINO IF IT BECOMES CLEAR THAT SHE DISCOVERED OR DEVELOPED A MAJOR TALENT THAT WON THE ROOKIE TOURNAMENT.
THAT'S THE NUMBER ONE REASON WHY TSUKINO SNEAKED INTO THE MAIN STORE EMPLOYMENT EXAMINATION TO FIND YOU GUYS. IT'S WHY SHE'S PUT SO MUCH ENERGY INTO THE ROOKIE TOURNAMENT.
Guh
Guh, guh...
...I, I... CALLED TSUKINO... DUMMY...
I... I... GUUH...

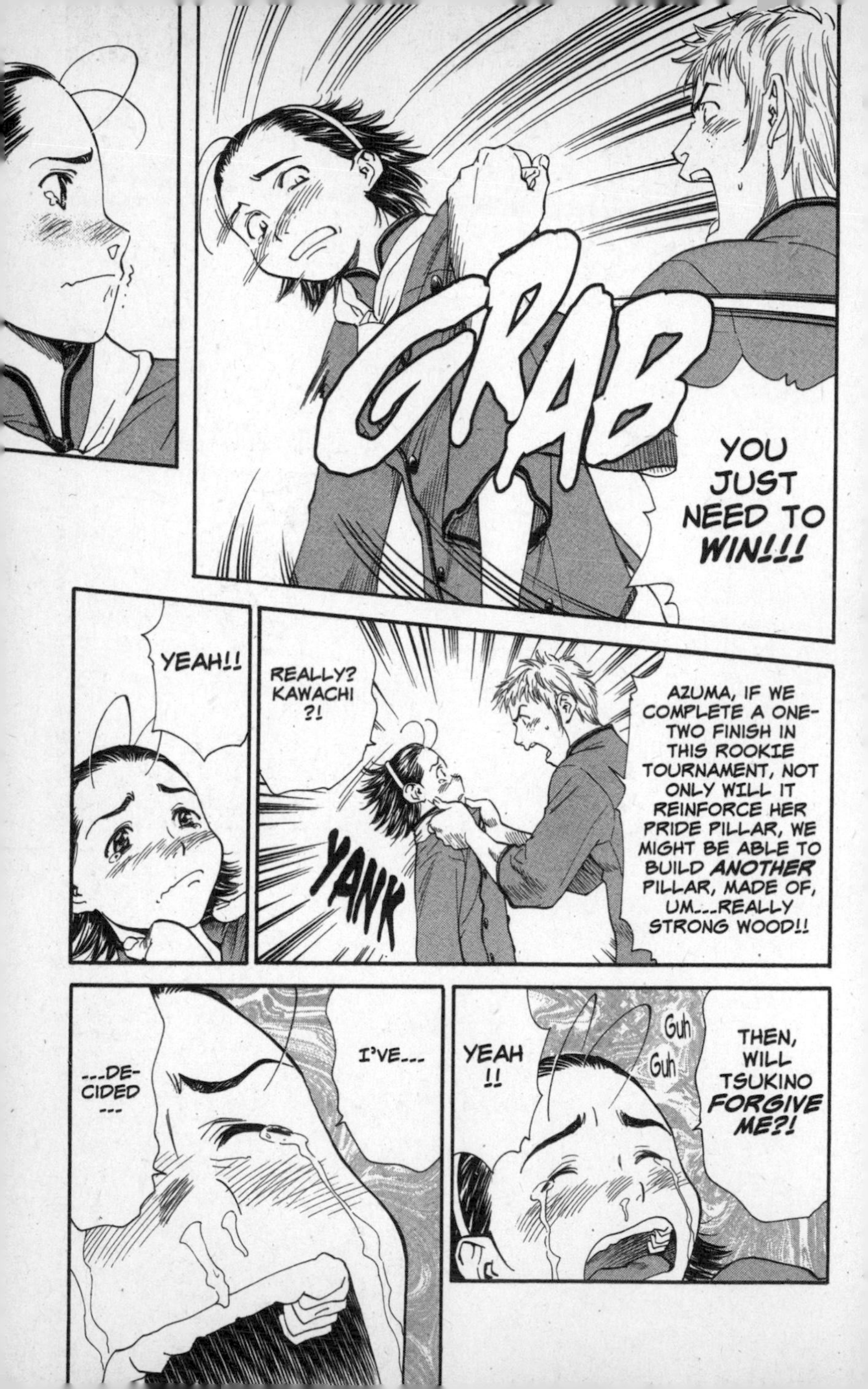
GRAB
YOU JUST NEED TO WIN!!!
AZUMA, IF WE COMPLETE A ONE-TWO FINISH IN THIS ROOKIE TOURNAMENT, NOT ONLY WILL IT REINFORCE HER PRIDE PILLAR, WE MIGHT BE ABLE TO BUILD ANOTHER PILLAR, MADE OF, UM...REALLY STRONG WOOD!!
REALLY? KAWACHI ?!
YANK
YEAH!!
THEN, WILL TSUKINO FORGIVE ME?!
Guh
Guh
YEAH !!
I'VE...
...DE-CIDED...

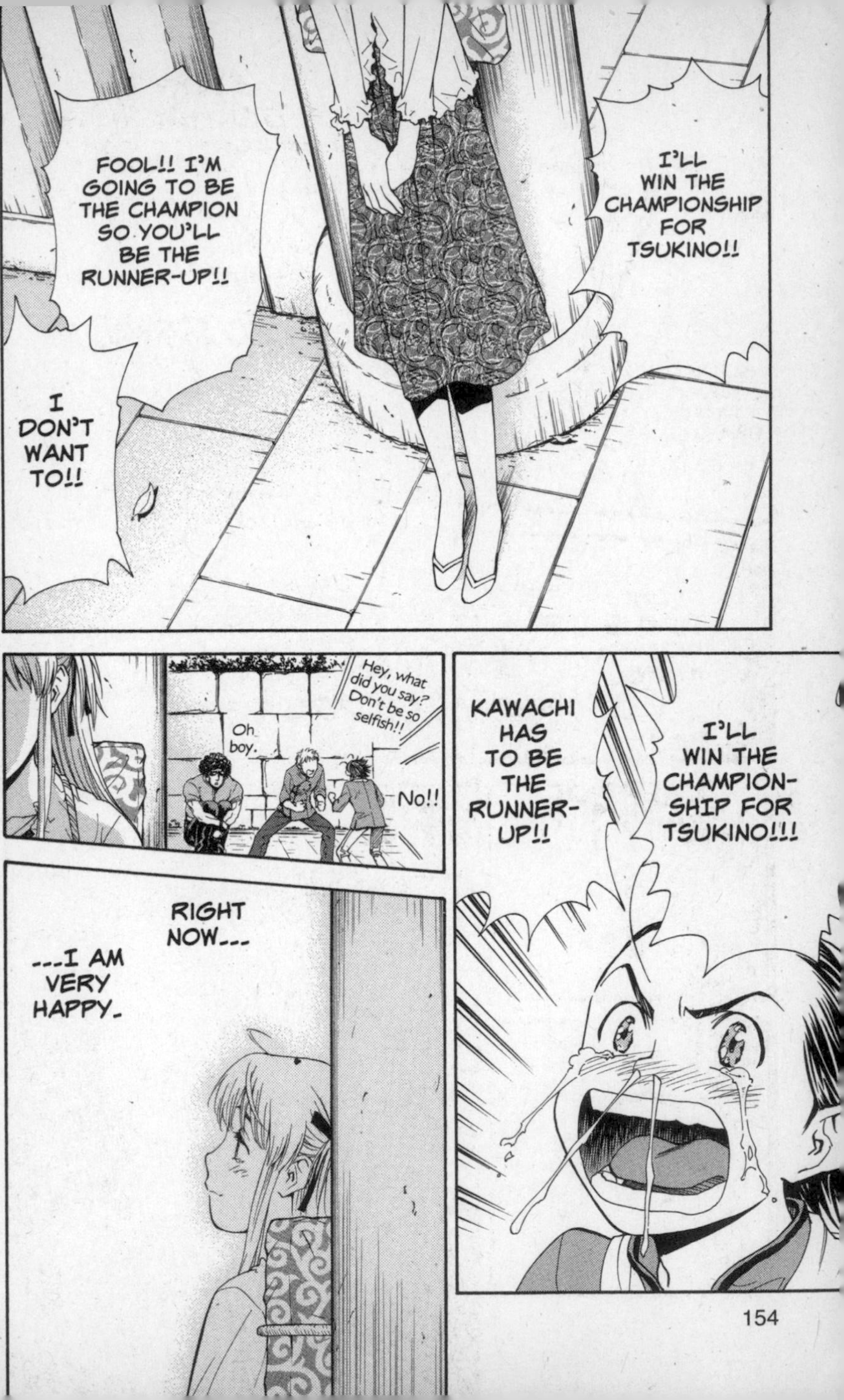
I'LL WIN THE CHAMPIONSHIP FOR TSUKINO!!
FOOL!! I'M GOING TO BE THE CHAMPION SO YOU'LL BE THE RUNNER-UP!!
I DON'T WANT TO!!
I'LL WIN THE CHAMPIONSHIP FOR TSUKINO!!!
KAWACHI HAS TO BE THE RUNNER-UP!!
Hey, what did you say? Don't be so selfish!!
No!!
Oh boy.
RIGHT NOW...
...I AM VERY HAPPY.

Story 24: A Difficult Subject

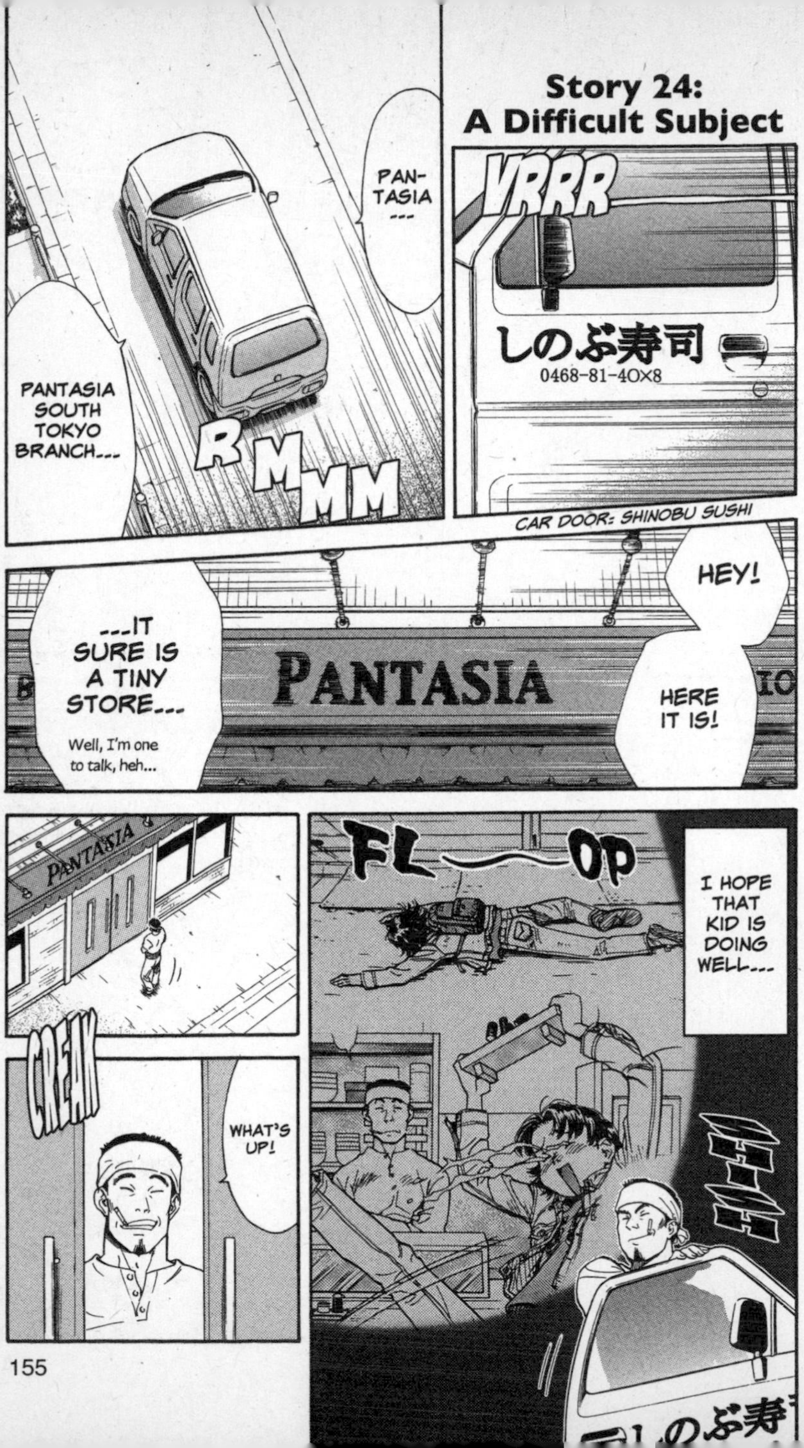
VRRR
しのぶ寿司
0468-81-40×8
CAR DOOR: SHINOBU SUSHI
PAN-TASIA---
PANTASIA SOUTH TOKYO BRANCH---
RMMM
HEY!
HERE IT IS!
PANTASIA
---IT SURE IS A TINY STORE---
Well, I'm one to talk, heh...
FL—OP
I HOPE THAT KID IS DOING WELL---
しのぶ寿
PANTASIA
CREAK
WHAT'S UP!

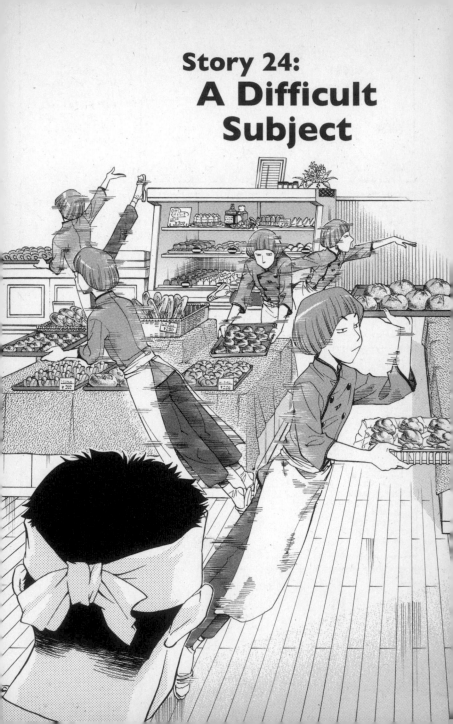

Story 24: A Difficult Subject

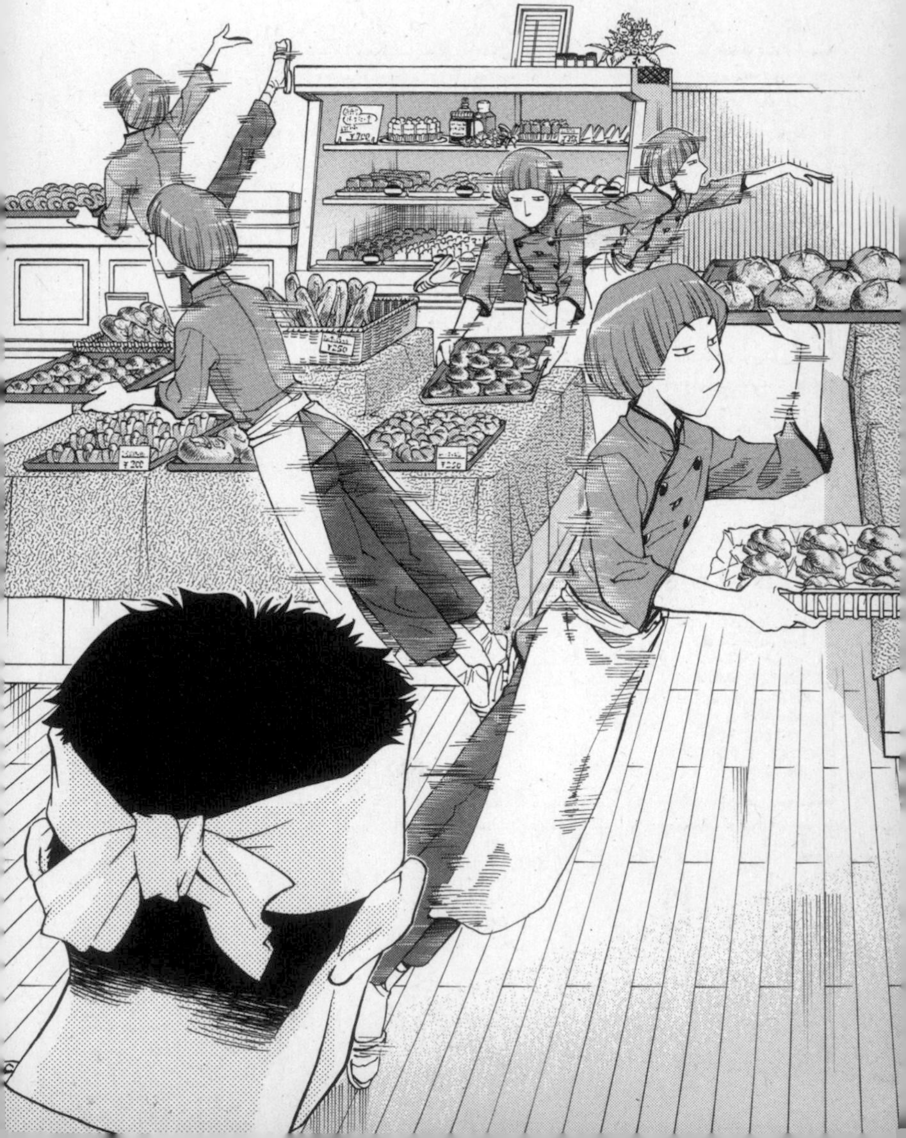

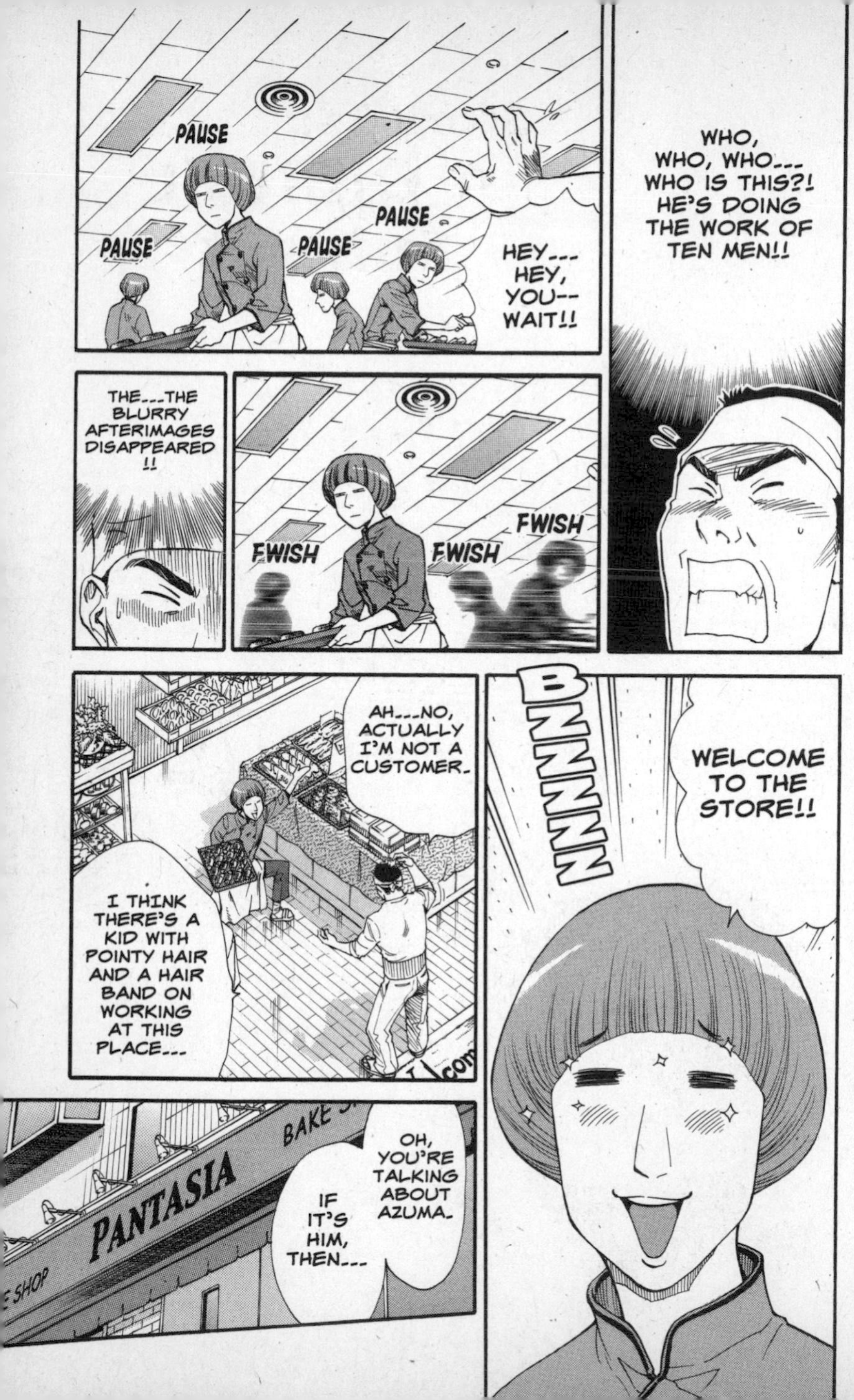
WHO, WHO, WHO... WHO IS THIS?! HE'S DOING THE WORK OF TEN MEN!!
PAUSE
HEY... HEY, YOU-- WAIT!!
PAUSE
PAUSE
PAUSE
FWISH
FWISH
FWISH
THE...THE BLURRY AFTERIMAGES DISAPPEARED!!
BNNNNN
WELCOME TO THE STORE!!
AH...NO, ACTUALLY I'M NOT A CUSTOMER.
I THINK THERE'S A KID WITH POINTY HAIR AND A HAIR BAND ON WORKING AT THIS PLACE...
OH, YOU'RE TALKING ABOUT AZUMA.
IF IT'S HIM, THEN...
PANTASIA

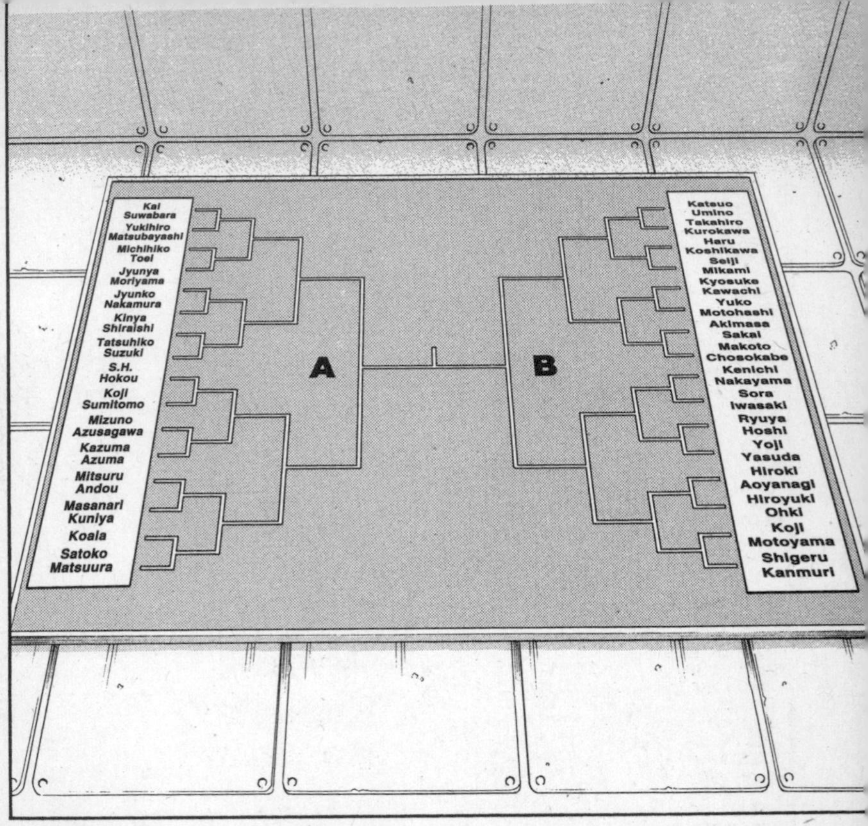
Katsuo Umino
Takahiro Kurokawa
Haru Koshikawa
Seiji Mikami
Kyosuke Kawachi
Yuko Motohashi
Akimasa Sakai
Makoto Chosokabe
Kenichi Nakayama
Sora Iwasaki
Ryuya Hoshi
Yoji Yasuda
Hiroki Aoyanagi
Hiroyuki Ohki
Koji Motoyama
Shigeru Kanmuri
B
A
Kai Suwabara
Yukihiro Matsubayashi
Michihiko Toei
Jyunya Moriyama
Jyunko Nakamura
Kinya Shiraishi
Tatsuhiko Suzuki
S.H. Hokou
Koji Sumitomo
Mizuno Azusagawa
Kazuma Azuma
Mitsuru Andou
Masanari Kuniya
Koala
Satoko Matsuura
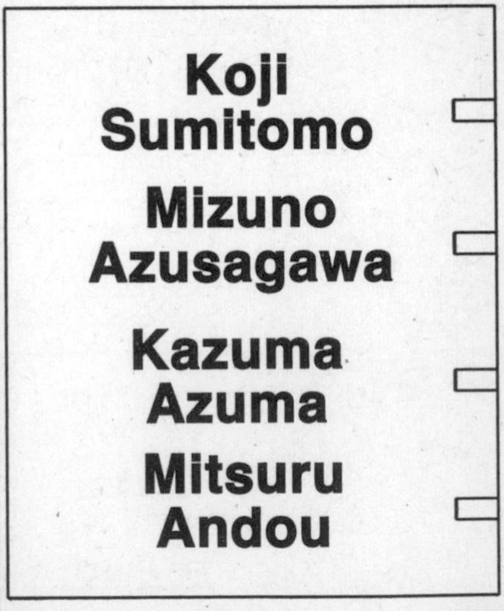
Koji Sumitomo
Mizuno Azusagawa
Kazuma Azuma
Mitsuru Andou
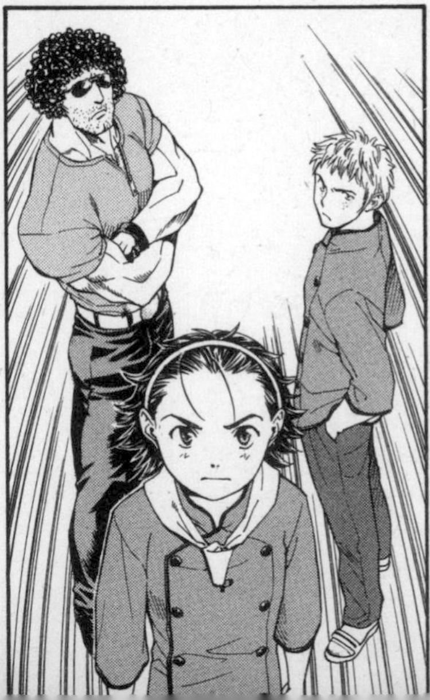

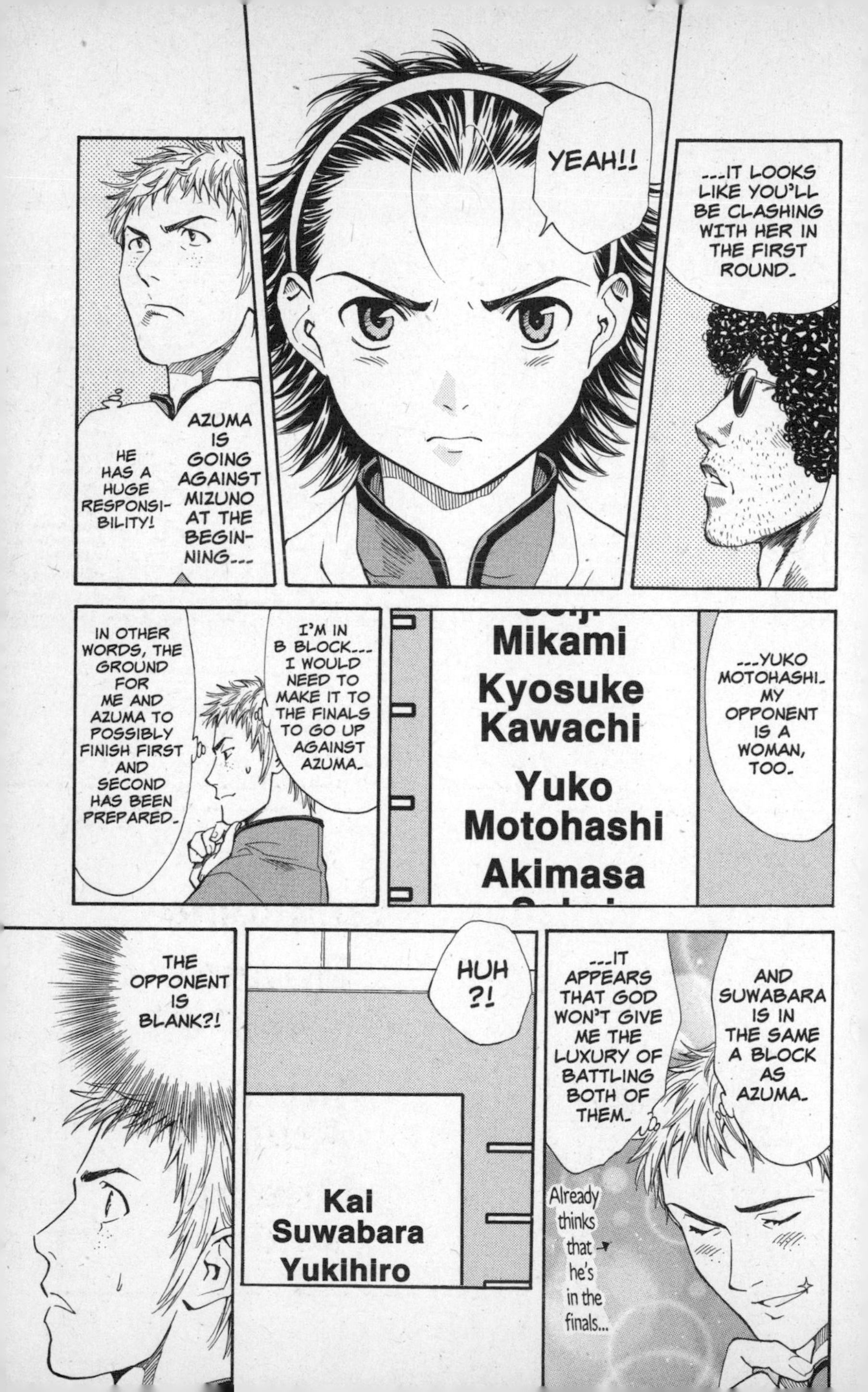
...IT LOOKS LIKE YOU'LL BE CLASHING WITH HER IN THE FIRST ROUND.
YEAH!!
AZUMA IS GOING AGAINST MIZUNO AT THE BEGINNING...
HE HAS A HUGE RESPONSI-BILITY!
...YUKO MOTOHASHI. MY OPPONENT IS A WOMAN, TOO.
Mikami
Kyosuke Kawachi
Yuko Motohashi
Akimasa
I'M IN B BLOCK... I WOULD NEED TO MAKE IT TO THE FINALS TO GO UP AGAINST AZUMA.
IN OTHER WORDS, THE GROUND FOR ME AND AZUMA TO POSSIBLY FINISH FIRST AND SECOND HAS BEEN PREPARED.
AND SUWABARA IS IN THE SAME A BLOCK AS AZUMA.
...IT APPEARS THAT GOD WON'T GIVE ME THE LUXURY OF BATTLING BOTH OF THEM.
Already thinks that he's in the finals...
HUH ?!
Kai
Suwabara
Yukihiro
THE OPPONENT IS BLANK?!

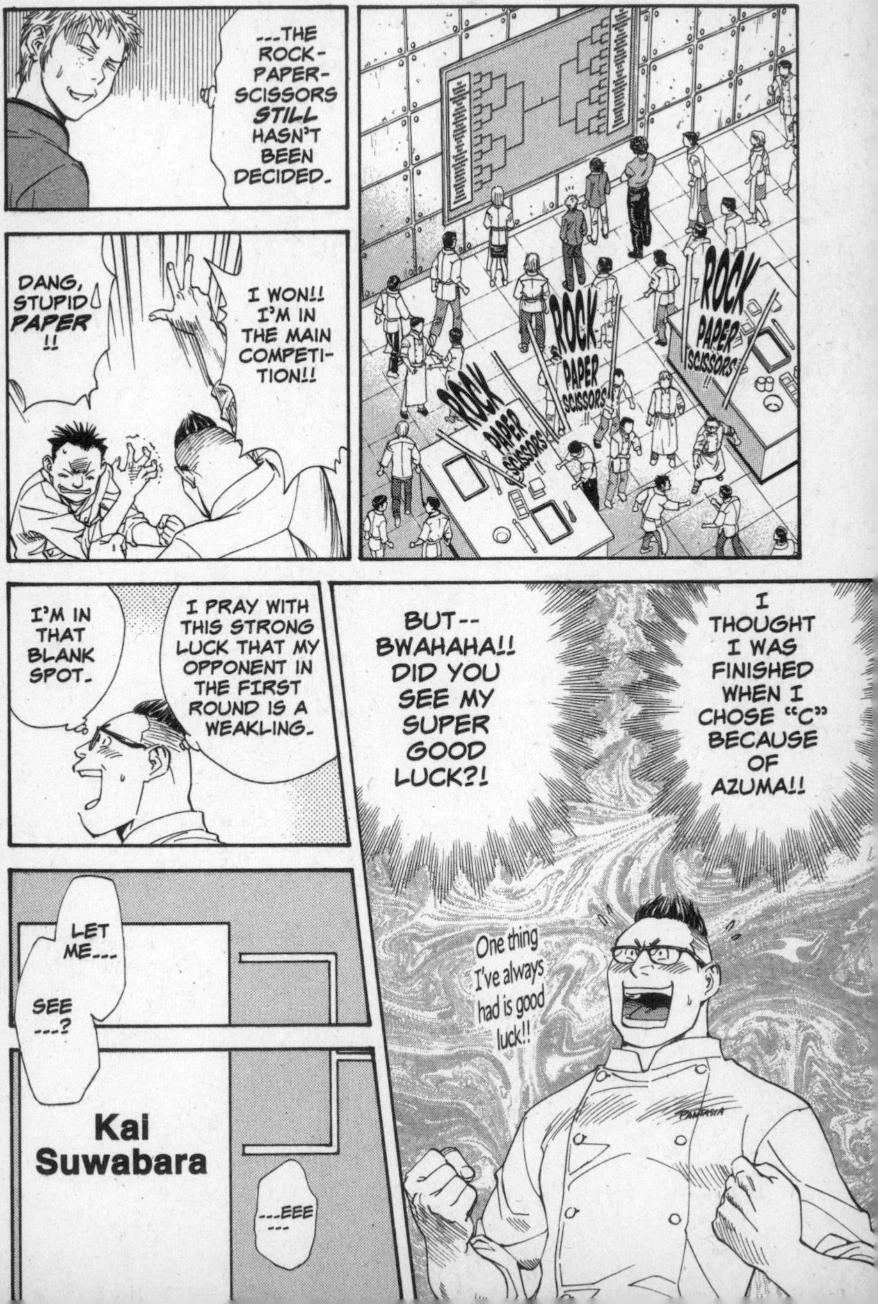
ROCK PAPER SCISSORS !!
ROCK PAPER SCISSORS !!
ROCK PAPER SCISSORS !!
---THE ROCK-PAPER-SCISSORS STILL HASN'T BEEN DECIDED.
I WON!! I'M IN THE MAIN COMPETITION!!
DANG, STUPID PAPER !!
I THOUGHT I WAS FINISHED WHEN I CHOSE "C" BECAUSE OF AZUMA!!
BUT-- BWAHAHA!! DID YOU SEE MY SUPER GOOD LUCK?!
One thing I've always had is good luck!!
I PRAY WITH THIS STRONG LUCK THAT MY OPPONENT IN THE FIRST ROUND IS A WEAKLING.
I'M IN THAT BLANK SPOT.
LET ME---
SEE ---?
Kai Suwabara
---EEE ---

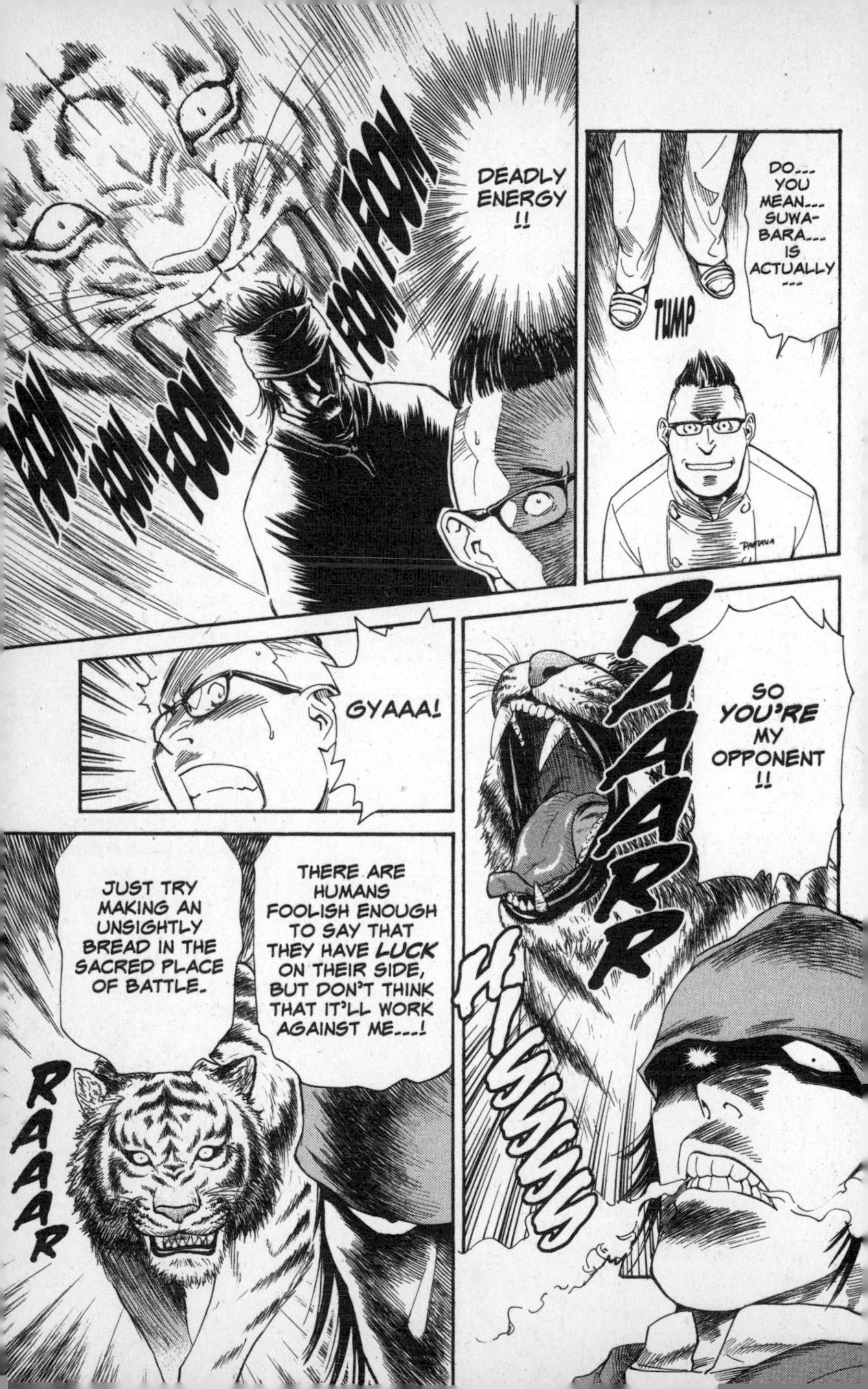
DO... YOU MEAN... SUWA-BARA... IS ACTUALLY ---
TUMP
DEADLY ENERGY !!
FOOM FOOM
FOOM FOOM FOOM
SO YOU'RE MY OPPONENT !!
RAAAARR
GYAAA!
THERE ARE HUMANS FOOLISH ENOUGH TO SAY THAT THEY HAVE LUCK ON THEIR SIDE, BUT DON'T THINK THAT IT'LL WORK AGAINST ME...!
JUST TRY MAKING AN UNSIGHTLY BREAD IN THE SACRED PLACE OF BATTLE.
RAAAR

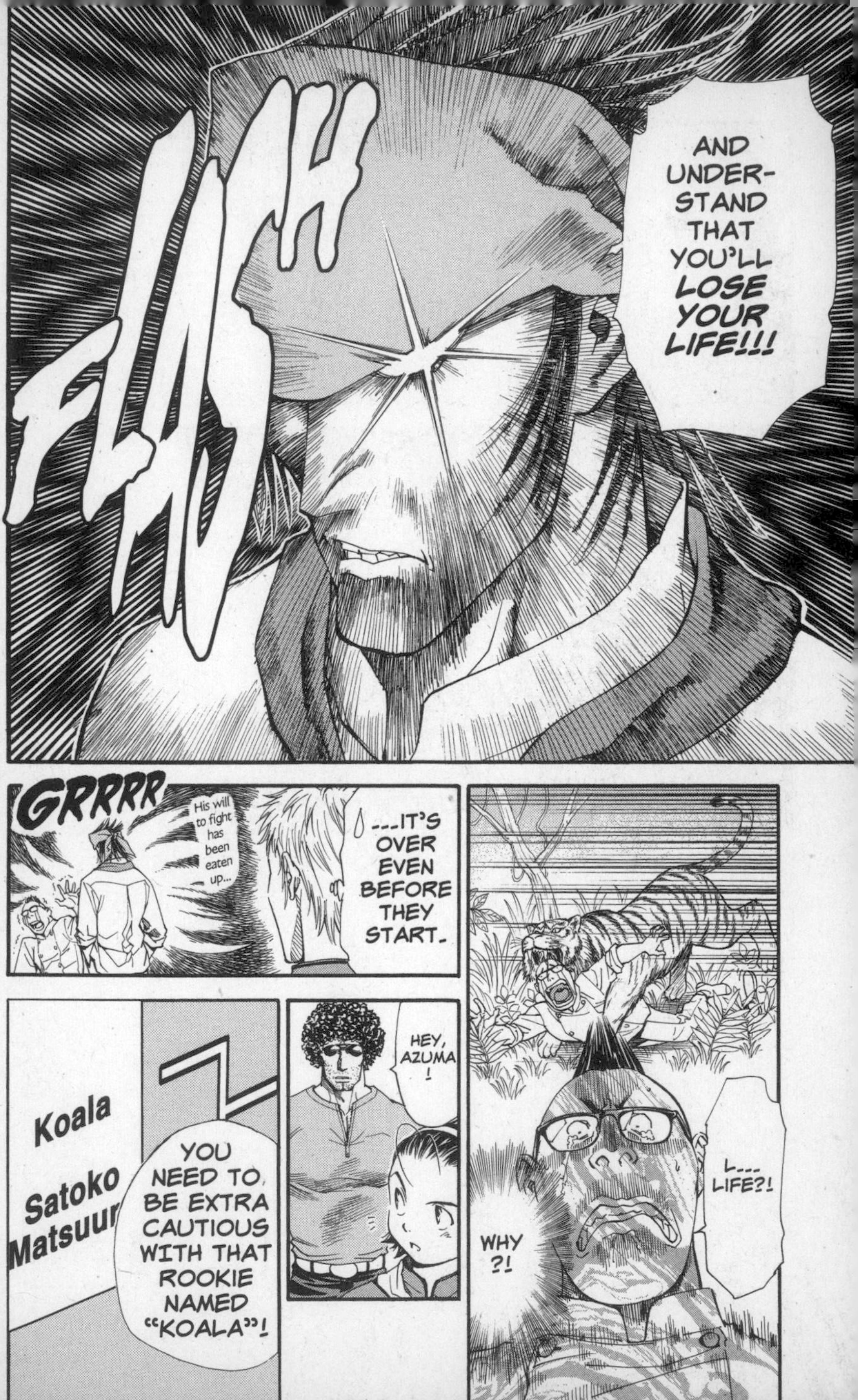
AND UNDER-STAND THAT YOU'LL LOSE YOUR LIFE!!!
FLASH
L... LIFE?!
WHY ?!
...IT'S OVER EVEN BEFORE THEY START.
His will to fight has been eaten up...
GRRRR
HEY, AZUMA!
YOU NEED TO BE EXTRA CAUTIOUS WITH THAT ROOKIE NAMED "KOALA"!
Koala
Satoko Matsuur

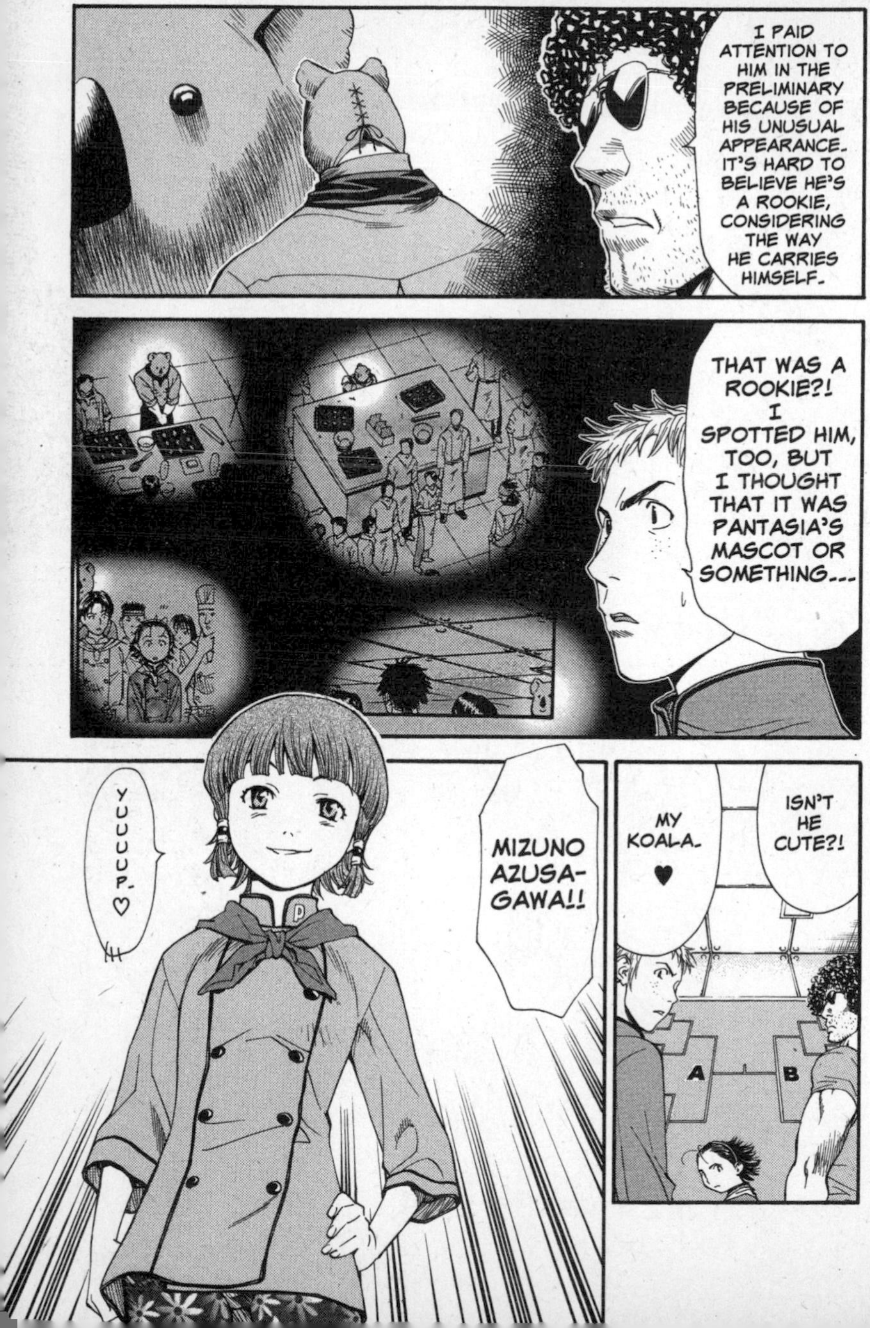
I PAID ATTENTION TO HIM IN THE PRELIMINARY BECAUSE OF HIS UNUSUAL APPEARANCE. IT'S HARD TO BELIEVE HE'S A ROOKIE, CONSIDERING THE WAY HE CARRIES HIMSELF.
THAT WAS A ROOKIE?! I SPOTTED HIM, TOO, BUT I THOUGHT THAT IT WAS PANTASIA'S MASCOT OR SOMETHING...
ISN'T HE CUTE?!
MY KOALA. ♥
A
B
MIZUNO AZUSA-GAWA!!
YUUUUP. ♡

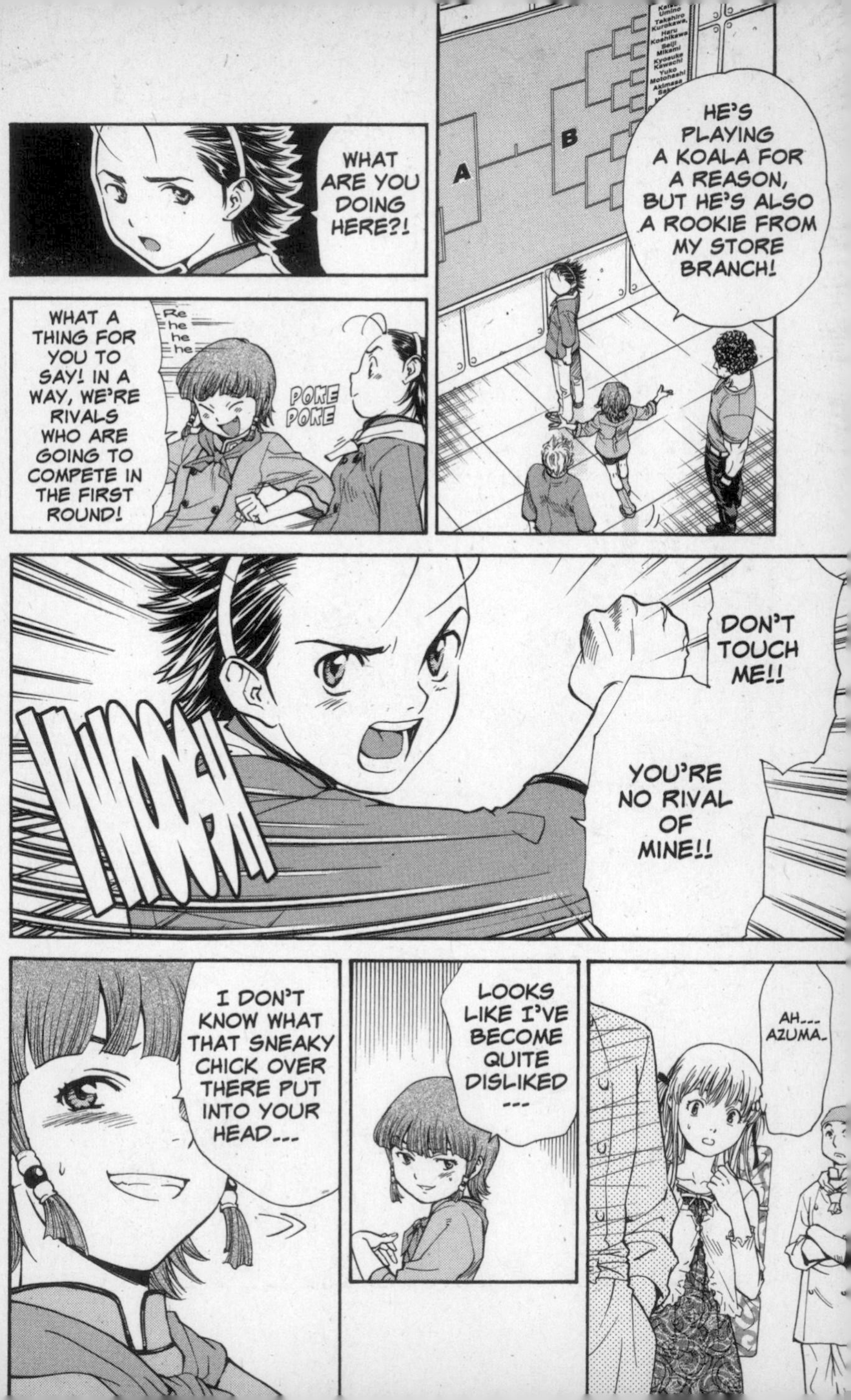
Umino
Takahiro Kurokawa,
Haru Koshikawa
Seiji Mikami
Kyosuke Kawachi
Yuko Motohashi
Akimasa
B
A
HE'S PLAYING A KOALA FOR A REASON, BUT HE'S ALSO A ROOKIE FROM MY STORE BRANCH!
WHAT ARE YOU DOING HERE?!
Re he he he
WHAT A THING FOR YOU TO SAY! IN A WAY, WE'RE RIVALS WHO ARE GOING TO COMPETE IN THE FIRST ROUND!
POKE POKE
DON'T TOUCH ME!!
YOU'RE NO RIVAL OF MINE!!
WHOOSH
AH... AZUMA...
LOOKS LIKE I'VE BECOME QUITE DISLIKED...
I DON'T KNOW WHAT THAT SNEAKY CHICK OVER THERE PUT INTO YOUR HEAD...

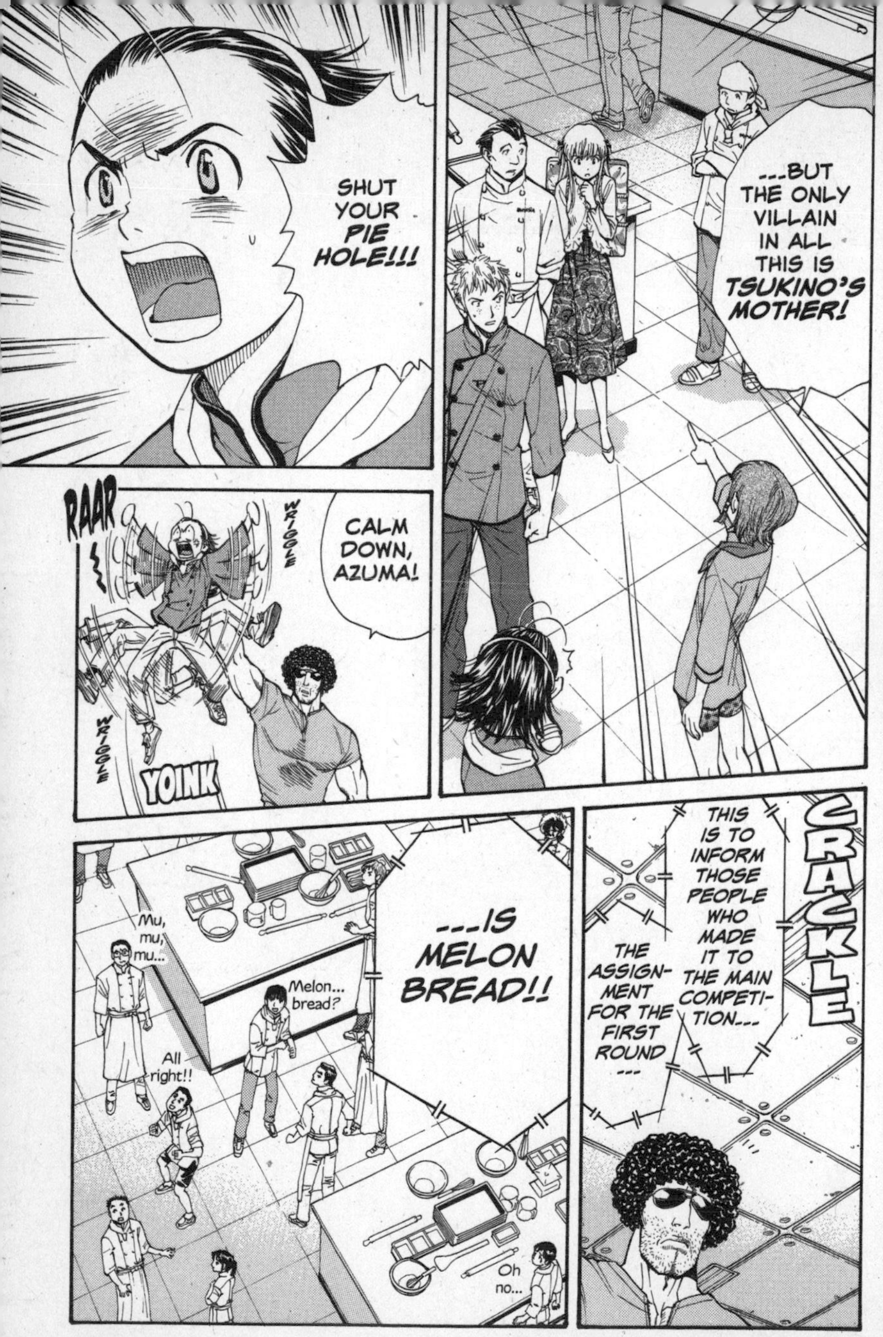
...BUT THE ONLY VILLAIN IN ALL THIS IS TSUKINO'S MOTHER!
SHUT YOUR PIE HOLE!!!
CALM DOWN, AZUMA!
WRIGGLE
RAAR
WRIGGLE
YOINK
CRACKLE
THIS IS TO INFORM THOSE PEOPLE WHO MADE IT TO THE MAIN COMPETITION...
THE ASSIGNMENT FOR THE FIRST ROUND...
...IS MELON BREAD!!
Melon... bread?
Mu, mu, mu...
All right!!
Oh no...

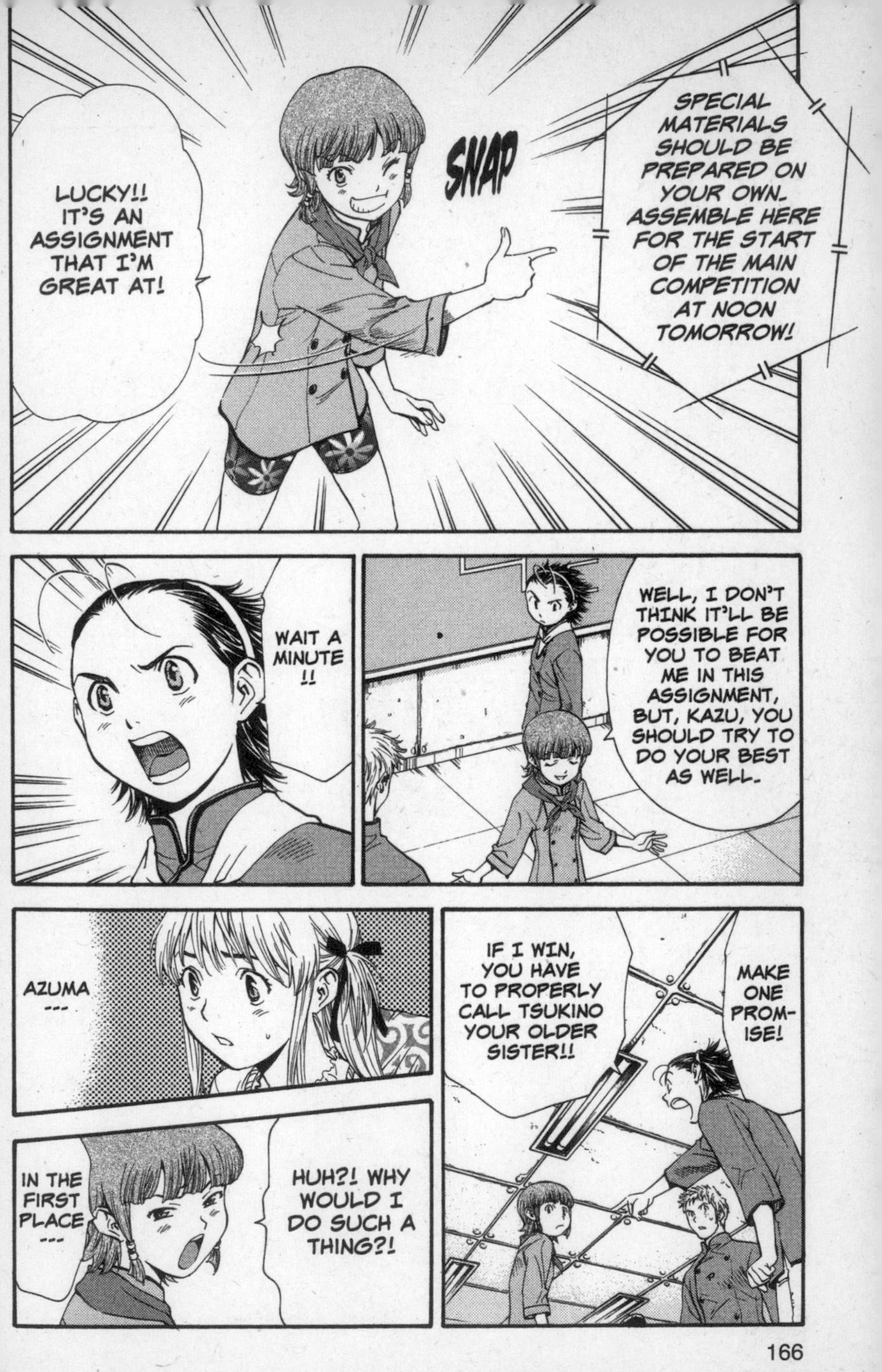
SPECIAL MATERIALS SHOULD BE PREPARED ON YOUR OWN. ASSEMBLE HERE FOR THE START OF THE MAIN COMPETITION AT NOON TOMORROW!
SNAP
LUCKY!! IT'S AN ASSIGNMENT THAT I'M GREAT AT!
WELL, I DON'T THINK IT'LL BE POSSIBLE FOR YOU TO BEAT ME IN THIS ASSIGNMENT, BUT, KAZU, YOU SHOULD TRY TO DO YOUR BEST AS WELL.
WAIT A MINUTE !!
MAKE ONE PROM-ISE!
IF I WIN, YOU HAVE TO PROPERLY CALL TSUKINO YOUR OLDER SISTER!!
AZUMA ---
HUH?! WHY WOULD I DO SUCH A THING?!
IN THE FIRST PLACE ---

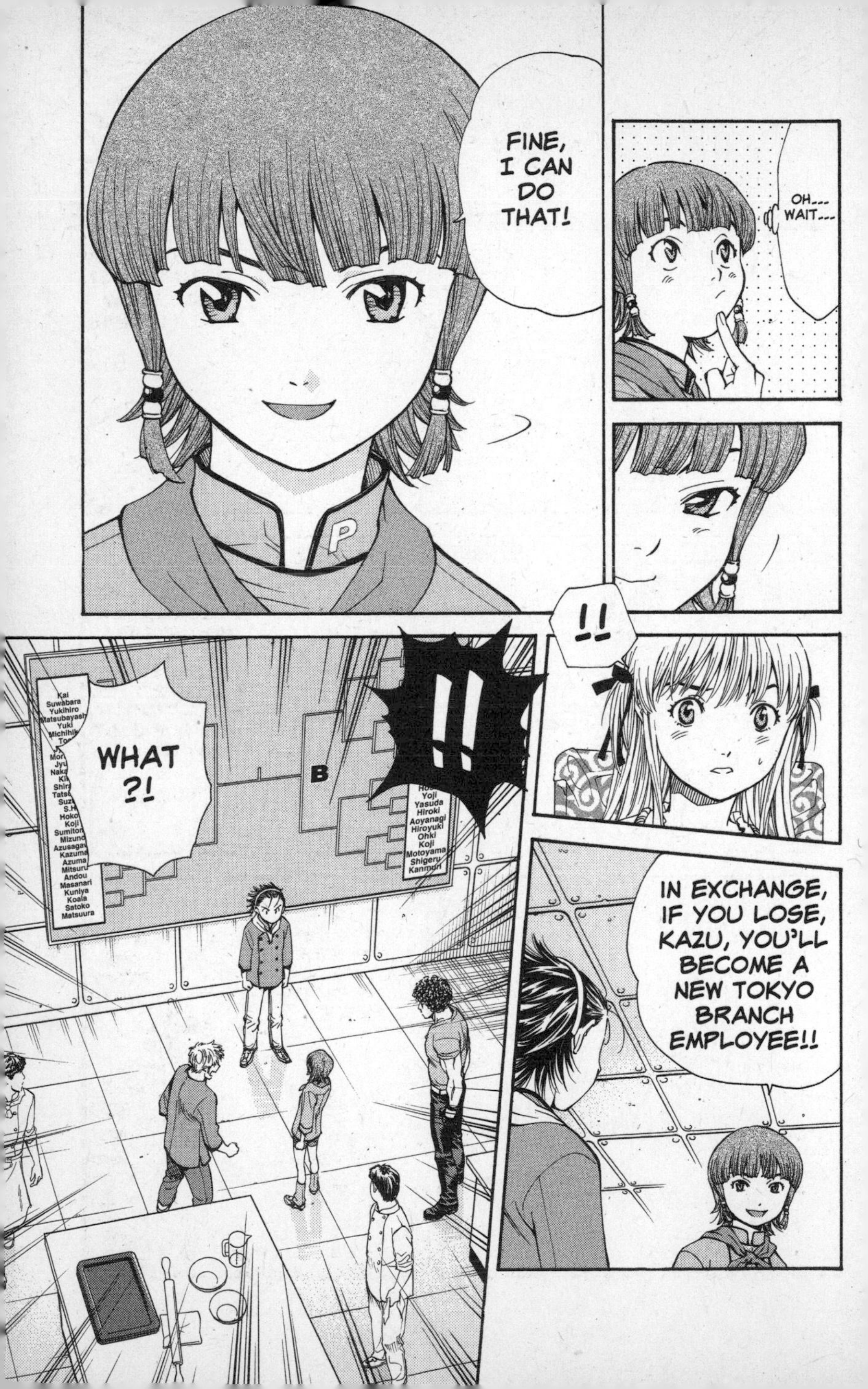
OH... WAIT...
FINE, I CAN DO THAT!
!!
!!
IN EXCHANGE, IF YOU LOSE, KAZU, YOU'LL BECOME A NEW TOKYO BRANCH EMPLOYEE!!
!!
WHAT?!

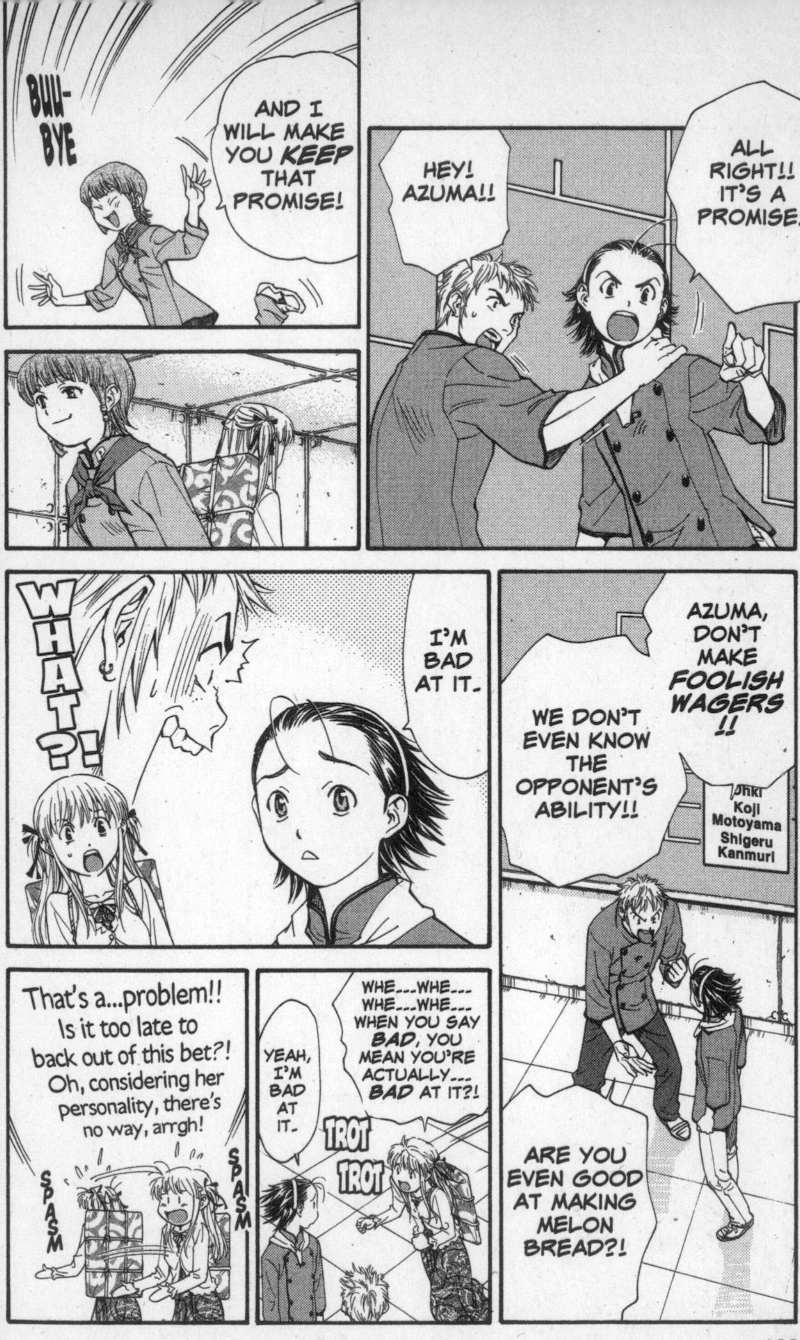
ALL RIGHT!! IT'S A PROMISE!
HEY! AZUMA!!
AND I WILL MAKE YOU KEEP THAT PROMISE!
BUU-BYE
AZUMA, DON'T MAKE FOOLISH WAGERS!!
WE DON'T EVEN KNOW THE OPPONENT'S ABILITY!!
Koji Motoyama
Shigeru Kanmuri
ARE YOU EVEN GOOD AT MAKING MELON BREAD?!
I'M BAD AT IT.
WHAT?!
WHE...WHE... WHE...WHE... WHEN YOU SAY BAD, YOU MEAN YOU'RE ACTUALLY... BAD AT IT?!
YEAH, I'M BAD AT IT.
TROT
TROT
That's a...problem!! Is it too late to back out of this bet?! Oh, considering her personality, there's no way, arrgh!
SPASM
SPASM

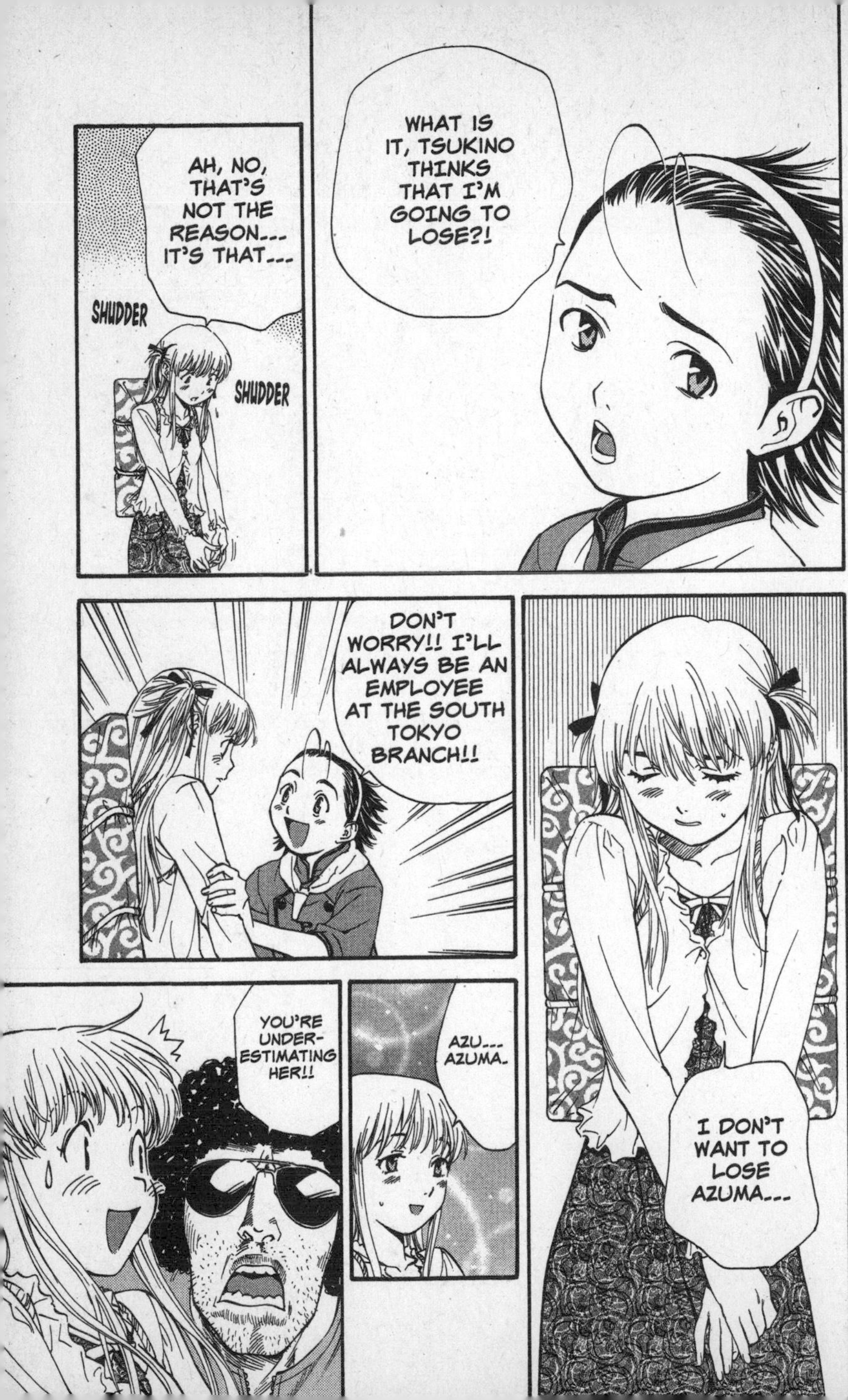
WHAT IS IT, TSUKINO THINKS THAT I'M GOING TO LOSE?!
AH, NO, THAT'S NOT THE REASON... IT'S THAT...
SHUDDER
SHUDDER
I DON'T WANT TO LOSE AZUMA...
DON'T WORRY!! I'LL ALWAYS BE AN EMPLOYEE AT THE SOUTH TOKYO BRANCH!!
AZU... AZUMA.
YOU'RE UNDER-ESTIMATING HER!!

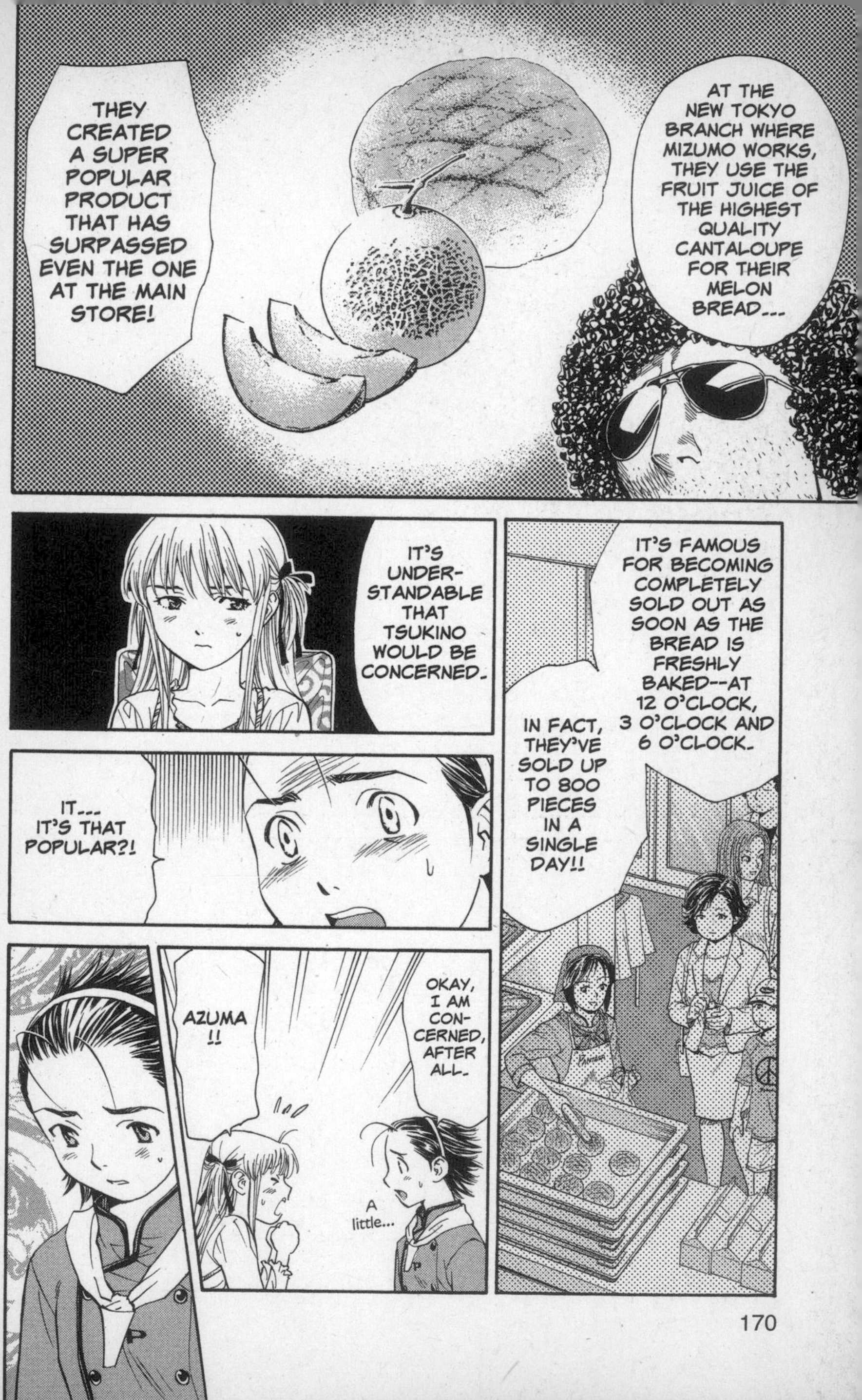
AT THE NEW TOKYO BRANCH WHERE MIZUMO WORKS, THEY USE THE FRUIT JUICE OF THE HIGHEST QUALITY CANTALOUPE FOR THEIR MELON BREAD...
THEY CREATED A SUPER POPULAR PRODUCT THAT HAS SURPASSED EVEN THE ONE AT THE MAIN STORE!
IT'S FAMOUS FOR BECOMING COMPLETELY SOLD OUT AS SOON AS THE BREAD IS FRESHLY BAKED--AT 12 O'CLOCK, 3 O'CLOCK AND 6 O'CLOCK.
IN FACT, THEY'VE SOLD UP TO 800 PIECES IN A SINGLE DAY!!
IT'S UNDERSTANDABLE THAT TSUKINO WOULD BE CONCERNED.
IT... IT'S THAT POPULAR?!
OKAY, I AM CONCERNED, AFTER ALL.
AZUMA!!
A little...

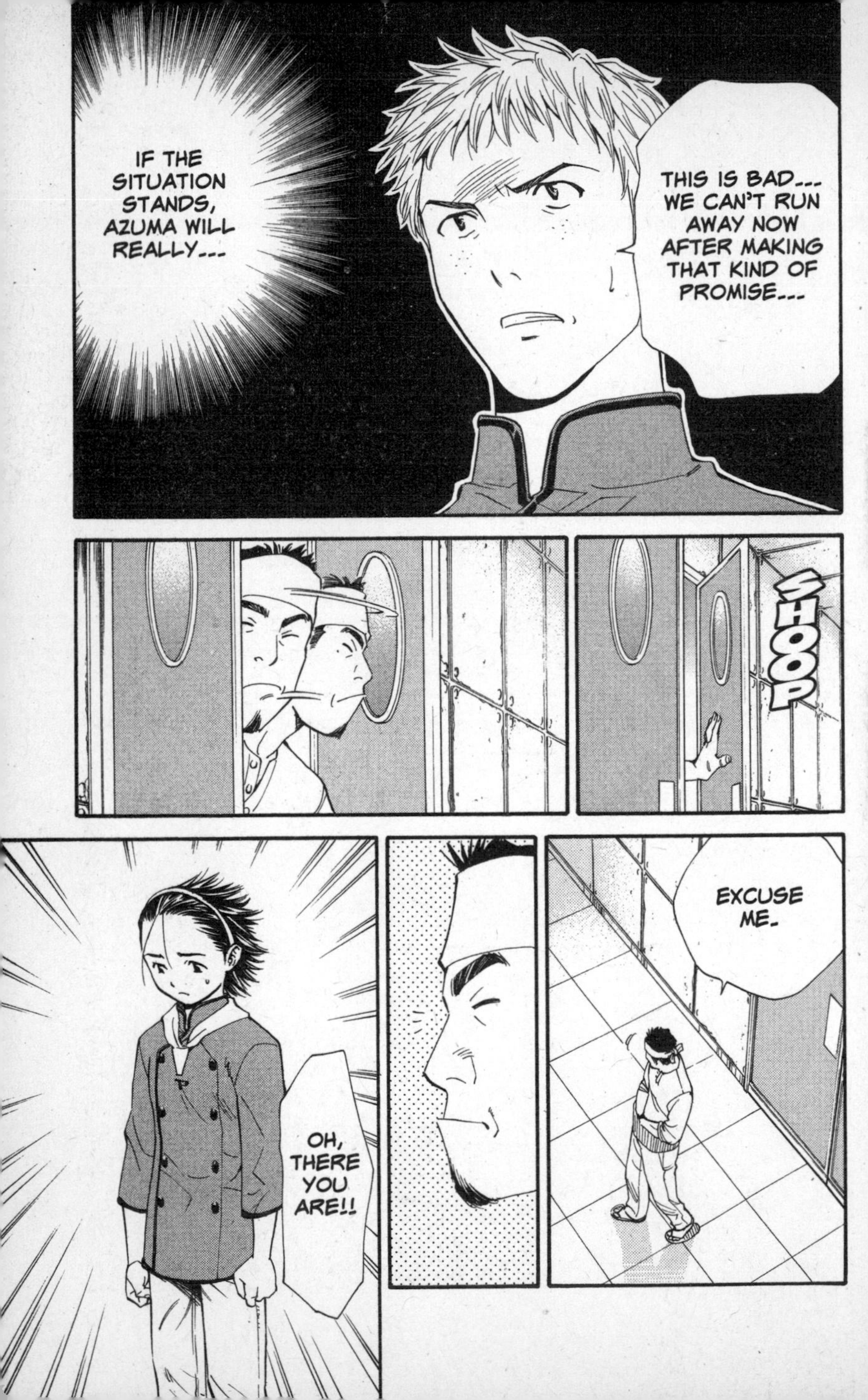
THIS IS BAD... WE CAN'T RUN AWAY NOW AFTER MAKING THAT KIND OF PROMISE...
IF THE SITUATION STANDS, AZUMA WILL REALLY...
SHOOP
EXCUSE ME.
OH, THERE YOU ARE!!

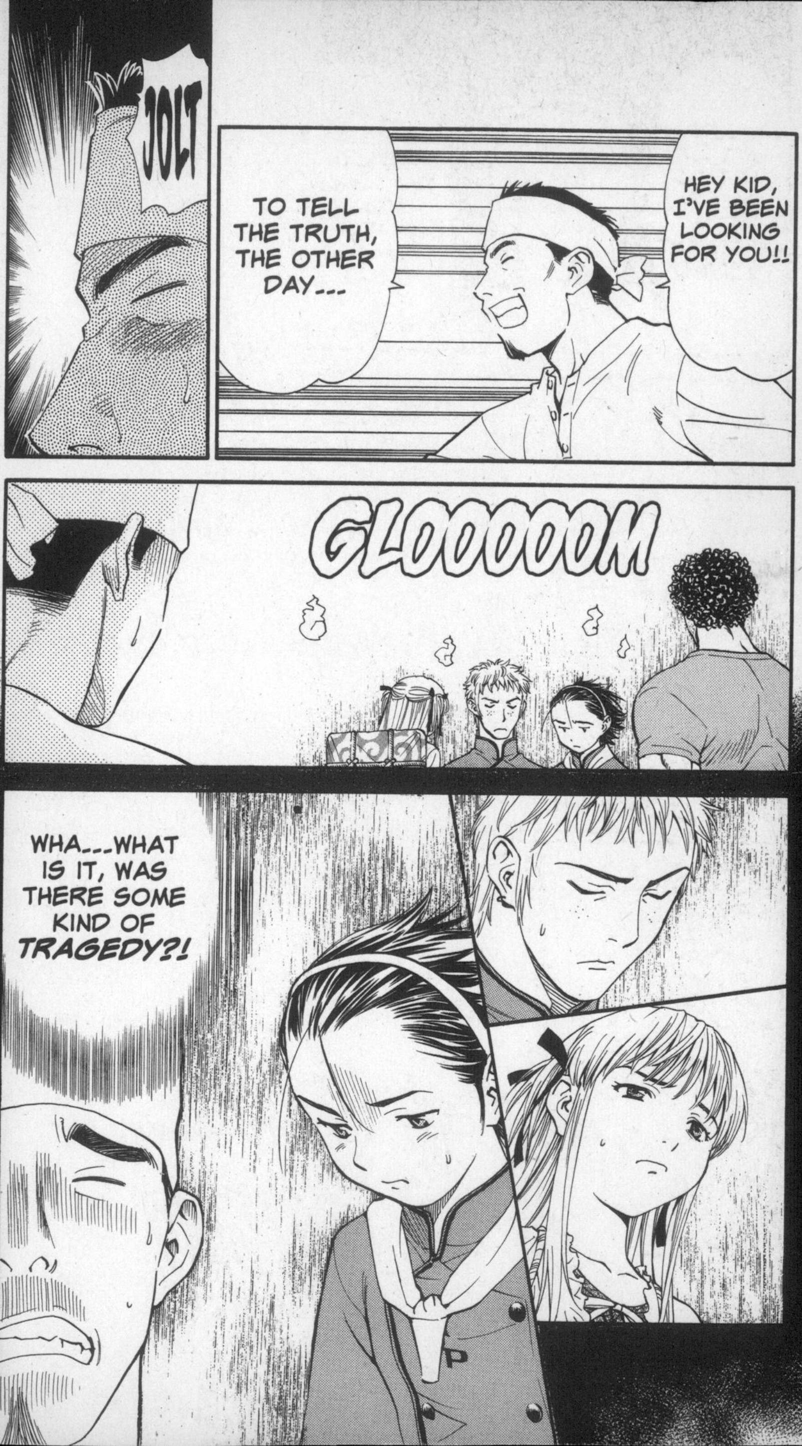
HEY KID, I'VE BEEN LOOKING FOR YOU!!
TO TELL THE TRUTH, THE OTHER DAY...
JOLT
GLOOOOOM
WHA...WHAT IS IT, WAS THERE SOME KIND OF TRAGEDY?!

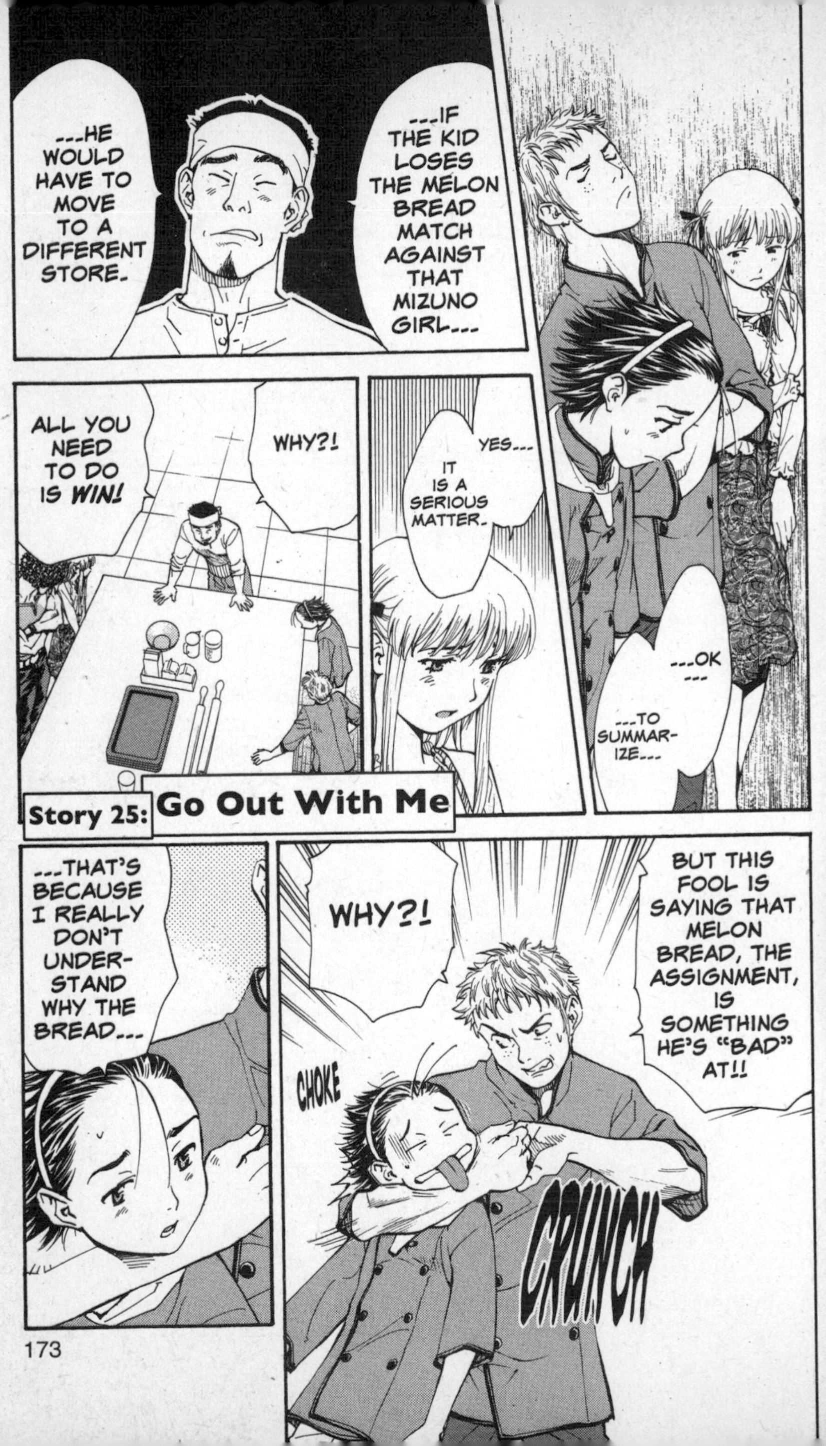
...OK...
...TO SUMMARIZE...
...IF THE KID LOSES THE MELON BREAD MATCH AGAINST THAT MIZUNO GIRL...
...HE WOULD HAVE TO MOVE TO A DIFFERENT STORE.
YES... IT IS A SERIOUS MATTER.
WHY?!
ALL YOU NEED TO DO IS *WIN!*
Story 25: Go Out With Me
BUT THIS FOOL IS SAYING THAT MELON BREAD, THE ASSIGNMENT, IS SOMETHING HE'S "BAD" AT!!
WHY?!
CHOKE
CRUNCH
...THAT'S BECAUSE I REALLY DON'T UNDERSTAND WHY THE BREAD...

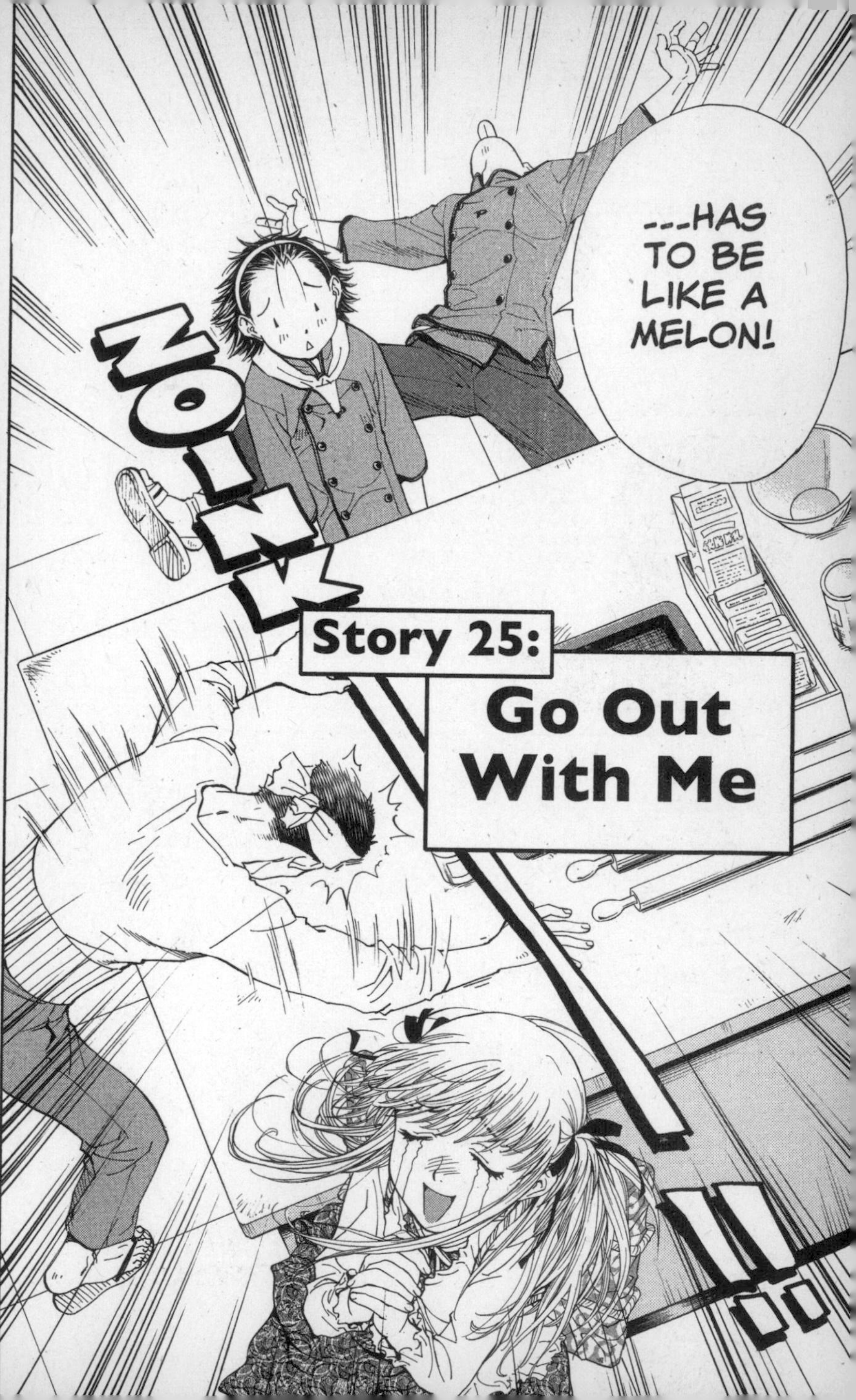
---HAS TO BE LIKE A MELON!
NOINK
Story 25:
Go Out With Me
!!

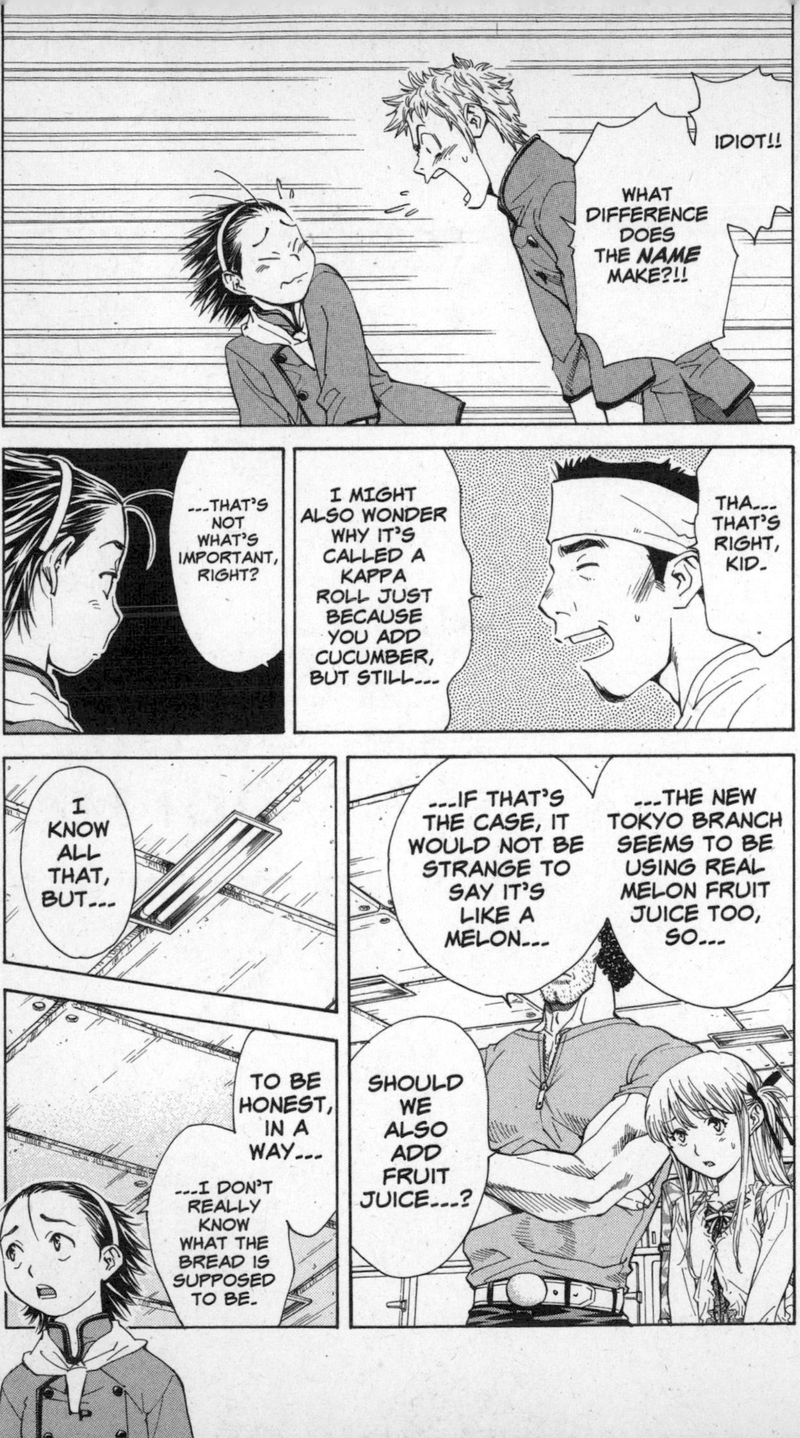
IDIOT!!
WHAT DIFFERENCE DOES THE *NAME* MAKE?!!
THA... THAT'S RIGHT, KID.
I MIGHT ALSO WONDER WHY IT'S CALLED A KAPPA ROLL JUST BECAUSE YOU ADD CUCUMBER, BUT STILL...
...THAT'S NOT WHAT'S IMPORTANT, RIGHT?
...THE NEW TOKYO BRANCH SEEMS TO BE USING REAL MELON FRUIT JUICE TOO, SO...
...IF THAT'S THE CASE, IT WOULD NOT BE STRANGE TO SAY IT'S LIKE A MELON...
SHOULD WE ALSO ADD FRUIT JUICE...?
I KNOW ALL THAT, BUT...
TO BE HONEST, IN A WAY...
...I DON'T REALLY KNOW WHAT THE BREAD IS SUPPOSED TO BE.

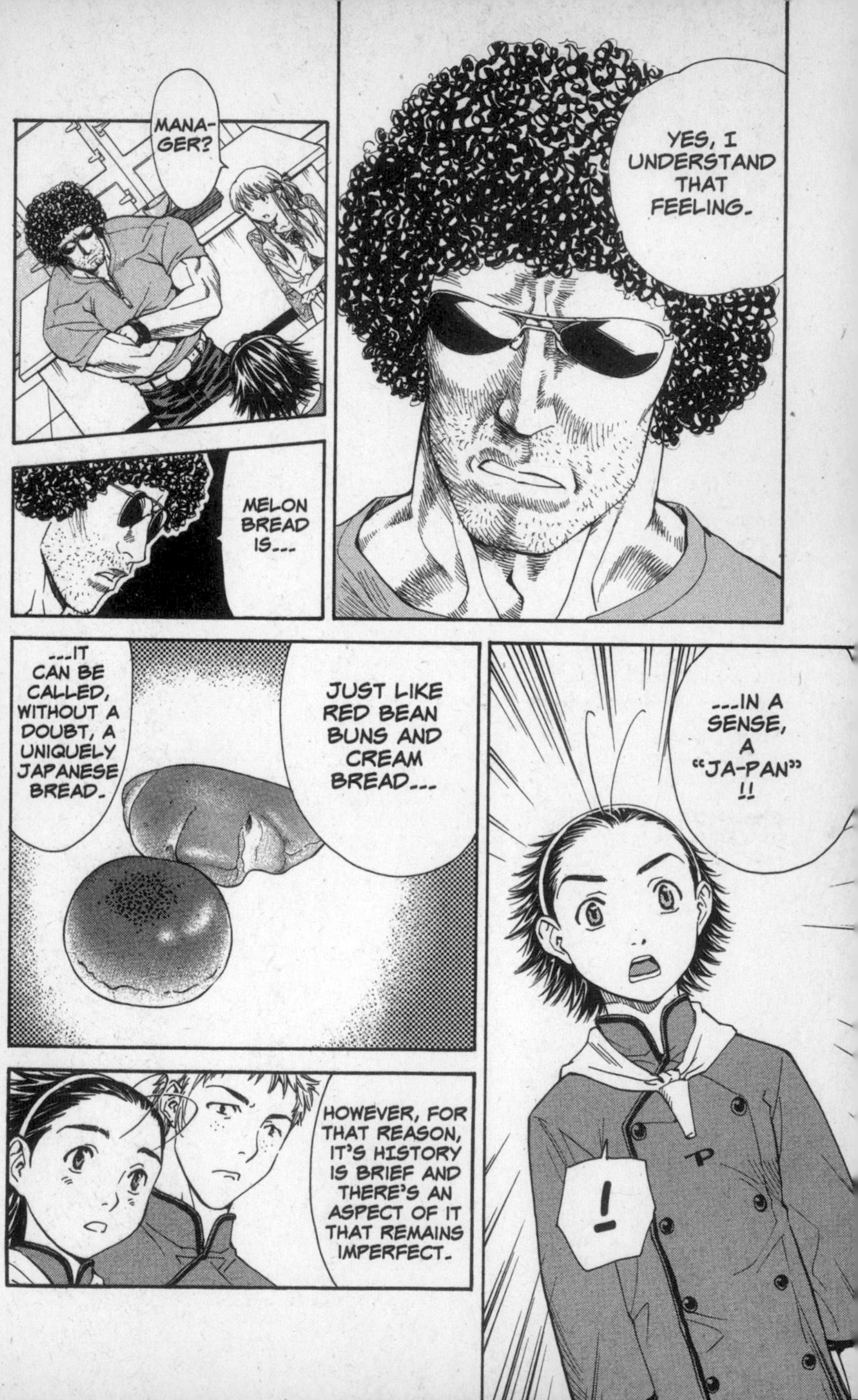
YES, I UNDERSTAND THAT FEELING.
MANA-GER?
MELON BREAD IS...
...IN A SENSE, A "JA-PAN" !!
!
JUST LIKE RED BEAN BUNS AND CREAM BREAD...
...IT CAN BE CALLED, WITHOUT A DOUBT, A UNIQUELY JAPANESE BREAD.
HOWEVER, FOR THAT REASON, IT'S HISTORY IS BRIEF AND THERE'S AN ASPECT OF IT THAT REMAINS IMPERFECT.

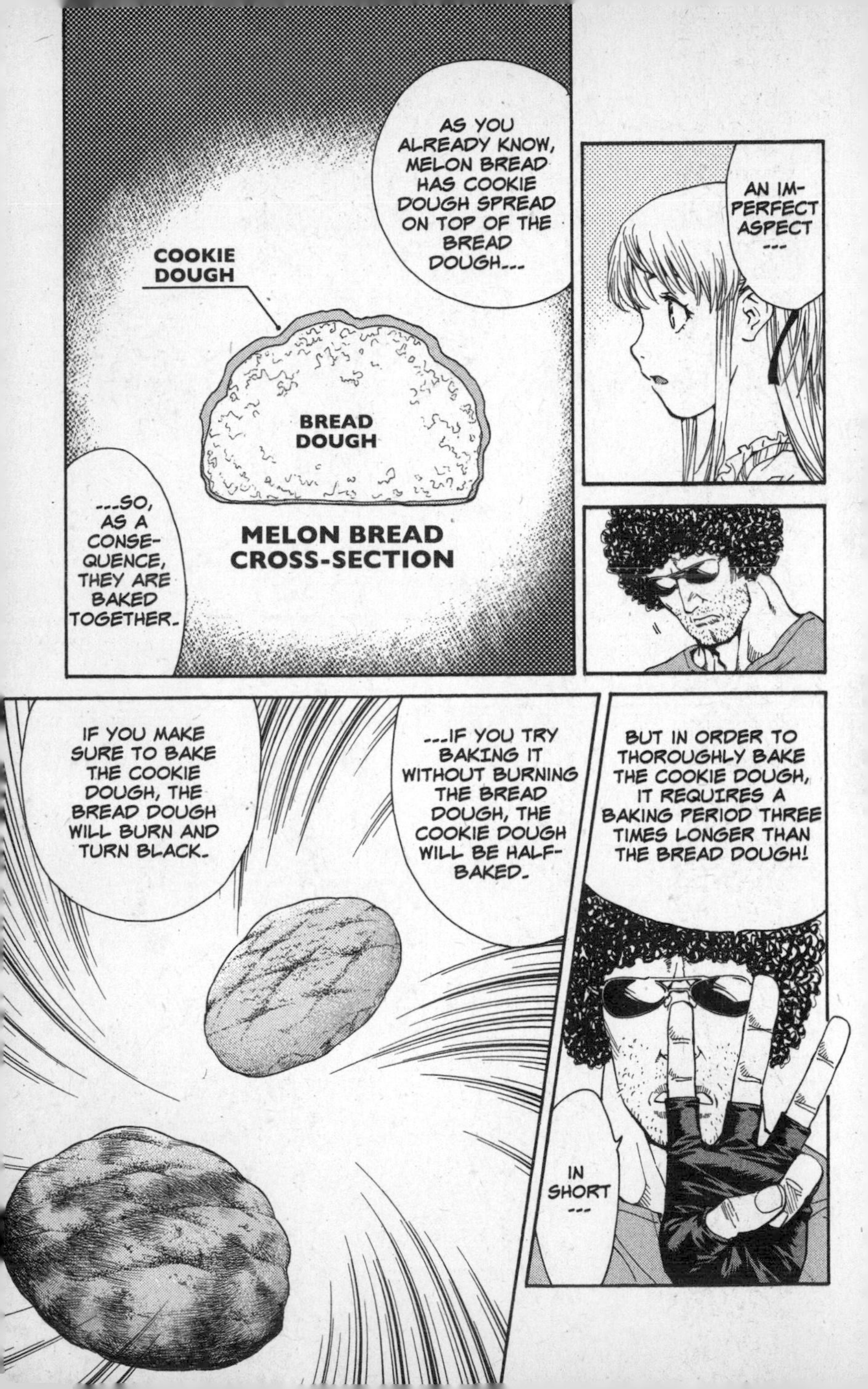
AN IMPERFECT ASPECT ---
AS YOU ALREADY KNOW, MELON BREAD HAS COOKIE DOUGH SPREAD ON TOP OF THE BREAD DOUGH...
COOKIE DOUGH
BREAD DOUGH
MELON BREAD CROSS-SECTION
...SO, AS A CONSEQUENCE, THEY ARE BAKED TOGETHER.
BUT IN ORDER TO THOROUGHLY BAKE THE COOKIE DOUGH, IT REQUIRES A BAKING PERIOD THREE TIMES LONGER THAN THE BREAD DOUGH!
IN SHORT ---
...IF YOU TRY BAKING IT WITHOUT BURNING THE BREAD DOUGH, THE COOKIE DOUGH WILL BE HALF-BAKED.
IF YOU MAKE SURE TO BAKE THE COOKIE DOUGH, THE BREAD DOUGH WILL BURN AND TURN BLACK.

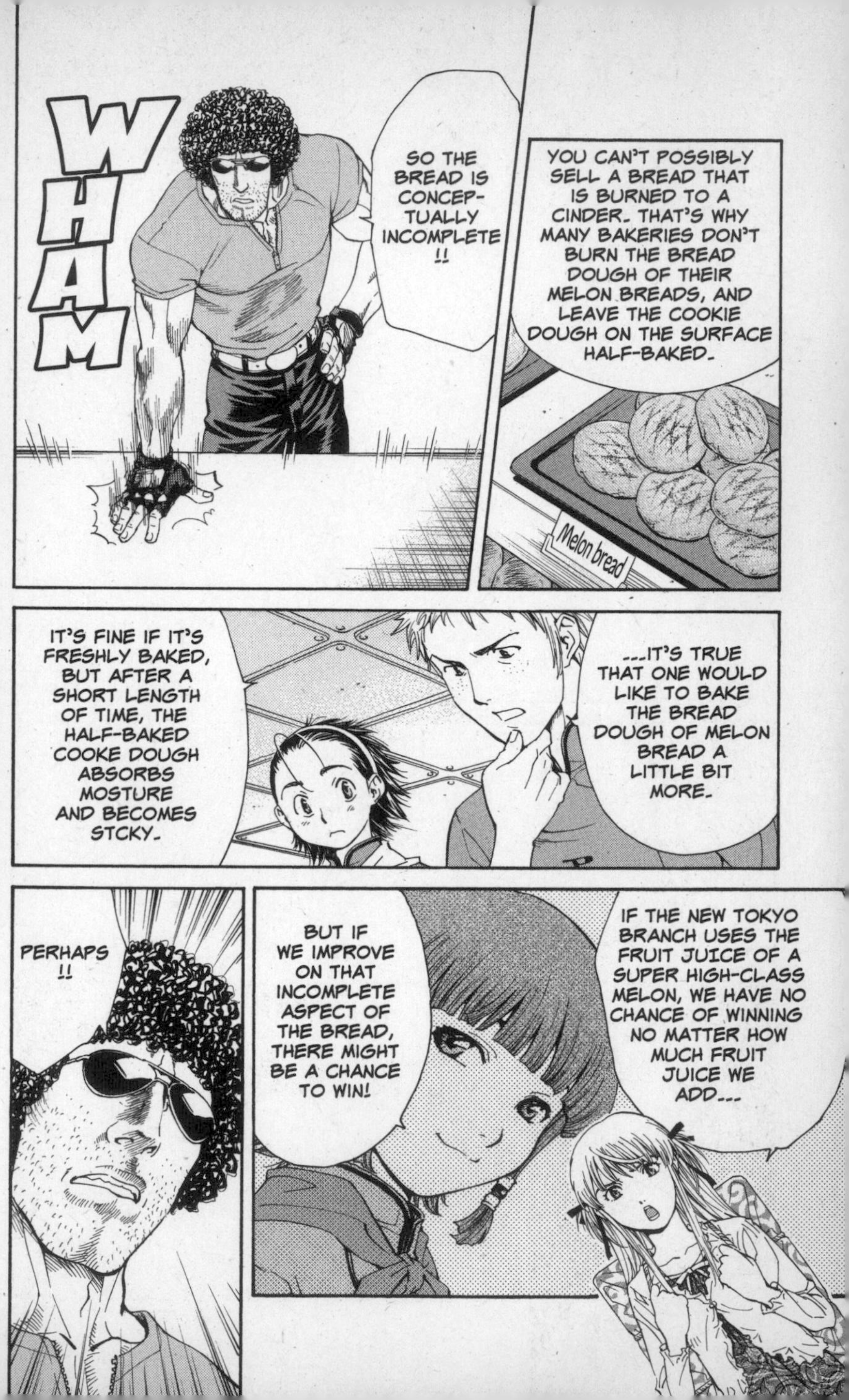
YOU CAN'T POSSIBLY SELL A BREAD THAT IS BURNED TO A CINDER. THAT'S WHY MANY BAKERIES DON'T BURN THE BREAD DOUGH OF THEIR MELON BREADS, AND LEAVE THE COOKIE DOUGH ON THE SURFACE HALF-BAKED.
Melon bread
WHAM
SO THE BREAD IS CONCEP-TUALLY INCOMPLETE!!
...IT'S TRUE THAT ONE WOULD LIKE TO BAKE THE BREAD DOUGH OF MELON BREAD A LITTLE BIT MORE.
IT'S FINE IF IT'S FRESHLY BAKED, BUT AFTER A SHORT LENGTH OF TIME, THE HALF-BAKED COOKE DOUGH ABSORBS MOSTURE AND BECOMES STCKY.
IF THE NEW TOKYO BRANCH USES THE FRUIT JUICE OF A SUPER HIGH-CLASS MELON, WE HAVE NO CHANCE OF WINNING NO MATTER HOW MUCH FRUIT JUICE WE ADD...
BUT IF WE IMPROVE ON THAT INCOMPLETE ASPECT OF THE BREAD, THERE MIGHT BE A CHANCE TO WIN!
PERHAPS!!

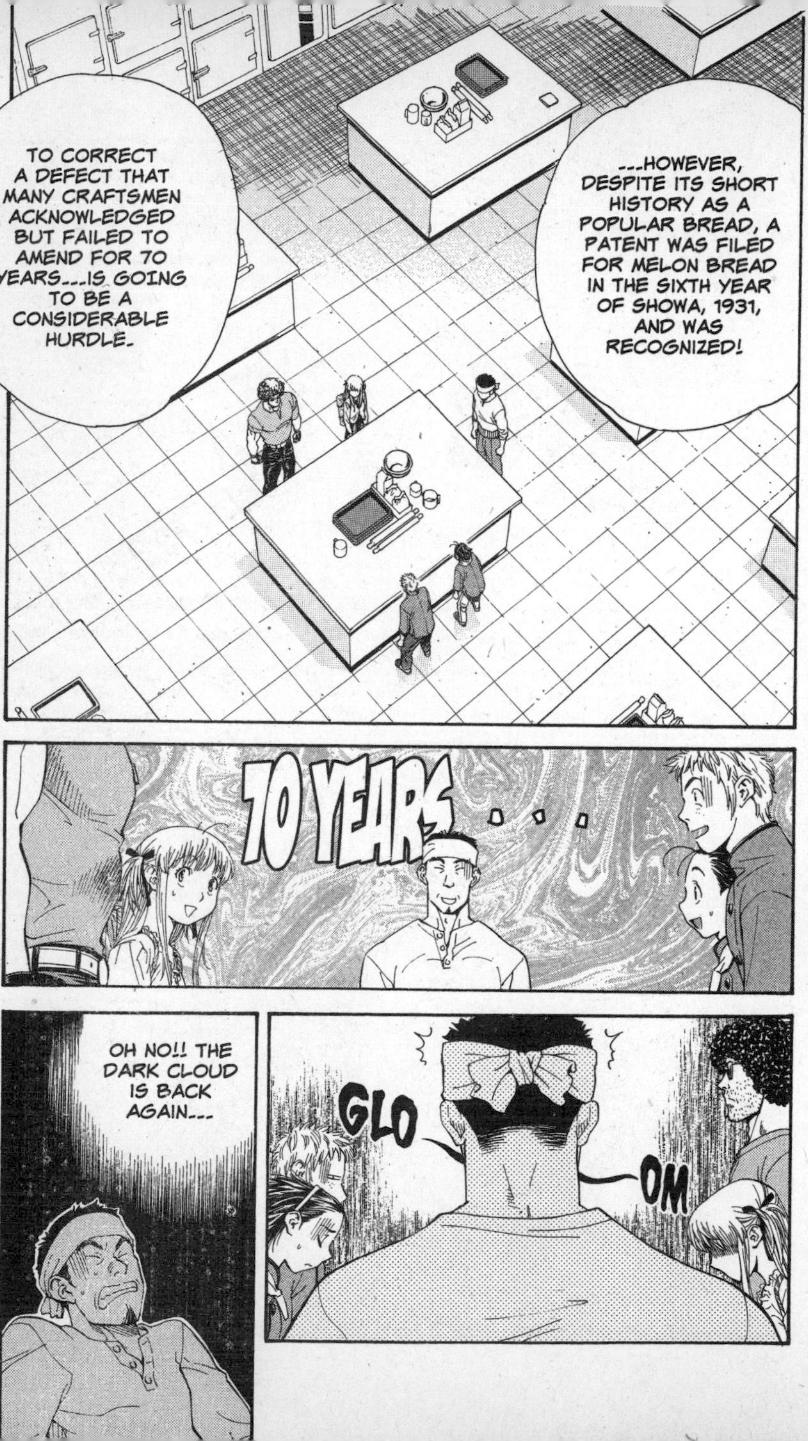
...HOWEVER, DESPITE ITS SHORT HISTORY AS A POPULAR BREAD, A PATENT WAS FILED FOR MELON BREAD IN THE SIXTH YEAR OF SHOWA, 1931, AND WAS RECOGNIZED!
TO CORRECT A DEFECT THAT MANY CRAFTSMEN ACKNOWLEDGED BUT FAILED TO AMEND FOR 70 YEARS...IS GOING TO BE A CONSIDERABLE HURDLE.
70 YEARS...
GLO
OM
OH NO!! THE DARK CLOUD IS BACK AGAIN...

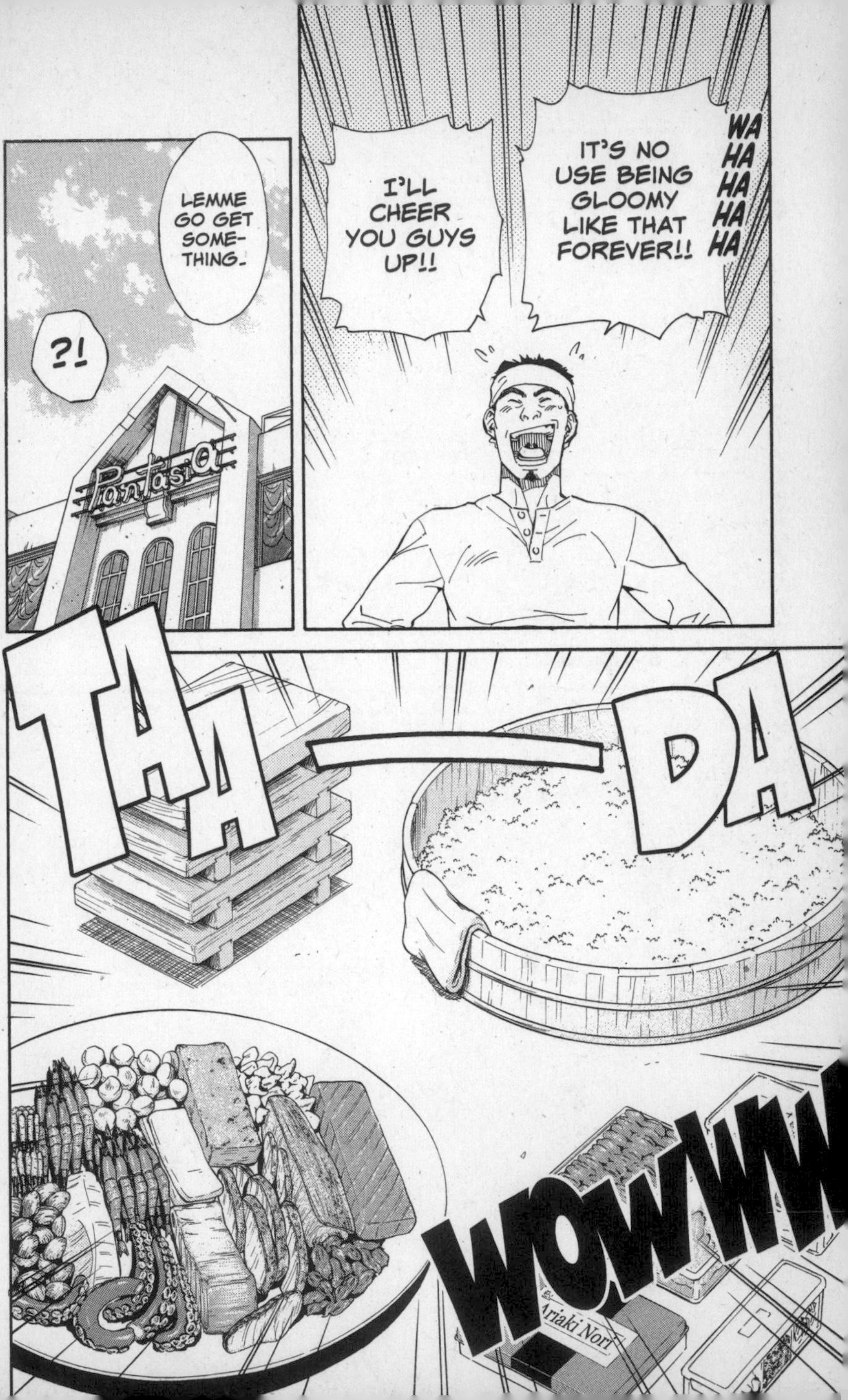
WA HA HA HA HA HA
IT'S NO USE BEING GLOOMY LIKE THAT FOREVER!!
I'LL CHEER YOU GUYS UP!!
LEMME GO GET SOME-THING.
?!
PantasiA
TA—DA
WOWWW
Ariaki Nori

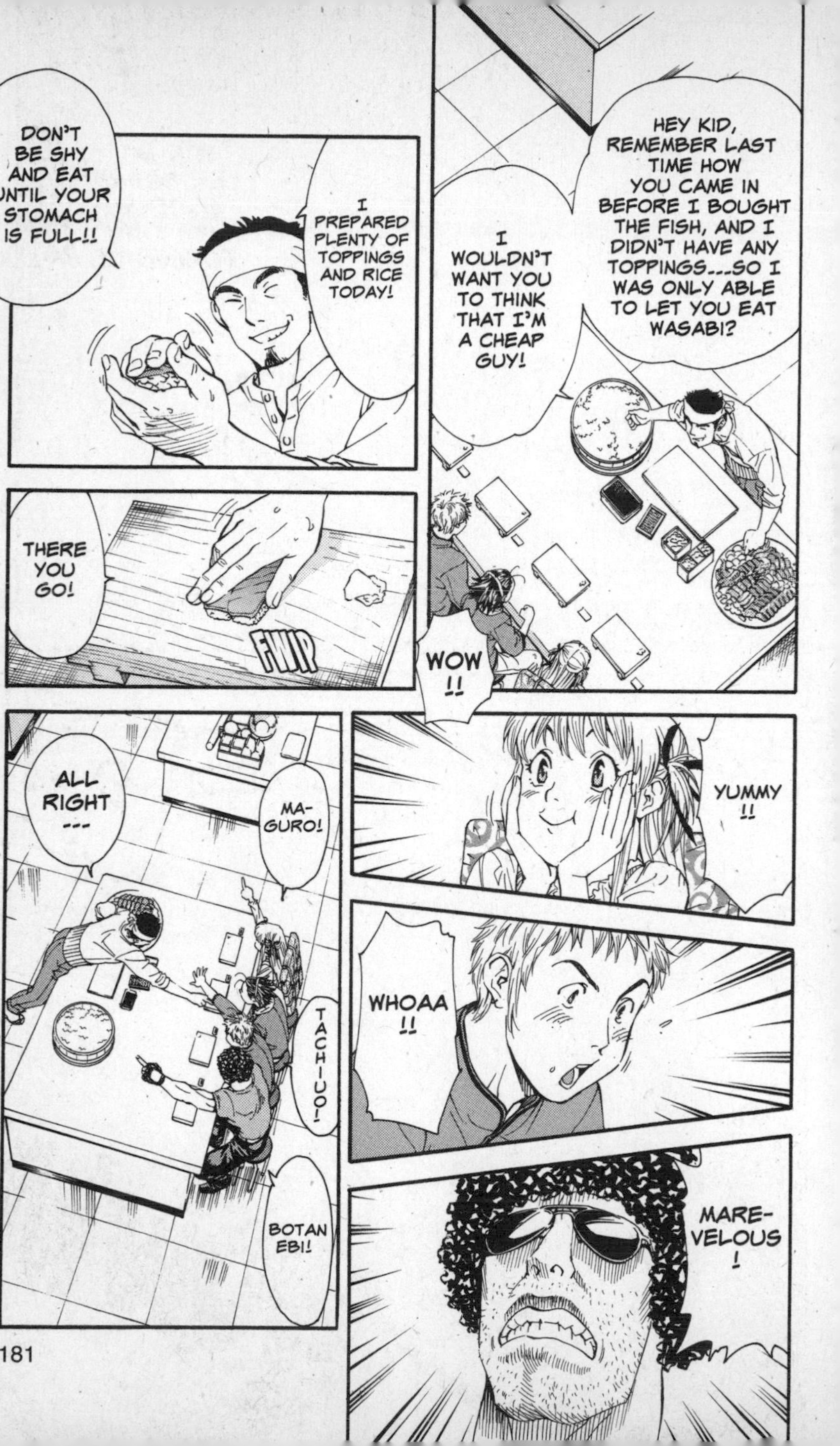
HEY KID, REMEMBER LAST TIME HOW YOU CAME IN BEFORE I BOUGHT THE FISH, AND I DIDN'T HAVE ANY TOPPINGS...SO I WAS ONLY ABLE TO LET YOU EAT WASABI?
I WOULDN'T WANT YOU TO THINK THAT I'M A CHEAP GUY!
WOW !!
I PREPARED PLENTY OF TOPPINGS AND RICE TODAY!
DON'T BE SHY AND EAT UNTIL YOUR STOMACH IS FULL!!
THERE YOU GO!
FWIP
YUMMY !!
WHOAA !!
MARE-VELOUS !
ALL RIGHT ...
MA-GURO!
TACHIUO!
BOTAN EBI!

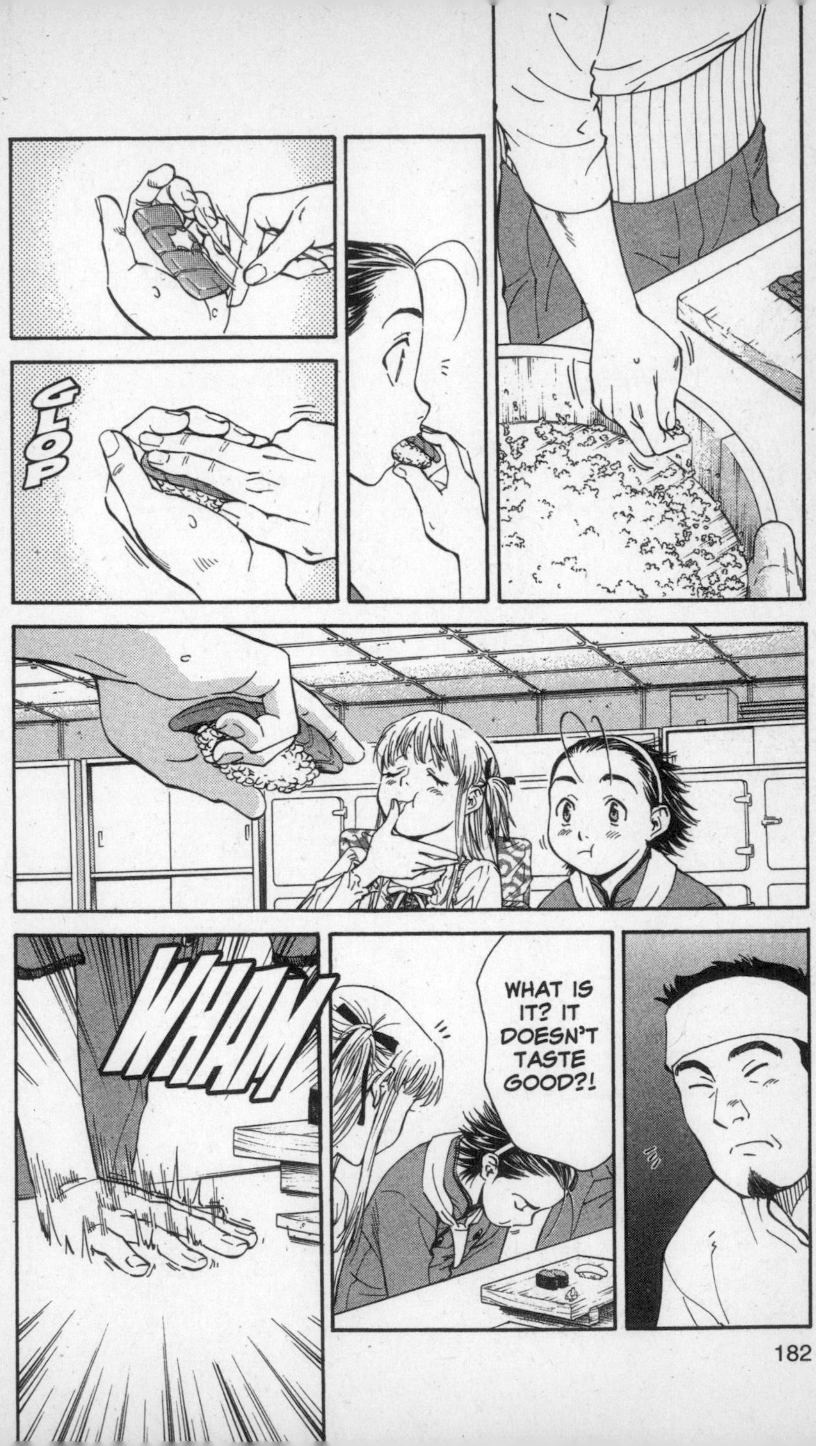
GLOP
WHAT IS IT? IT DOESN'T TASTE GOOD?!
WHAM

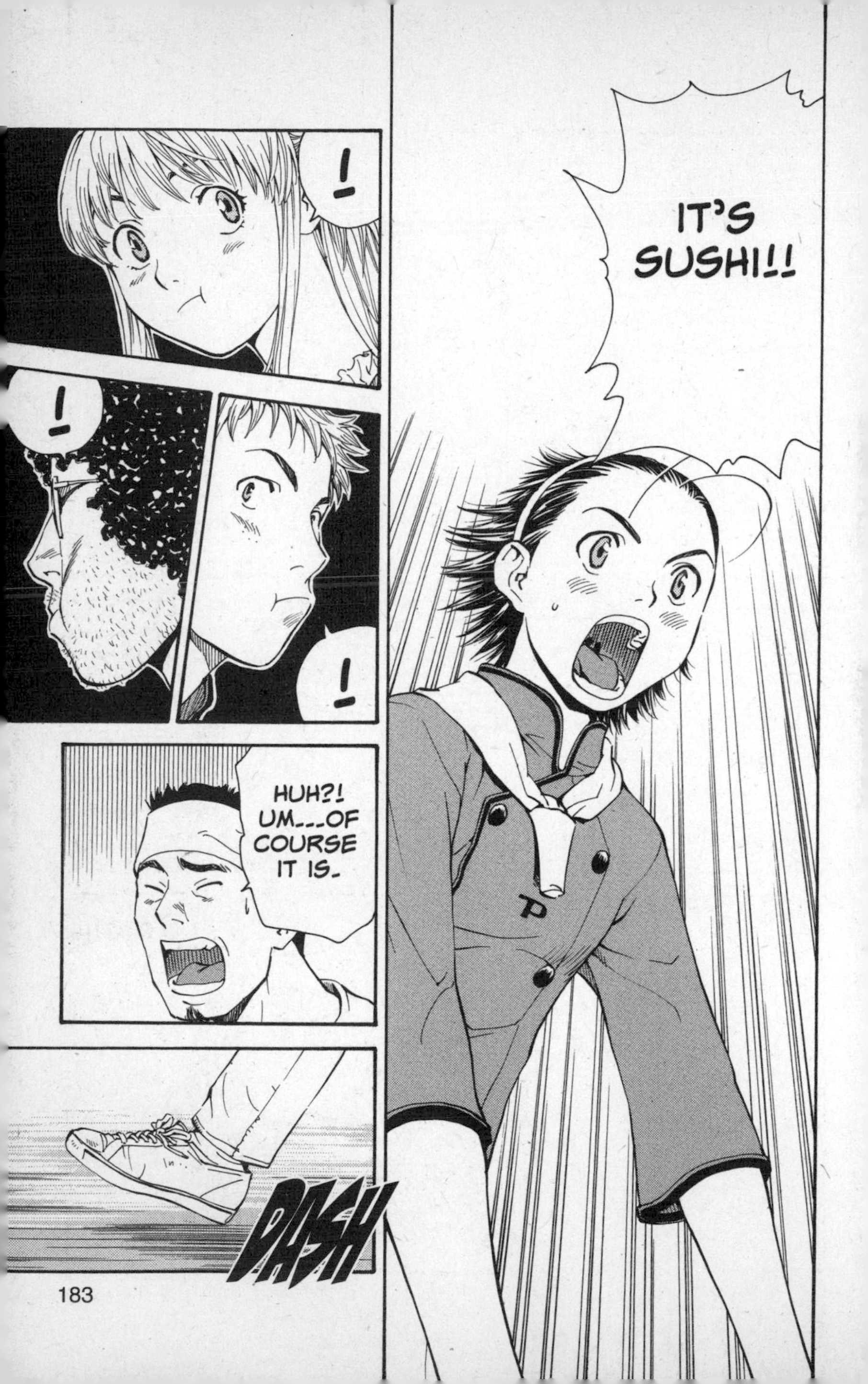
IT'S SUSHI!!
!
!
!
HUH?! UM...OF COURSE IT IS.
DASH

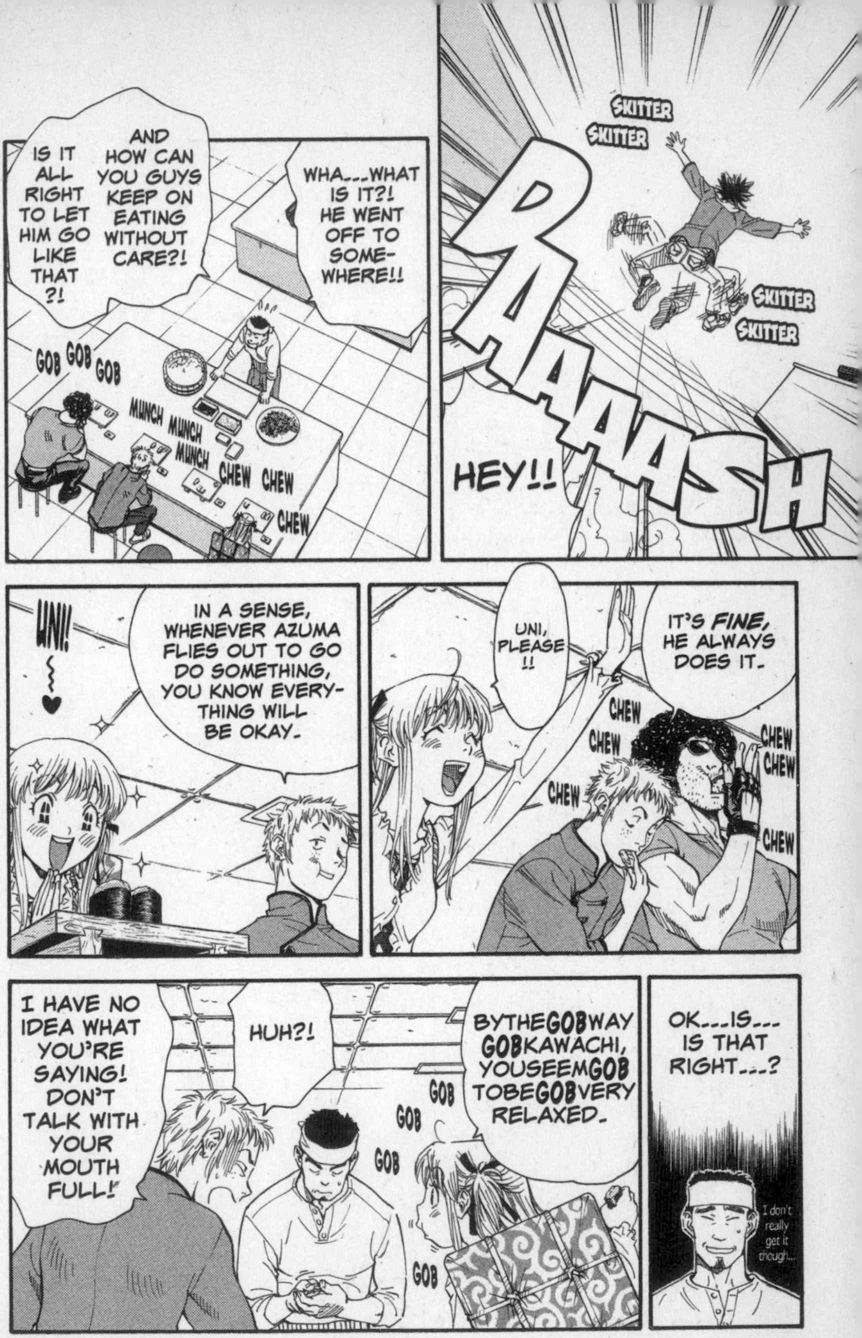
SKITTER
SKITTER
RAAAASH
SKITTER
SKITTER
HEY!!
WHA...WHAT IS IT?! HE WENT OFF TO SOME-WHERE!!
AND HOW CAN YOU GUYS KEEP ON EATING WITHOUT CARE?!
IS IT ALL RIGHT TO LET HIM GO LIKE THAT?!
GOB GOB GOB
MUNCH MUNCH MUNCH
CHEW CHEW CHEW
IT'S FINE, HE ALWAYS DOES IT.
UNI, PLEASE!!
CHEW CHEW CHEW CHEW CHEW CHEW
IN A SENSE, WHENEVER AZUMA FLIES OUT TO GO DO SOMETHING, YOU KNOW EVERY-THING WILL BE OKAY.
UNI!
OK...IS...IS THAT RIGHT...?
I don't really get it though...
BYTHEGOBWAY GOBKAWACHI, YOUSEEMGOB TOBEGOBVERY RELAXED.
GOB GOB GOB GOB
HUH?!
I HAVE NO IDEA WHAT YOU'RE SAYING! DON'T TALK WITH YOUR MOUTH FULL!

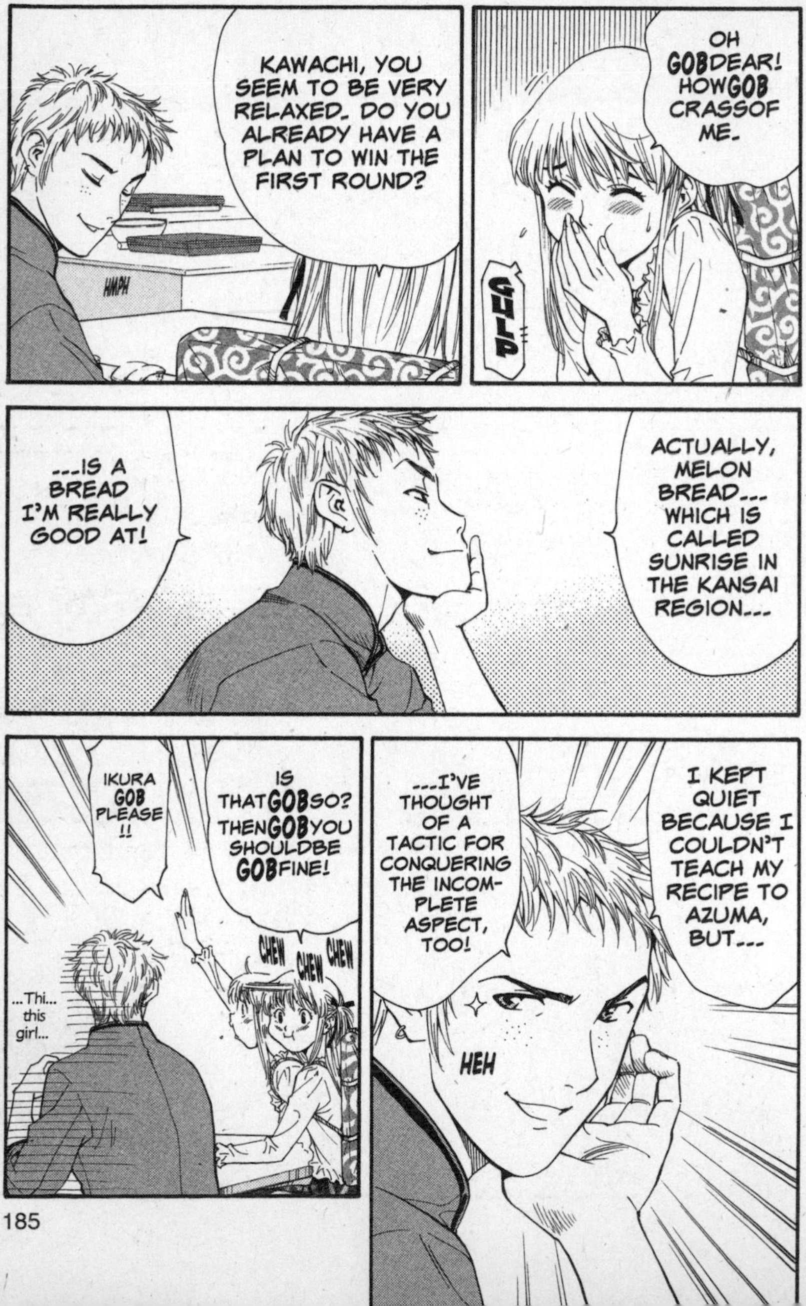
OH GOBDEAR! HOWGOB CRASSOF ME.
GULP
KAWACHI, YOU SEEM TO BE VERY RELAXED. DO YOU ALREADY HAVE A PLAN TO WIN THE FIRST ROUND?
HMPH
ACTUALLY, MELON BREAD... WHICH IS CALLED SUNRISE IN THE KANSAI REGION...
...IS A BREAD I'M REALLY GOOD AT!
I KEPT QUIET BECAUSE I COULDN'T TEACH MY RECIPE TO AZUMA, BUT...
...I'VE THOUGHT OF A TACTIC FOR CONQUERING THE INCOMPLETE ASPECT, TOO!
HEH
IS THATGOBSO? THENGOBYOU SHOULDBE GOBFINE!
IKURA GOB PLEASE !!
CHEW CHEW CHEW
...Thi... this girl...

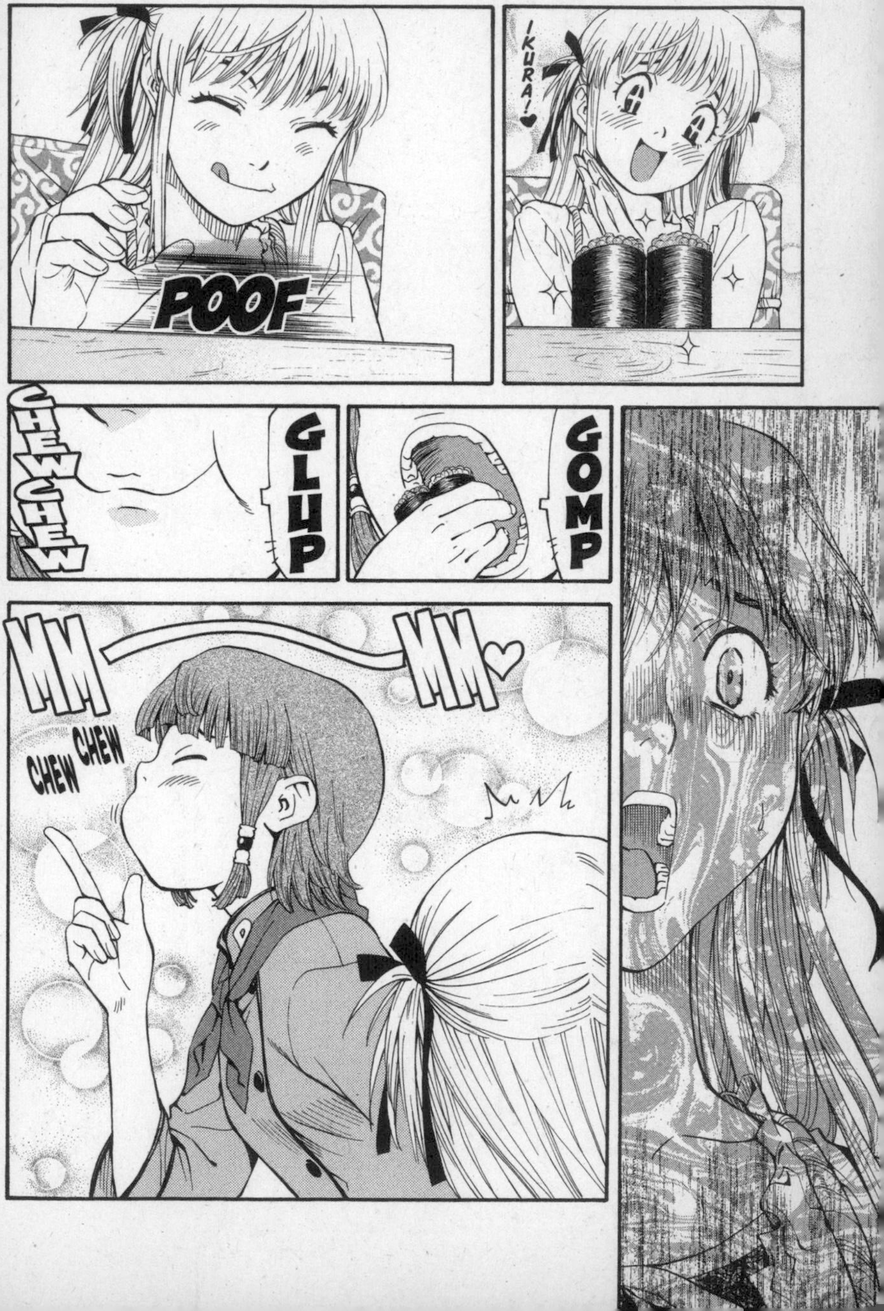
IKURA!♥
POOF
GOMP
GLUP
CHEW CHEW
MM MM♥
CHEW CHEW

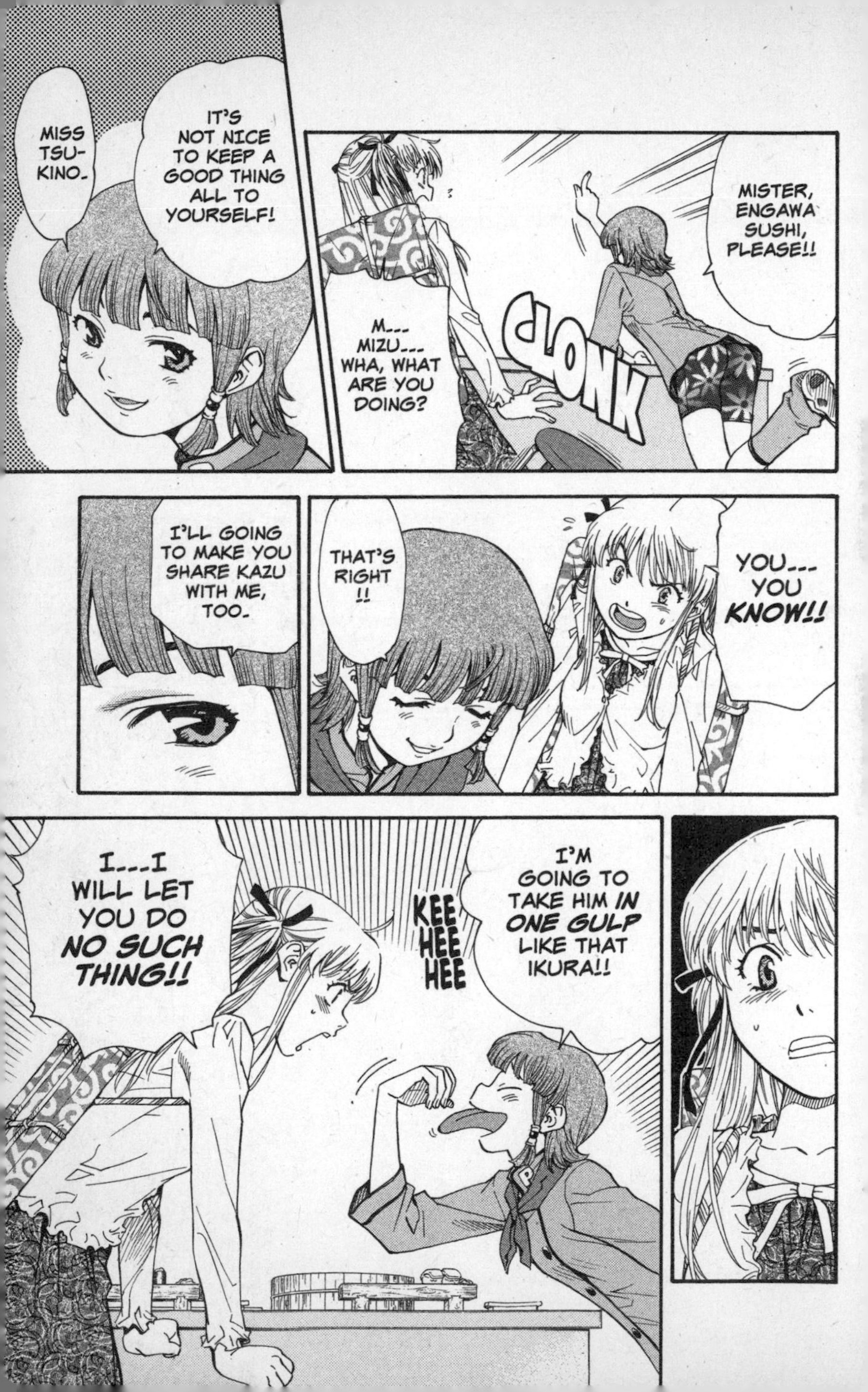
MISTER, ENGAWA SUSHI, PLEASE!!
CLONK
M... MIZU... WHA, WHAT ARE YOU DOING?
IT'S NOT NICE TO KEEP A GOOD THING ALL TO YOURSELF!
MISS TSU-KINO.
YOU... YOU KNOW!!
THAT'S RIGHT!!
I'LL GOING TO MAKE YOU SHARE KAZU WITH ME, TOO.
I'M GOING TO TAKE HIM IN ONE GULP LIKE THAT IKURA!!
KEE HEE HEE
I...I WILL LET YOU DO NO SUCH THING!!

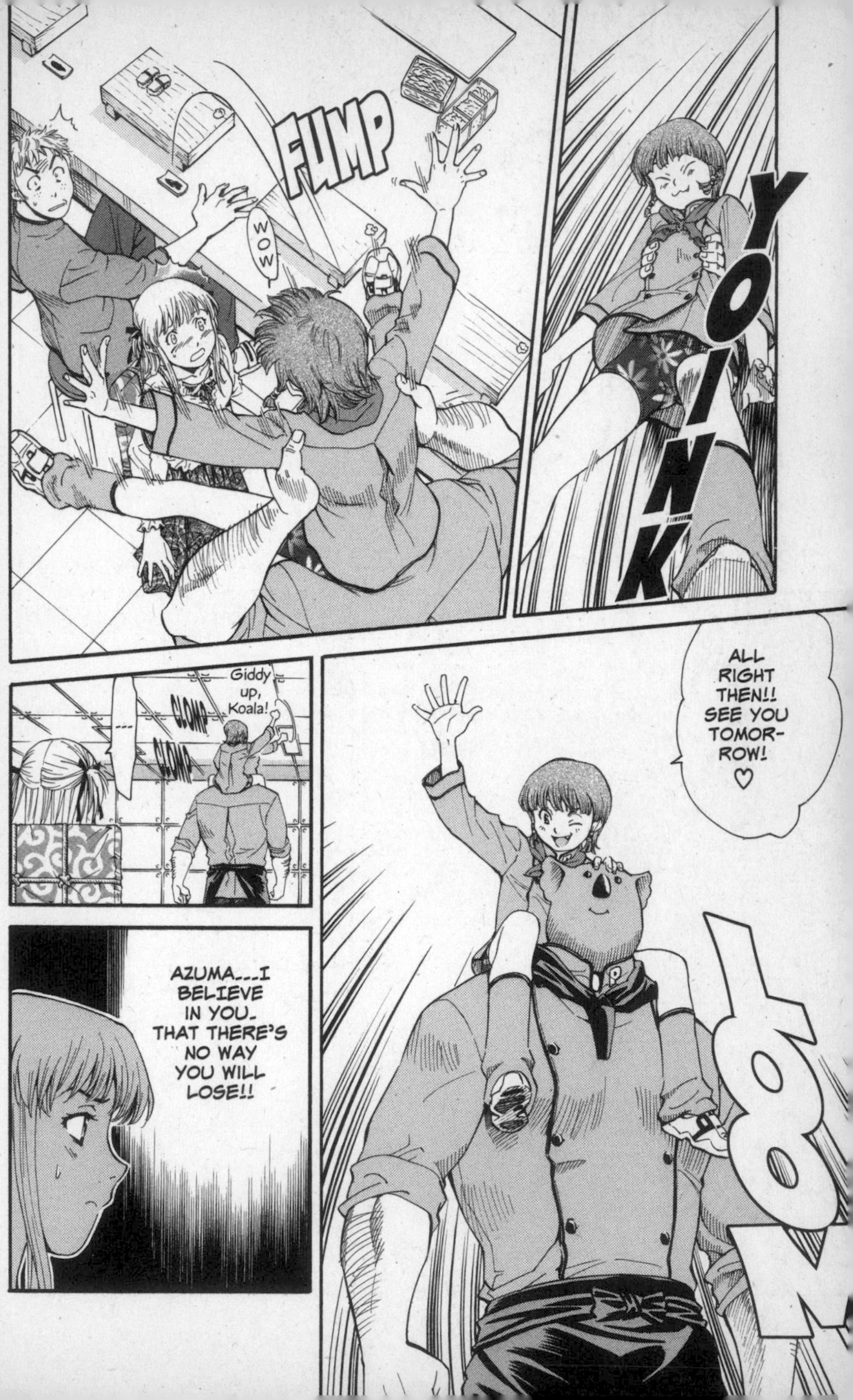
YOINK
FUMP
WOW
ALL RIGHT THEN!! SEE YOU TOMORROW! ♡
Giddy up, Koala!
...
CLOMP
CLOMP
AZUMA...I BELIEVE IN YOU. THAT THERE'S NO WAY YOU WILL LOSE!!

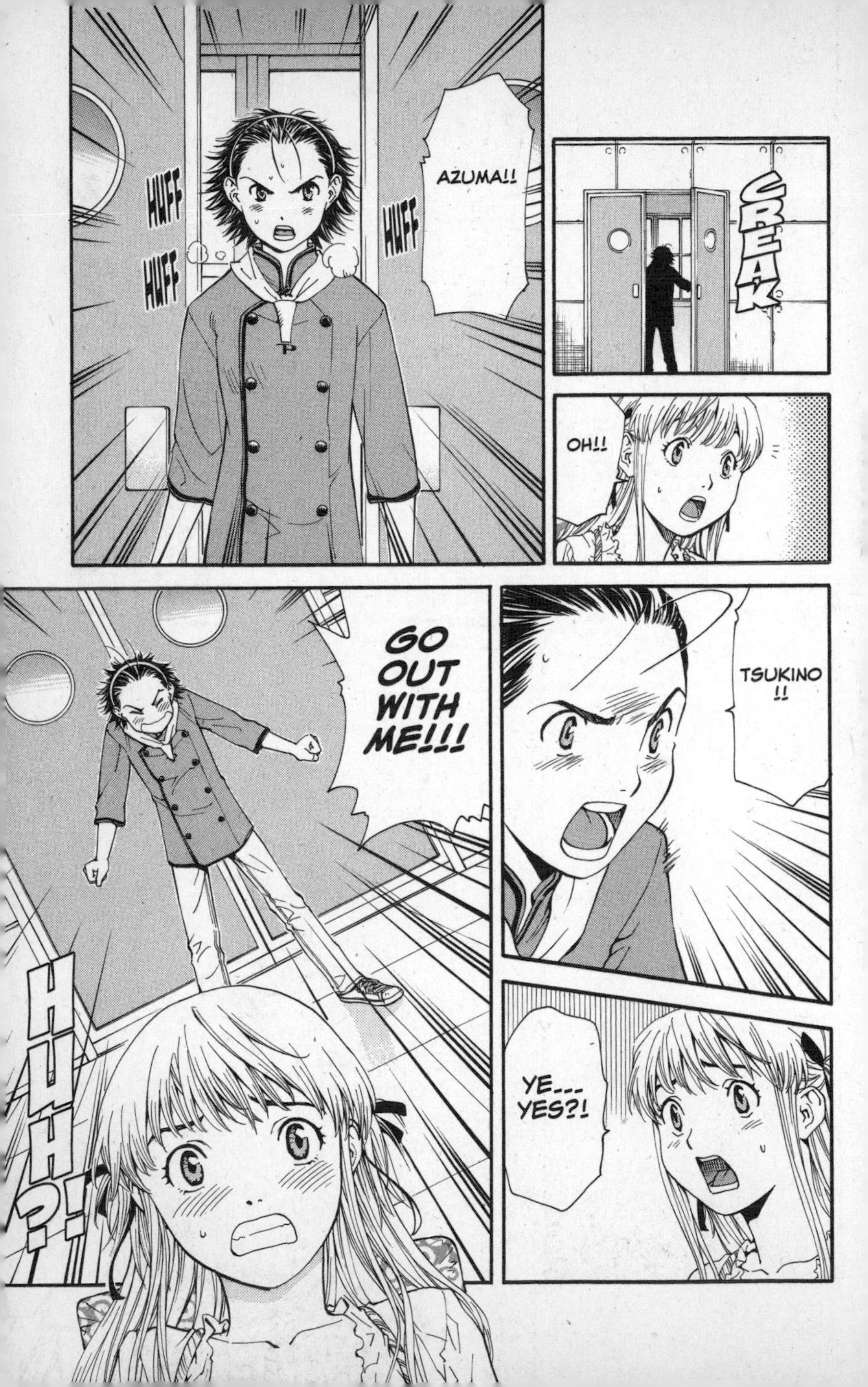
CREAK
OH!!
HUFF
HUFF
HUFF
AZUMA!!
TSUKINO!!
YE... YES?!
GO OUT WITH ME!!!
HUUH?!

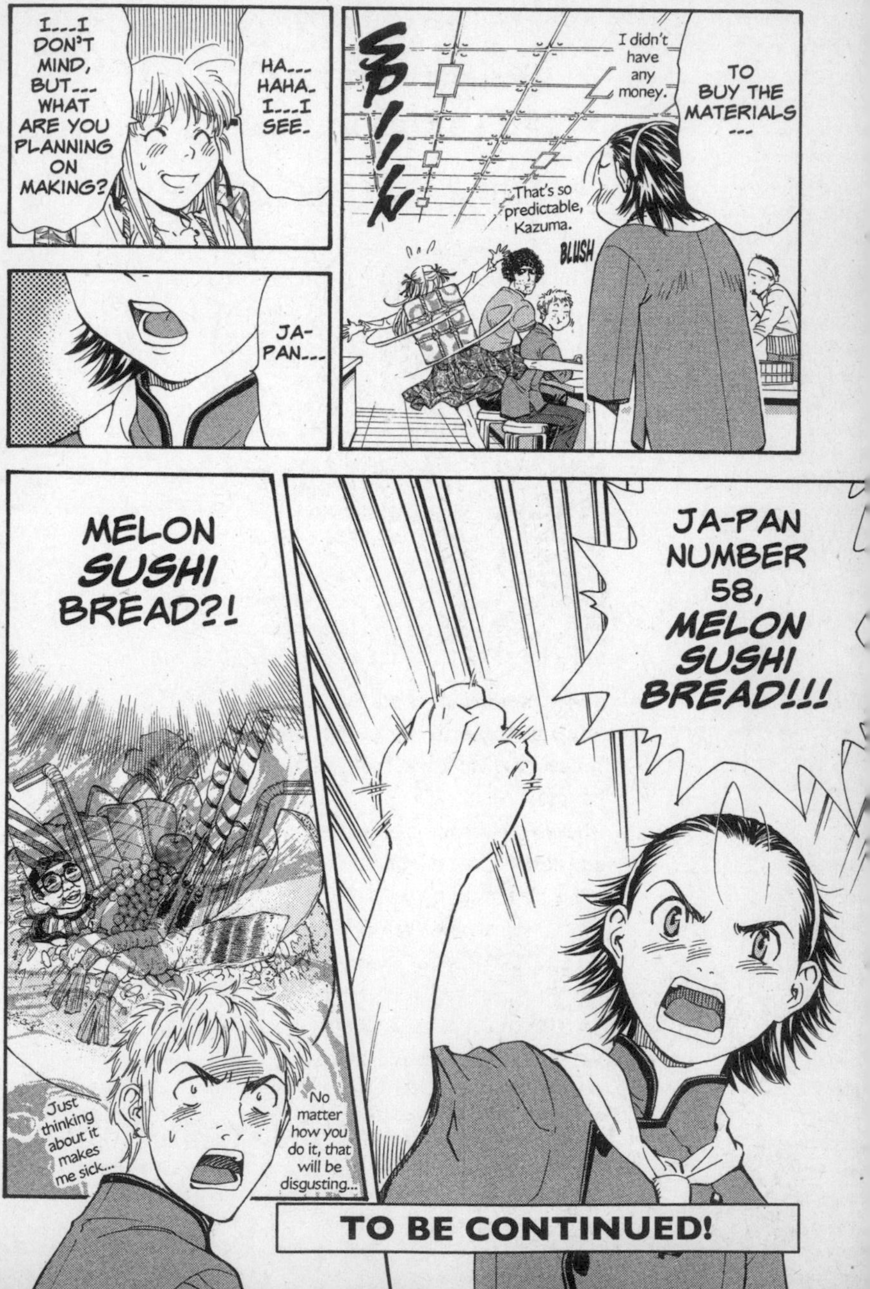
TO BUY THE MATERIALS...
I didn't have any money.
SPIN
That's so predictable, Kazuma.
BLUSH
HA... HAHA. I...I SEE.
I...I DON'T MIND, BUT... WHAT ARE YOU PLANNING ON MAKING?
JA-PAN...
JA-PAN NUMBER 58, MELON SUSHI BREAD!!!
TO BE CONTINUED!
MELON SUSHI BREAD?!
No matter how you do it, that will be disgusting...
Just thinking about it makes me sick...

Freshly Baked!!
Mini Information

—— Loaves of Bread ——

Some loaves of bread are rounded at the top and some are perfectly square. Rounded loaves are called "English Bread," and have been popular for years.

However, because the mountain-shaped loaves are round, they could not be piled on top of each other, and took up a lot of space. That's why square loaves were created—to make them easier to pile.

To us, they are mere loaves of bread, but to the craftsmen who make them, they are works of art.

BUT MY TEARS FLOW LIKE RAIN. THAT'S BECAUSE I'M A GIRL.

YAKITATE!! JAPAN
VOL. 3

STORY AND ART BY
TAKASHI HASHIGUCHI

English Adaptation/Drew Williams
Translation/Noritaka Minami
Touch-up Art & Lettering/Steve Dutro
Cover Design/Yukiko Whitley
Editor/Kit Fox

Managing Editor/Annette Roman
Editorial Director/Elizabeth Kawasaki
Editor in Chief/Alvin Lu
Sr. Director of Acquisitions/Rika Inouye
Sr. VP of Marketing/Liza Coppola
Exec. VP of Sales & Marketing/John Easum
Publisher/Hyoe Narita

Published by VIZ Media, LLC
P.O. Box 77010
San Francisco, CA 94107

10 9 8 7 6 5 4 3 2 1
First printing, January 2007

VIZ
MEDIA
www.viz.com   store.viz.com

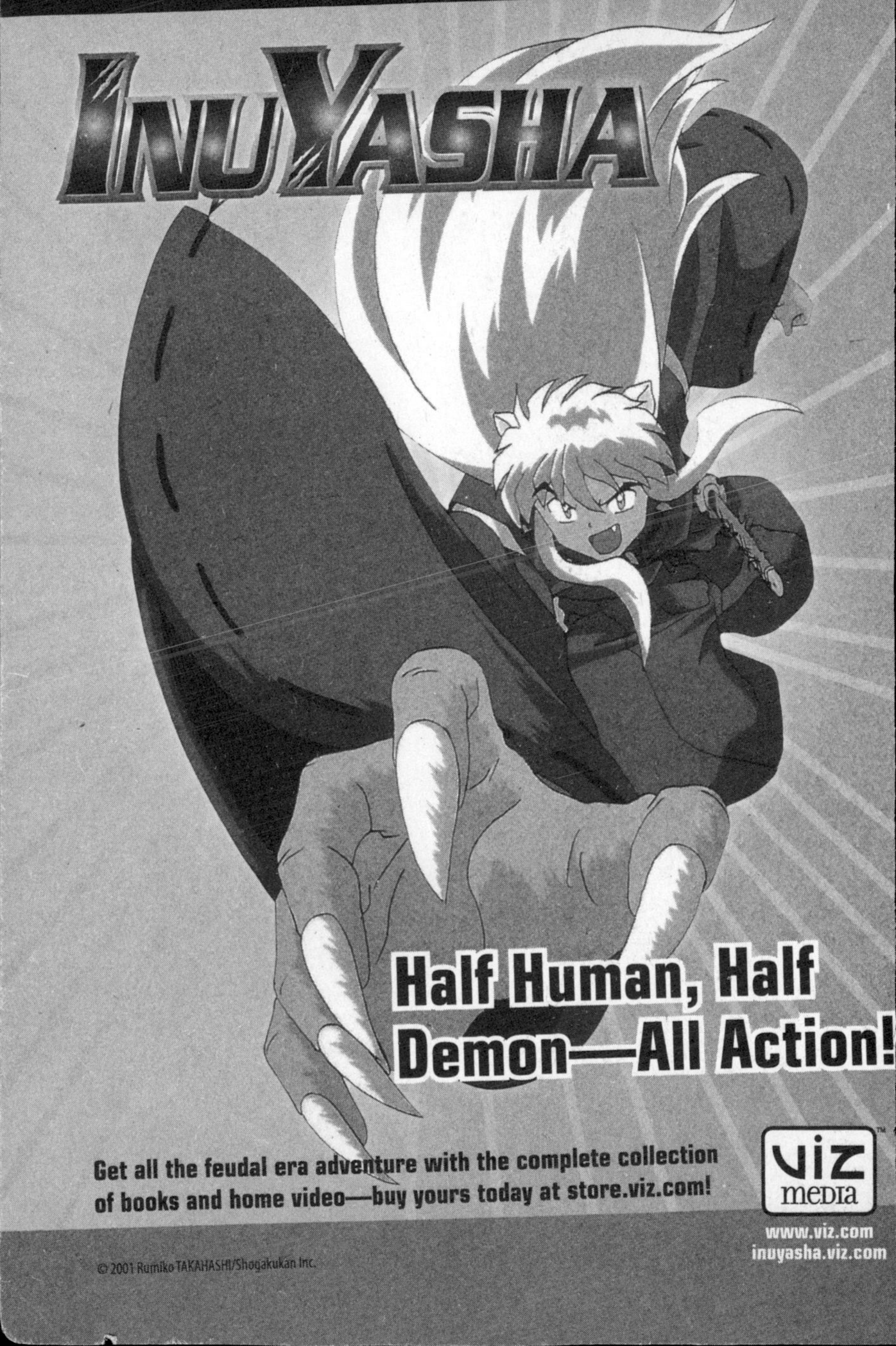
INUYASHA
Half Human, Half
Demon—All Action!
Get all the feudal era adventure with the complete collection
of books and home video—buy yours today at store.viz.com!
VIZ media
www.viz.com
inuyasha.viz.com
© 2001 Rumiko TAKAHASHI/Shogakukan Inc.

INUYASHA

Read the action from the start with the original manga series

Full color adaptation of the popular TV series

Art book with cel art, paintings, character profiles and more

TV SERIES & MOVIES ON DVD!

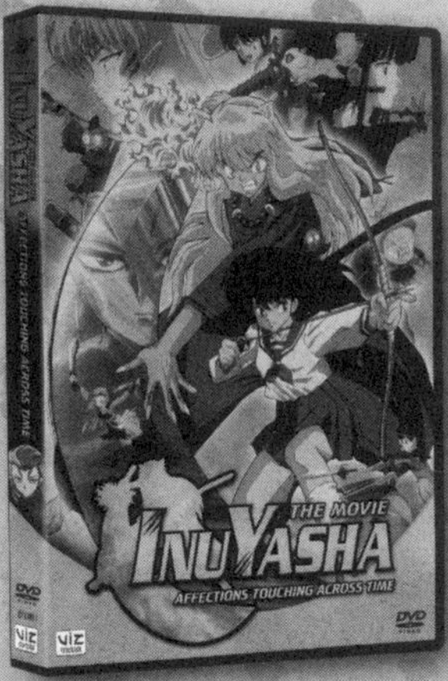
INUYASHA
INUYASHA THE MOVIE
AFFECTIONS TOUCHING ACROSS TIME
DVD
VIZ

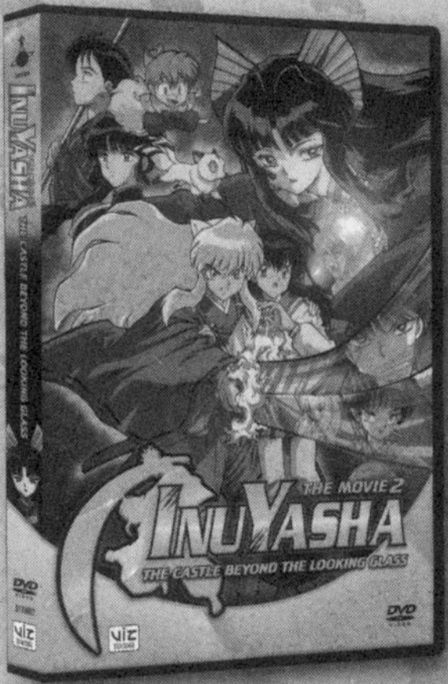
INUYASHA
INUYASHA THE MOVIE 2
THE CASTLE BEYOND THE LOOKING GLASS
DVD
VIZ

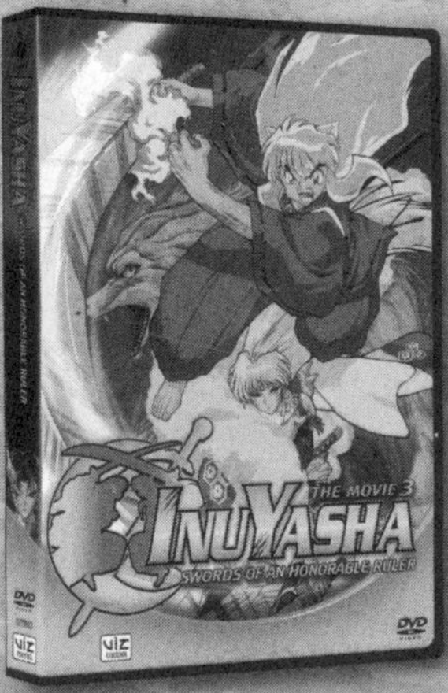
INUYASHA
INUYASHA THE MOVIE 3
SWORDS OF AN HONORABLE RULER
DVD
VIZ

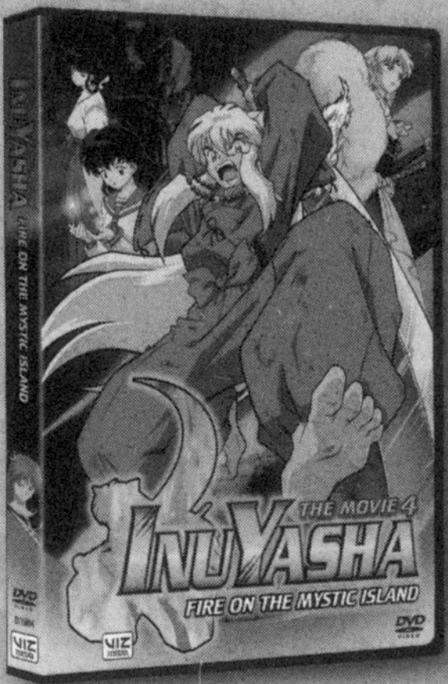
INUYASHA
FIRE ON THE MYSTIC ISLAND
INUYASHA THE MOVIE 4
FIRE ON THE MYSTIC ISLAND
DVD
VIZ

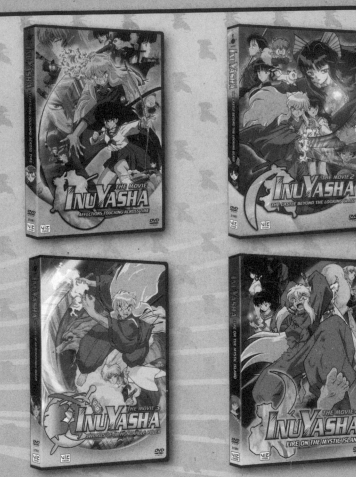

See more of the action in Inuyasha full-length movies

VIZ MEDIA™

www.viz.com
inuyasha.viz.com

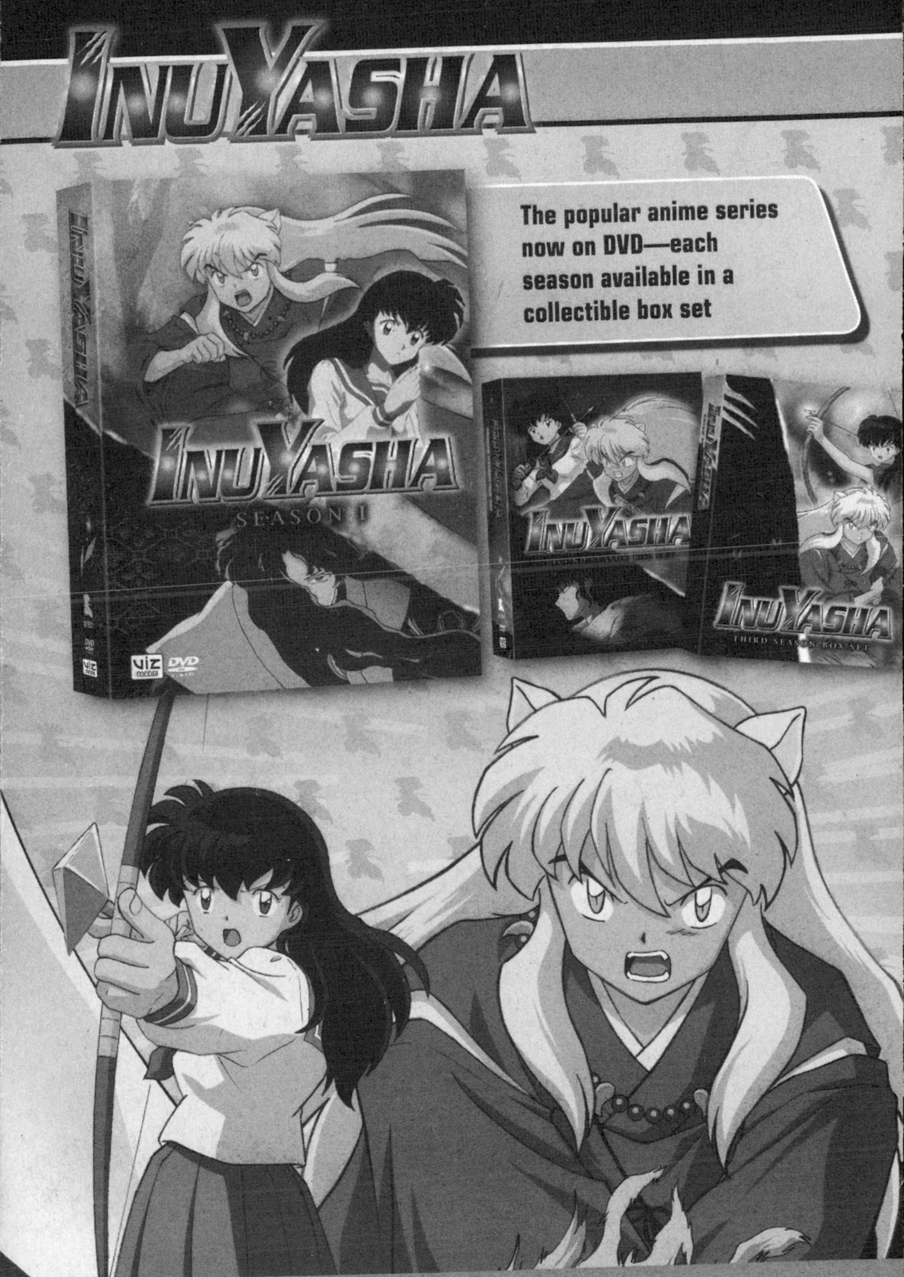
INUYASHA
The popular anime series now on DVD—each season available in a collectible box set
INUYASHA
SEASON 1
INUYASHA
INUYASHA
THIRD SEASON BOX SET

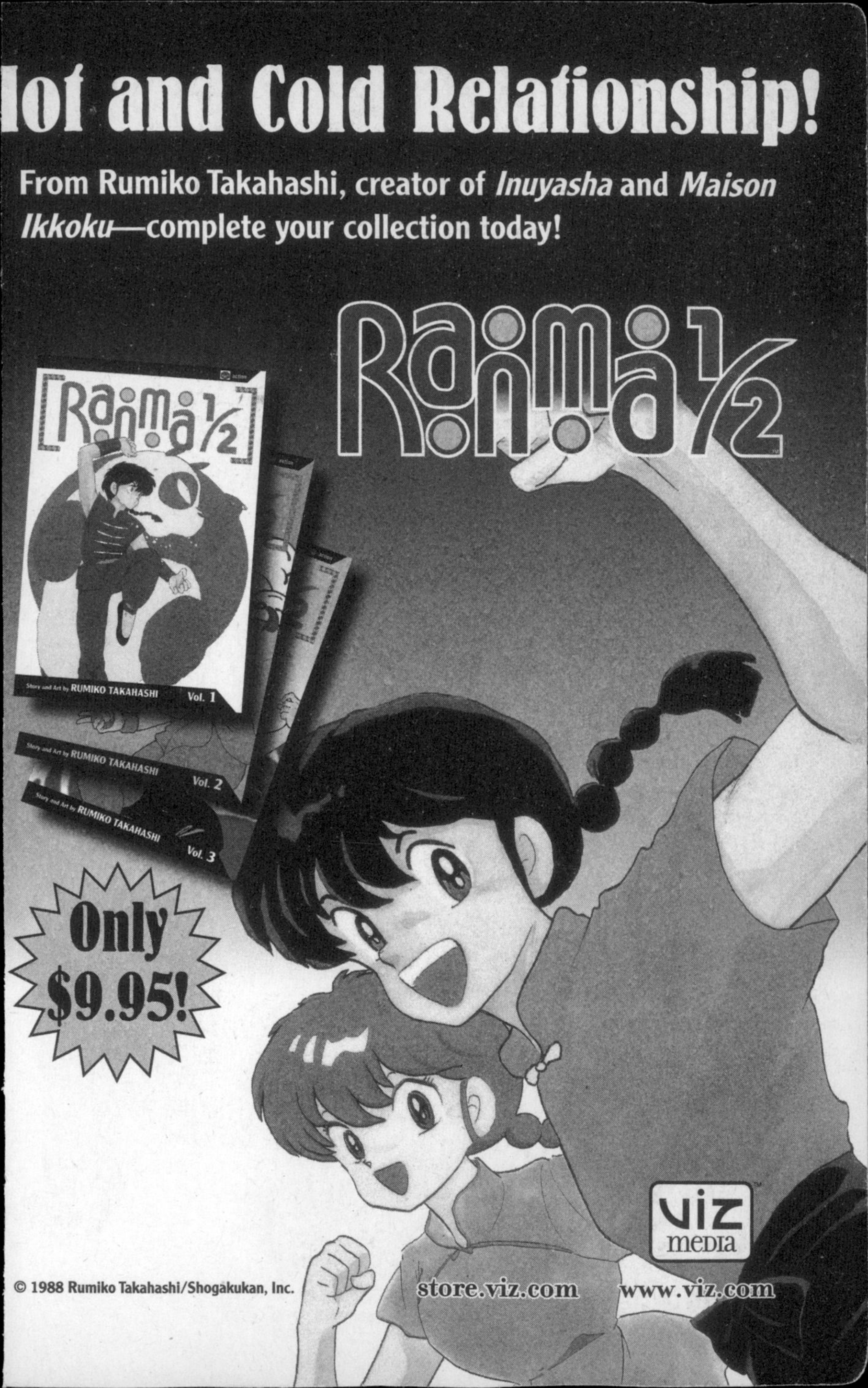
lot and Cold Relationship!
From Rumiko Takahashi, creator of Inuyasha and Maison Ikkoku—complete your collection today!
Ranma 1/2
Story and Art by RUMIKO TAKAHASHI Vol. 1
Story and Art by RUMIKO TAKAHASHI Vol. 2
Story and Art by RUMIKO TAKAHASHI Vol. 3
Only $9.95!
viz media
© 1988 Rumiko Takahashi/Shogakukan, Inc.
store.viz.com
www.viz.com

A Comedy that Redefines a

Due to an unfortunate accident, when martial artist Ranma gets splashed with cold water, he becomes a buxom young girl! Hot water reverses the effect, but when blamed for offenses both real and imagined, and pursued by lovesick suitors of both genders, what's a half-boy, half-girl to do?

A full TV season in each DVD box set

Only $119.98 each!

LOVE MANGA?
LET US KNOW WHAT YOU THINK!

HELP US MAKE THE MANGA
YOU LOVE BETTER!